LOVELESS

Volume 3

TOKYOPOP®

HAMBURG // LONDON // LOS ANGELES // TOKYO

Loveless Vol. 3
Created by Yun Kouga

Translation - Ray Yoshimoto
English Adaptation - Christine Boylan
Retouch and Lettering - Jihye "Sophia" Hong
Cover Design - Al-Insan Lashley

Editor - Lillian Diaz-Przybyl
Digital Imaging Manager - Chris Buford
Pre-Production Supervisor - Erika Terriquez
Art Director - Anne Marie Horne
Production Manager - Liz Brizzi
Managing Editor - Vy Nguyen
VP of Production - Ron Klamert
Editor-In-Chief - Rob Tokar
Publisher - Mike Kiley
President and C.O.O. - John Parker
C.E.O. and Chief Creative Officer - Stuart Levy

A **TOKYOPOP** Manga

TOKYOPOP Inc.
5900 Wilshire Blvd. Suite 2000
Los Angeles, CA 90036

E-mail: info@TOKYOPOP.com
Come visit us online at www.TOKYOPOP.com

ISBN:1-59816-223-3

First TOKYOPOP printing: October 2006
10 9 8 7 6 5 4 3 2
Printed in the USA

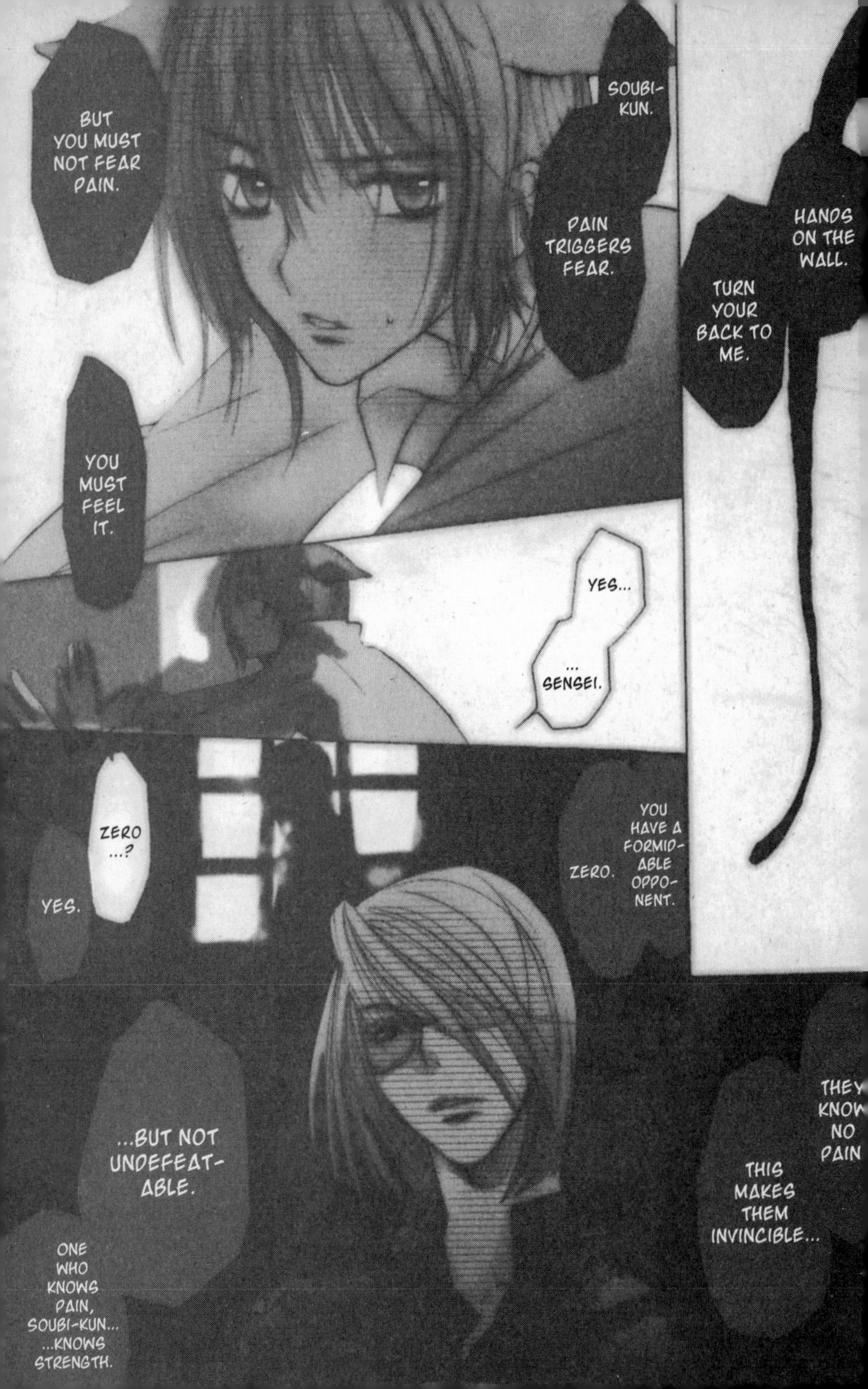
HANDS ON THE WALL.
TURN YOUR BACK TO ME.
SOUBI-KUN.
PAIN TRIGGERS FEAR.
BUT YOU MUST NOT FEAR PAIN.
YOU MUST FEEL IT.
YES...
...SENSEI.
YOU HAVE A FORMIDABLE OPPONENT.
ZERO.
ZERO ...?
YES.
THEY KNOW NO PAIN
THIS MAKES THEM INVINCIBLE...
...BUT NOT UNDEFEATABLE.
ONE WHO KNOWS PAIN, SOUBI-KUN... ...KNOWS STRENGTH.

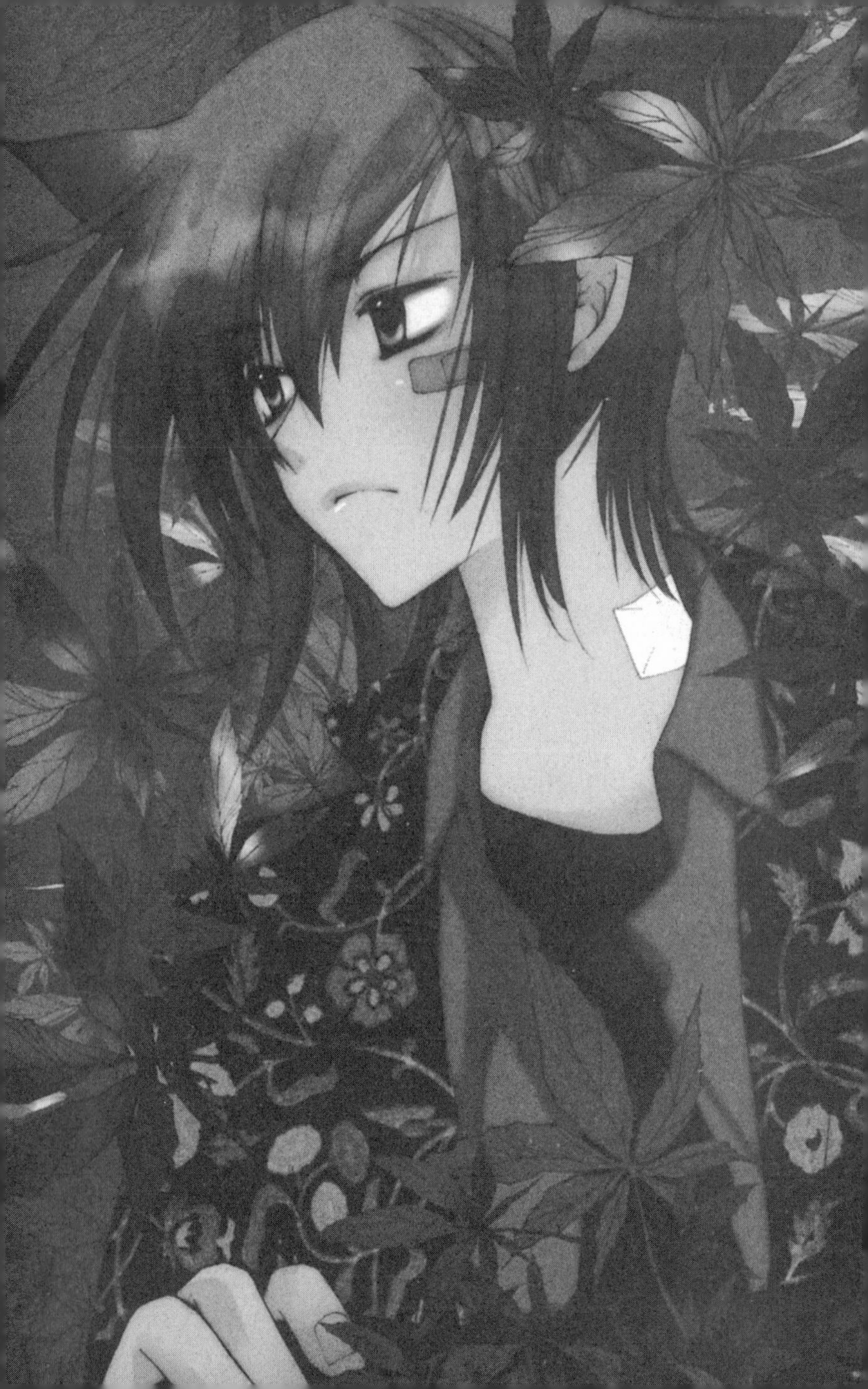

The Volume of the Absolute Toy Master II

Chapter6

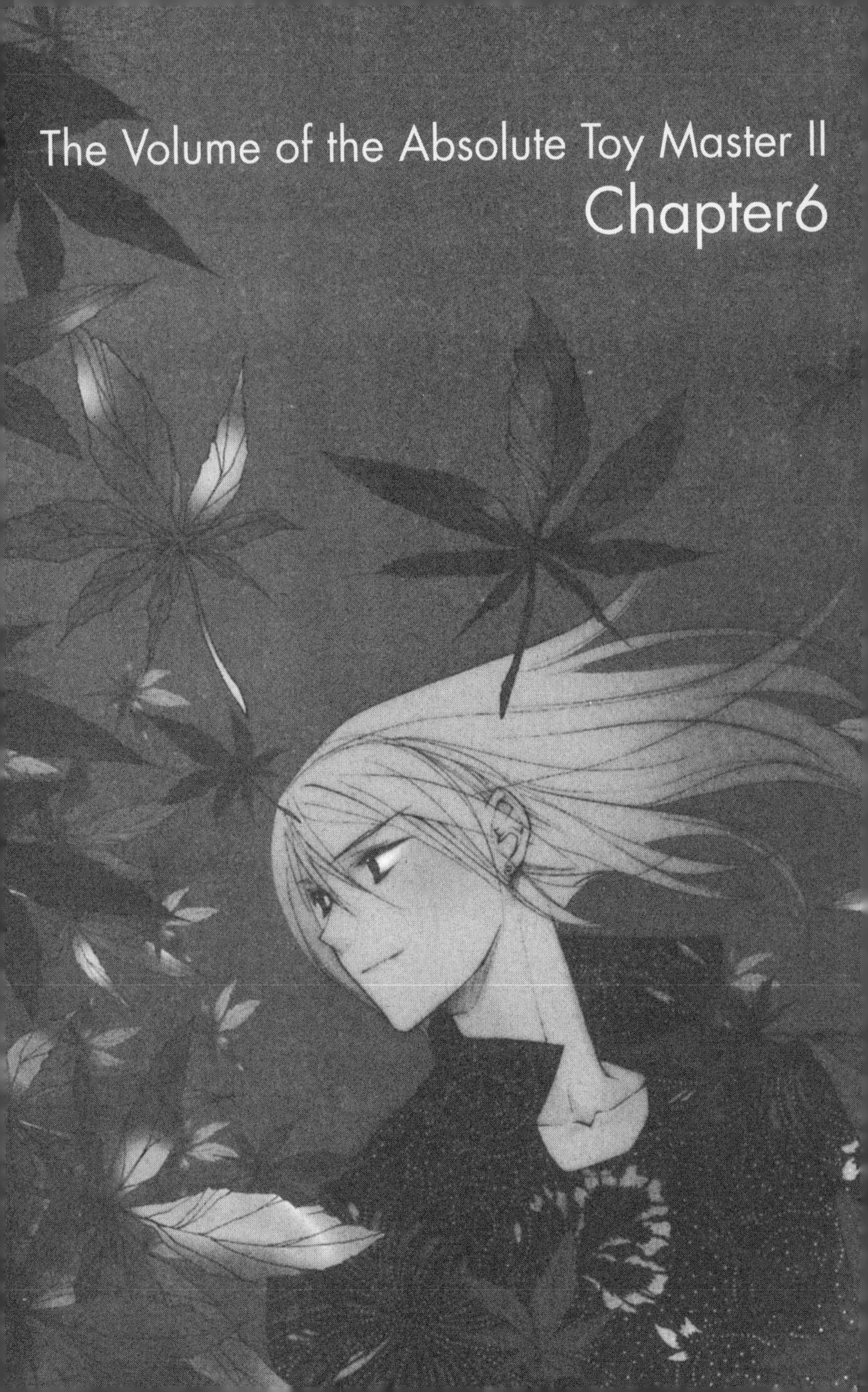

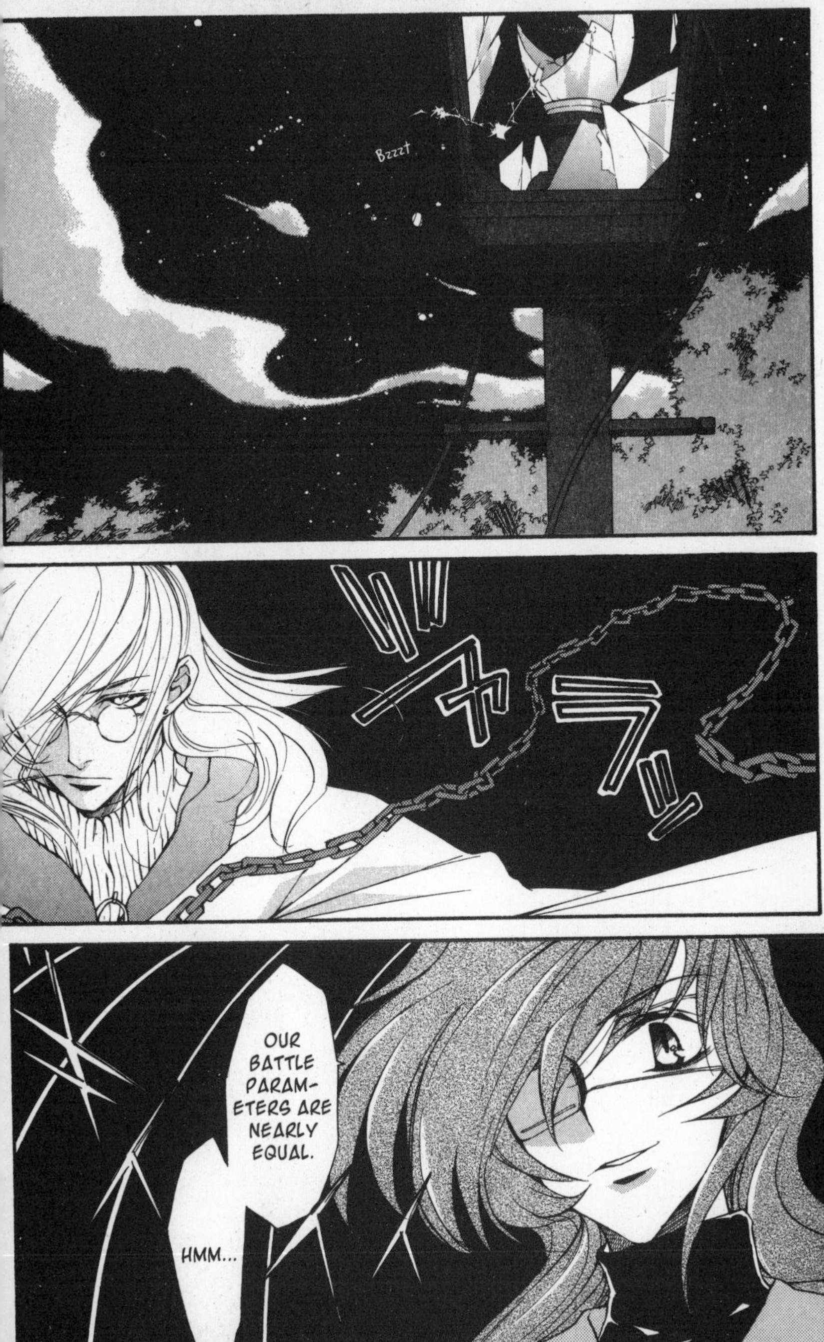
Bzzzt
OUR BATTLE PARAM- ETERS ARE NEARLY EQUAL.
HMM...

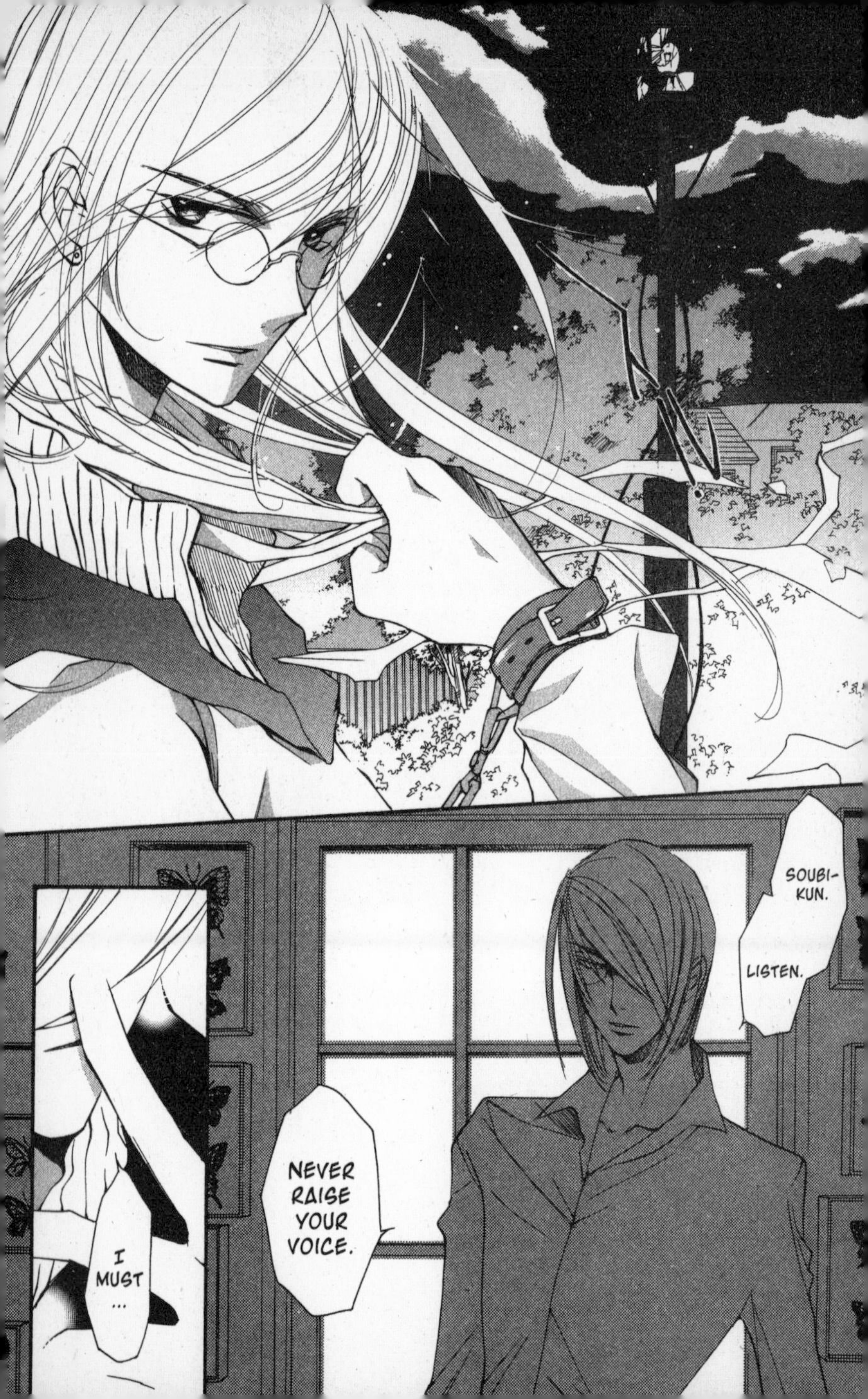
SOUBI-KUN.
LISTEN.
NEVER RAISE YOUR VOICE.
I MUST ...

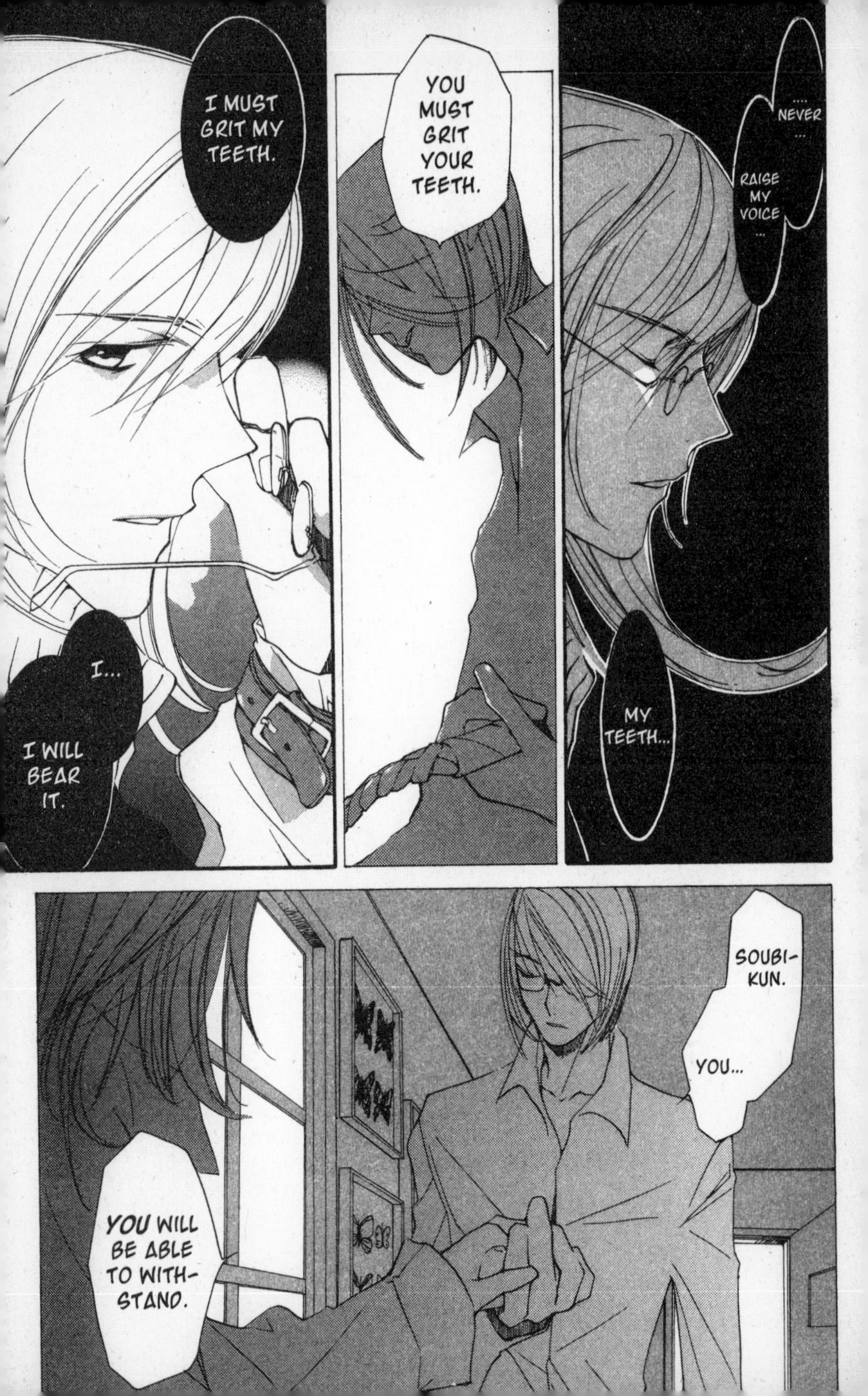

...NEVER...
RAISE MY VOICE...
MY TEETH...
YOU MUST GRIT YOUR TEETH.
I MUST GRIT MY TEETH.
I...
I WILL BEAR IT.
SOUBI-KUN.
YOU...
YOU WILL BE ABLE TO WITH-STAND.

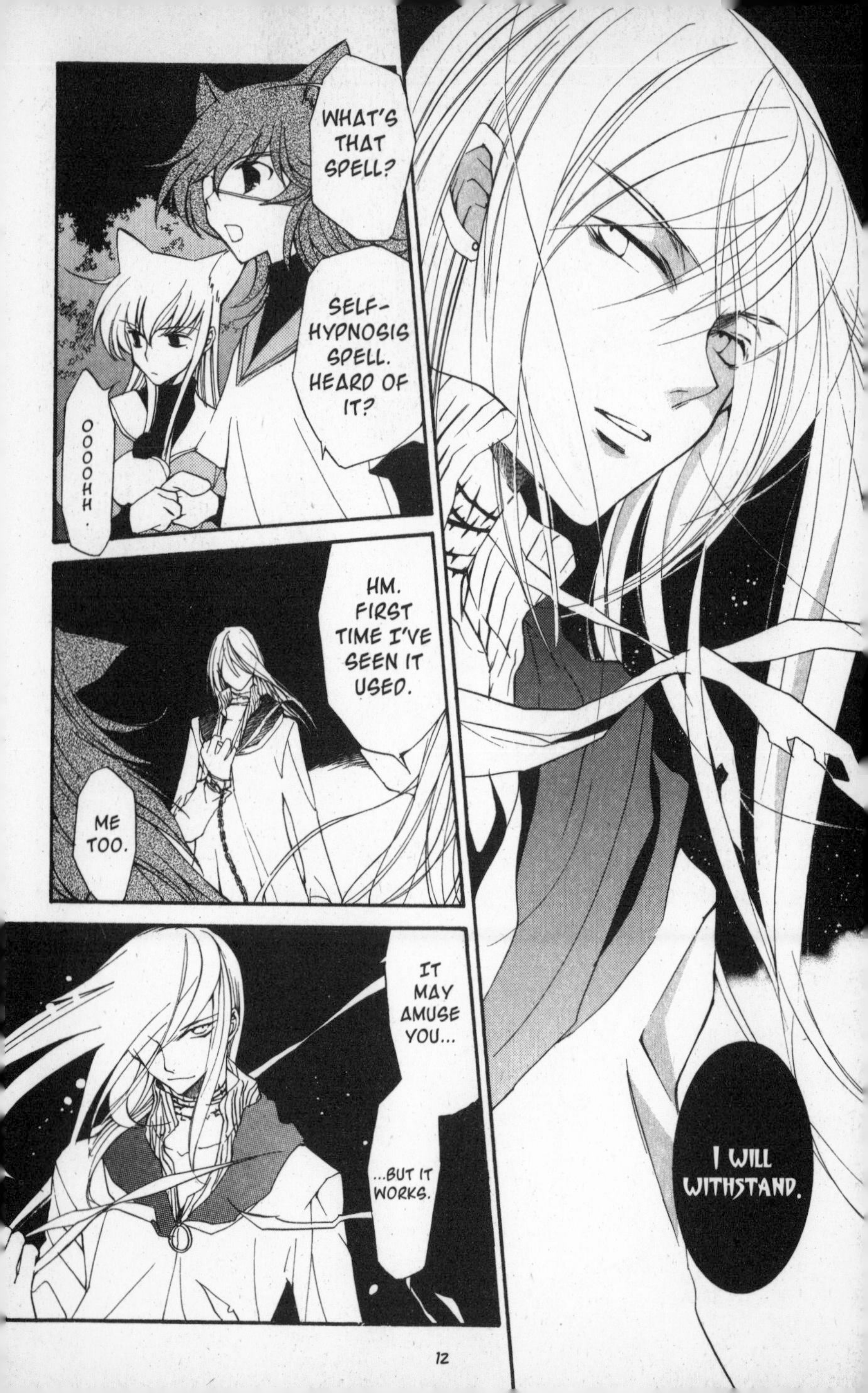

I WILL WITHSTAND.
WHAT'S THAT SPELL?
SELF-HYPNOSIS SPELL. HEARD OF IT?
OOOOHH.
HM. FIRST TIME I'VE SEEN IT USED.
ME TOO.
IT MAY AMUSE YOU...
...BUT IT WORKS.

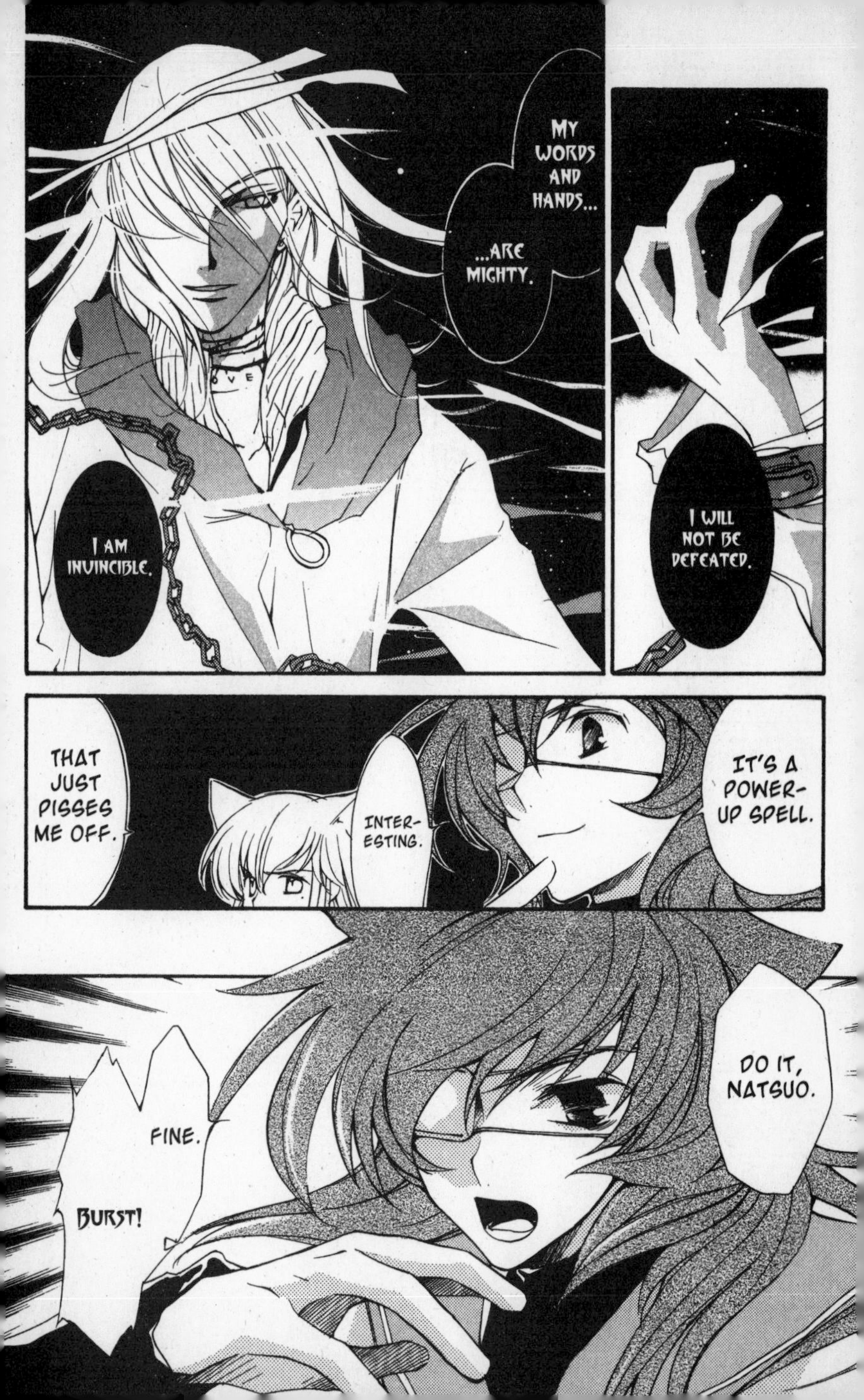
I WILL NOT BE DEFEATED.
MY WORDS AND HANDS...
...ARE MIGHTY.
I AM INVINCIBLE.
IT'S A POWER-UP SPELL.
INTER-ESTING.
THAT JUST PISSES ME OFF.
DO IT, NATSUO.
FINE.
BURST!

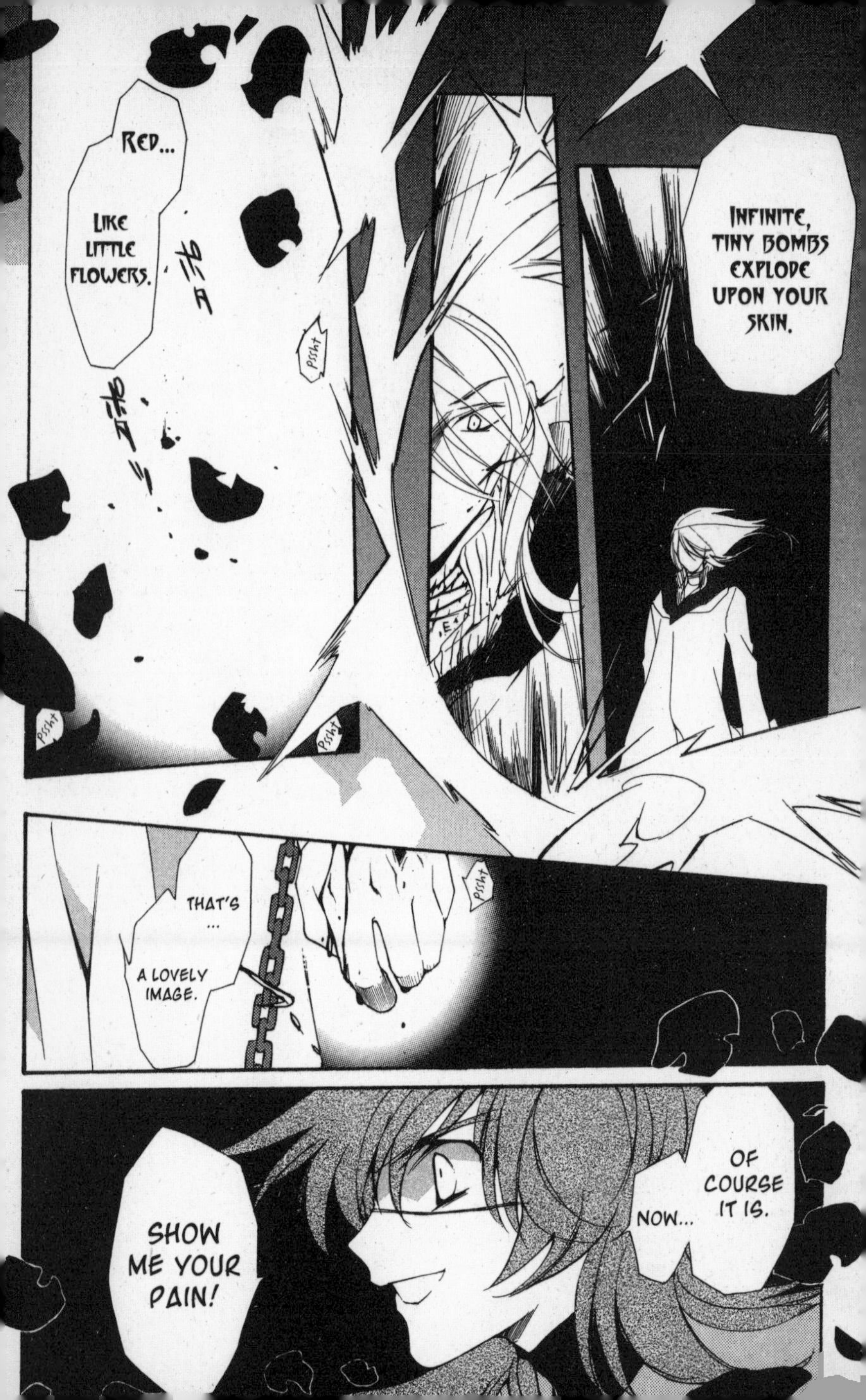
Infinite, tiny bombs explode upon your skin.
Red...
Like little flowers.
Pssht
Pssht
Pssht
Pssht
That's ... a lovely image.
Of course it is.
Now...
Show me your pain!

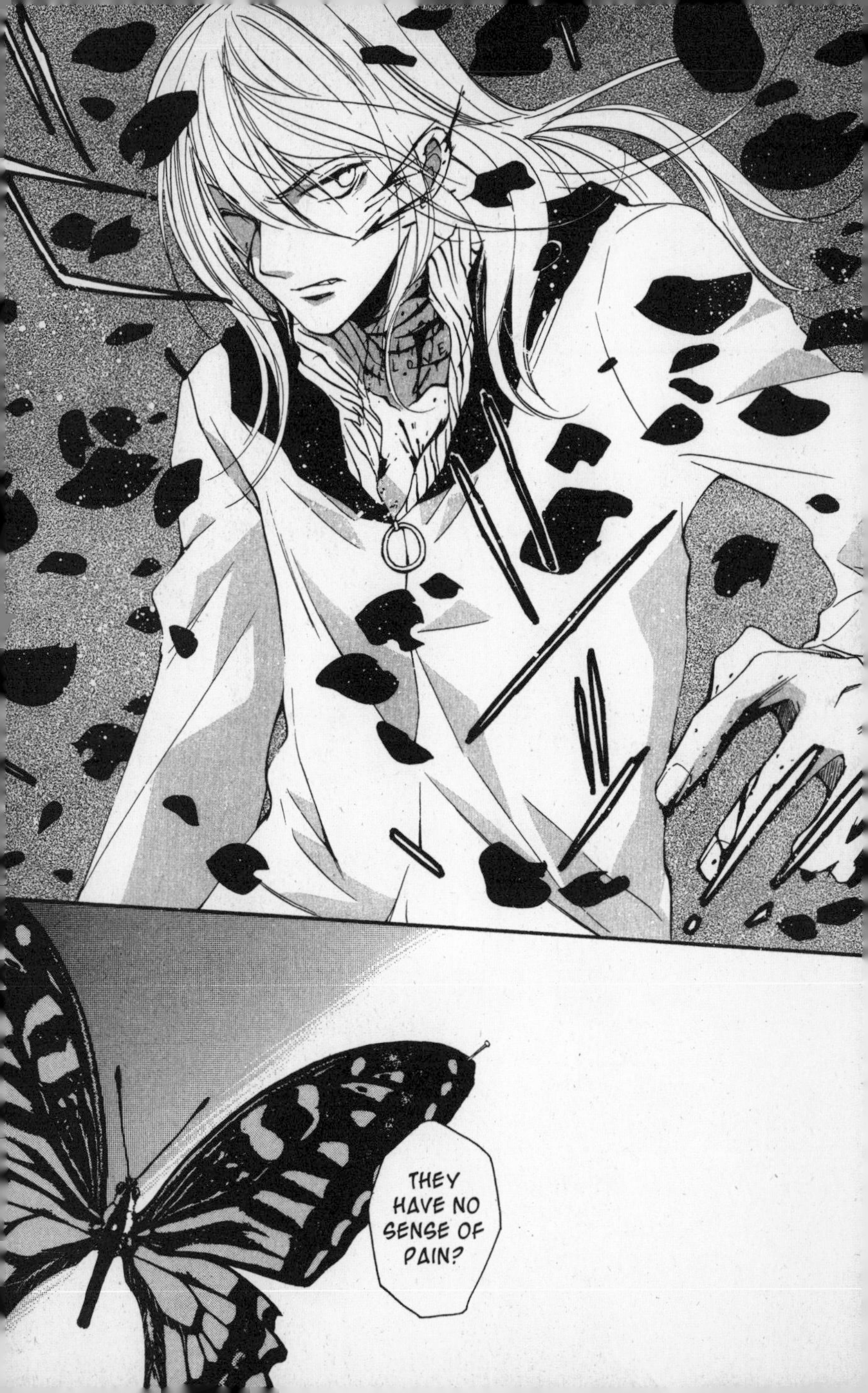
LOVE
THEY HAVE NO SENSE OF PAIN?

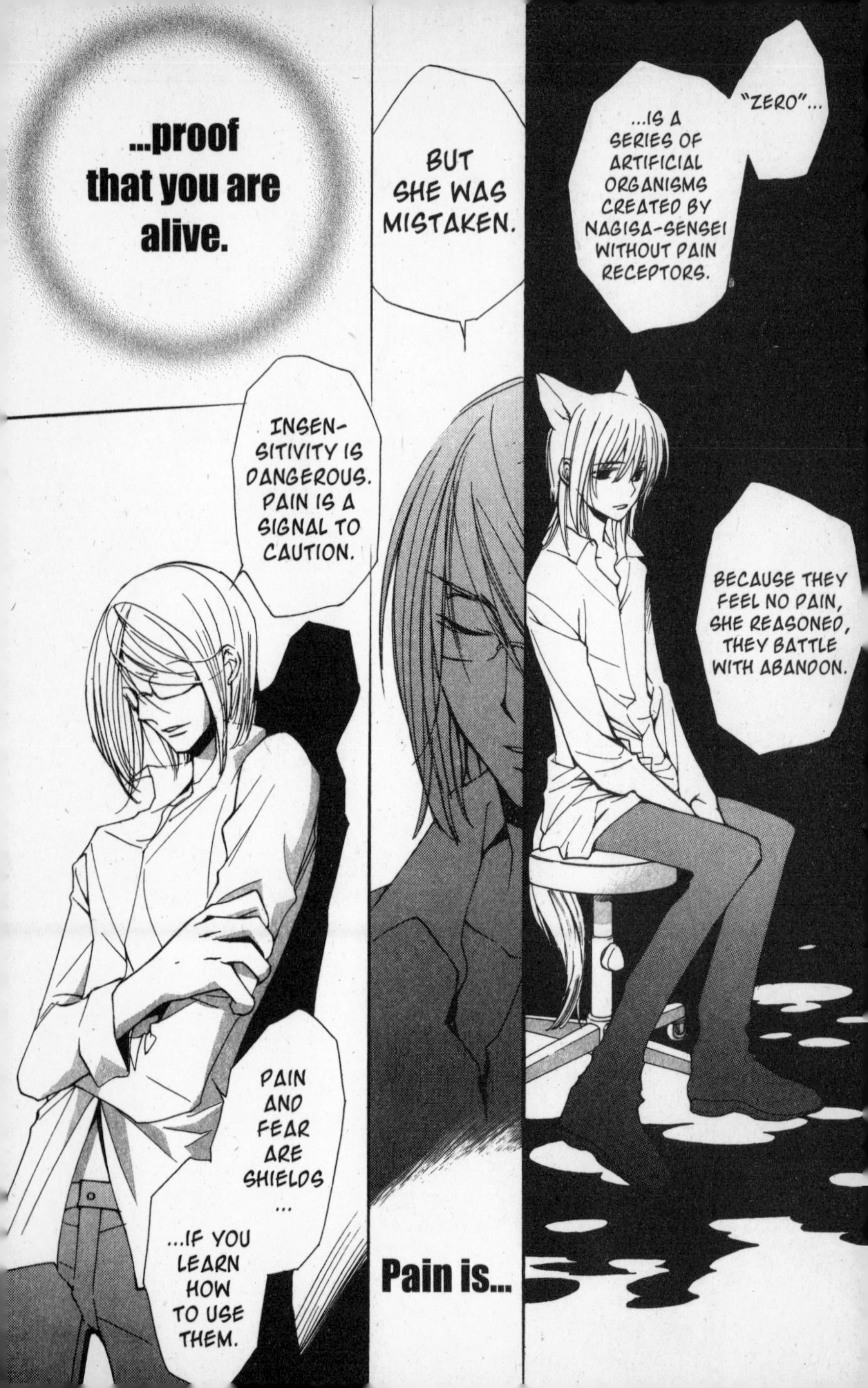
"ZERO"...
...IS A SERIES OF ARTIFICIAL ORGANISMS CREATED BY NAGISA-SENSEI WITHOUT PAIN RECEPTORS.
BECAUSE THEY FEEL NO PAIN, SHE REASONED, THEY BATTLE WITH ABANDON.
BUT SHE WAS MISTAKEN.
Pain is...
...proof that you are alive.
INSEN-SITIVITY IS DANGEROUS. PAIN IS A SIGNAL TO CAUTION.
PAIN AND FEAR ARE SHIELDS...
...IF YOU LEARN HOW TO USE THEM.

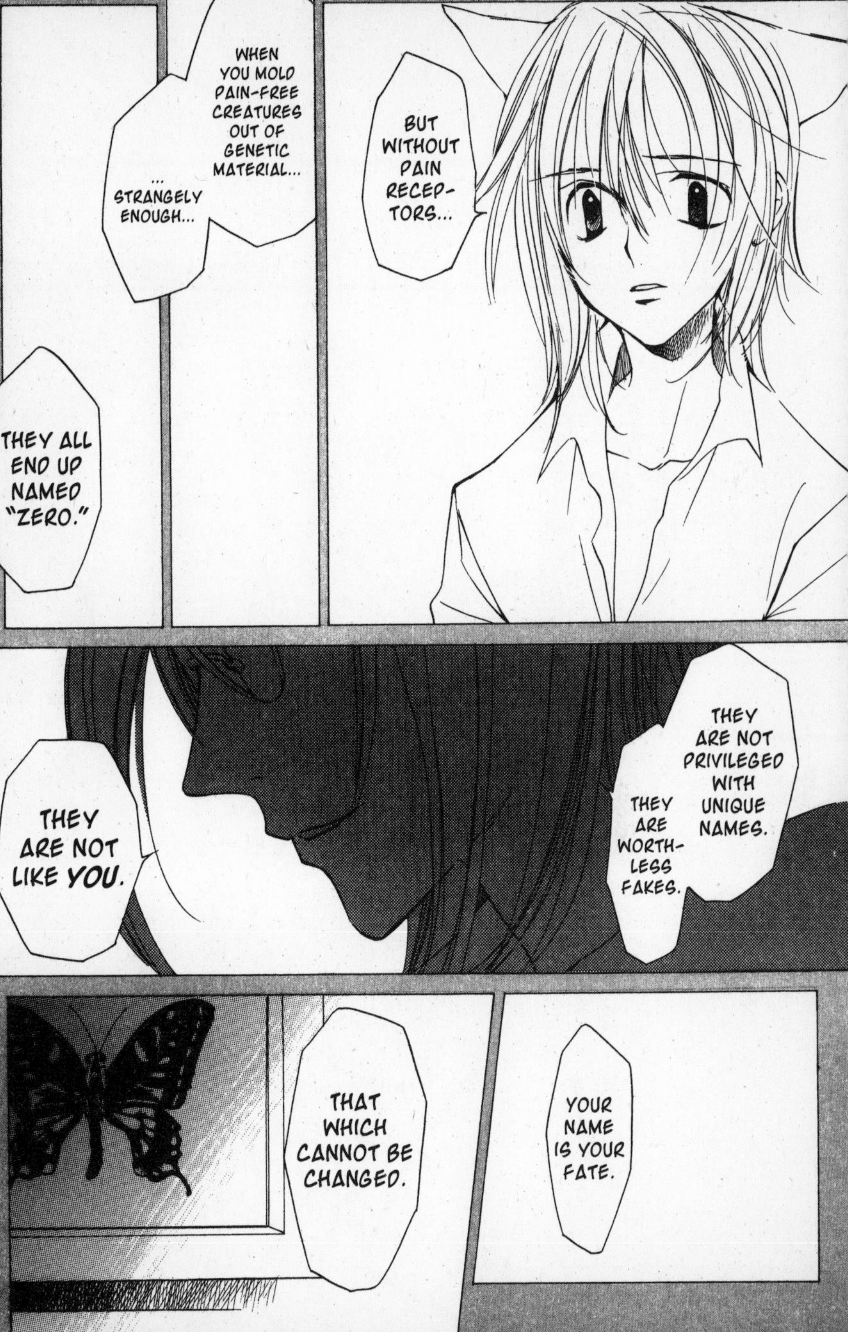

BUT WITHOUT PAIN RECEPTORS...
WHEN YOU MOLD PAIN-FREE CREATURES OUT OF GENETIC MATERIAL...
...STRANGELY ENOUGH...
THEY ALL END UP NAMED "ZERO."
THEY ARE NOT PRIVILEGED WITH UNIQUE NAMES.
THEY ARE WORTHLESS FAKES.
THEY ARE NOT LIKE *YOU*.
YOUR NAME IS YOUR FATE.
THAT WHICH CANNOT BE CHANGED.

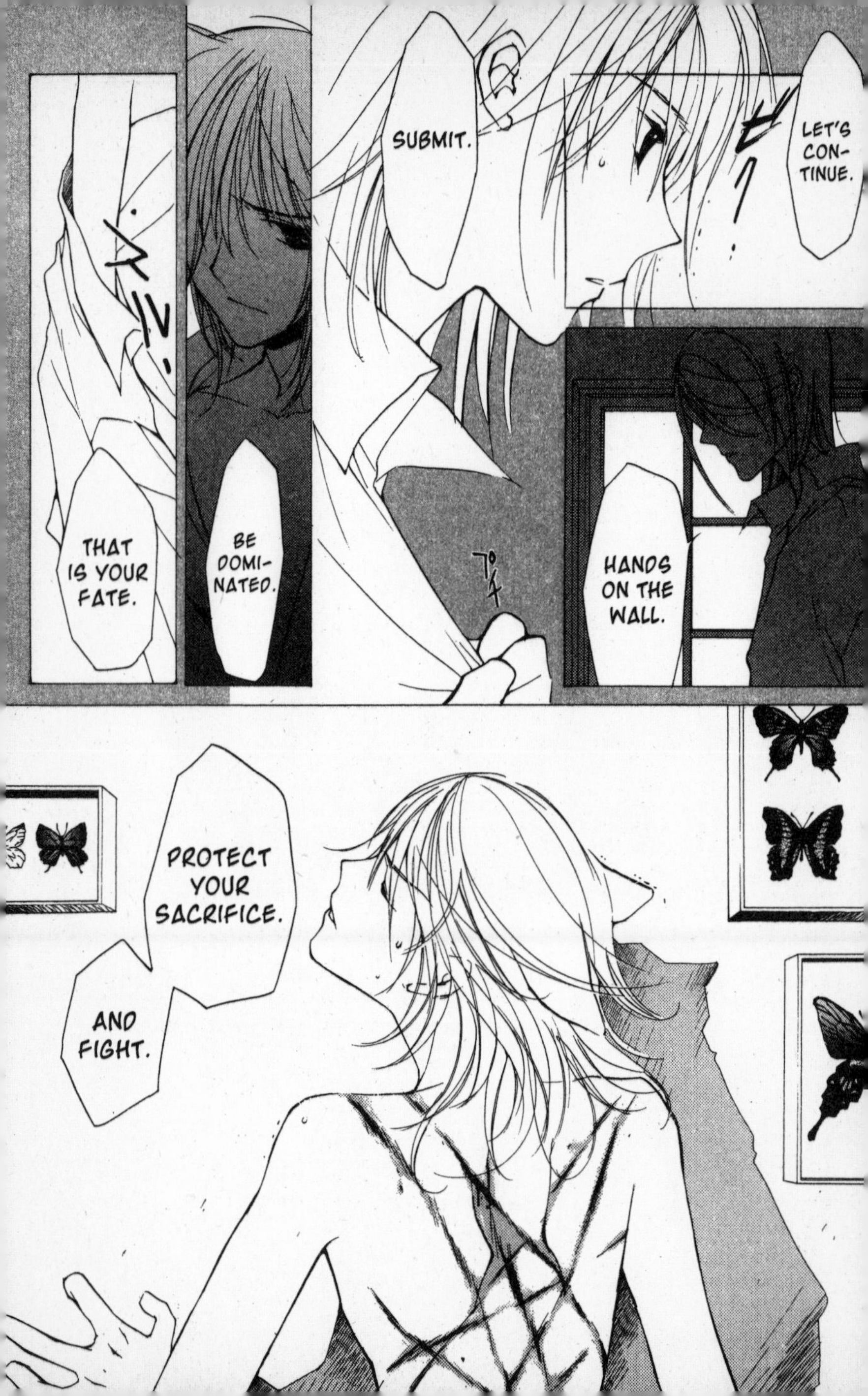
LET'S CON-TINUE.
HANDS ON THE WALL.
SUBMIT.
BE DOMI-NATED.
THAT IS YOUR FATE.
PROTECT YOUR SACRIFICE.
AND FIGHT.

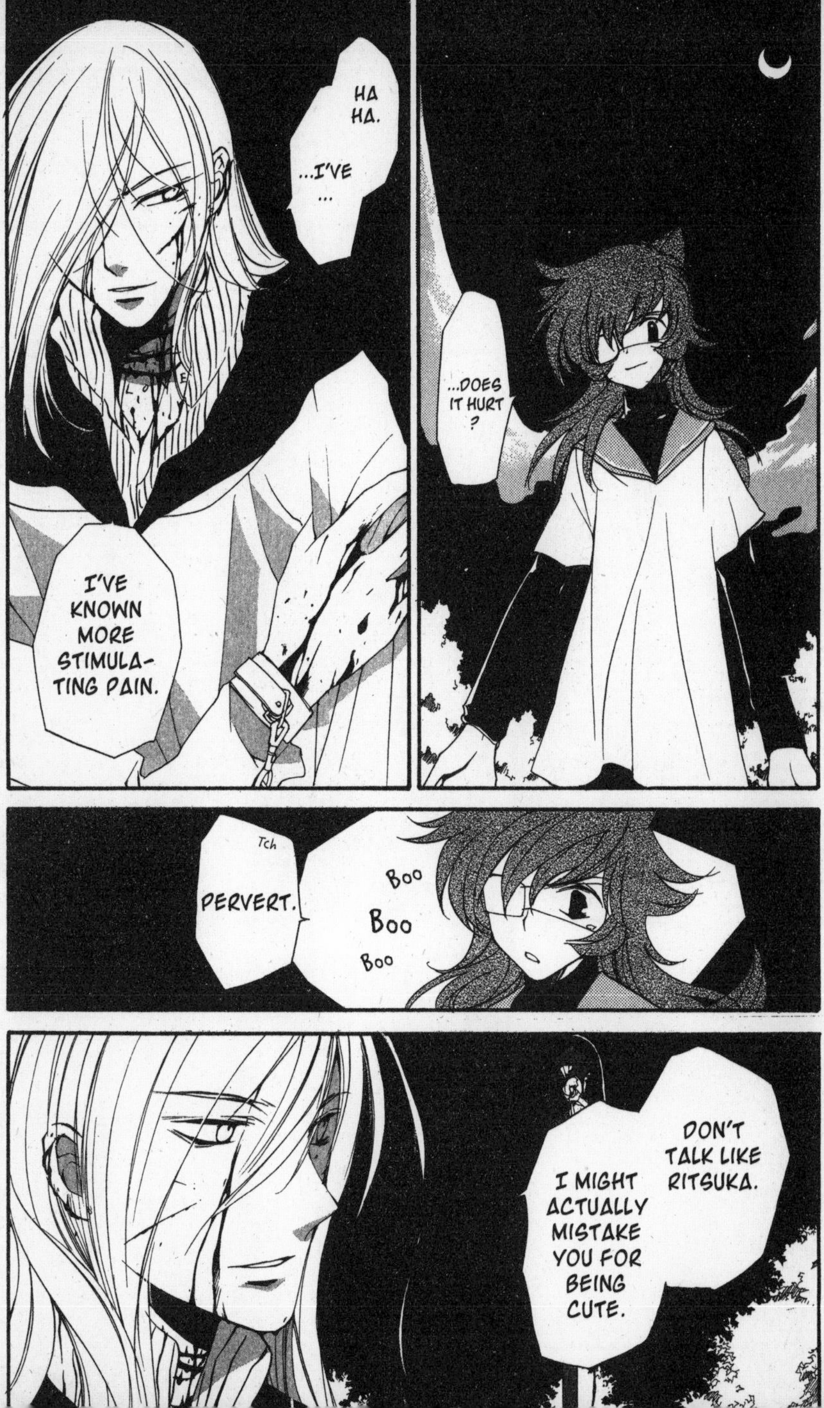
...DOES IT HURT?
HA HA.
...I'VE ...
I'VE KNOWN MORE STIMULATING PAIN.
Boo Boo Boo
Tch
PERVERT.
DON'T TALK LIKE RITSUKA.
I MIGHT ACTUALLY MISTAKE YOU FOR BEING CUTE.

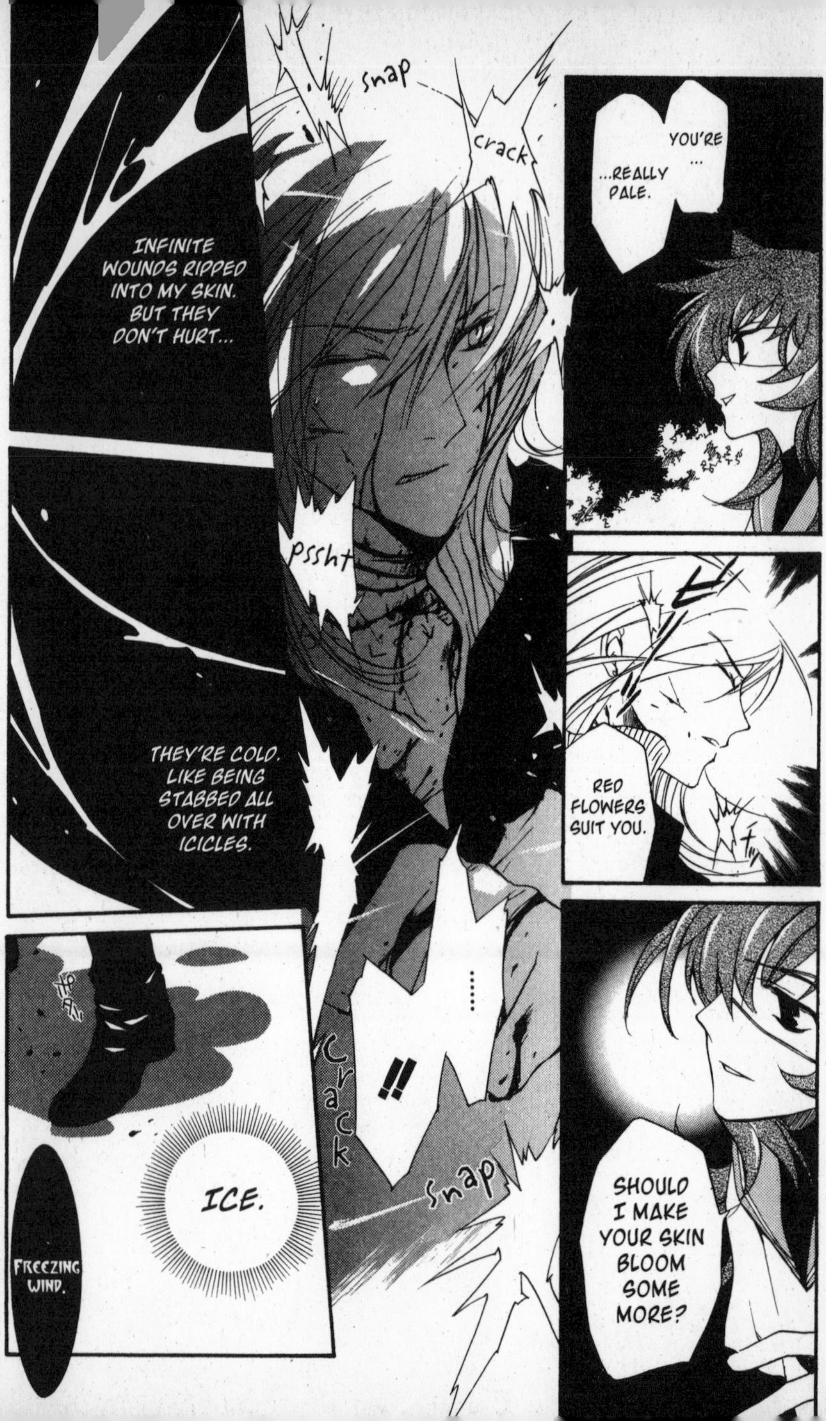
YOU'RE ...
...REALLY PALE.
RED FLOWERS SUIT YOU.
SHOULD I MAKE YOUR SKIN BLOOM SOME MORE?
snap
crack
pssht
......
!!
crack
snap
INFINITE WOUNDS RIPPED INTO MY SKIN. BUT THEY DON'T HURT...
THEY'RE COLD. LIKE BEING STABBED ALL OVER WITH ICICLES.
ICE.
FREEZING WIND.

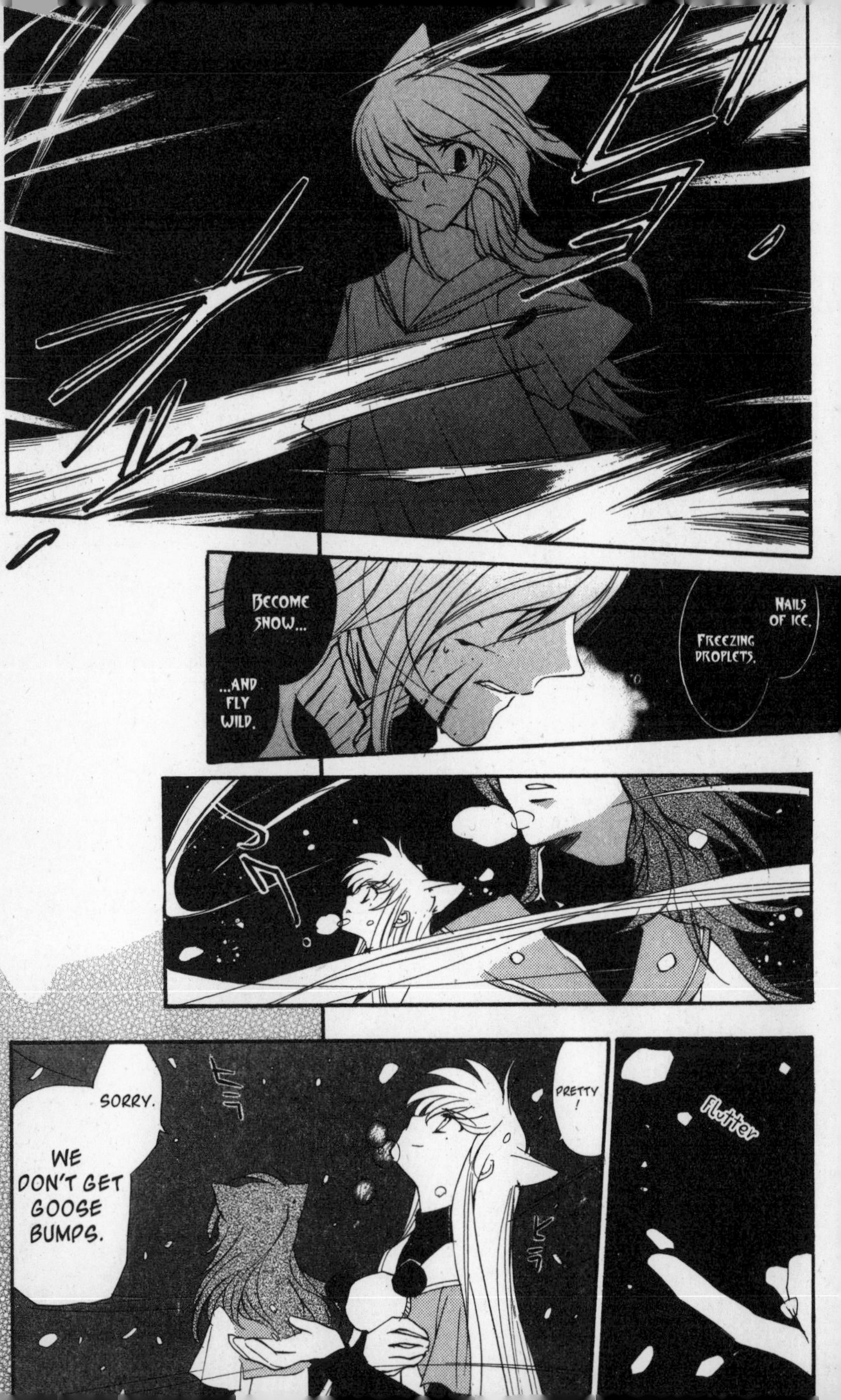
Nails of ice.
Freezing droplets.
Become snow...
...and fly wild.
Flutter
Pretty!
Sorry.
We don't get goose bumps.

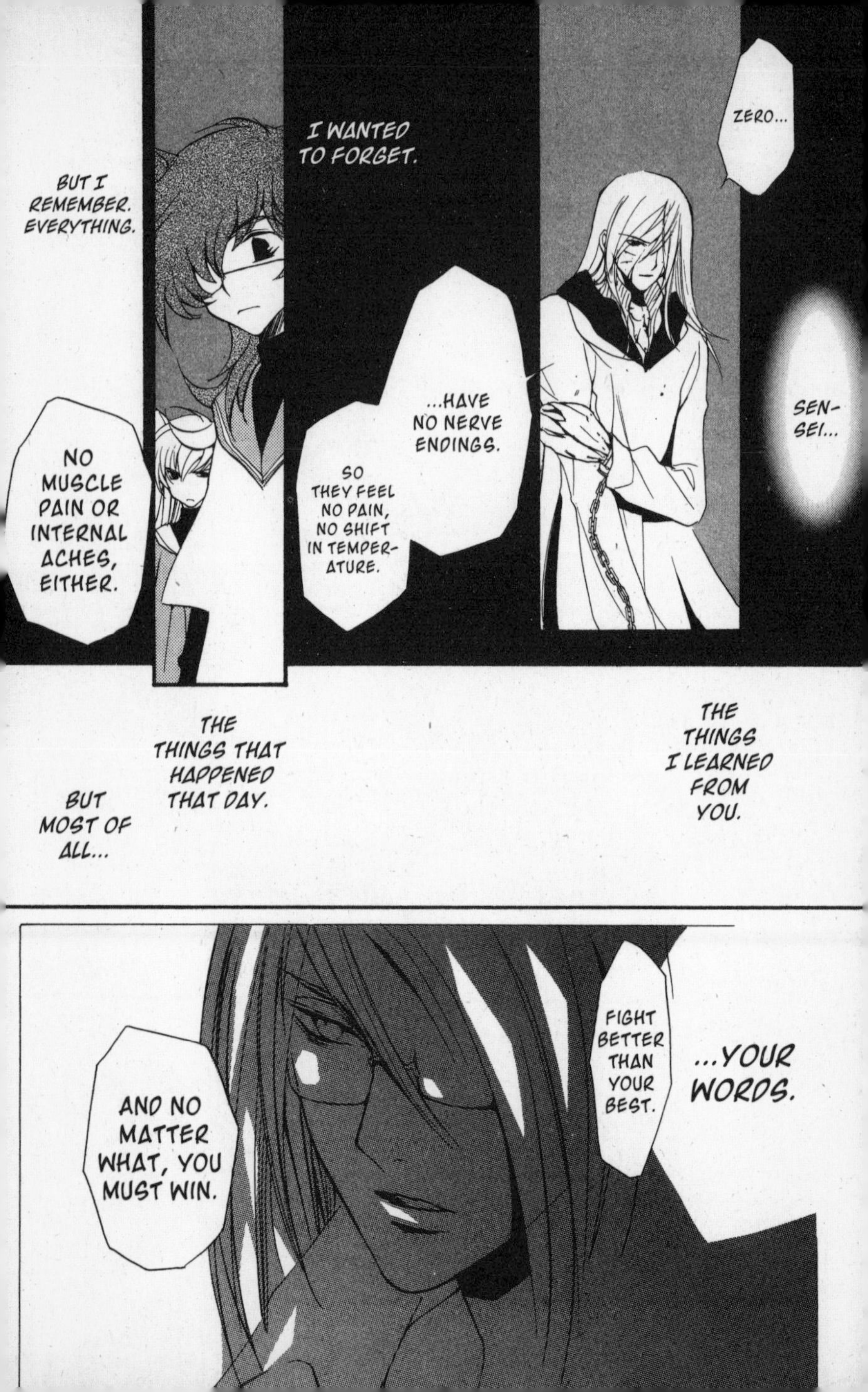
ZERO...
SEN-SEI...
I WANTED TO FORGET.
...HAVE NO NERVE ENDINGS.
SO THEY FEEL NO PAIN, NO SHIFT IN TEMPERATURE.
BUT I REMEMBER. EVERYTHING.
NO MUSCLE PAIN OR INTERNAL ACHES, EITHER.
THE THINGS I LEARNED FROM YOU.
THE THINGS THAT HAPPENED THAT DAY.
BUT MOST OF ALL...
...YOUR WORDS.
FIGHT BETTER THAN YOUR BEST.
AND NO MATTER WHAT, YOU MUST WIN.

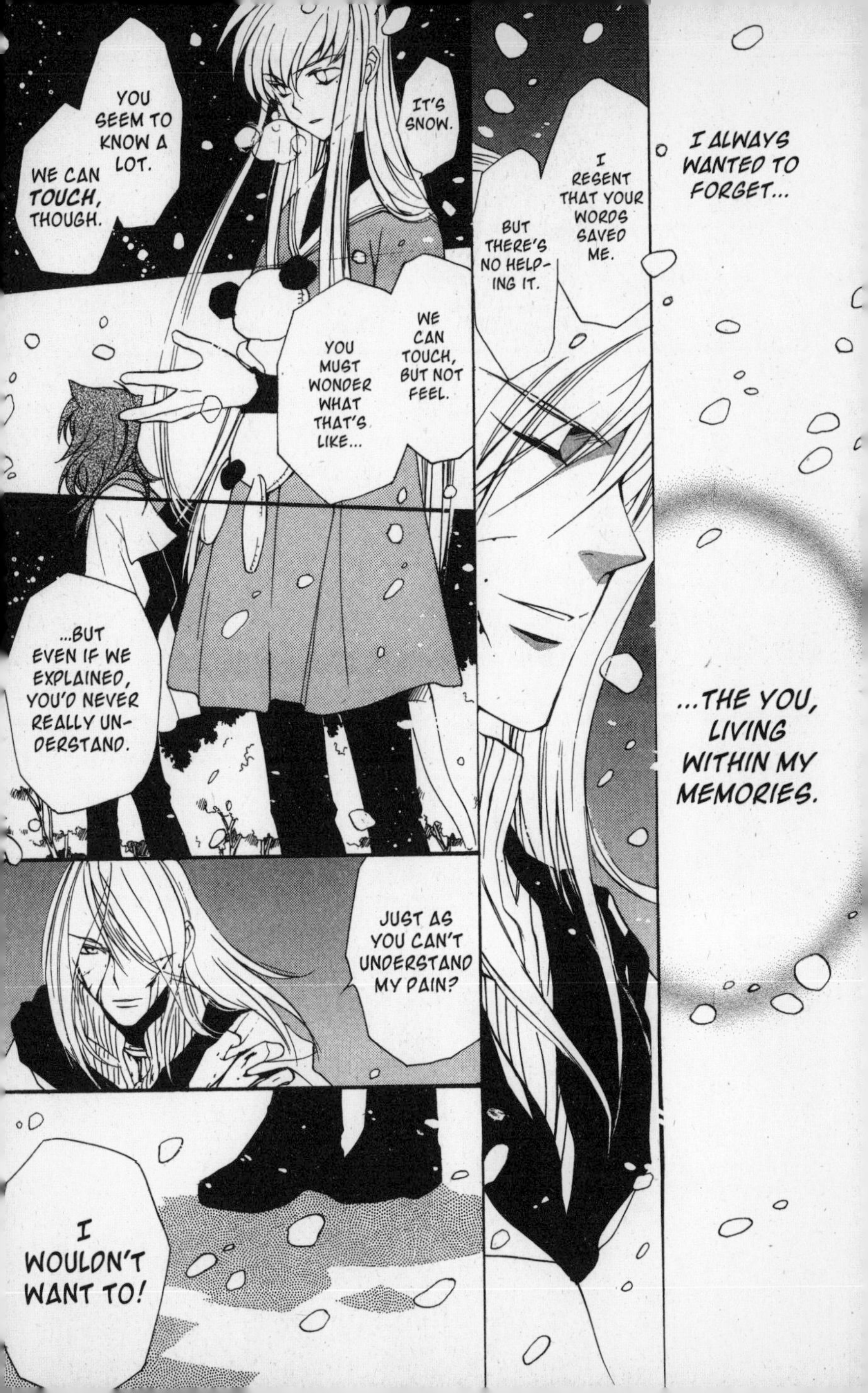
I ALWAYS WANTED TO FORGET...
...THE YOU, LIVING WITHIN MY MEMORIES.
I RESENT THAT YOUR WORDS SAVED ME.
BUT THERE'S NO HELPING IT.
IT'S SNOW.
YOU SEEM TO KNOW A LOT.
WE CAN *TOUCH*, THOUGH.
WE CAN TOUCH, BUT NOT FEEL.
YOU MUST WONDER WHAT THAT'S LIKE...
...BUT EVEN IF WE EXPLAINED, YOU'D NEVER REALLY UNDERSTAND.
JUST AS YOU CAN'T UNDERSTAND MY PAIN?
I WOULDN'T WANT TO!

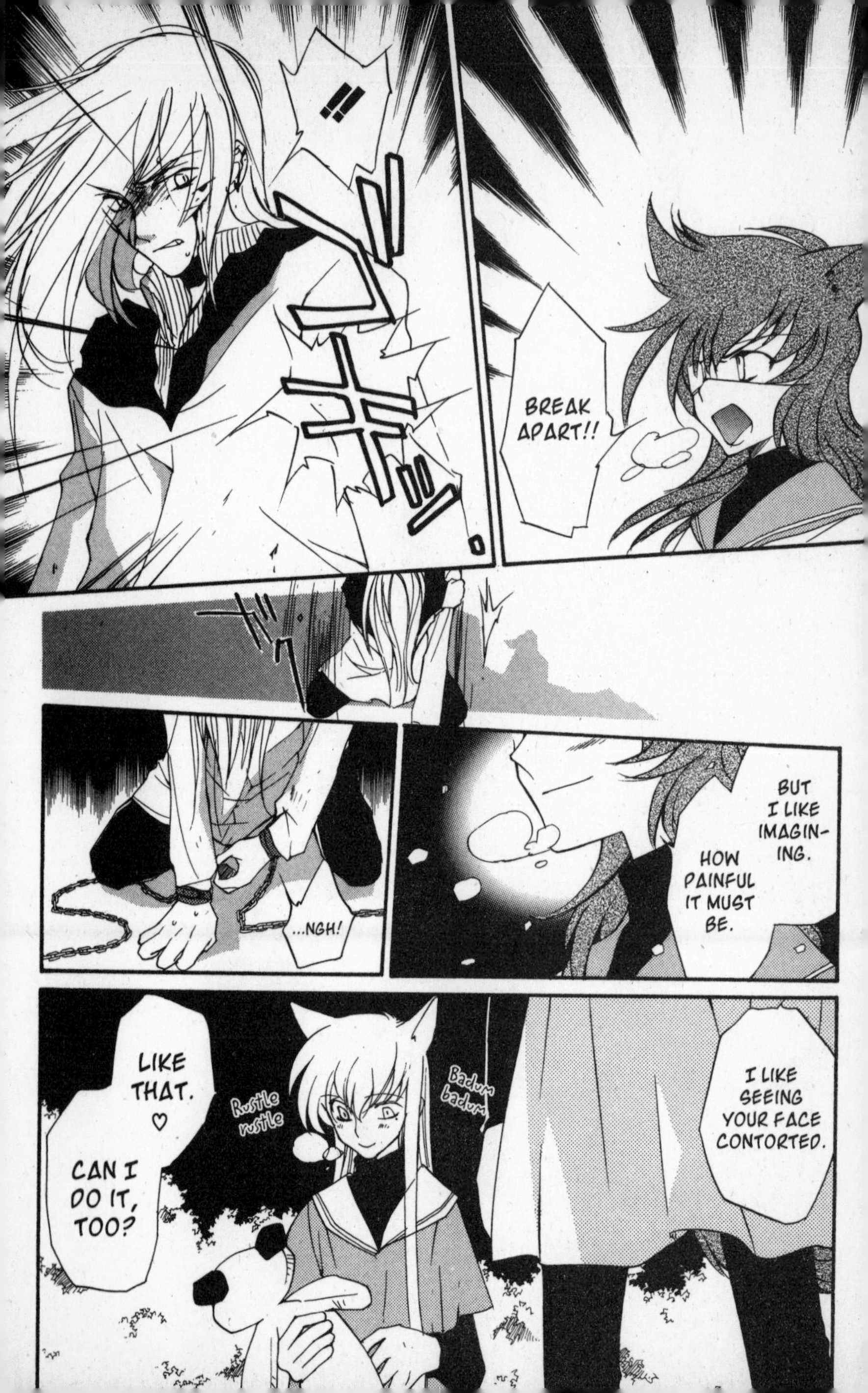
BREAK APART!!
!!
BUT I LIKE IMAGINING.
HOW PAINFUL IT MUST BE.
...NGH!
I LIKE SEEING YOUR FACE CONTORTED.
Badum badum
Rustle rustle
LIKE THAT. ♡
CAN I DO IT, TOO?

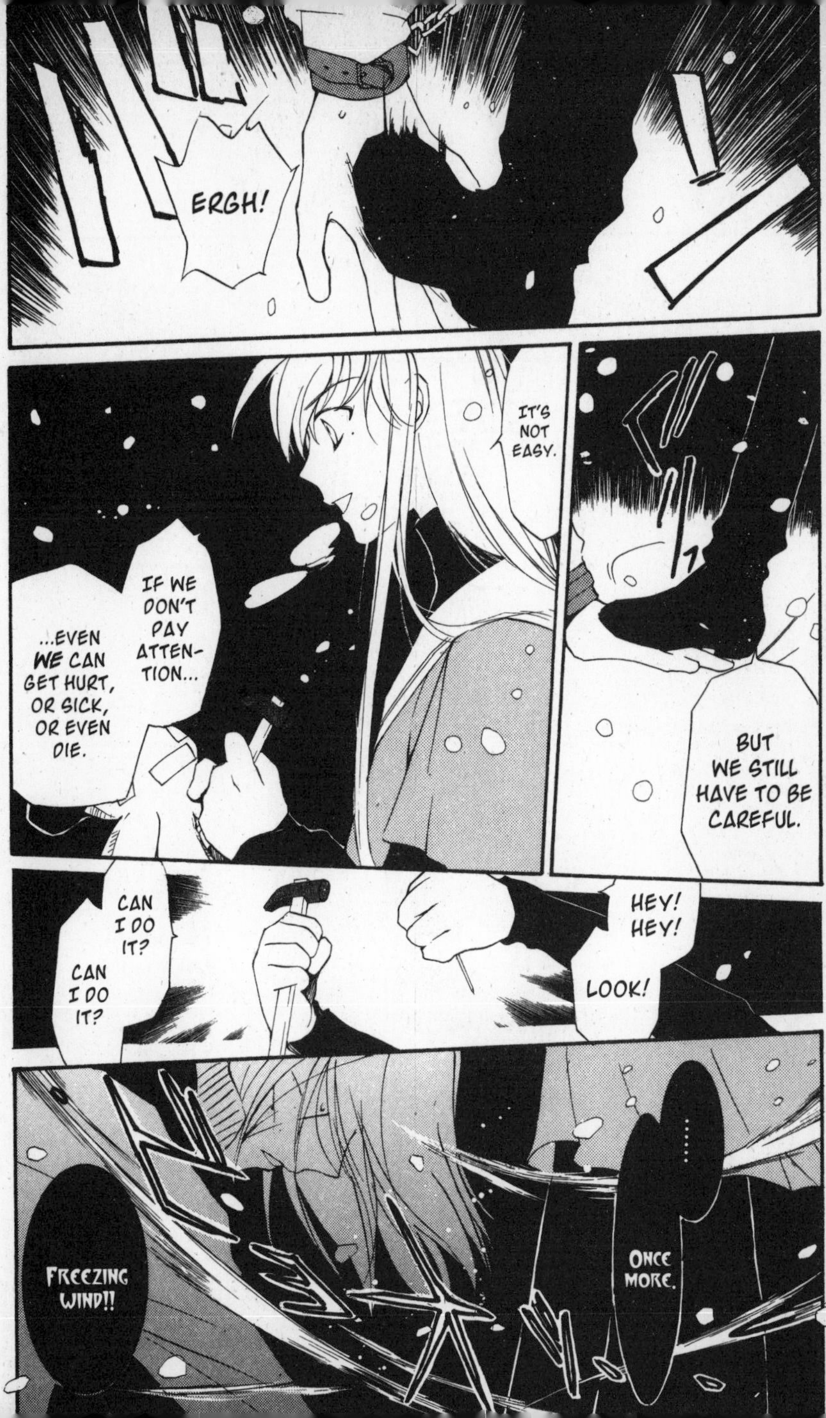
ERGH!
BUT WE STILL HAVE TO BE CAREFUL.
IT'S NOT EASY.
IF WE DON'T PAY ATTENTION...
...EVEN WE CAN GET HURT, OR SICK, OR EVEN DIE.
HEY! HEY!
LOOK!
CAN I DO IT?
CAN I DO IT?
......
ONCE MORE.
FREEZING WIND!!

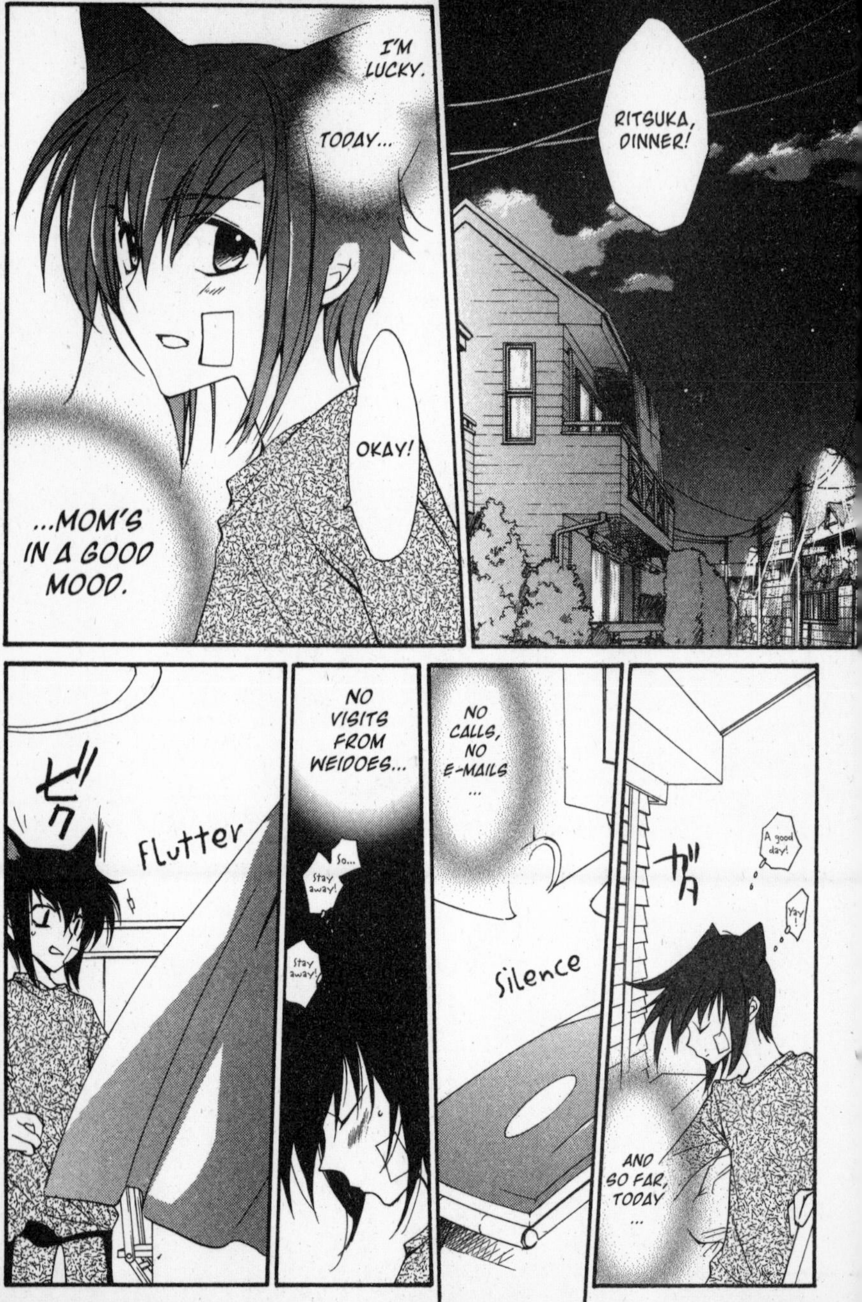

RITSUKA, DINNER!
I'M LUCKY.
TODAY...
OKAY!
...MOM'S IN A GOOD MOOD.
A good day!
Yay!
ガタ
AND SO FAR, TODAY ...
NO CALLS, NO E-MAILS ...
Silence
NO VISITS FROM WEIDOES...
So... Stay away!
Stay away!
ビク
Flutter

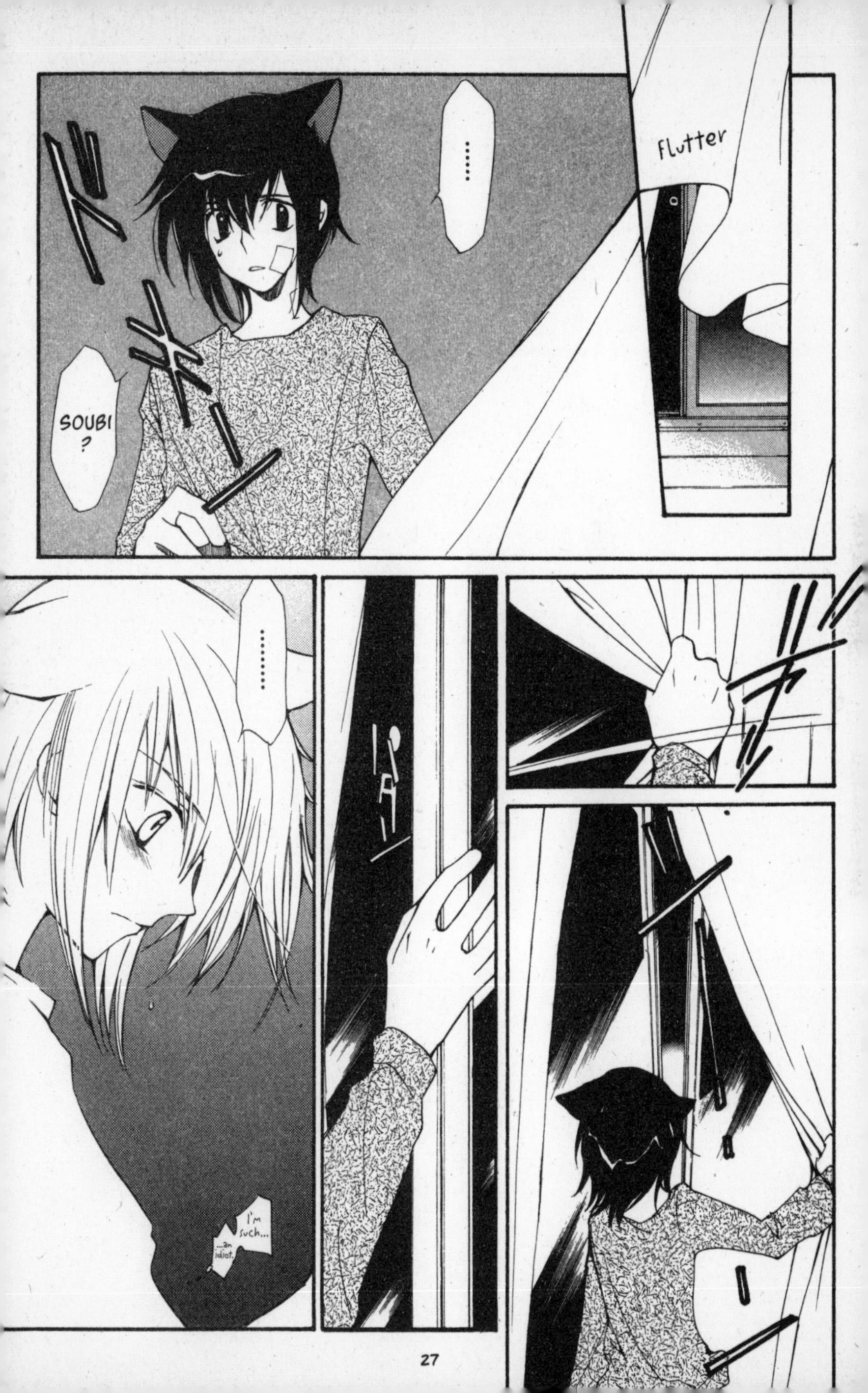
Flutter
......
SOUBI ?
......
I'm such...
...an idiot.

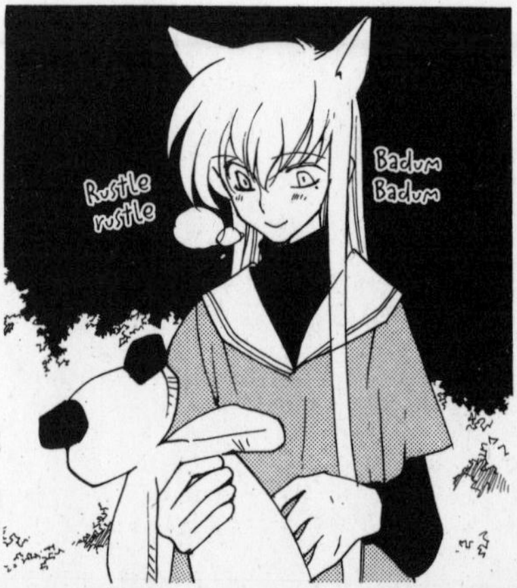
Badum
Badum
Rustle
rustle

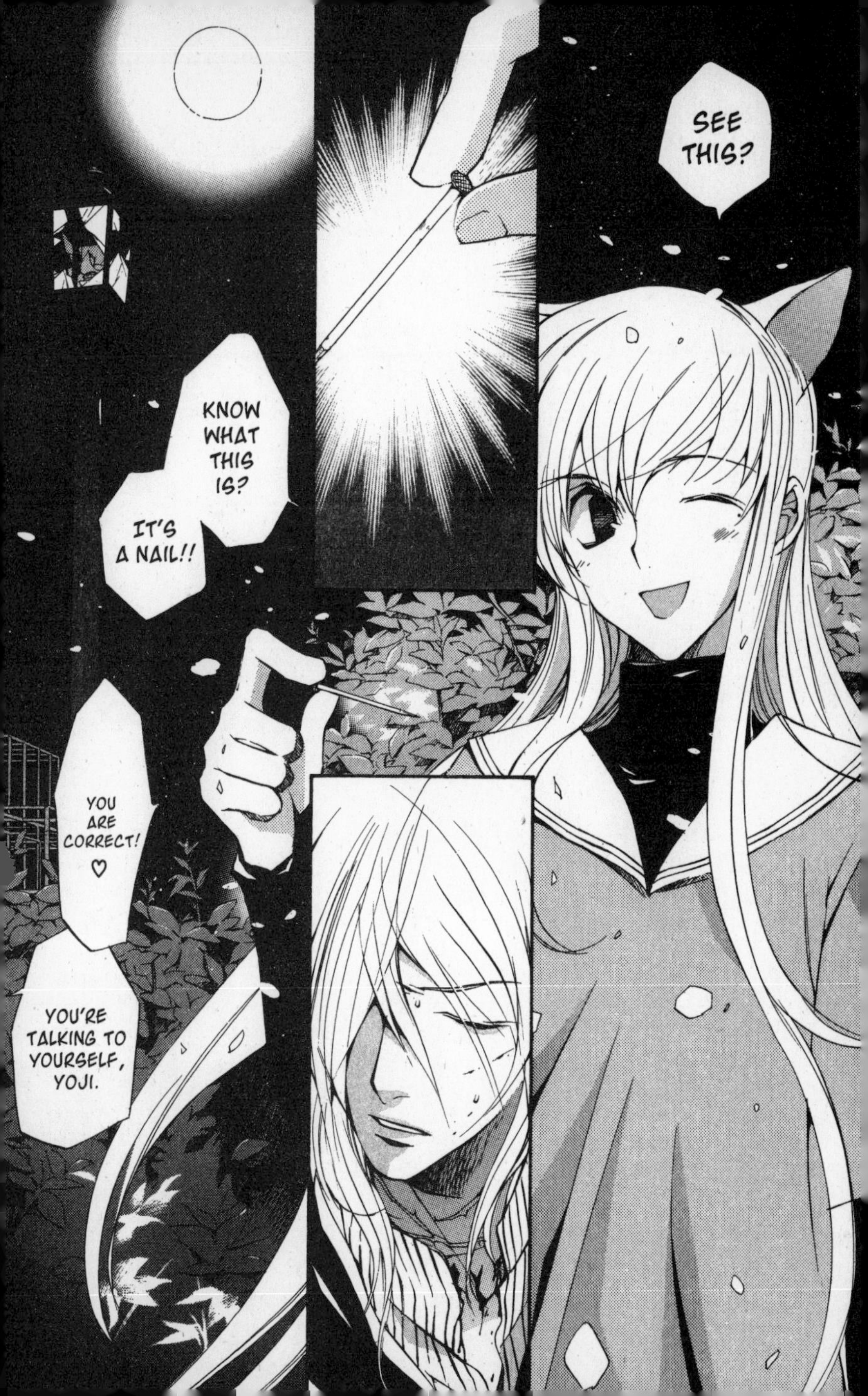
SEE THIS?
KNOW WHAT THIS IS?
IT'S A NAIL!!
YOU ARE CORRECT! ♡
YOU'RE TALKING TO YOURSELF, YOJI.

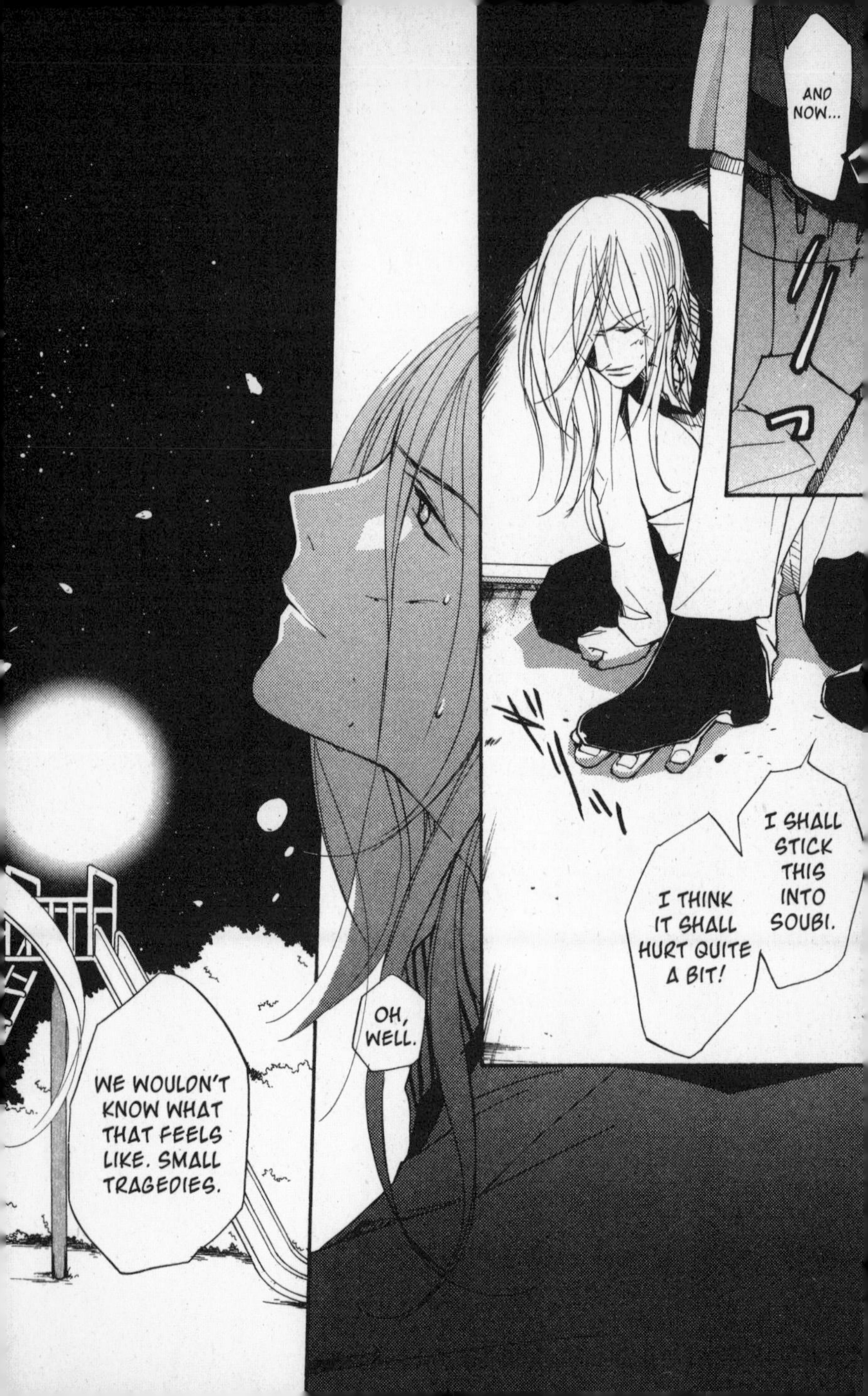
AND NOW...
I SHALL STICK THIS INTO SOUBI.
I THINK IT SHALL HURT QUITE A BIT!
OH, WELL.
WE WOULDN'T KNOW WHAT THAT FEELS LIKE. SMALL TRAGEDIES.

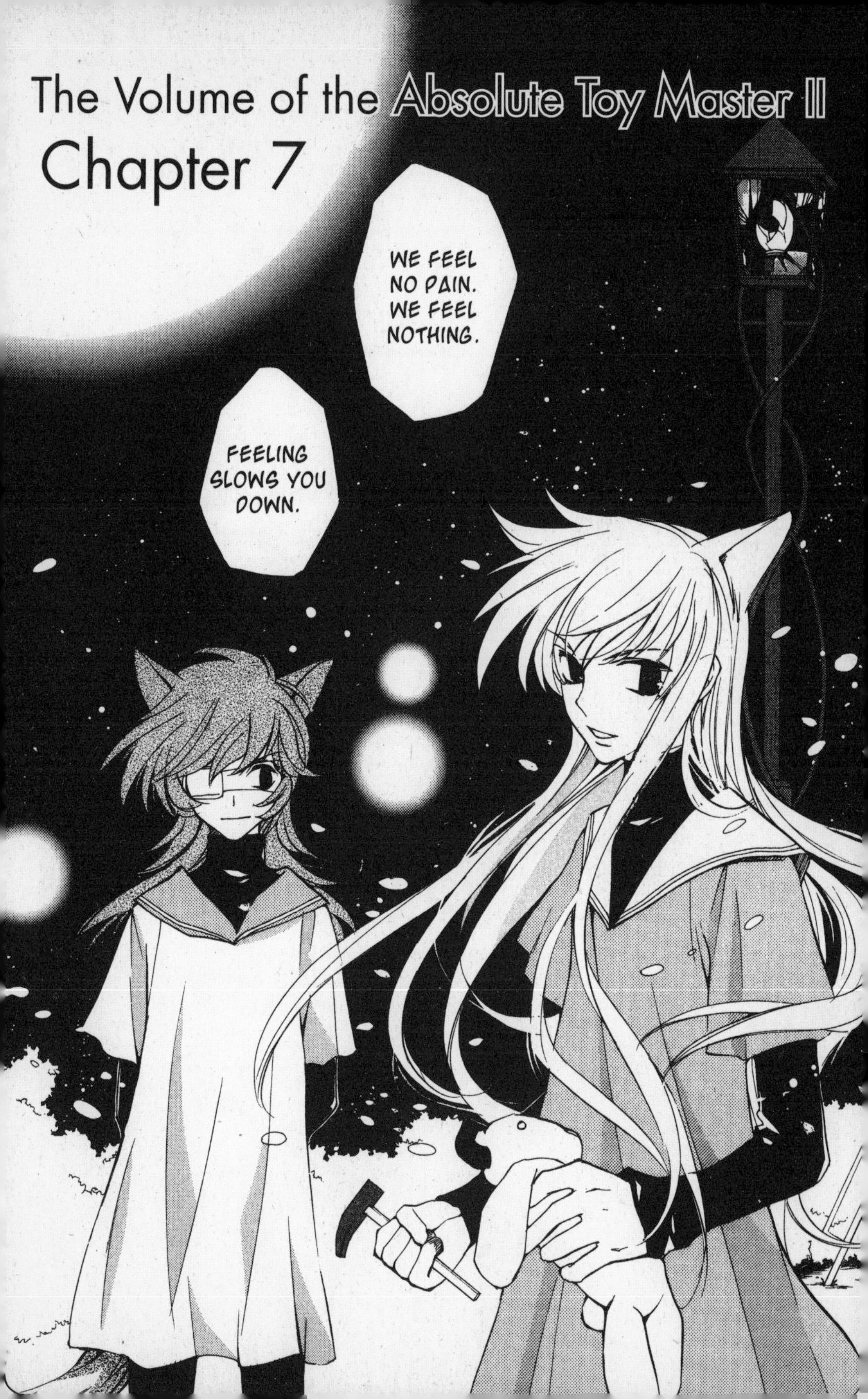
The Volume of the Absolute Toy Master II
Chapter 7
WE FEEL NO PAIN. WE FEEL NOTHING.
FEELING SLOWS YOU DOWN.

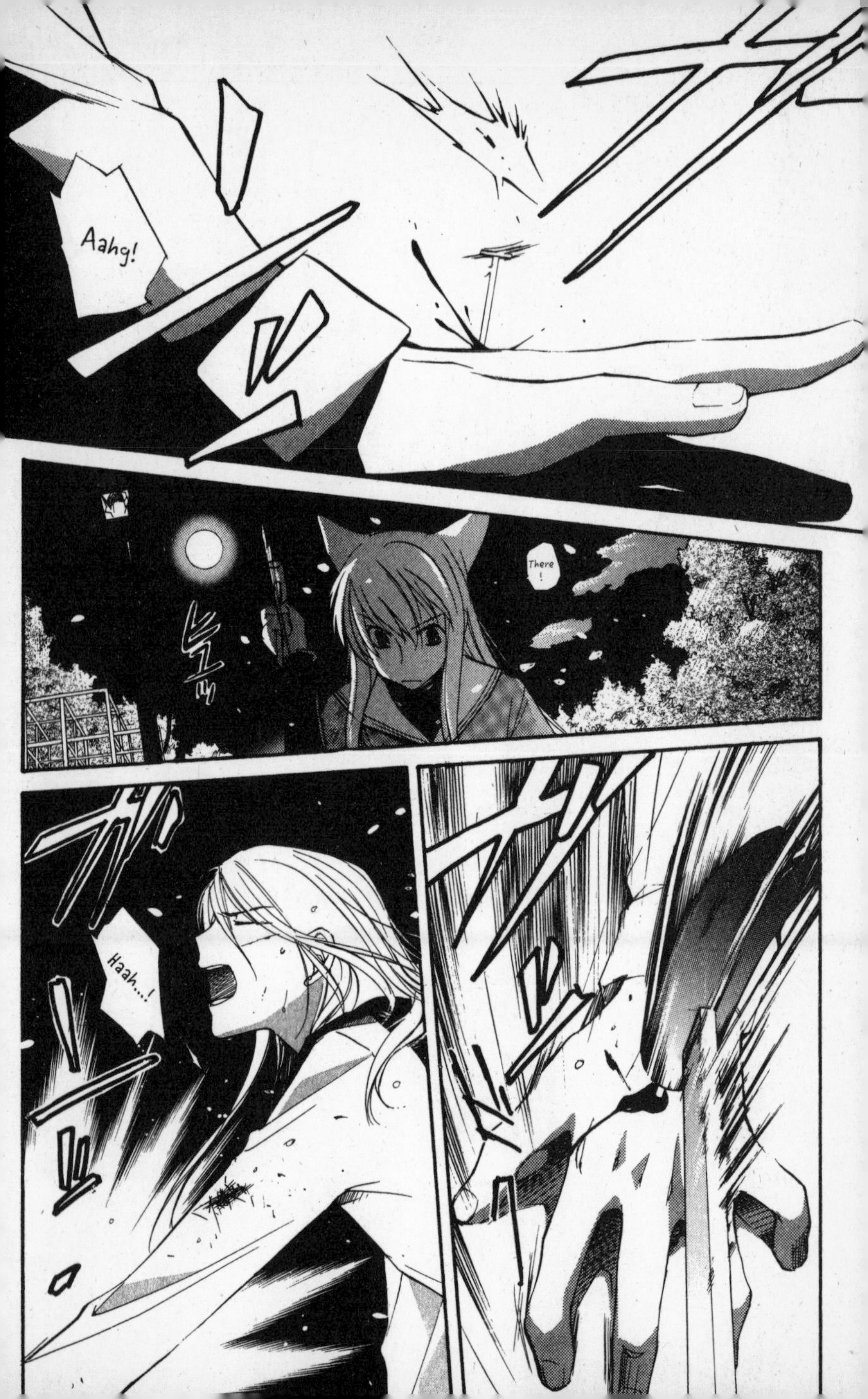
Aahg!
There!
Haaah...!

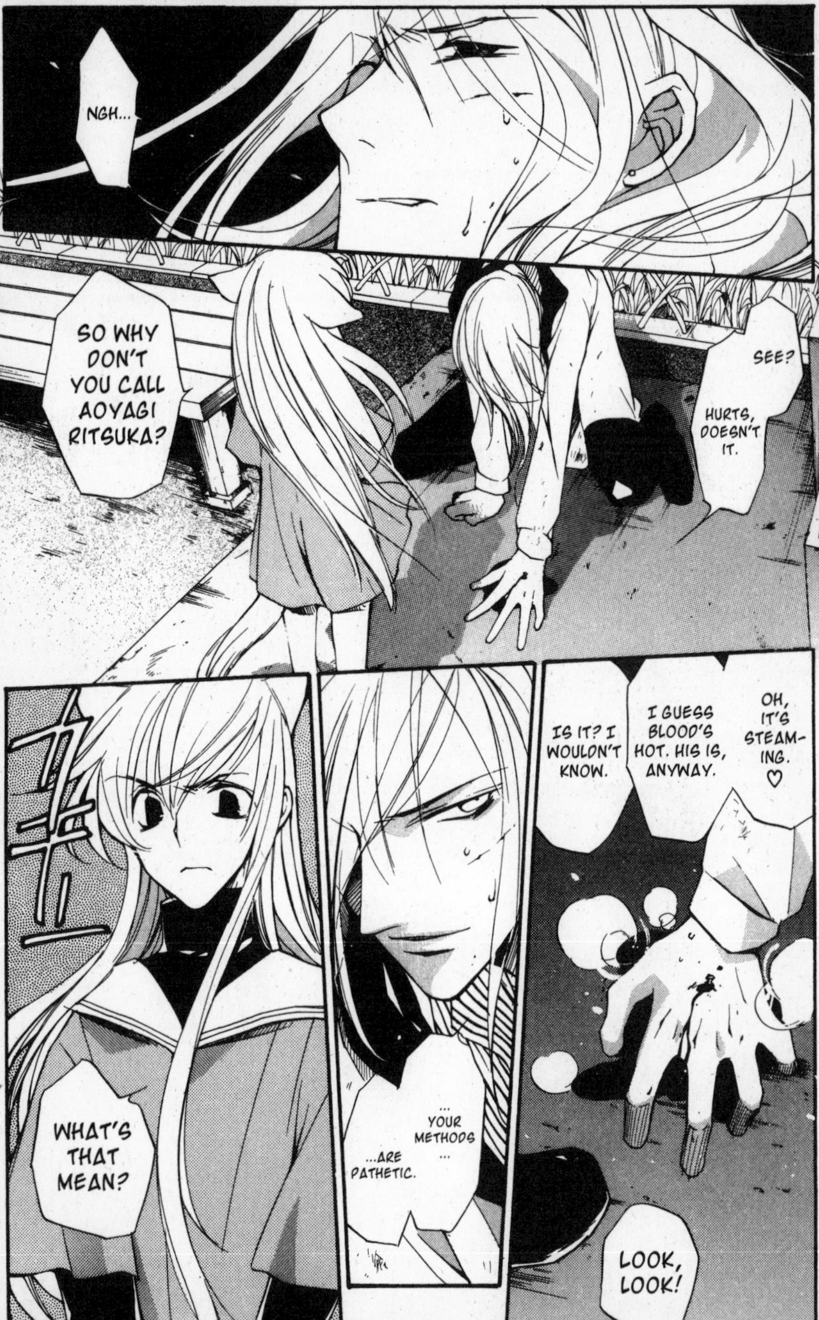
NGH...
SEE?
HURTS, DOESN'T IT.
SO WHY DON'T YOU CALL AOYAGI RITSUKA?
OH, IT'S STEAMING. ♡
I GUESS BLOOD'S HOT. HIS IS, ANYWAY.
IS IT? I WOULDN'T KNOW.
LOOK, LOOK!
...YOUR METHODS...
...ARE PATHETIC.
WHAT'S THAT MEAN?

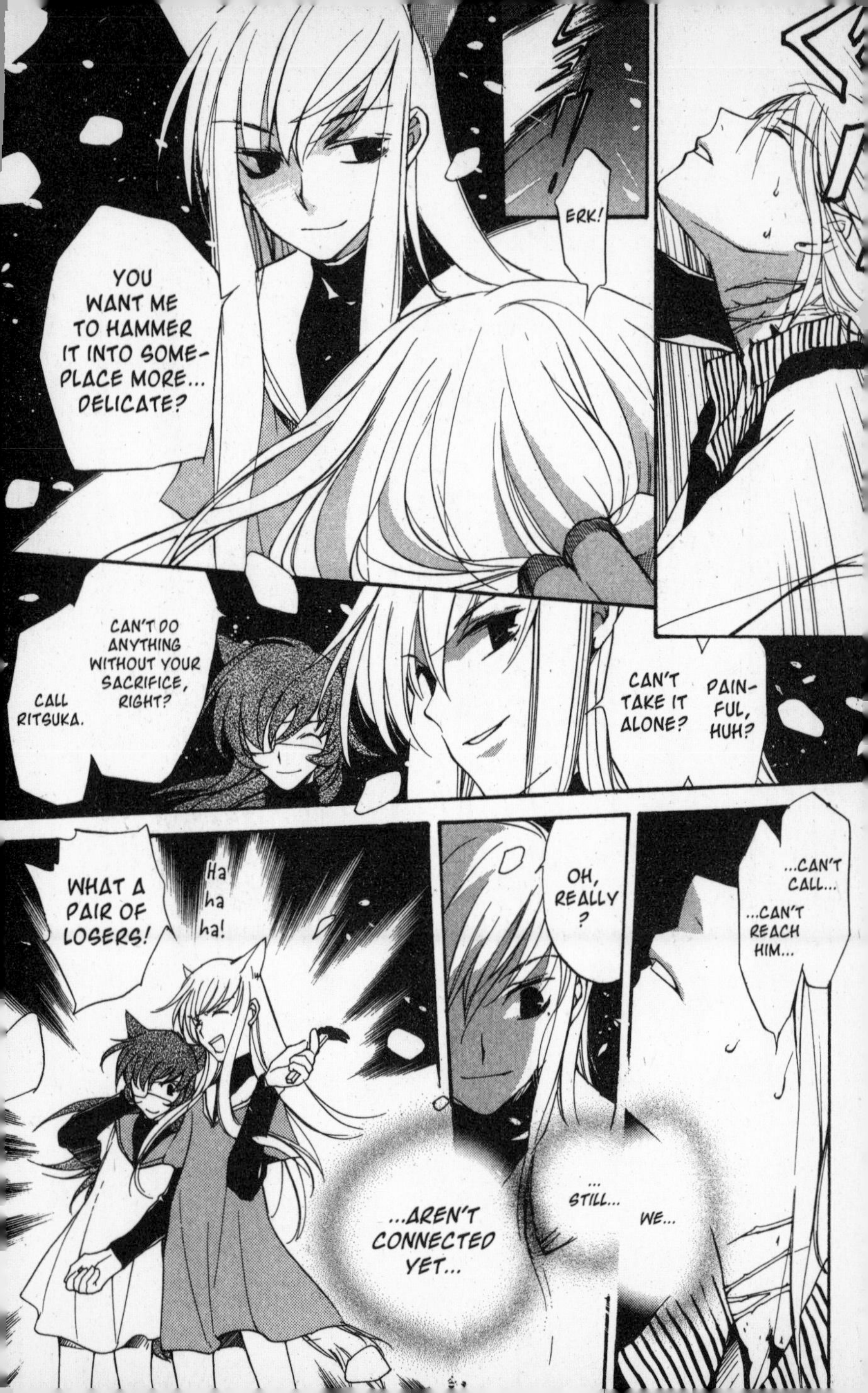

ERK!
YOU WANT ME TO HAMMER IT INTO SOME-PLACE MORE... DELICATE?
PAIN-FUL, HUH?
CAN'T TAKE IT ALONE?
CAN'T DO ANYTHING WITHOUT YOUR SACRIFICE, RIGHT?
CALL RITSUKA.
...CAN'T CALL...
...CAN'T REACH HIM...
WE...
... STILL...
...AREN'T CONNECTED YET...
OH, REALLY?
Ha ha ha!
WHAT A PAIR OF LOSERS!

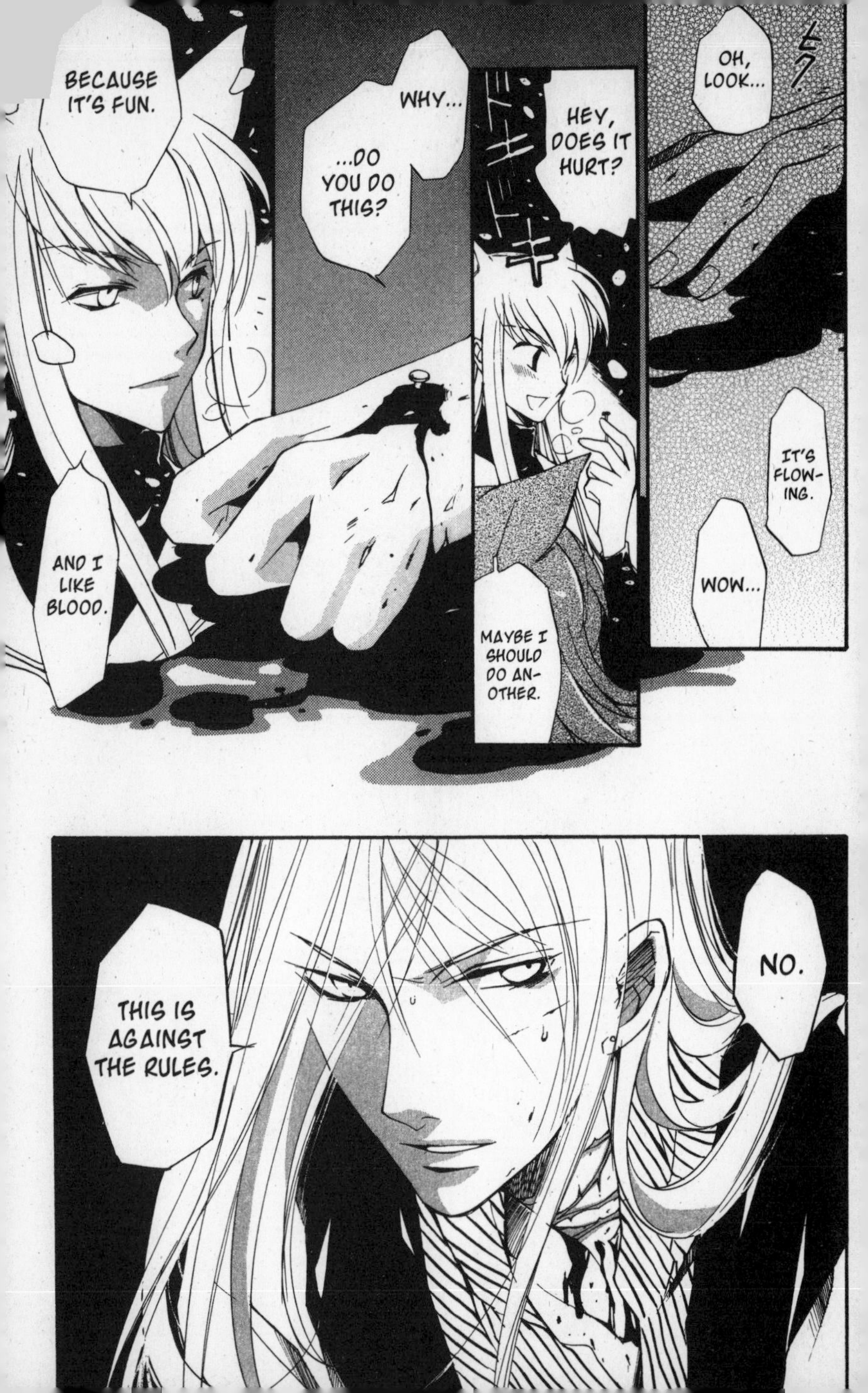
OH, LOOK...
IT'S FLOWING.
WOW...
HEY, DOES IT HURT?
MAYBE I SHOULD DO ANOTHER.
WHY...
...DO YOU DO THIS?
BECAUSE IT'S FUN.
AND I LIKE BLOOD.
NO.
THIS IS AGAINST THE RULES.

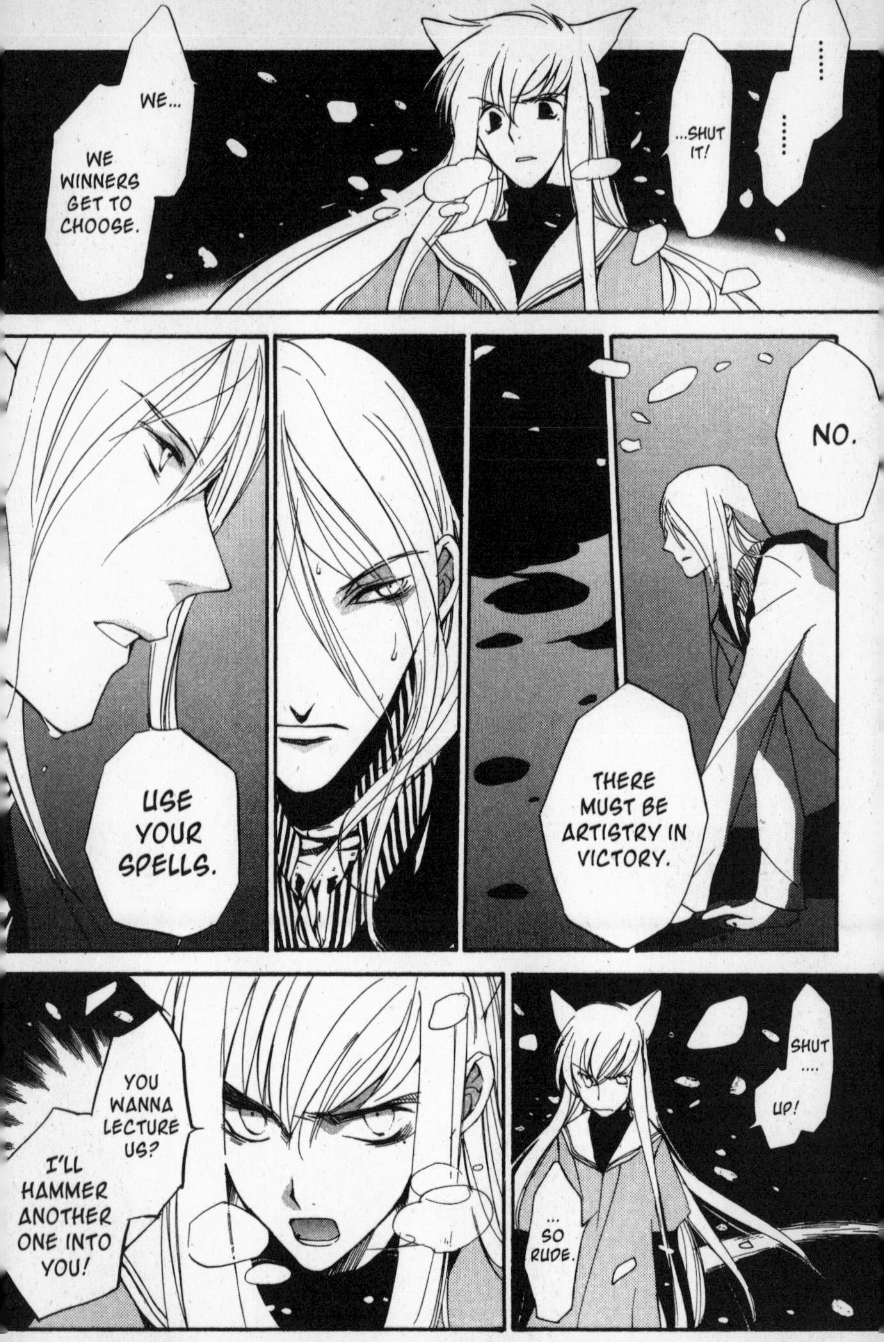
......
...SHUT IT!
WE...
WE WINNERS GET TO CHOOSE.
NO.
THERE MUST BE ARTISTRY IN VICTORY.
USE YOUR SPELLS.
SHUT .... UP!
... SO RUDE.
YOU WANNA LECTURE US?
I'LL HAMMER ANOTHER ONE INTO YOU!

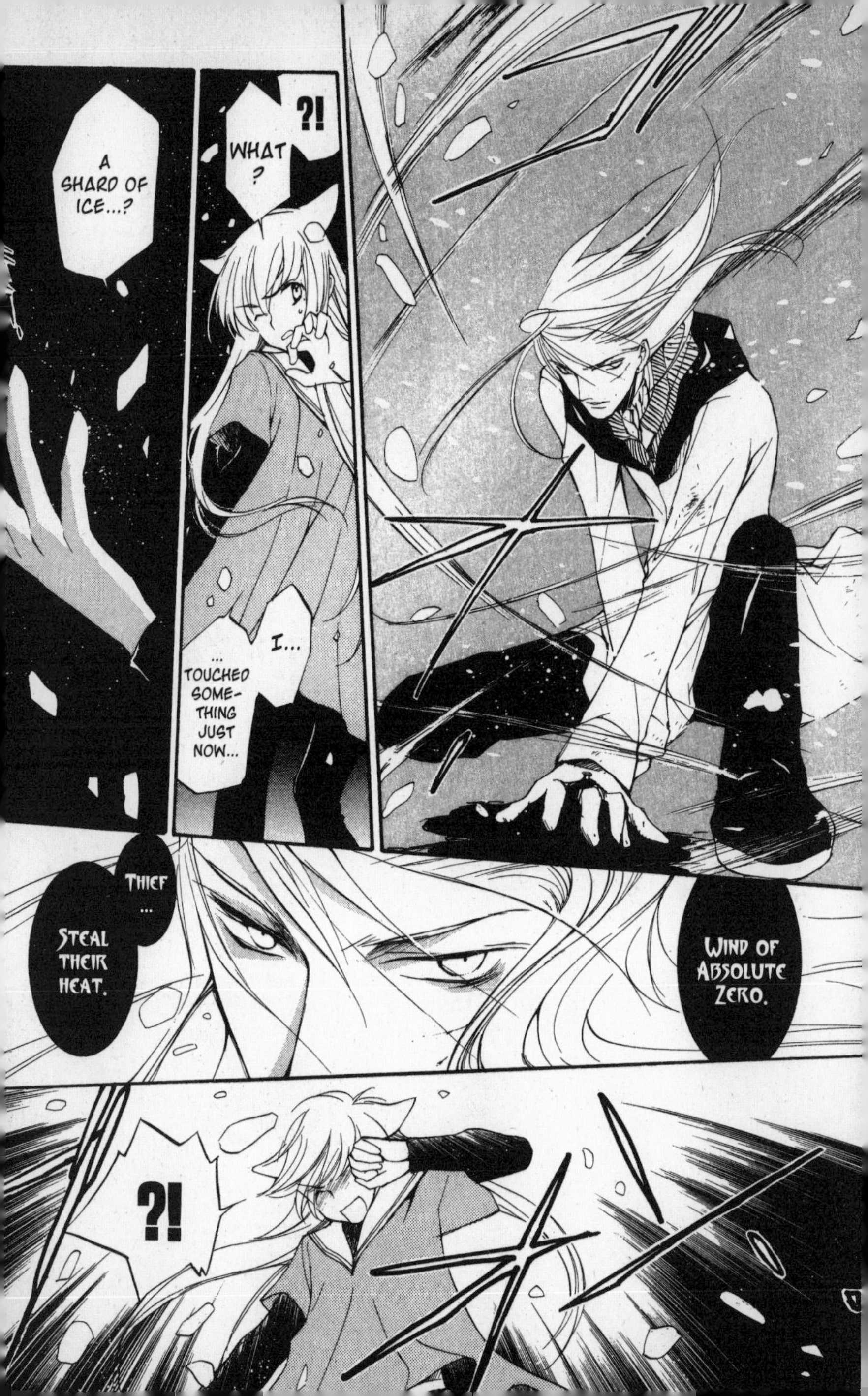
?!
WHAT ?
I...
...TOUCHED SOMETHING JUST NOW...
A SHARD OF ICE...?
WIND OF ABSOLUTE ZERO.
THIEF ...
STEAL THEIR HEAT.
?!

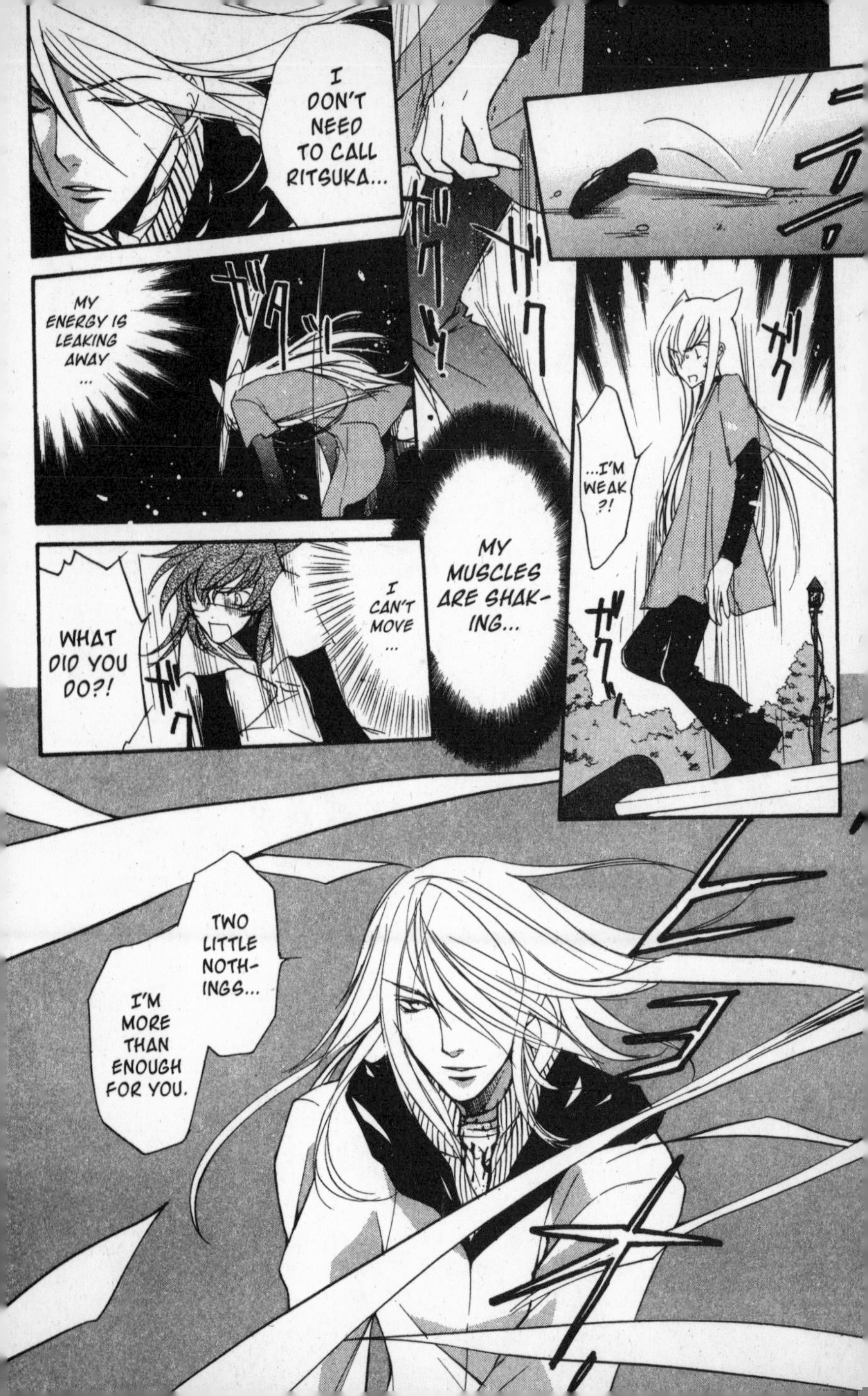
I DON'T NEED TO CALL RITSUKA...
...I'M WEAK ?!
MY MUSCLES ARE SHAK- ING...
MY ENERGY IS LEAKING AWAY ...
I CAN'T MOVE ...
WHAT DID YOU DO?!
TWO LITTLE NOTH- INGS...
I'M MORE THAN ENOUGH FOR YOU.

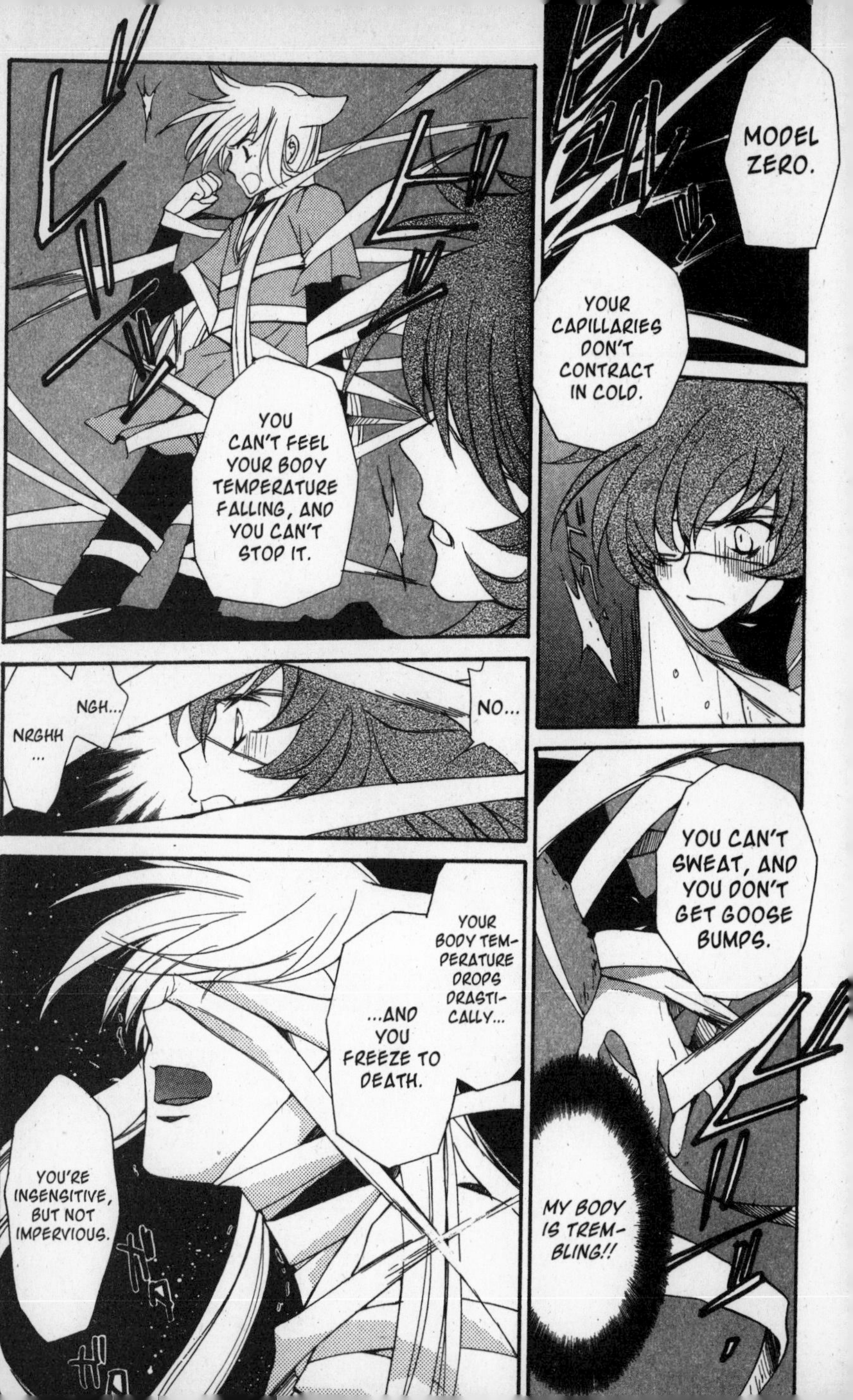
MODEL ZERO.
YOUR CAPILLARIES DON'T CONTRACT IN COLD.
YOU CAN'T FEEL YOUR BODY TEMPERATURE FALLING, AND YOU CAN'T STOP IT.
NO...
NGH...
NRGHH ...
YOU CAN'T SWEAT, AND YOU DON'T GET GOOSE BUMPS.
YOUR BODY TEMPERATURE DROPS DRASTICALLY...
...AND YOU FREEZE TO DEATH.
YOU'RE INSENSITIVE, BUT NOT IMPERVIOUS.
MY BODY IS TREMBLING!!

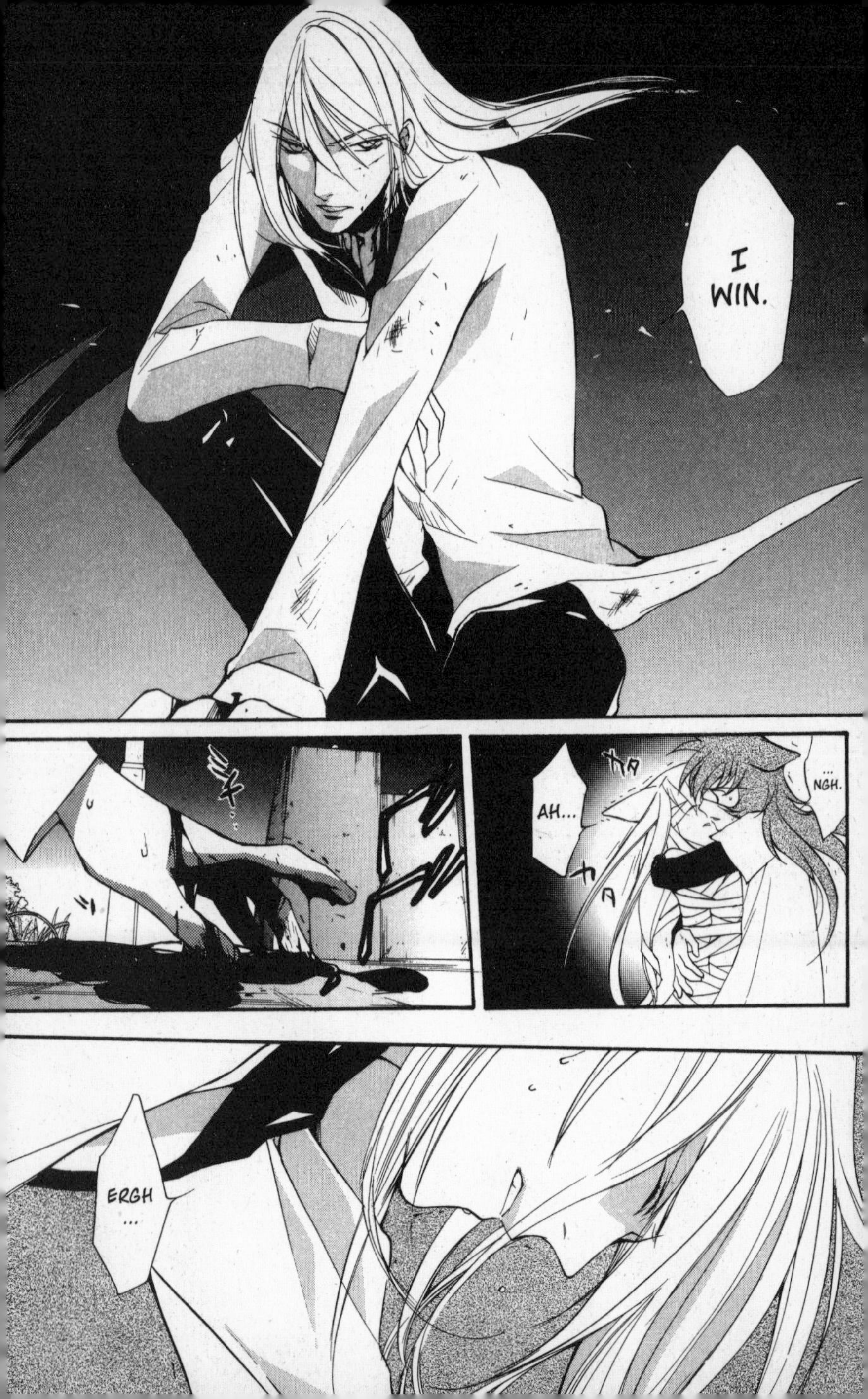
I WIN.
...NGH.
AH...
ERGH ...

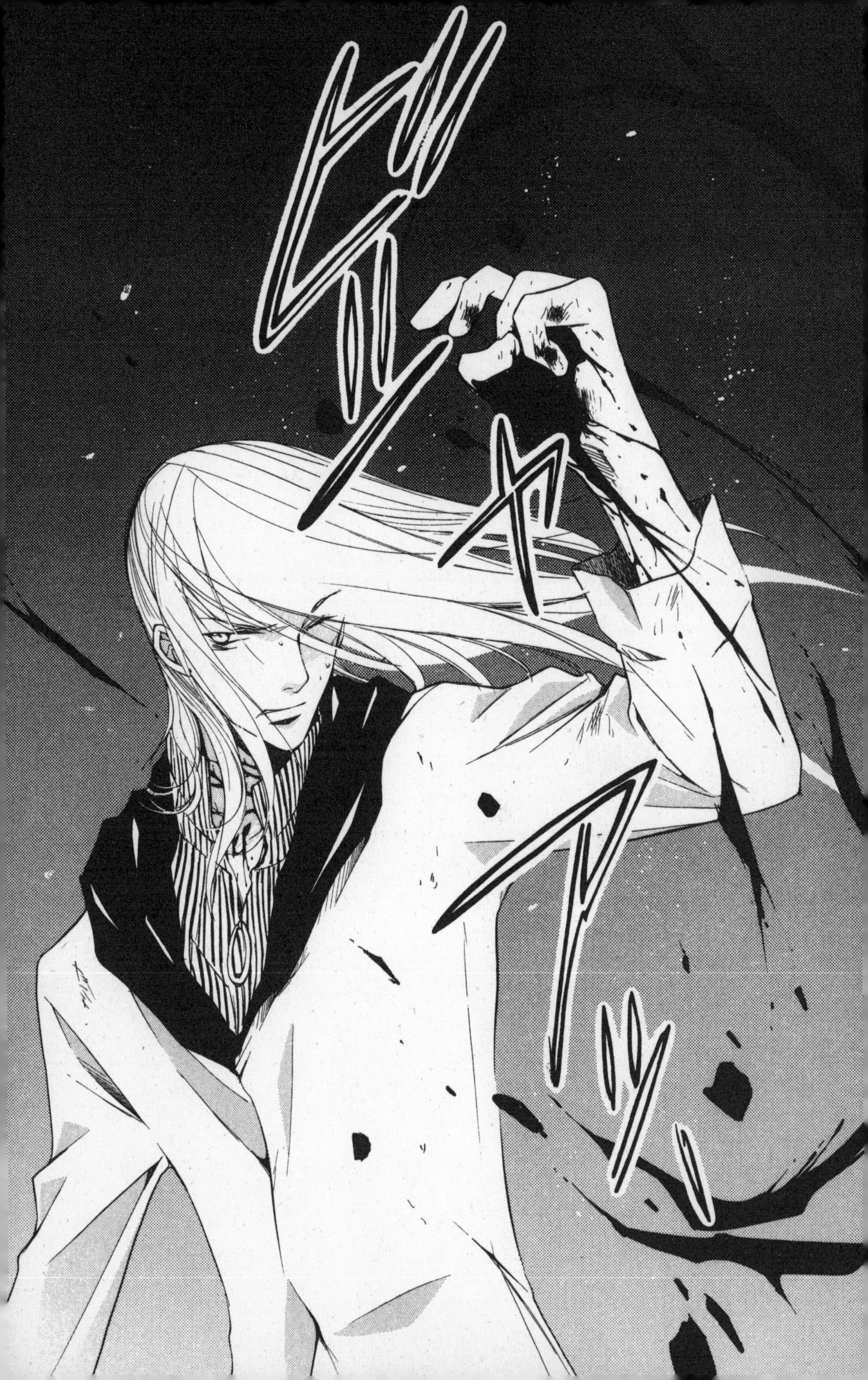

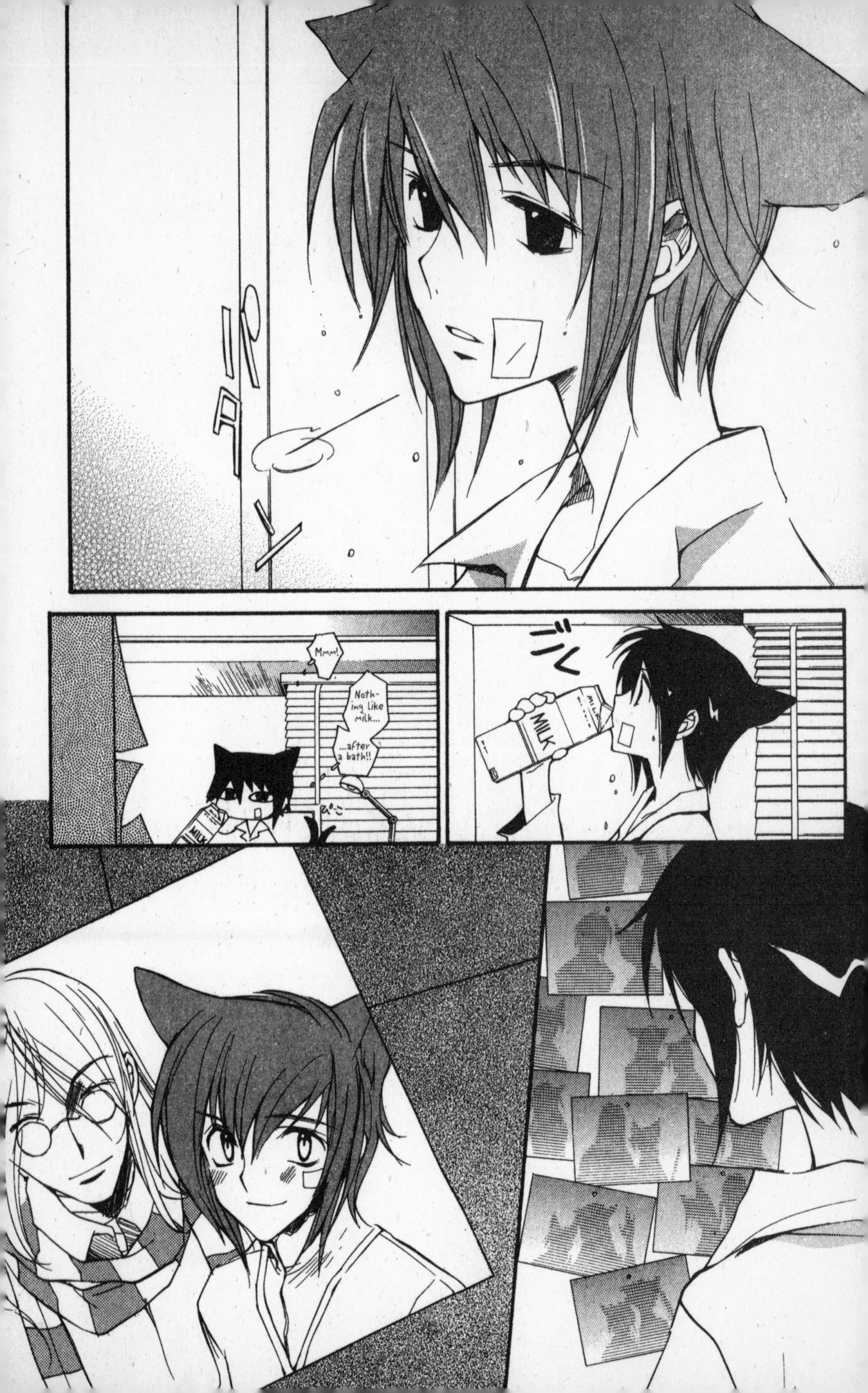
ごく
MILK
Mmm!
Nothing like milk...
...after a bath!!
ぴこ

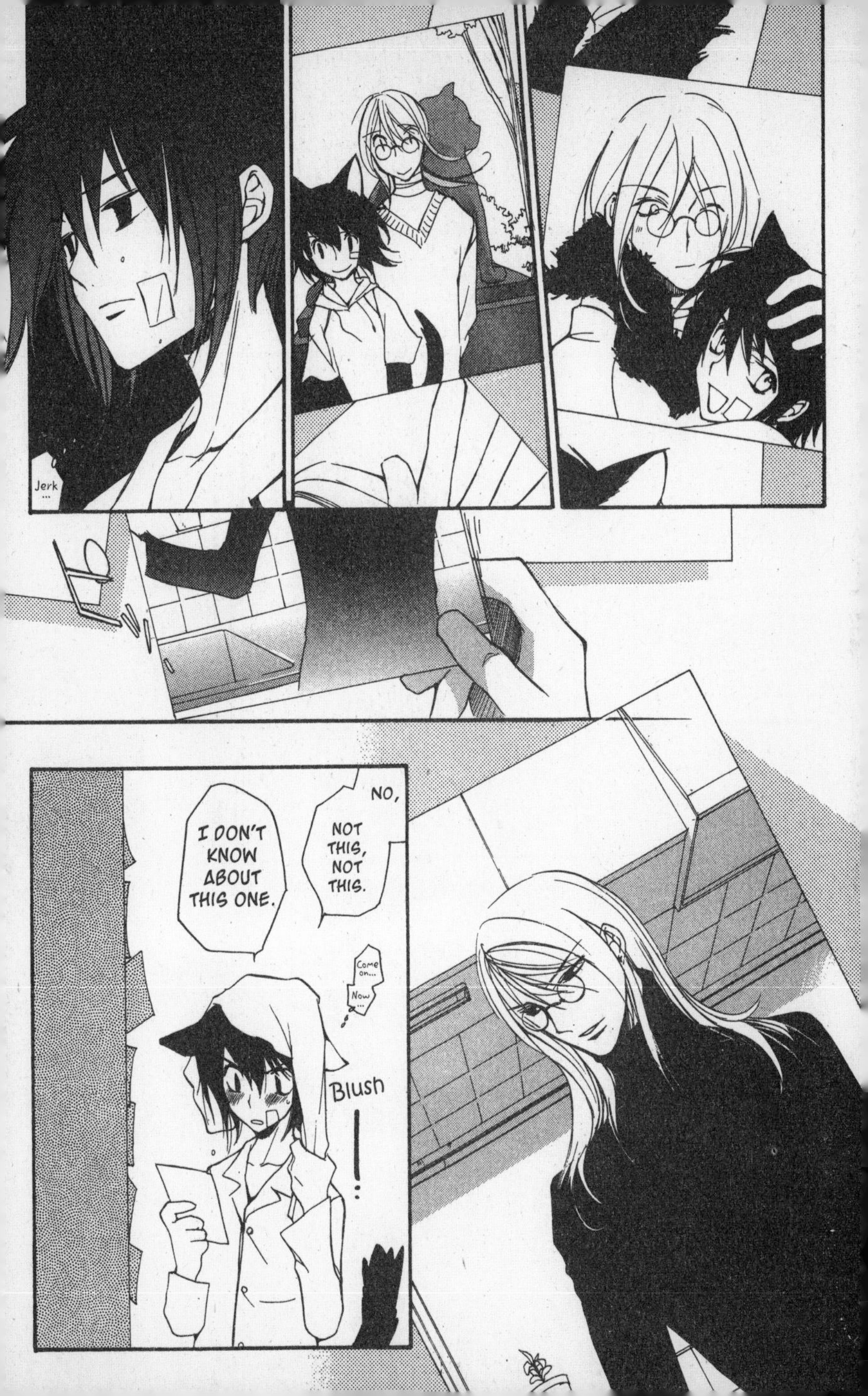
Jerk...
NO,
NOT THIS, NOT THIS.
I DON'T KNOW ABOUT THIS ONE.
Come on...
Now...
Blush
!

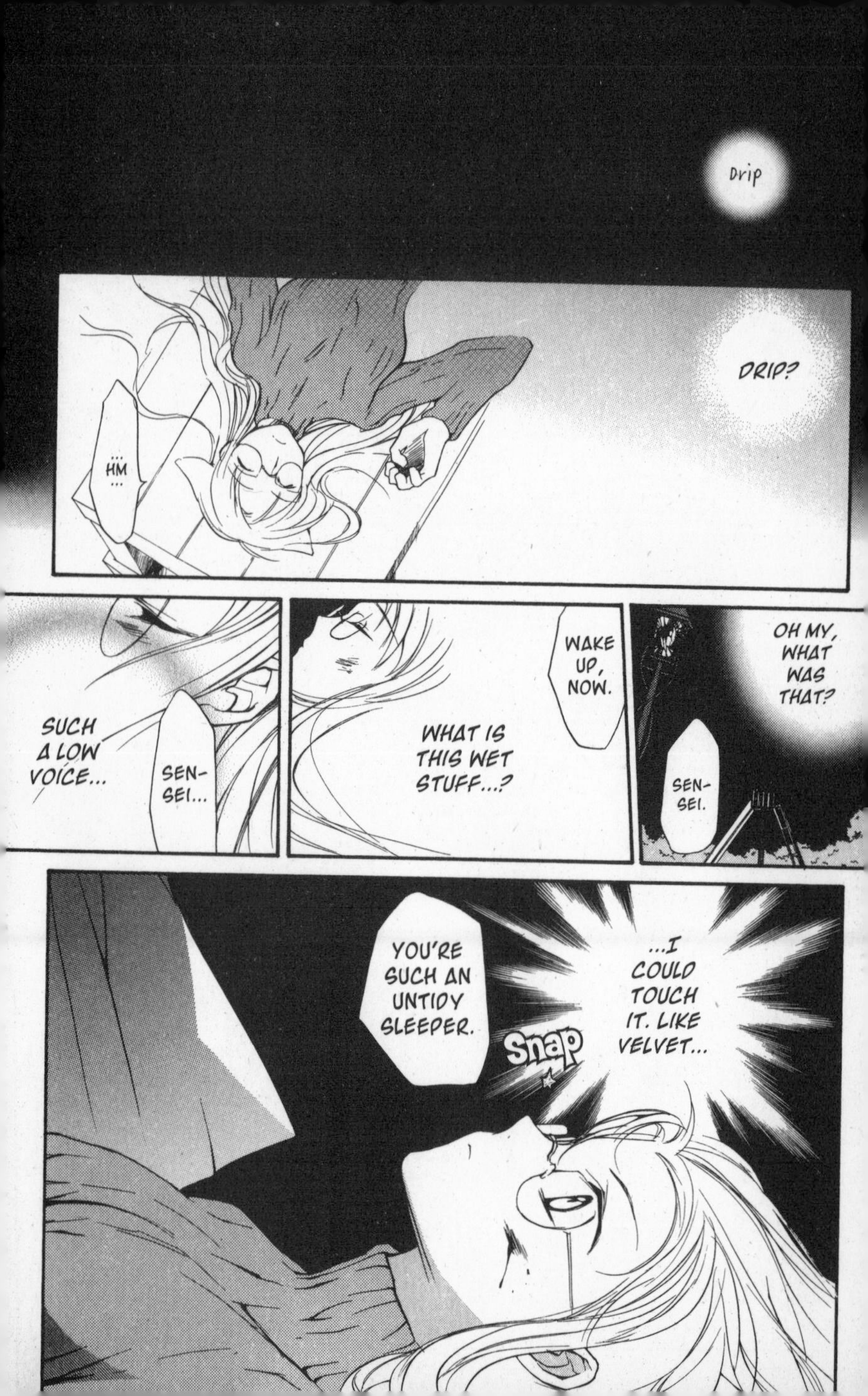
Drip
DRIP?
...HM...
OH MY, WHAT WAS THAT?
SEN-SEI.
WAKE UP, NOW.
WHAT IS THIS WET STUFF...?
SEN-SEI...
SUCH A LOW VOICE...
...I COULD TOUCH IT. LIKE VELVET...
Snap
YOU'RE SUCH AN UNTIDY SLEEPER.

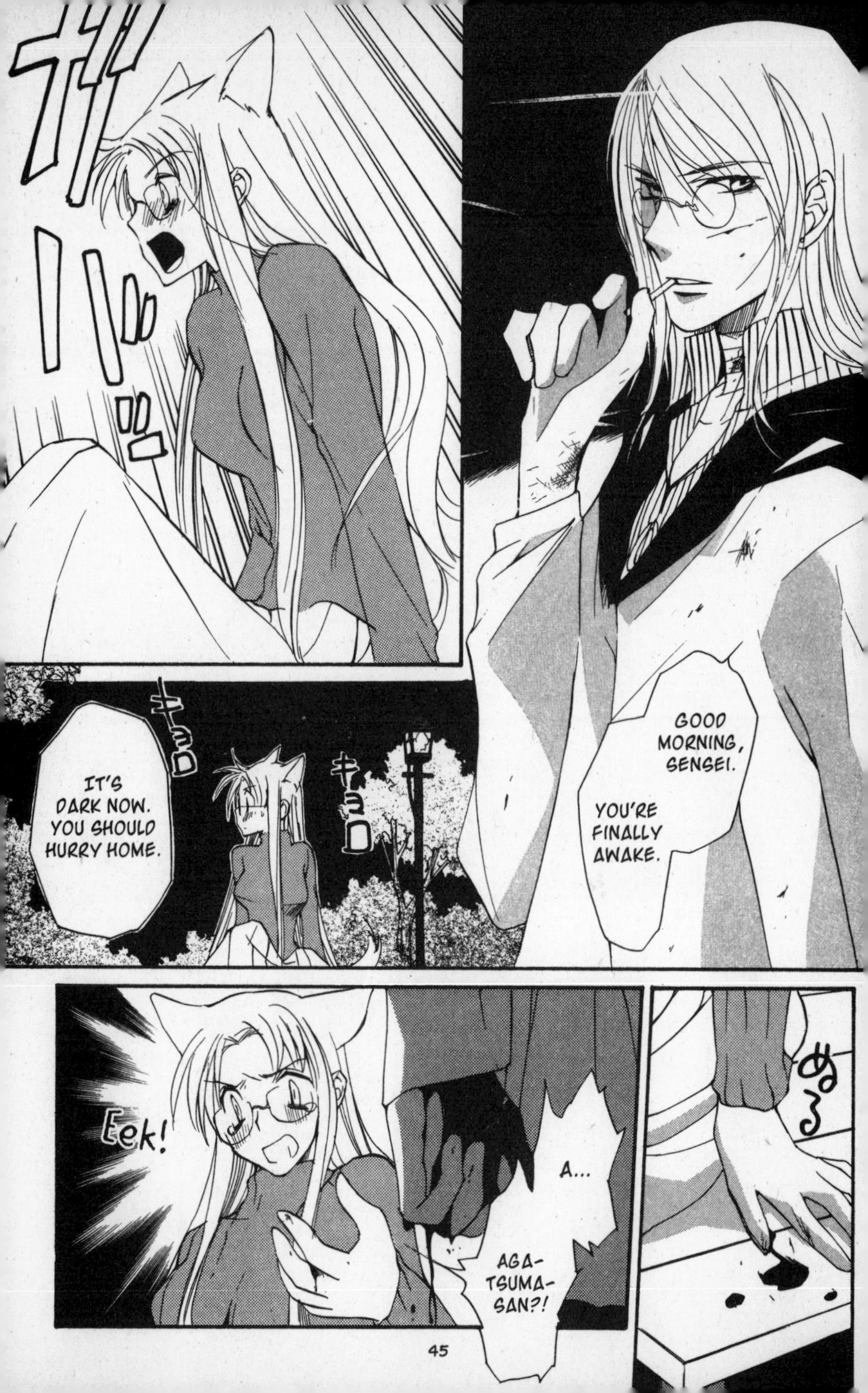
GOOD MORNING, SENSEI.
YOU'RE FINALLY AWAKE.
IT'S DARK NOW. YOU SHOULD HURRY HOME.
キョロ
キョロ
ぬる
A...
AGA-TSUMA-SAN?!
Eek!

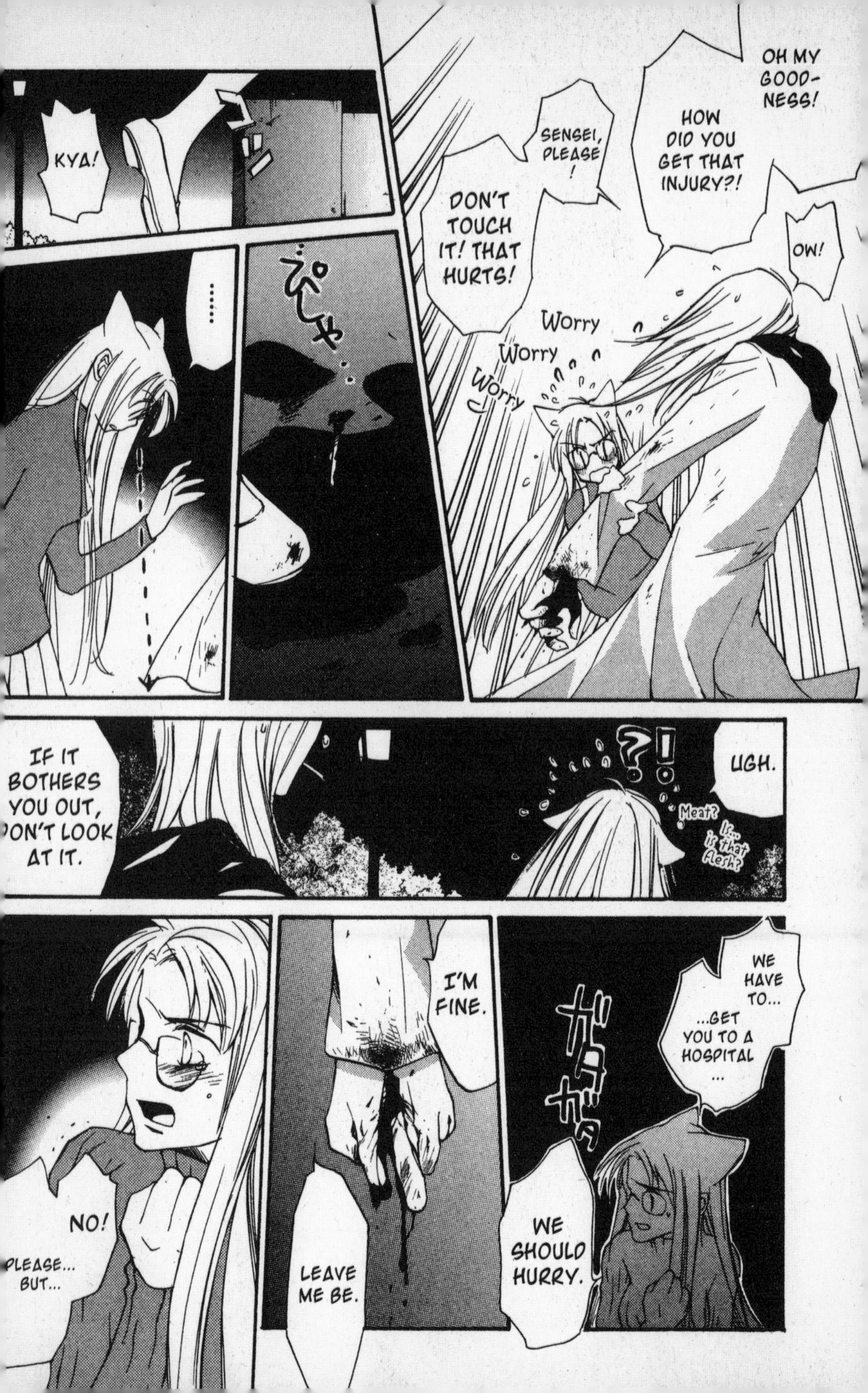
OH MY GOODNESS!
HOW DID YOU GET THAT INJURY?!
OW!
SENSEI, PLEASE!
DON'T TOUCH IT! THAT HURTS!
Worry
Worry
Worry
KYA!
ぴしゃ
......
UGH.
?!
Meat?
Is... is that flesh?
IF IT BOTHERS YOU OUT, DON'T LOOK AT IT.
WE HAVE TO...
...GET YOU TO A HOSPITAL...
ガタガタ
WE SHOULD HURRY.
I'M FINE.
LEAVE ME BE.
NO!
PLEASE... BUT...

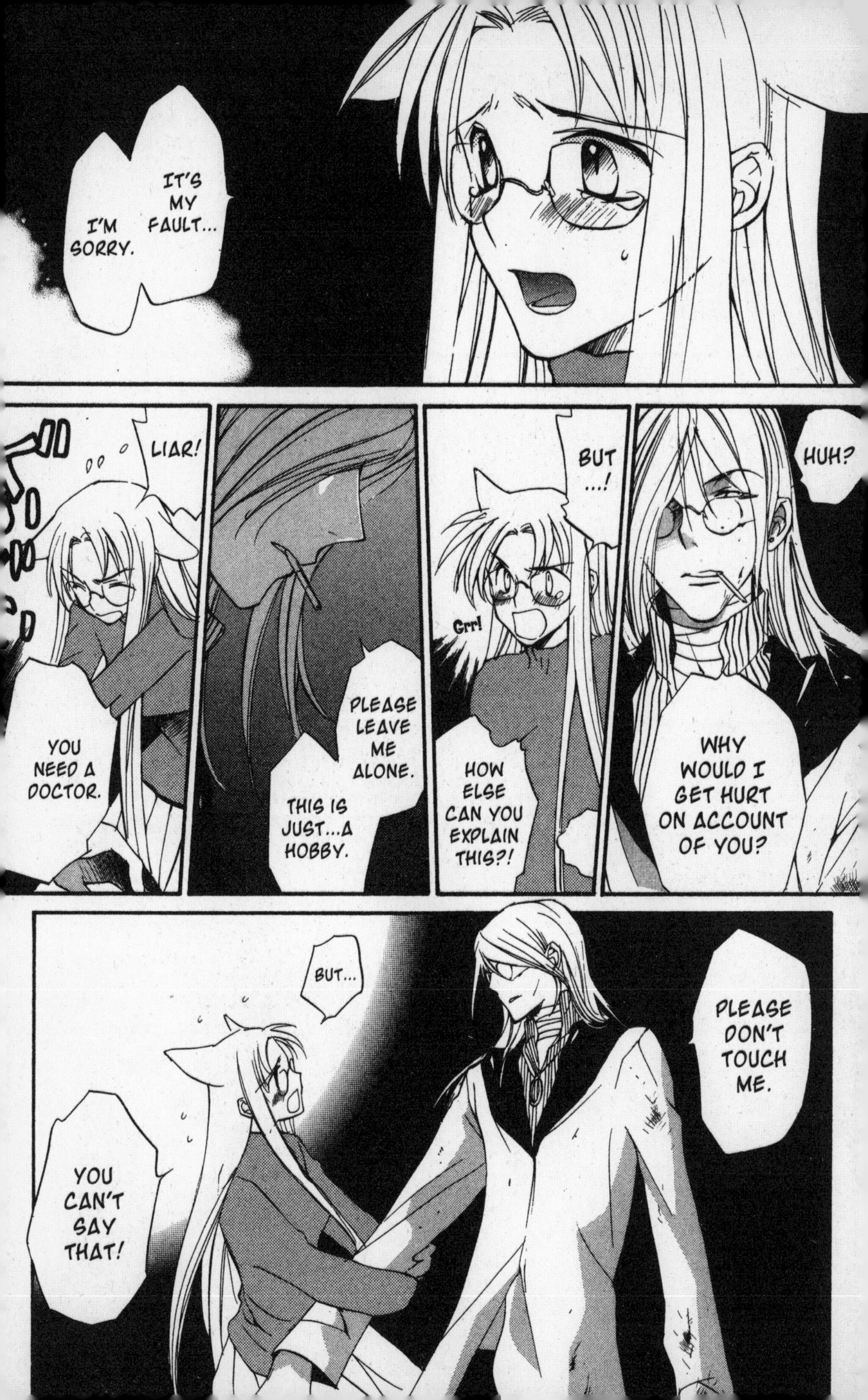
IT'S MY FAULT...
I'M SORRY.
HUH?
WHY WOULD I GET HURT ON ACCOUNT OF YOU?
BUT ...!
Grr!
HOW ELSE CAN YOU EXPLAIN THIS?!
PLEASE LEAVE ME ALONE.
THIS IS JUST...A HOBBY.
LIAR!
YOU NEED A DOCTOR.
PLEASE DON'T TOUCH ME.
BUT...
YOU CAN'T SAY THAT!

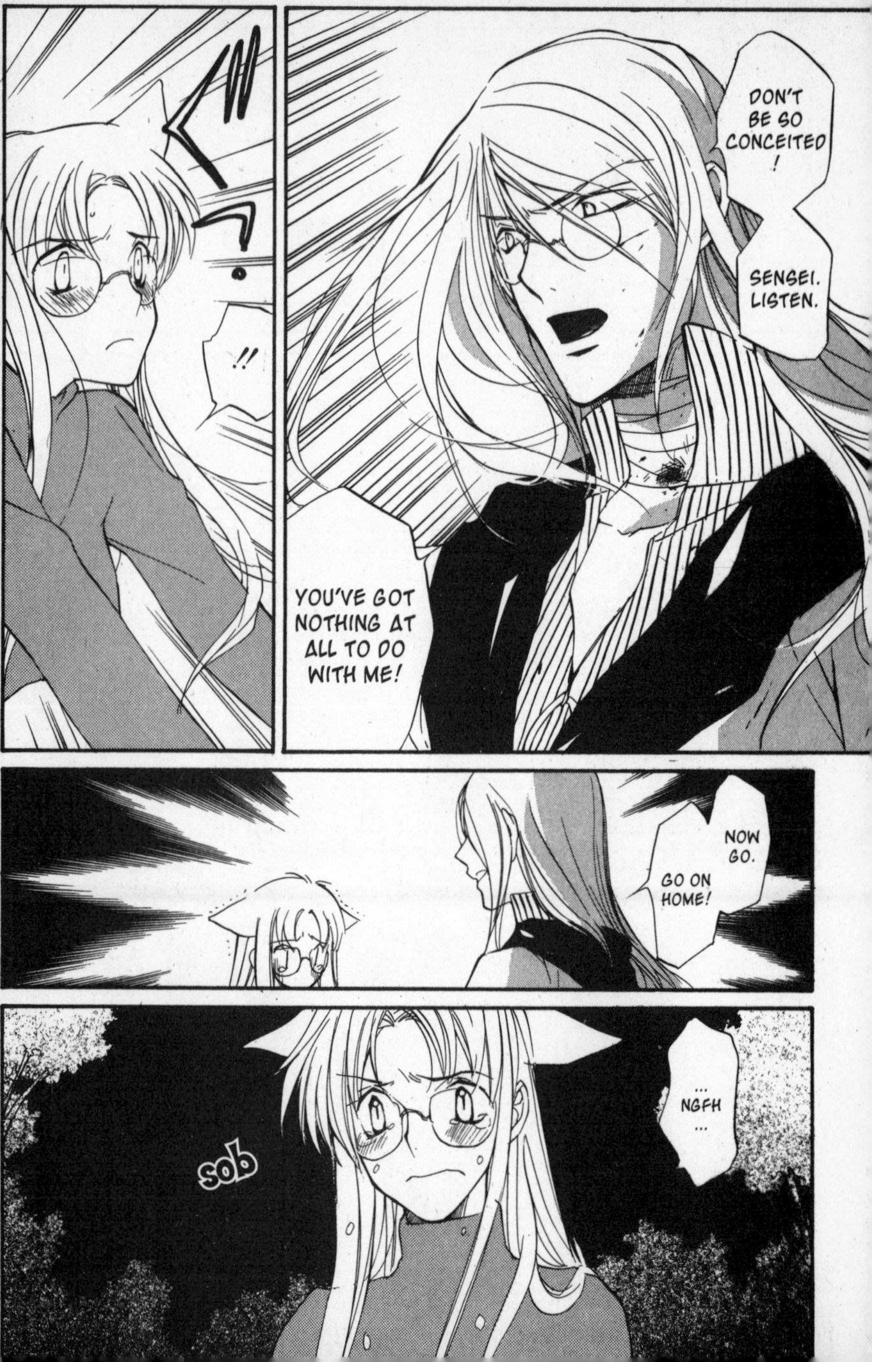
DON'T BE SO CONCEITED!
SENSEI. LISTEN.
YOU'VE GOT NOTHING AT ALL TO DO WITH ME!
!!
NOW GO.
GO ON HOME!
...NGFH...
sob

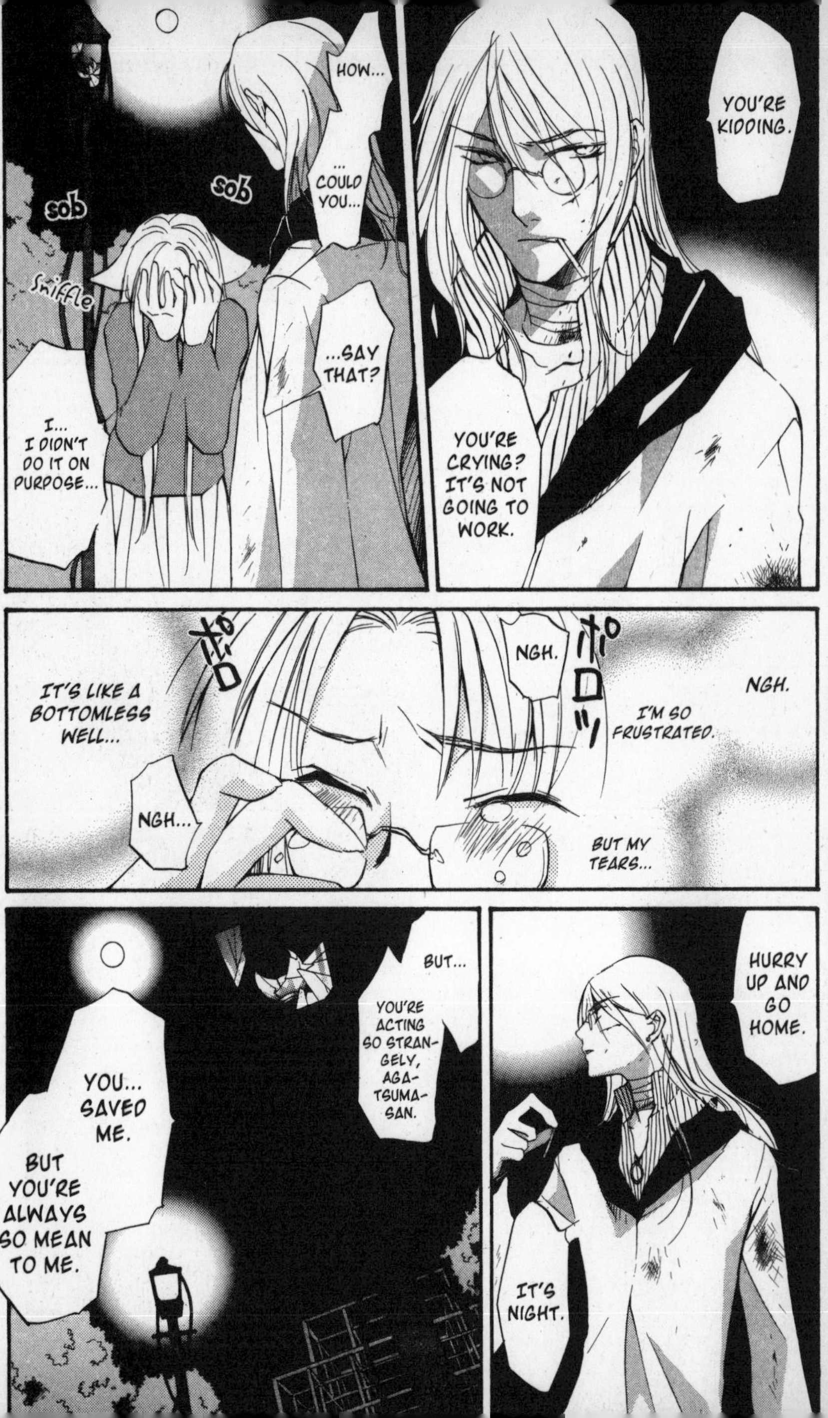
YOU'RE KIDDING.
YOU'RE CRYING? IT'S NOT GOING TO WORK.
HOW...
...COULD YOU...
...SAY THAT?
sob
sob
sniffle
I... I DIDN'T DO IT ON PURPOSE...
NGH.
I'M SO FRUSTRATED.
ポロッ
NGH.
BUT MY TEARS...
ポロ
IT'S LIKE A BOTTOMLESS WELL...
NGH...
HURRY UP AND GO HOME.
IT'S NIGHT.
BUT...
YOU'RE ACTING SO STRANGELY, AGATSUMA-SAN.
YOU... SAVED ME.
BUT YOU'RE ALWAYS SO MEAN TO ME.

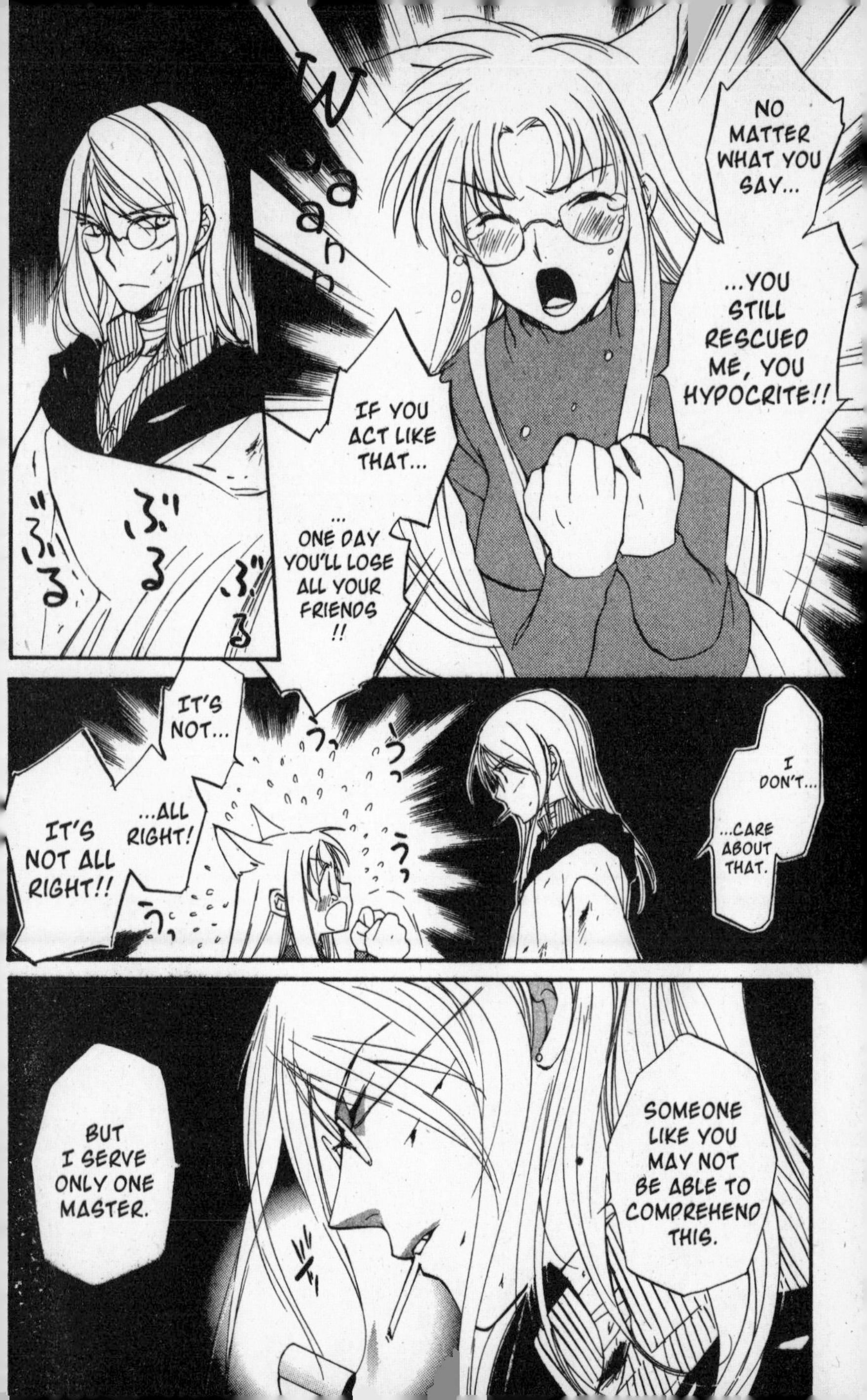
NO MATTER WHAT YOU SAY...
...YOU STILL RESCUED ME, YOU HYPOCRITE!!
Waaann
IF YOU ACT LIKE THAT...
... ONE DAY YOU'LL LOSE ALL YOUR FRIENDS !!
ぶる
ぶる
ぶる
I DON'T...
...CARE ABOUT THAT.
うっ
うっ
うっ
IT'S NOT...
...ALL RIGHT!
IT'S NOT ALL RIGHT!!
うっ
SOMEONE LIKE YOU MAY NOT BE ABLE TO COMPREHEND THIS.
BUT I SERVE ONLY ONE MASTER.

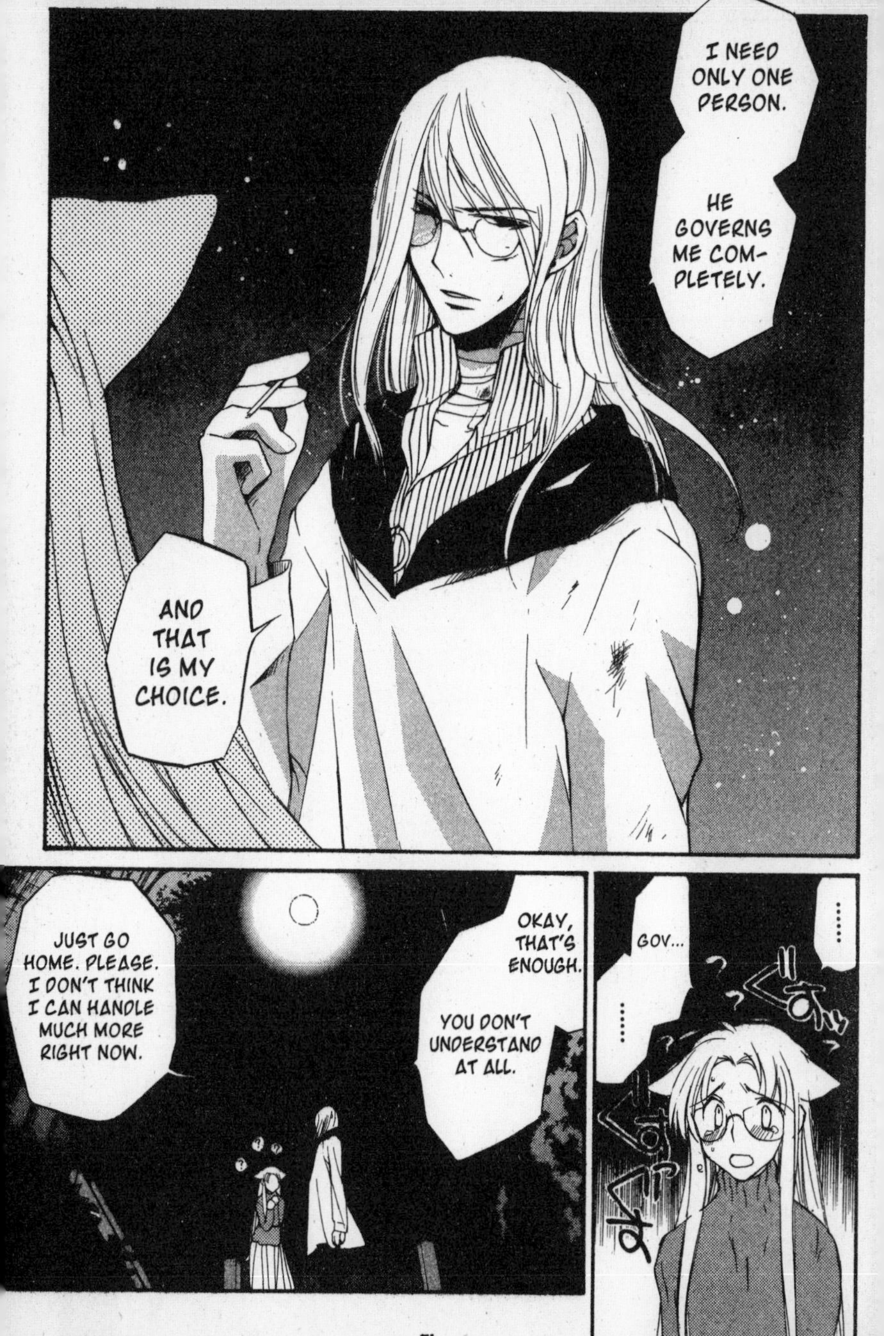

I NEED ONLY ONE PERSON.
HE GOVERNS ME COM-PLETELY.
AND THAT IS MY CHOICE.
......
GOV...
......
OKAY, THAT'S ENOUGH.
YOU DON'T UNDERSTAND AT ALL.
JUST GO HOME. PLEASE. I DON'T THINK I CAN HANDLE MUCH MORE RIGHT NOW.

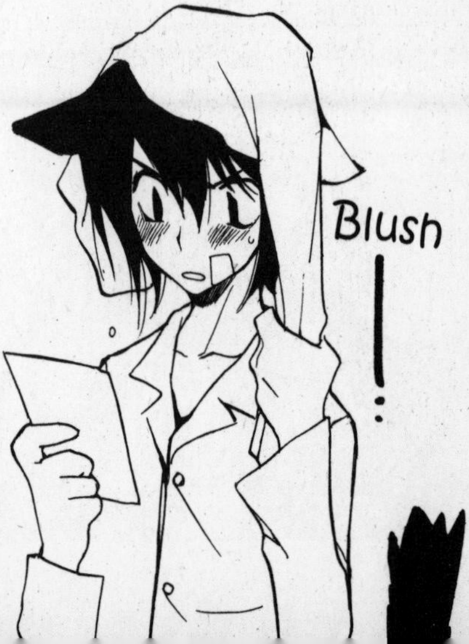
Blush
!!

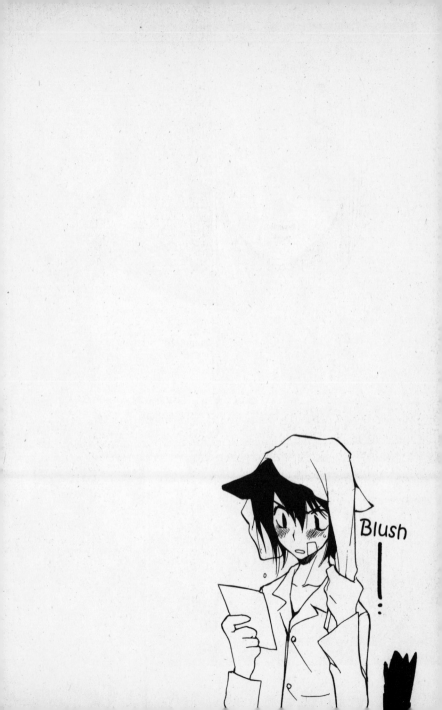

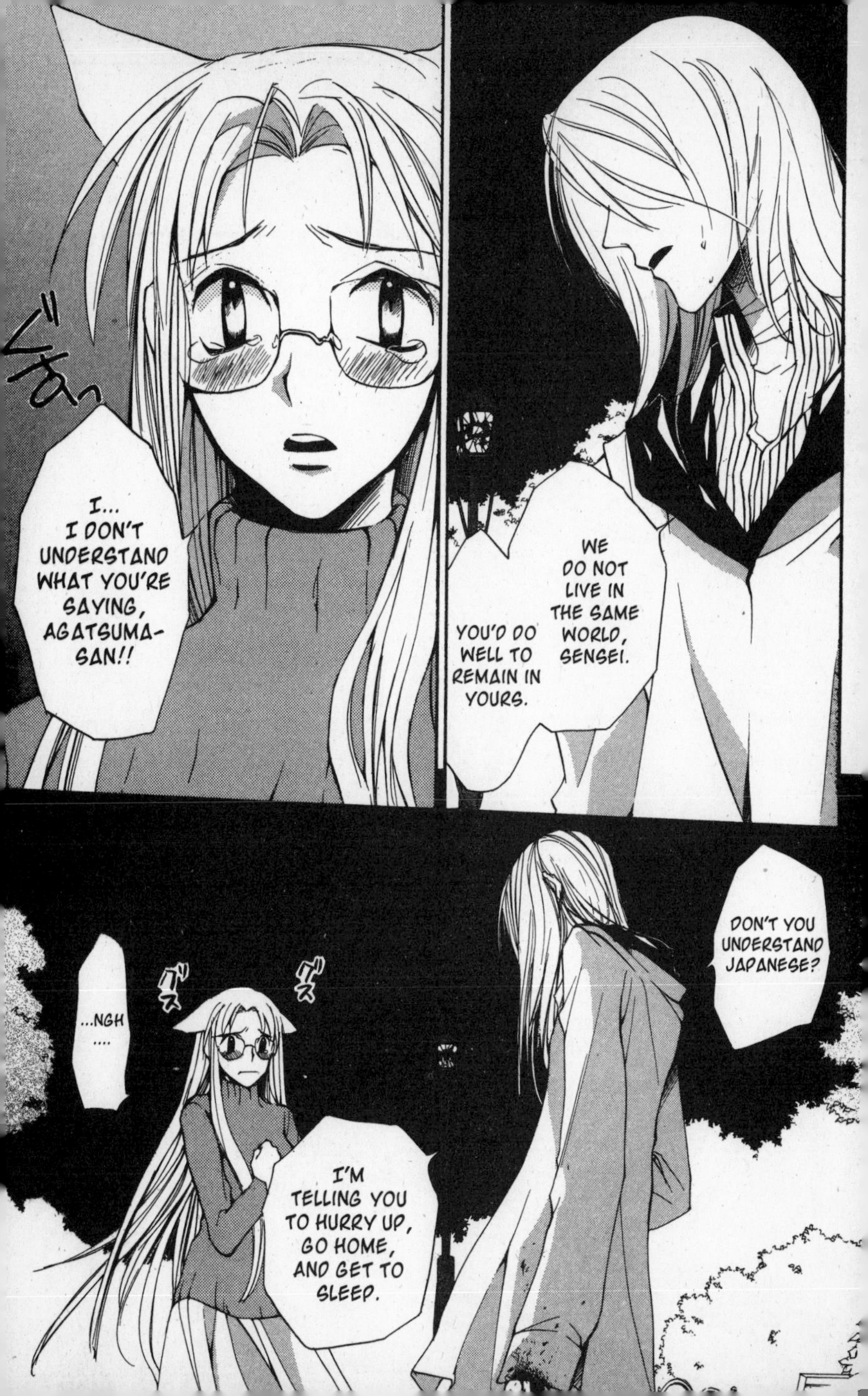
WE DO NOT LIVE IN THE SAME WORLD, SENSEI.
YOU'D DO WELL TO REMAIN IN YOURS.
I... I DON'T UNDERSTAND WHAT YOU'RE SAYING, AGATSUMA-SAN!!
DON'T YOU UNDERSTAND JAPANESE?
I'M TELLING YOU TO HURRY UP, GO HOME, AND GET TO SLEEP.
グス
グス
...NGH ....

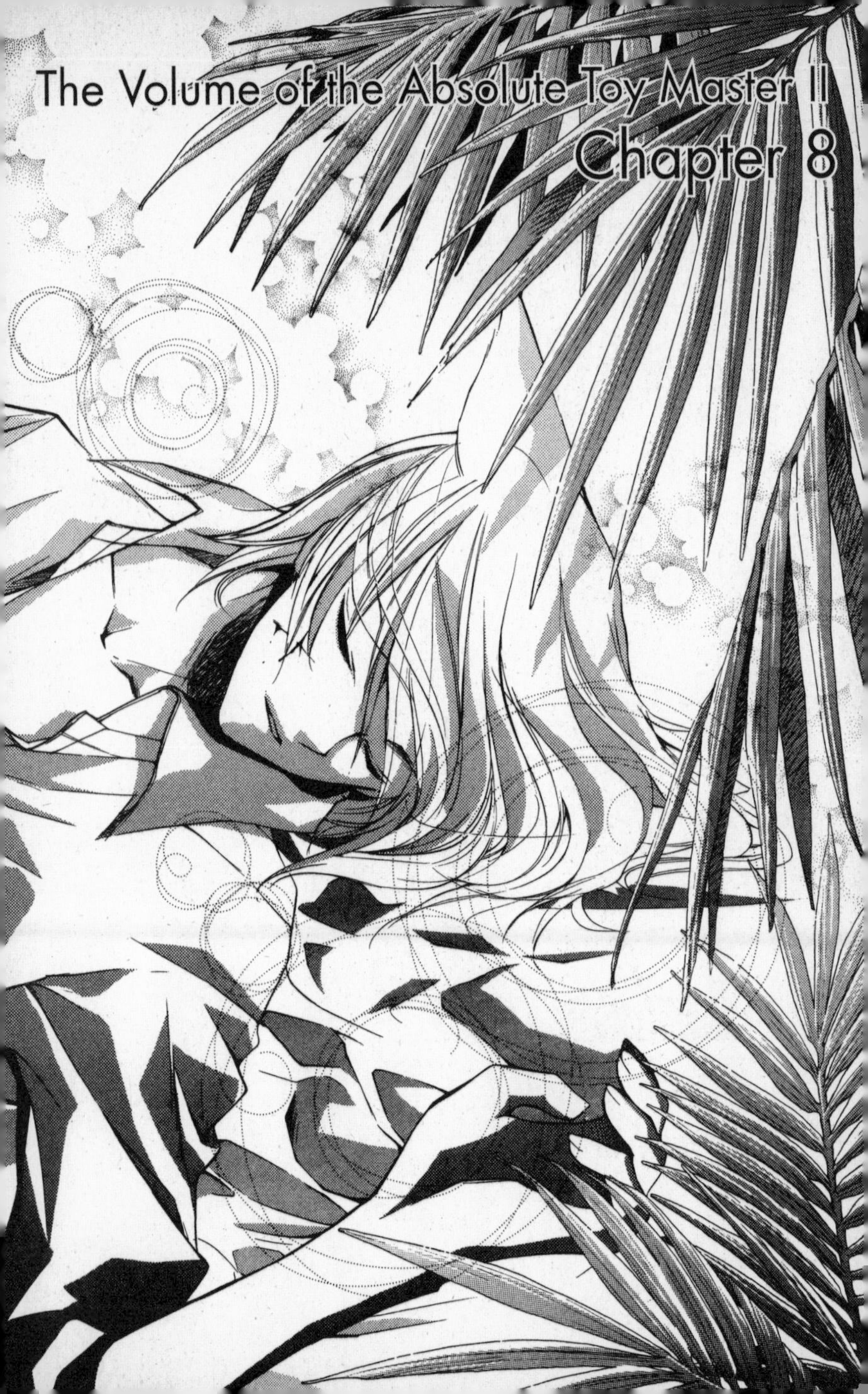
The Volume of the Absolute Toy Master II
Chapter 8

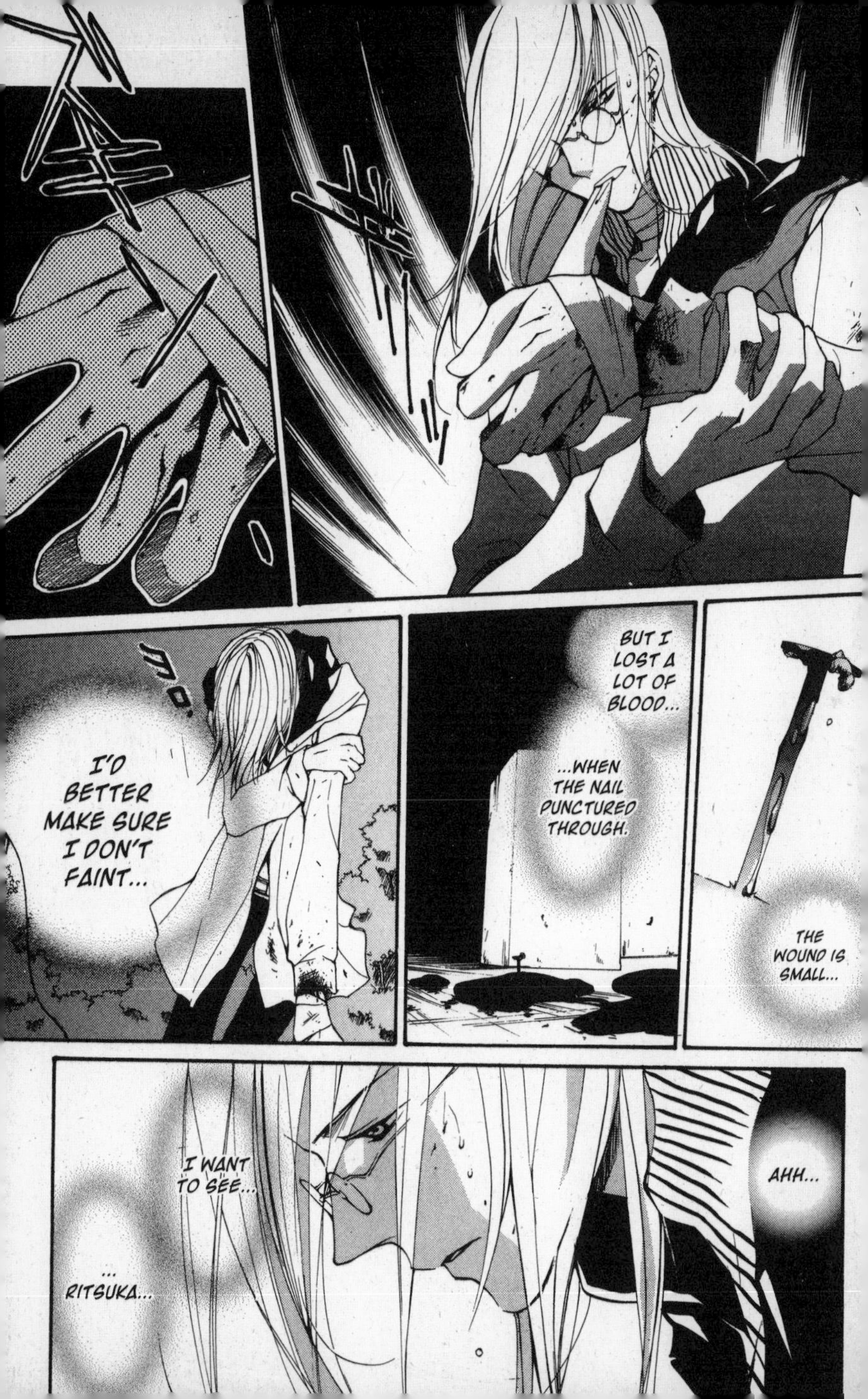
THE WOUND IS SMALL...
BUT I LOST A LOT OF BLOOD...
...WHEN THE NAIL PUNCTURED THROUGH.
I'D BETTER MAKE SURE I DON'T FAINT...
AHH...
I WANT TO SEE...
... RITSUKA...

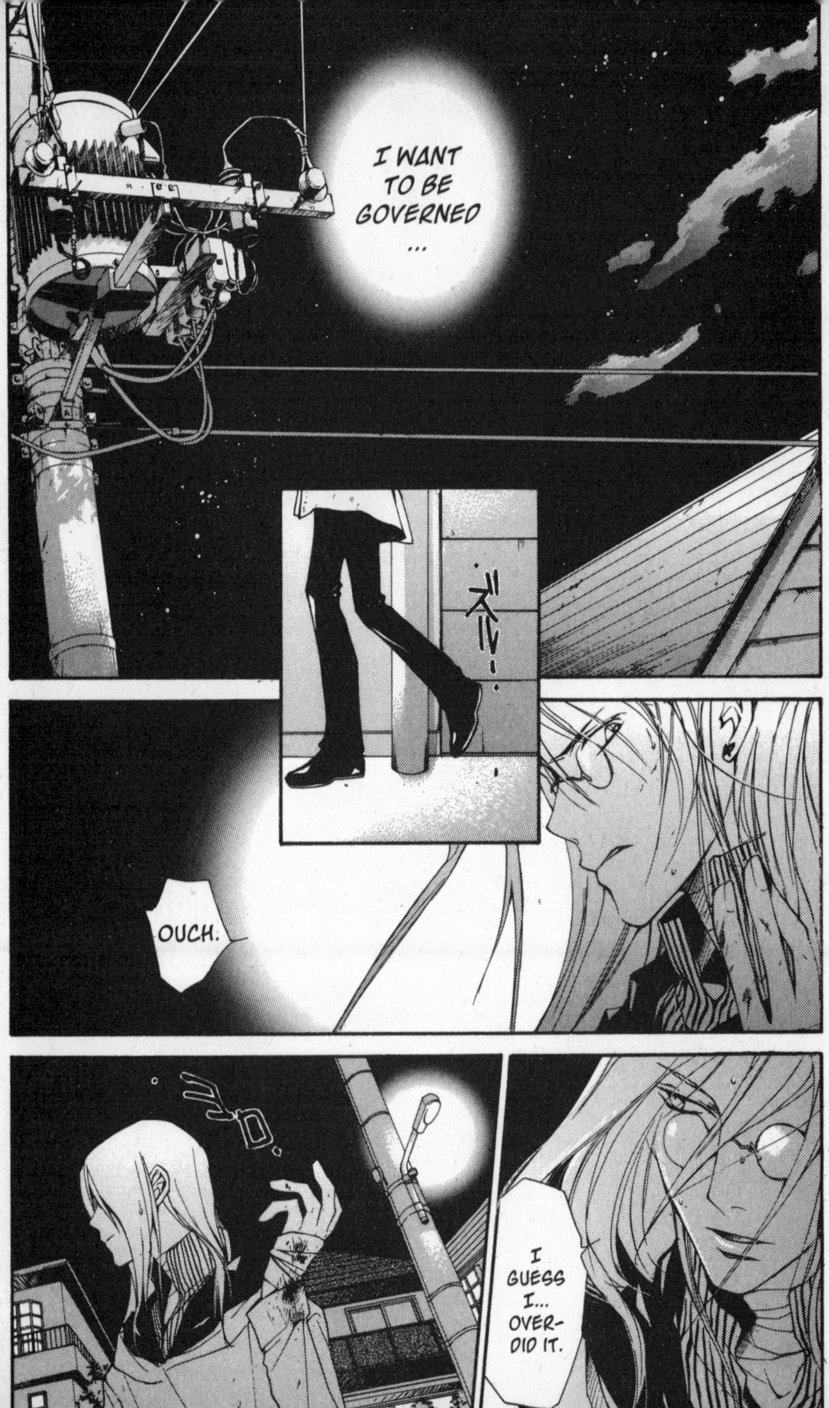
I WANT TO BE GOVERNED ...
ズル
OUCH.
I GUESS I... OVER-DID IT.

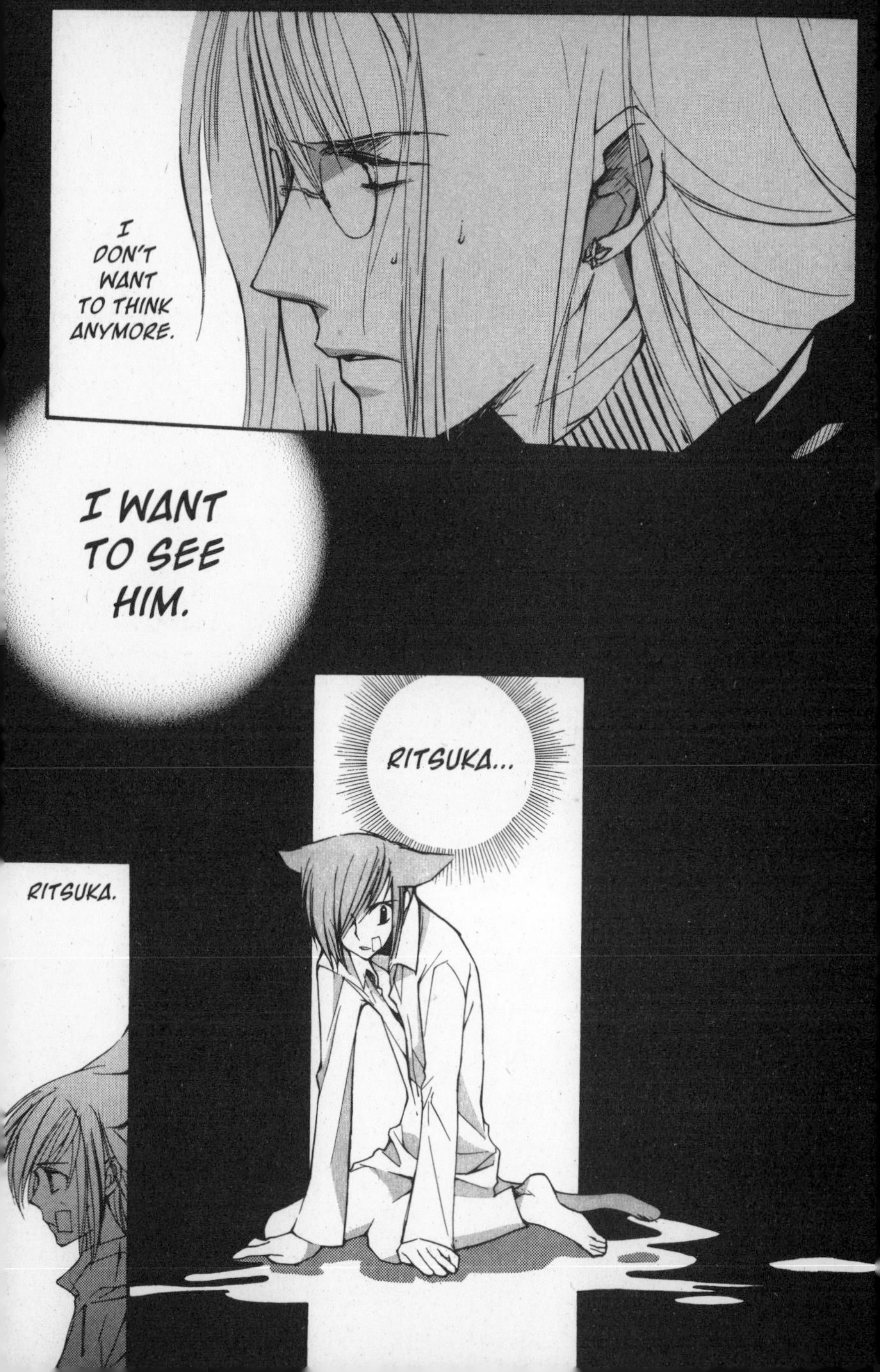
I DON'T WANT TO THINK ANYMORE.
I WANT TO SEE HIM.
RITSUKA...
RITSUKA.

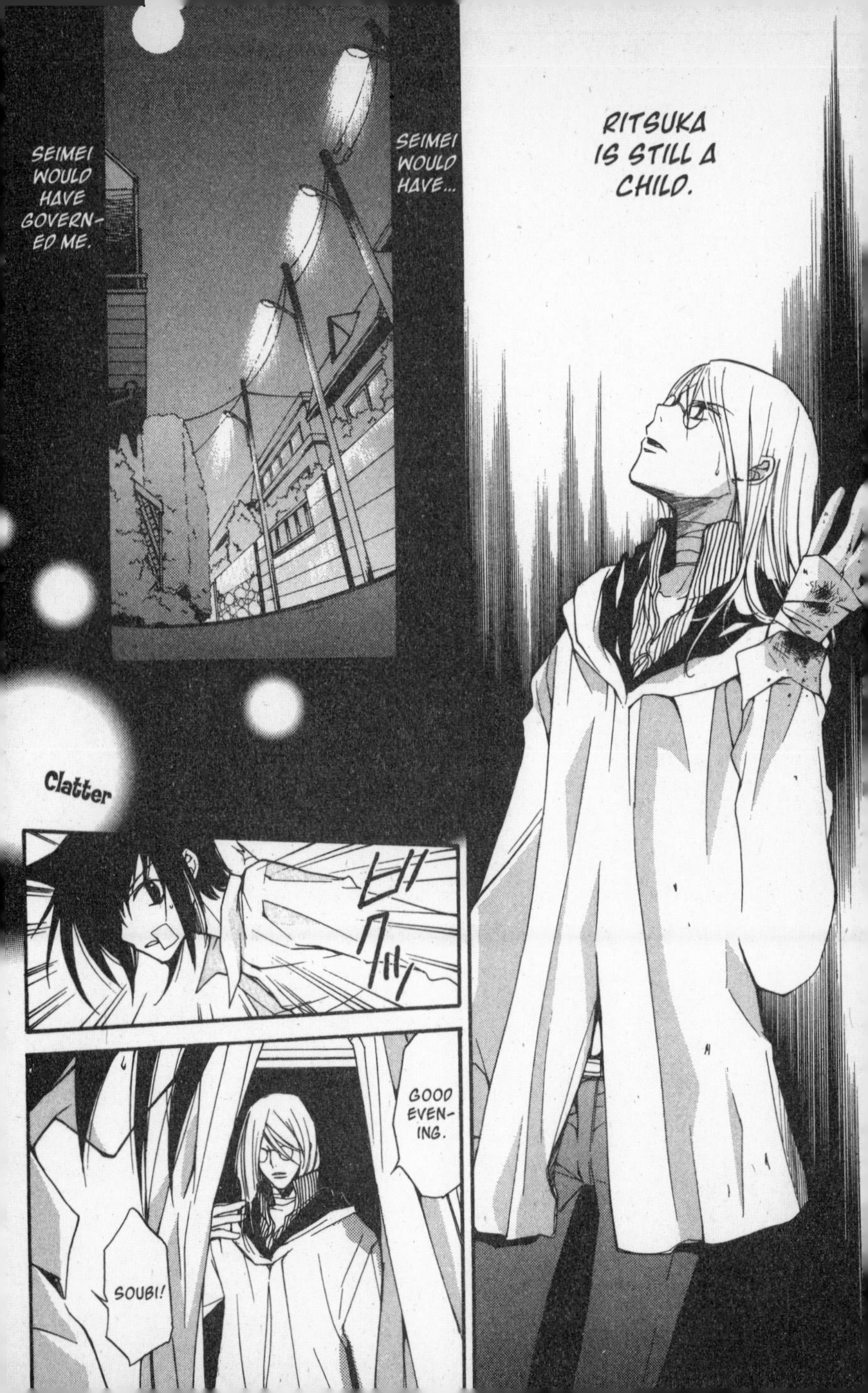
RITSUKA IS STILL A CHILD.
SEIMEI WOULD HAVE...
SEIMEI WOULD HAVE GOVERN-ED ME.
Clatter
GOOD EVEN-ING.
SOUBI!

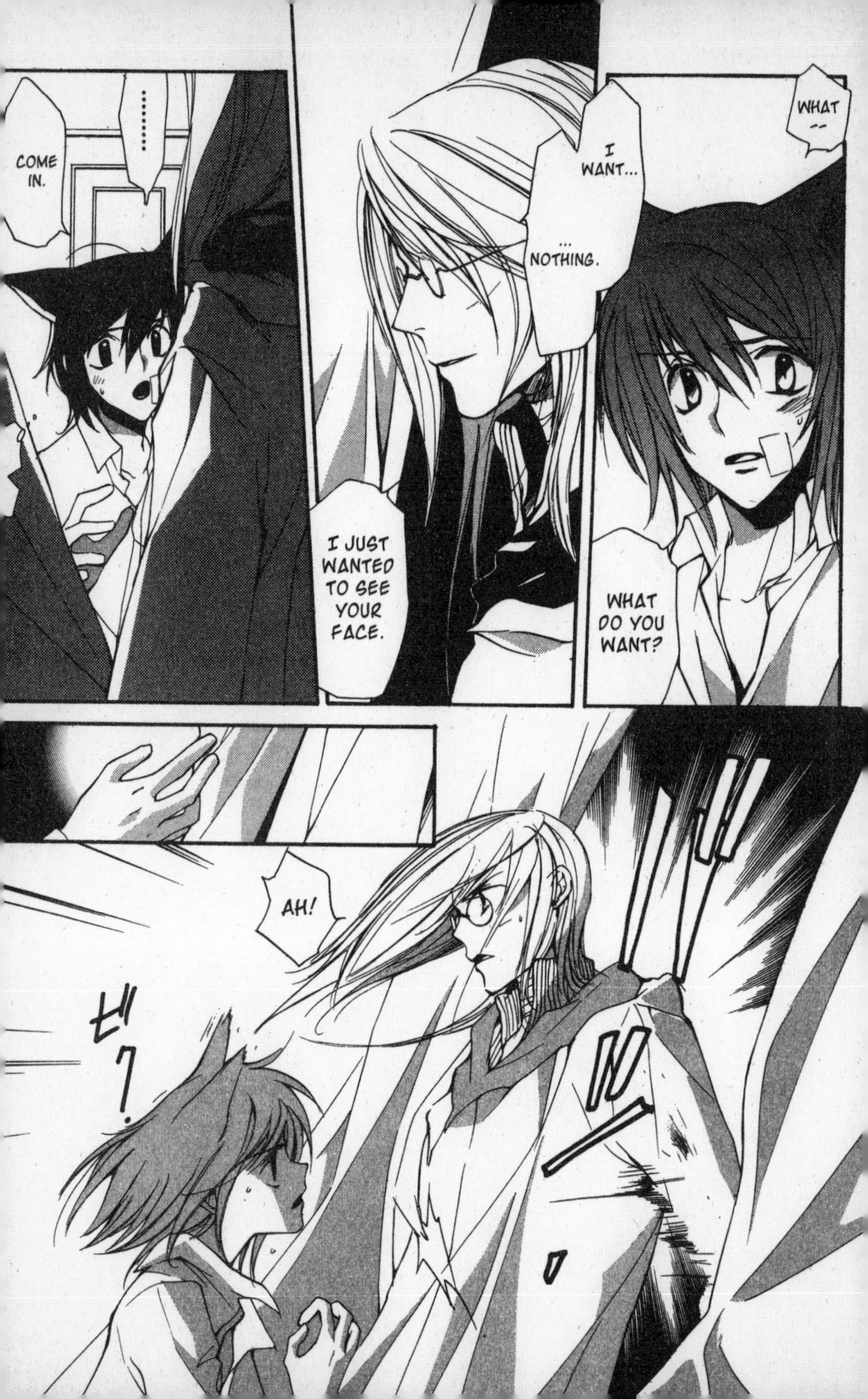
WHAT --
WHAT DO YOU WANT?
I WANT...
... NOTHING.
I JUST WANTED TO SEE YOUR FACE.
......
COME IN.
AH!
ビク!

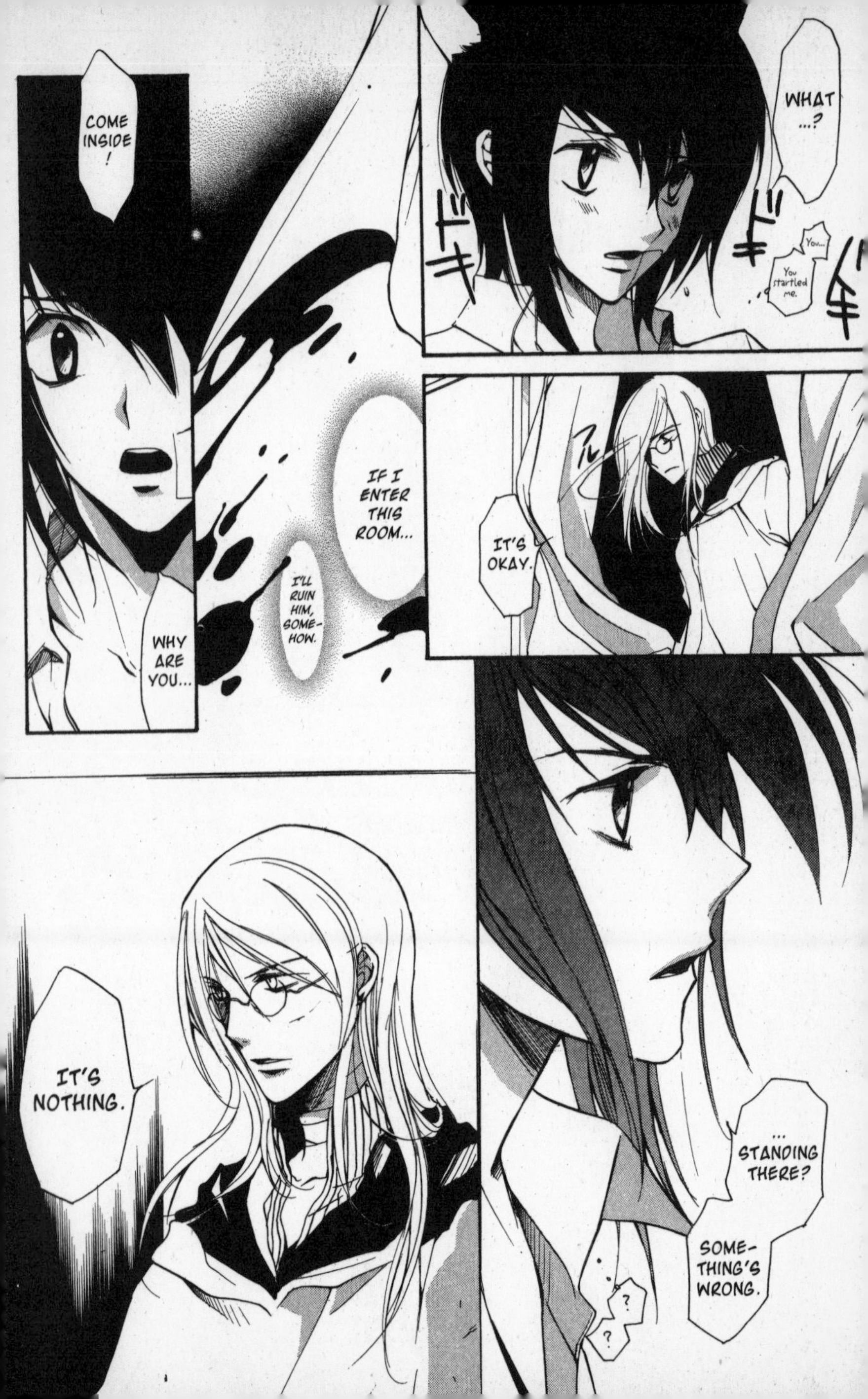
WHAT ...?
ドキ ドキ
You... You startled me.
IT'S OKAY.
COME INSIDE!
IF I ENTER THIS ROOM...
I'LL RUIN HIM, SOMEHOW.
WHY ARE YOU...
... STANDING THERE?
SOMETHING'S WRONG.
? ?
IT'S NOTHING.

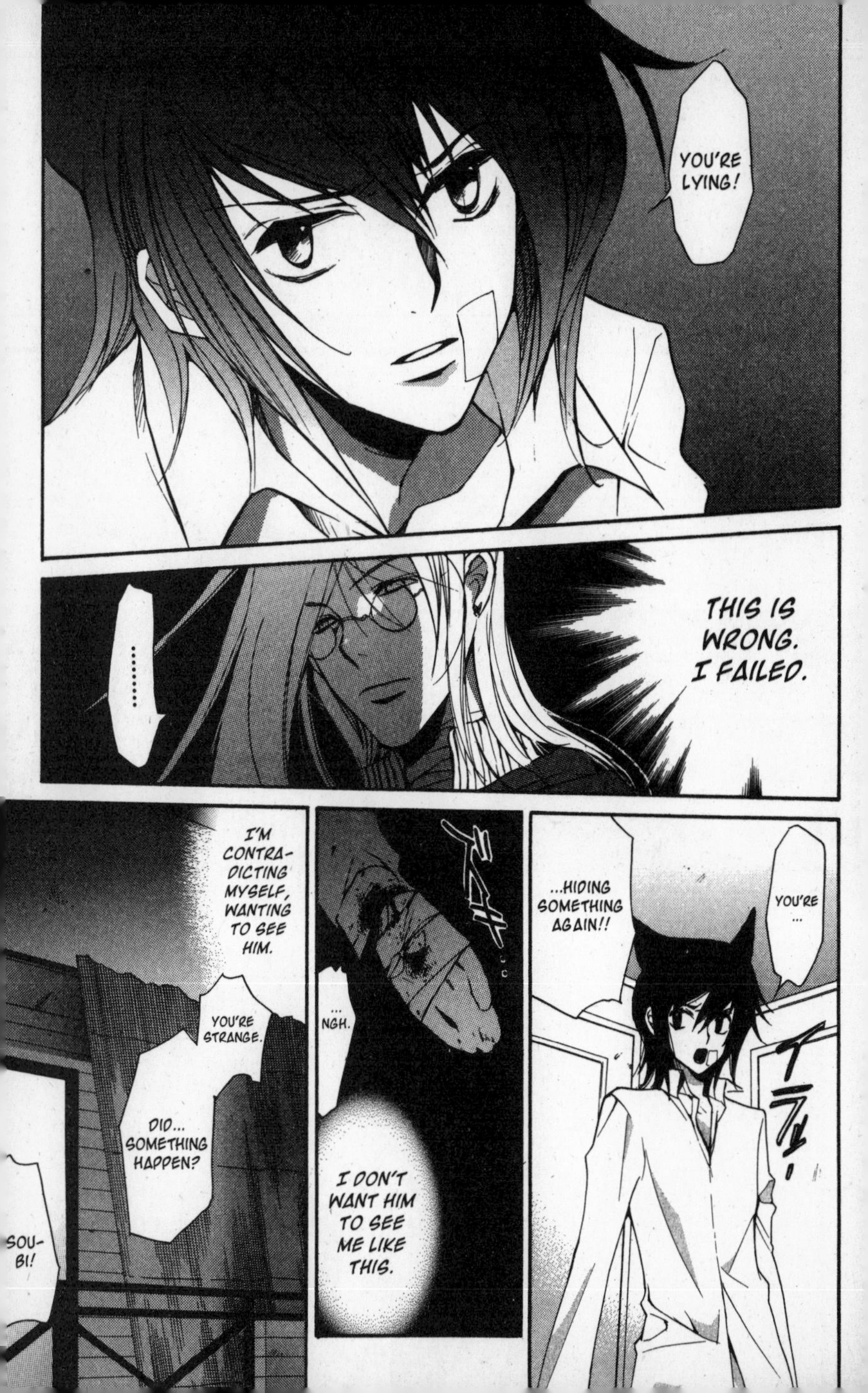
YOU'RE LYING!
THIS IS WRONG. I FAILED.
......
YOU'RE ...
...HIDING SOMETHING AGAIN!!
... NGH.
I DON'T WANT HIM TO SEE ME LIKE THIS.
I'M CONTRA-DICTING MYSELF, WANTING TO SEE HIM.
YOU'RE STRANGE.
DID... SOMETHING HAPPEN?
SOU-BI!

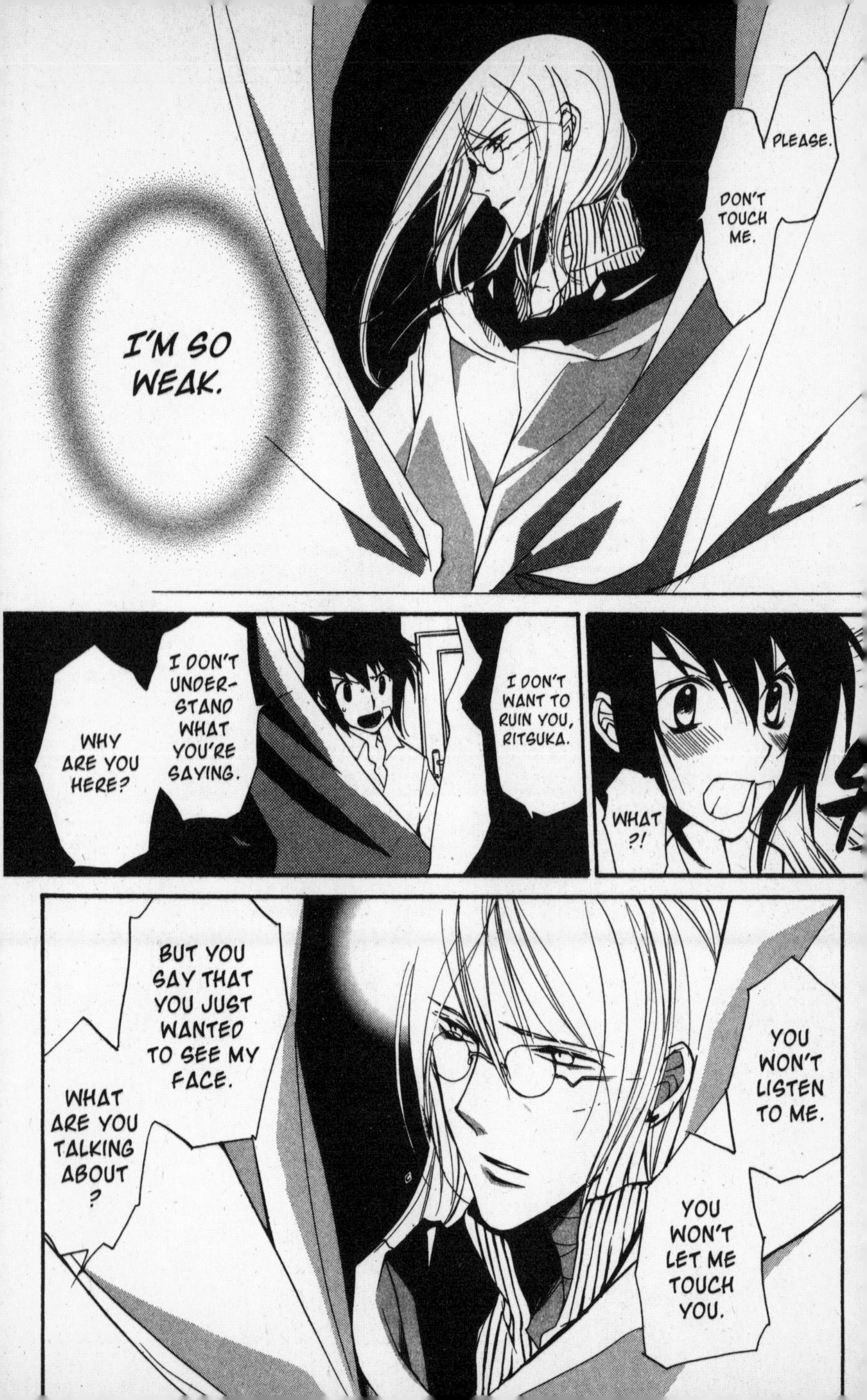
PLEASE.
DON'T TOUCH ME.
I'M SO WEAK.
I DON'T WANT TO RUIN YOU, RITSUKA.
WHAT?!
I DON'T UNDERSTAND WHAT YOU'RE SAYING.
WHY ARE YOU HERE?
YOU WON'T LISTEN TO ME.
YOU WON'T LET ME TOUCH YOU.
BUT YOU SAY THAT YOU JUST WANTED TO SEE MY FACE.
WHAT ARE YOU TALKING ABOUT?

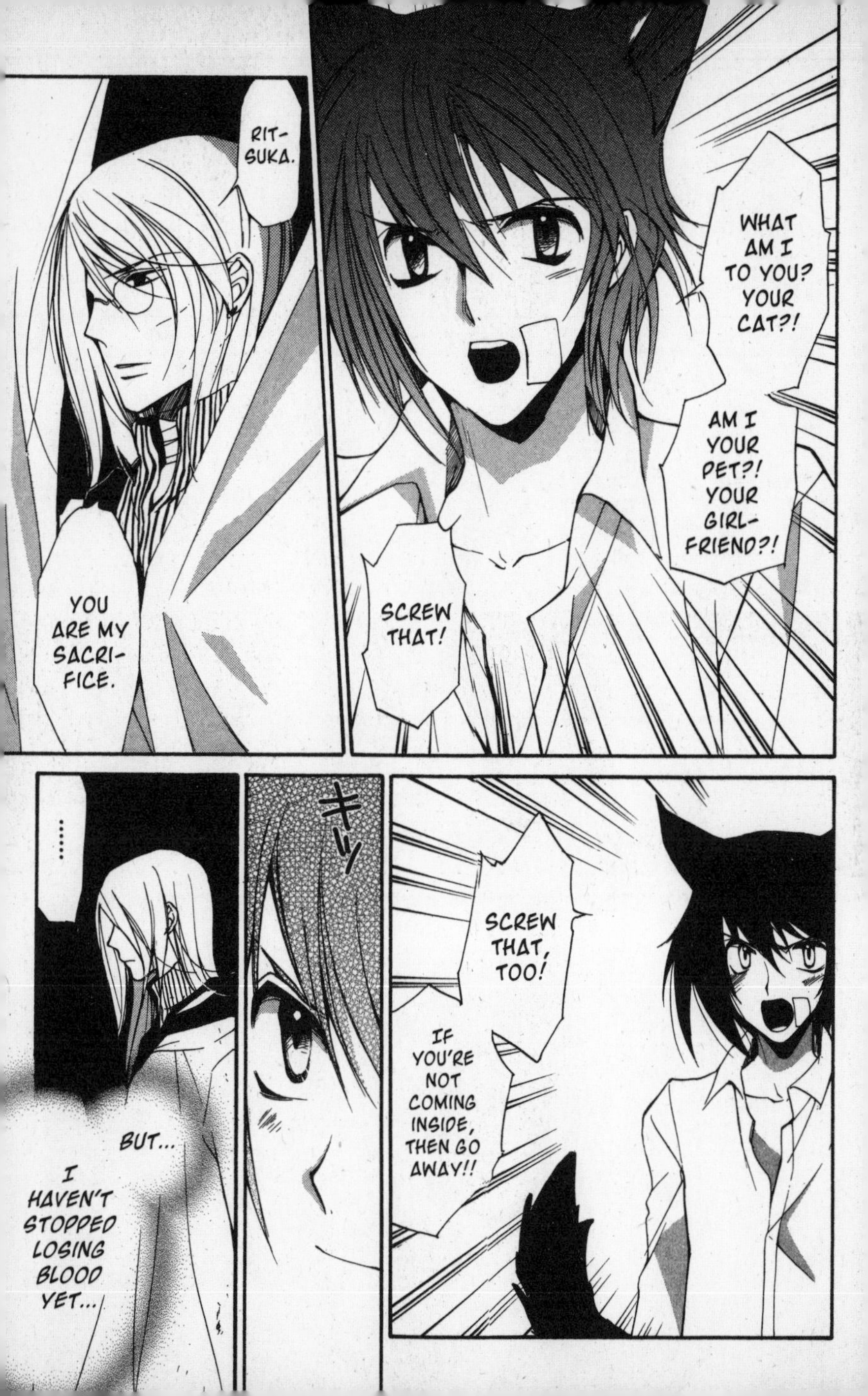
WHAT AM I TO YOU? YOUR CAT?!
AM I YOUR PET?! YOUR GIRL-FRIEND?!
SCREW THAT!
RIT-SUKA.
YOU ARE MY SACRI-FICE.
SCREW THAT, TOO!
IF YOU'RE NOT COMING INSIDE, THEN GO AWAY!!
キッ
......
BUT...
I HAVEN'T STOPPED LOSING BLOOD YET...

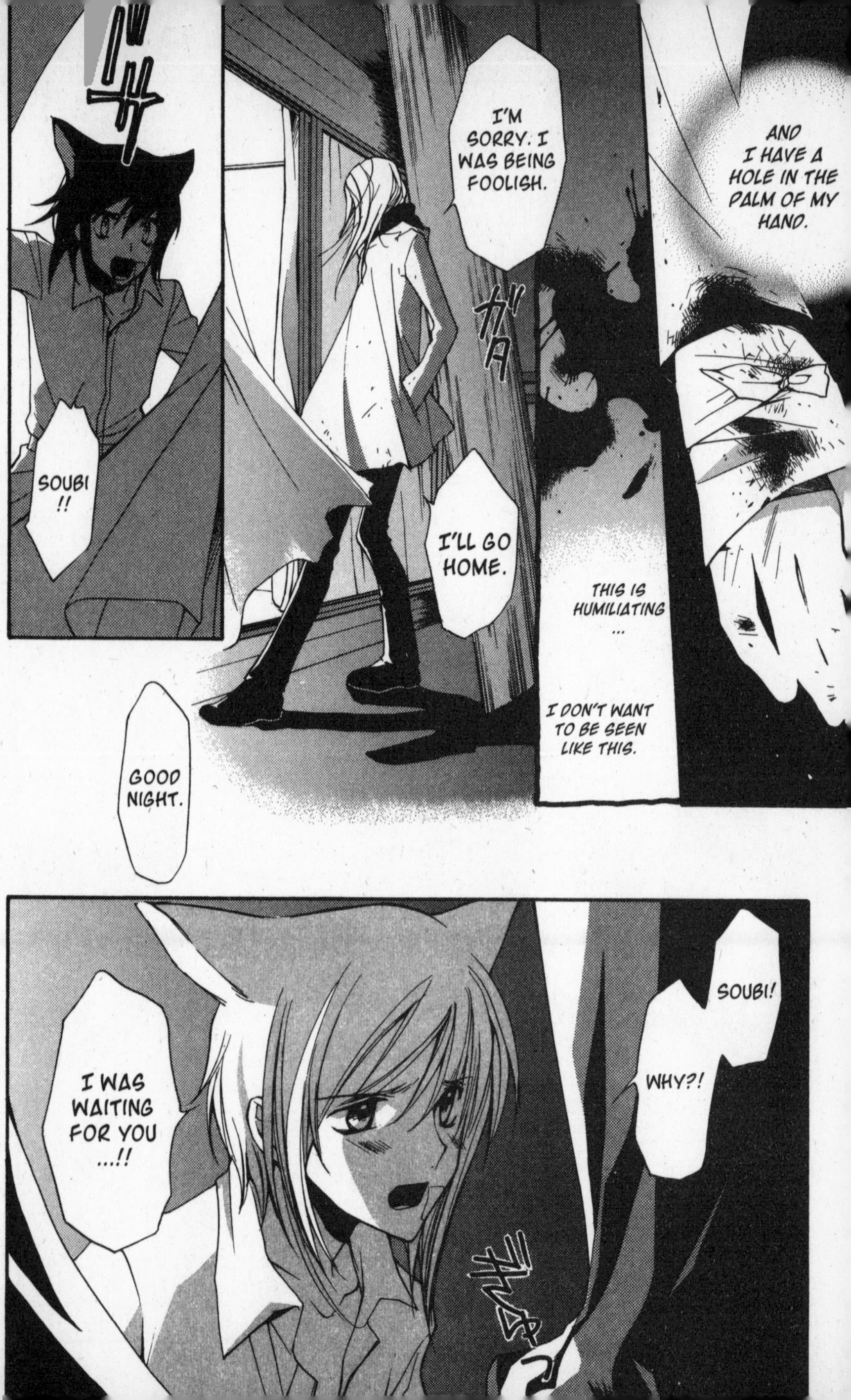
AND I HAVE A HOLE IN THE PALM OF MY HAND.
THIS IS HUMILIATING ...
I DON'T WANT TO BE SEEN LIKE THIS.
I'M SORRY. I WAS BEING FOOLISH.
I'LL GO HOME.
GOOD NIGHT.
SOUBI !!
SOUBI!
WHY?!
I WAS WAITING FOR YOU ...!!

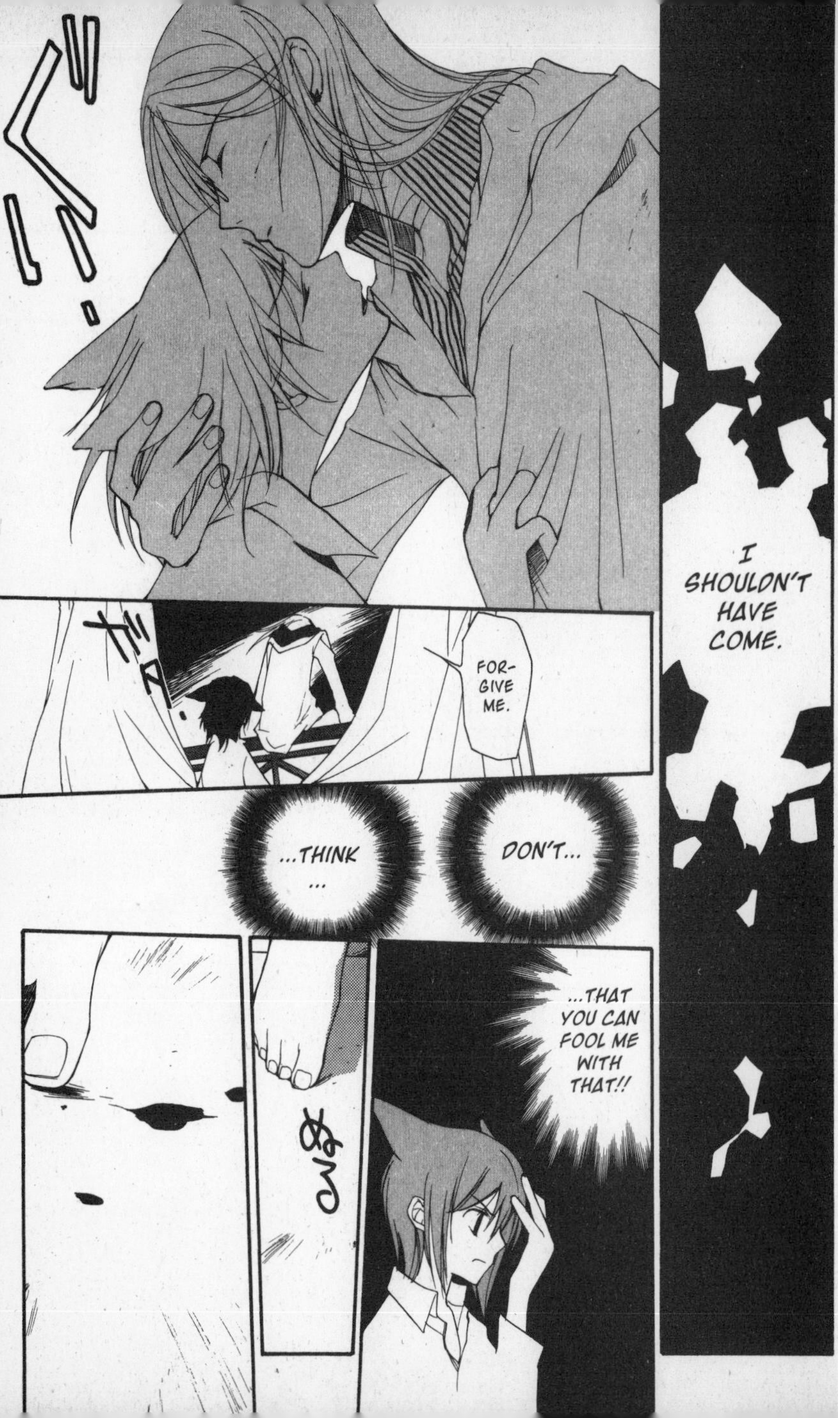
I SHOULDN'T HAVE COME.
FOR-GIVE ME.
DON'T...
...THINK ...
...THAT YOU CAN FOOL ME WITH THAT!!

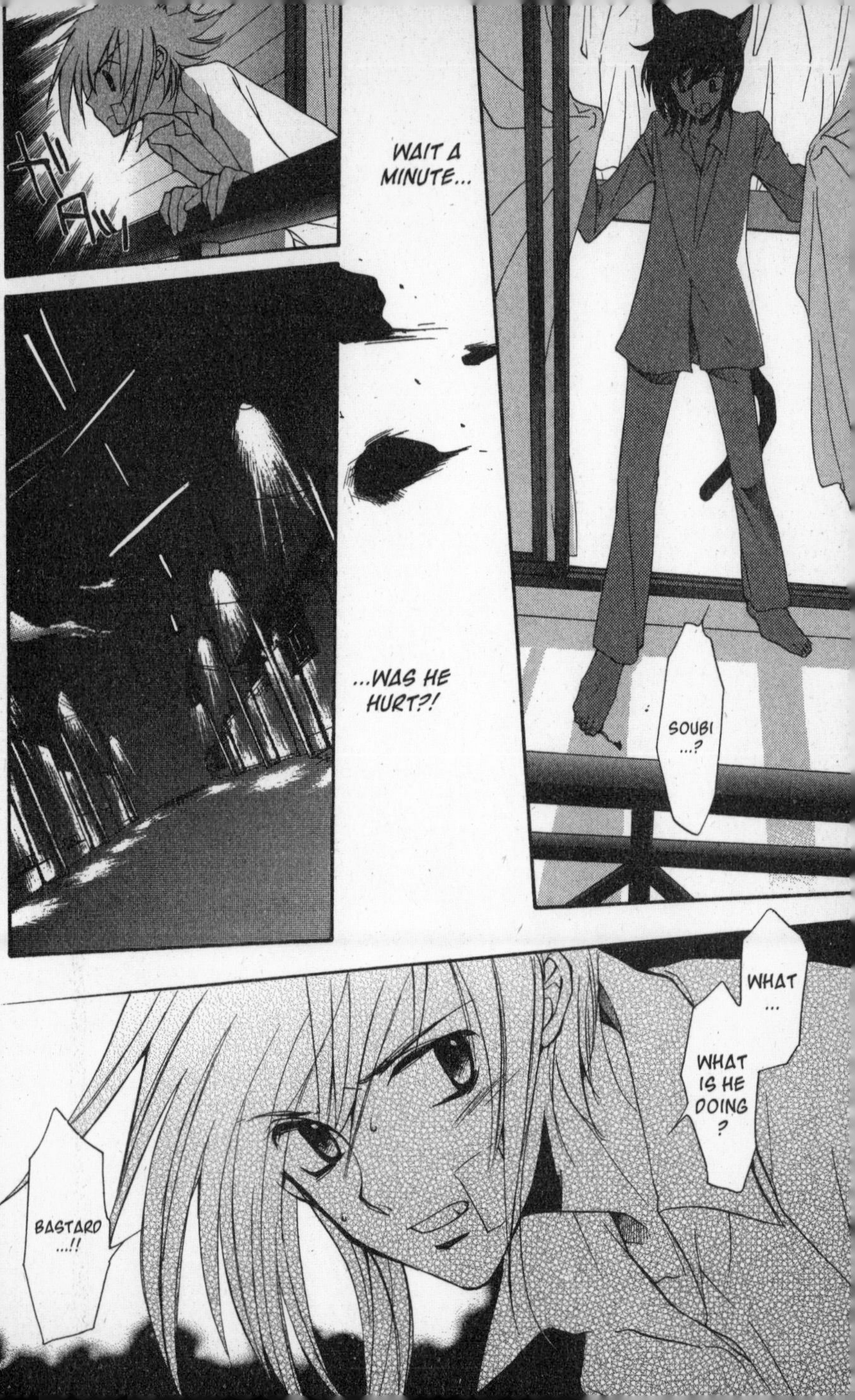
SOUBI ...?
WAIT A MINUTE...
...WAS HE HURT?!
WHAT ... WHAT IS HE DOING ?
BASTARD ...!!

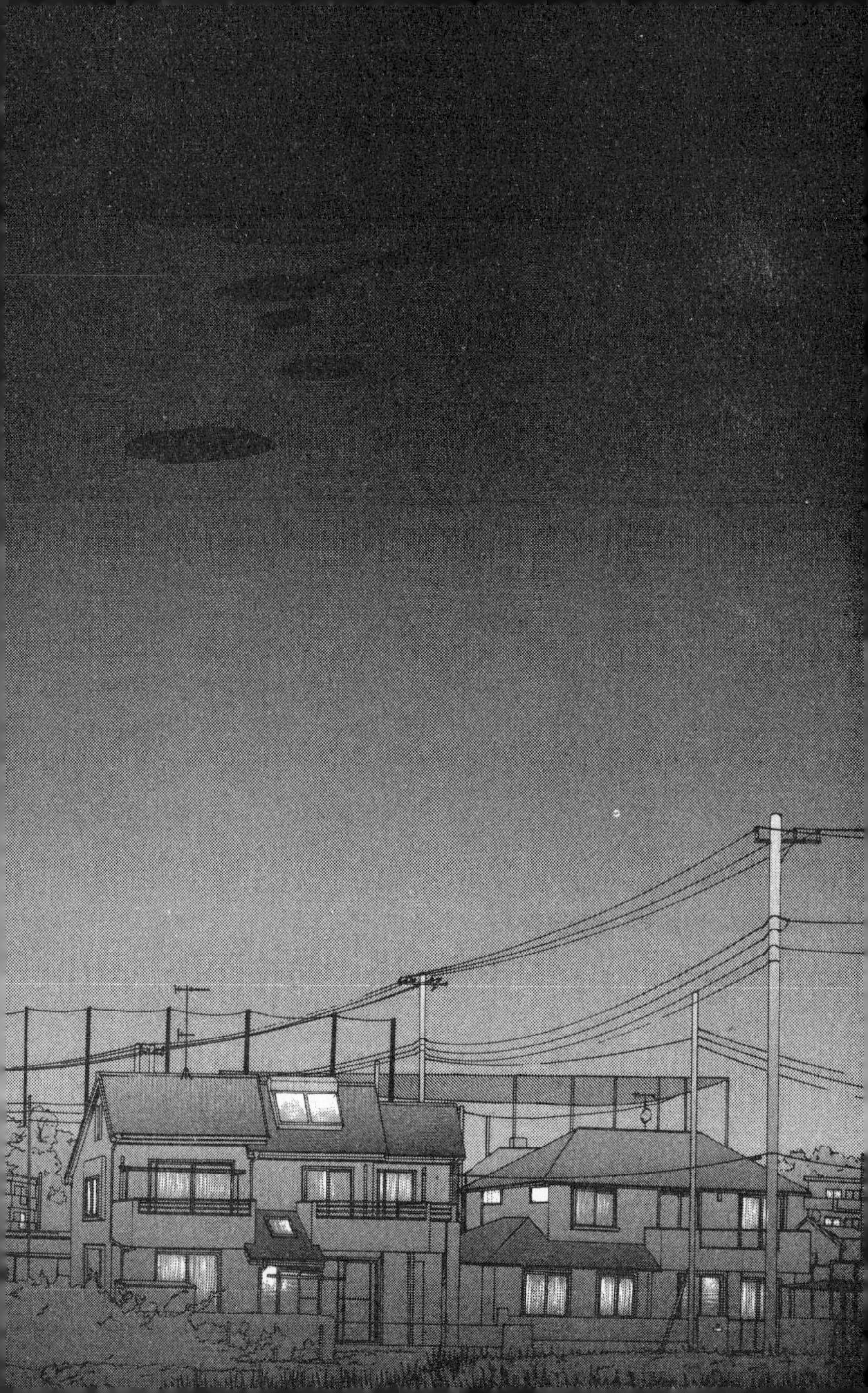

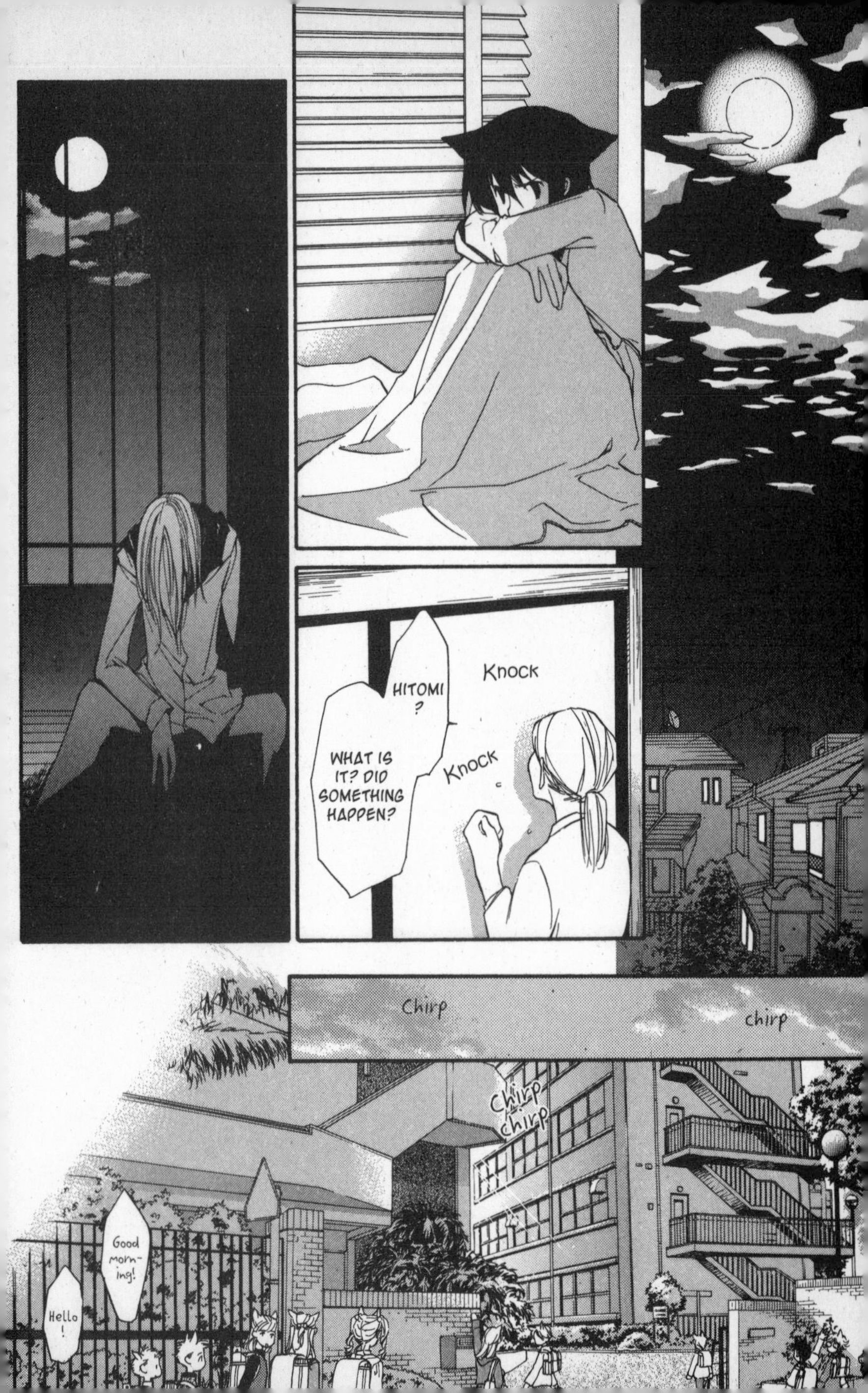
Knock
HITOMI?
Knock
WHAT IS IT? DID SOMETHING HAPPEN?
Chirp
chirp
Chirp chirp
Good morning!
Hello!

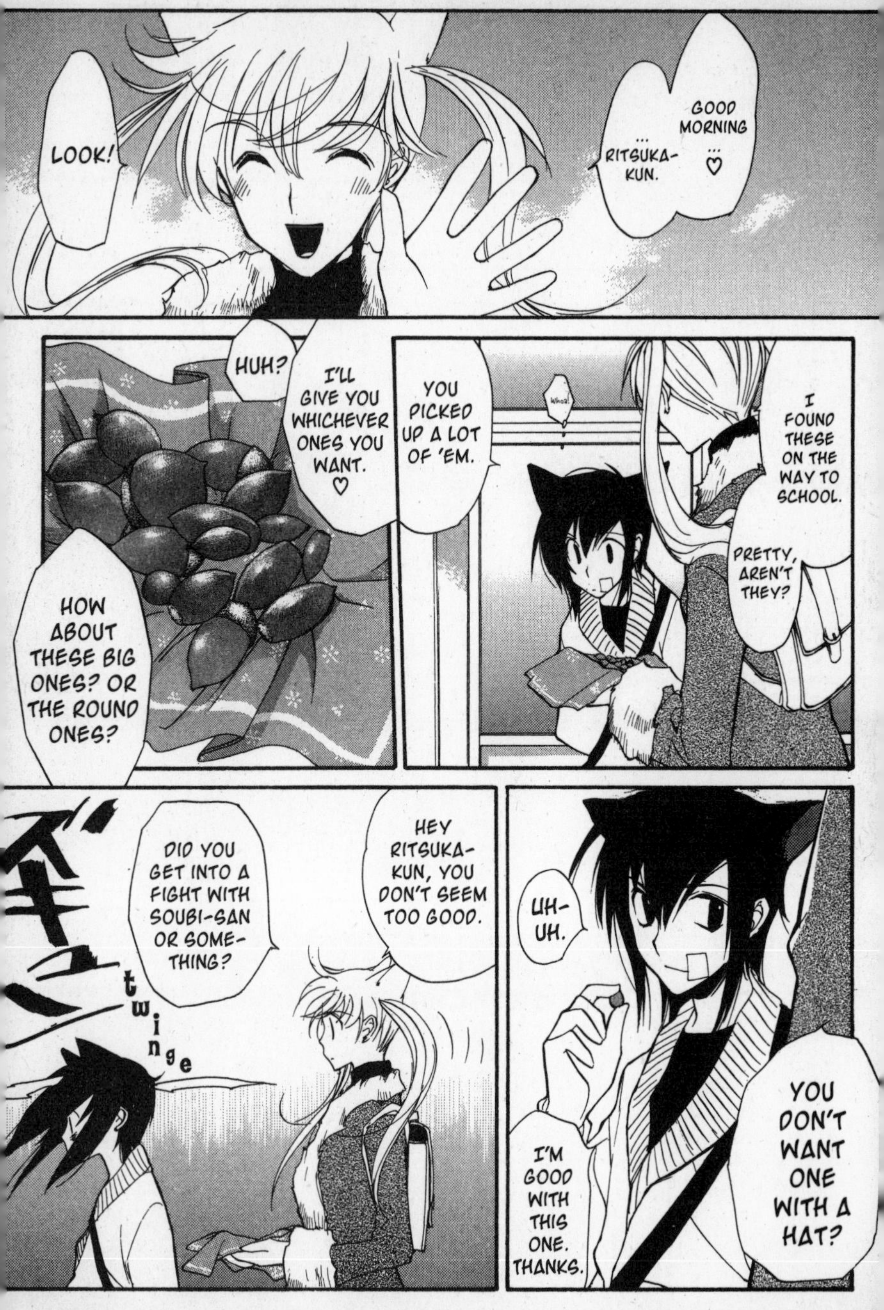
GOOD MORNING ... ♡
... RITSUKA-KUN.
LOOK!
I FOUND THESE ON THE WAY TO SCHOOL.
PRETTY, AREN'T THEY?
Whoa!
YOU PICKED UP A LOT OF 'EM.
I'LL GIVE YOU WHICHEVER ONES YOU WANT. ♡
HUH?
HOW ABOUT THESE BIG ONES? OR THE ROUND ONES?
UH-UH.
YOU DON'T WANT ONE WITH A HAT?
I'M GOOD WITH THIS ONE. THANKS.
HEY RITSUKA-KUN, YOU DON'T SEEM TOO GOOD.
DID YOU GET INTO A FIGHT WITH SOUBI-SAN OR SOMETHING?
twinge

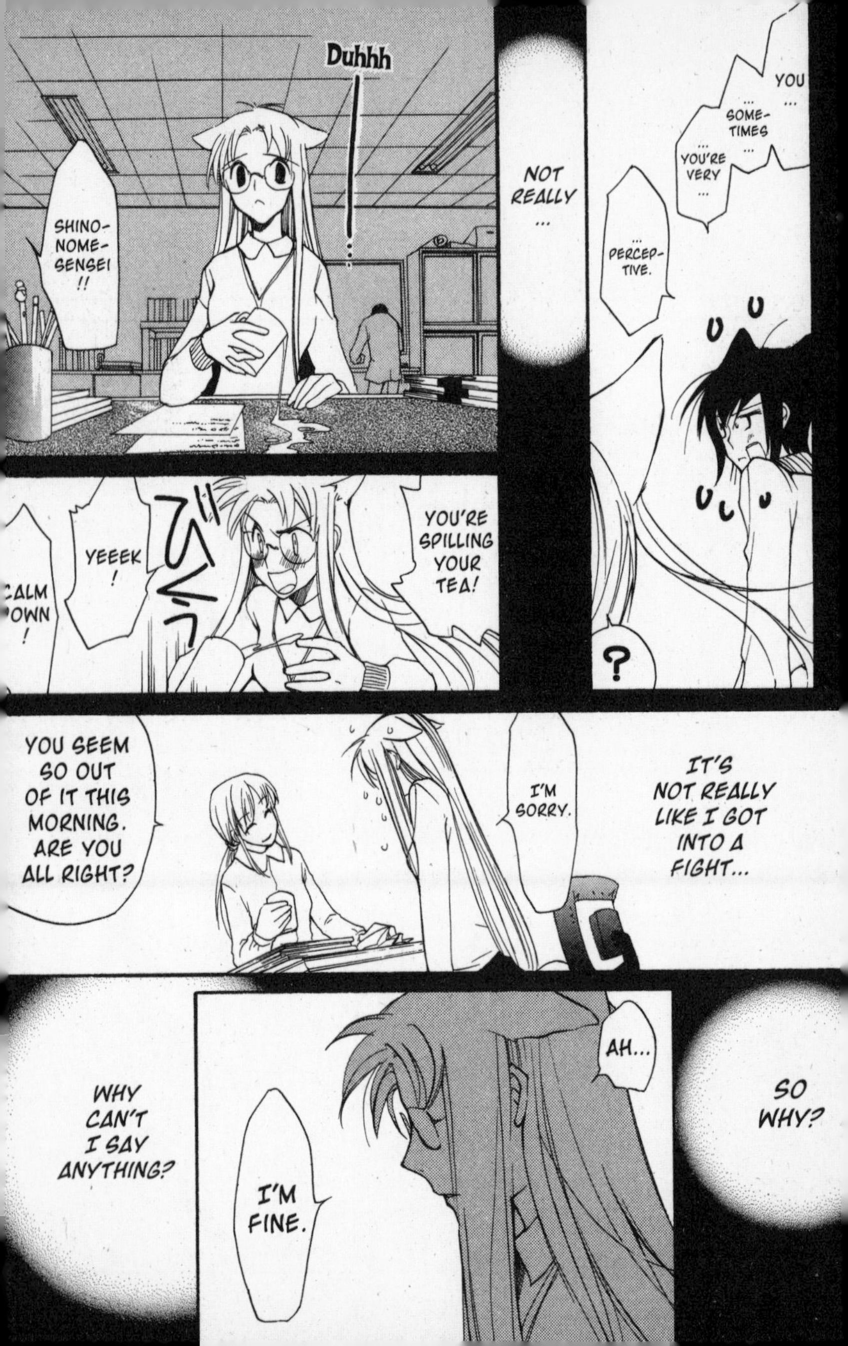

YOU ... SOME-TIMES ... YOU'RE VERY ...
... PERCEP-TIVE.
?
NOT REALLY ...
Duhhh
SHINONOME-SENSEI !!
YOU'RE SPILLING YOUR TEA!
びくっ
YEEEK!
CALM DOWN!
IT'S NOT REALLY LIKE I GOT INTO A FIGHT...
I'M SORRY.
YOU SEEM SO OUT OF IT THIS MORNING. ARE YOU ALL RIGHT?
SO WHY?
AH...
I'M FINE.
WHY CAN'T I SAY ANYTHING?

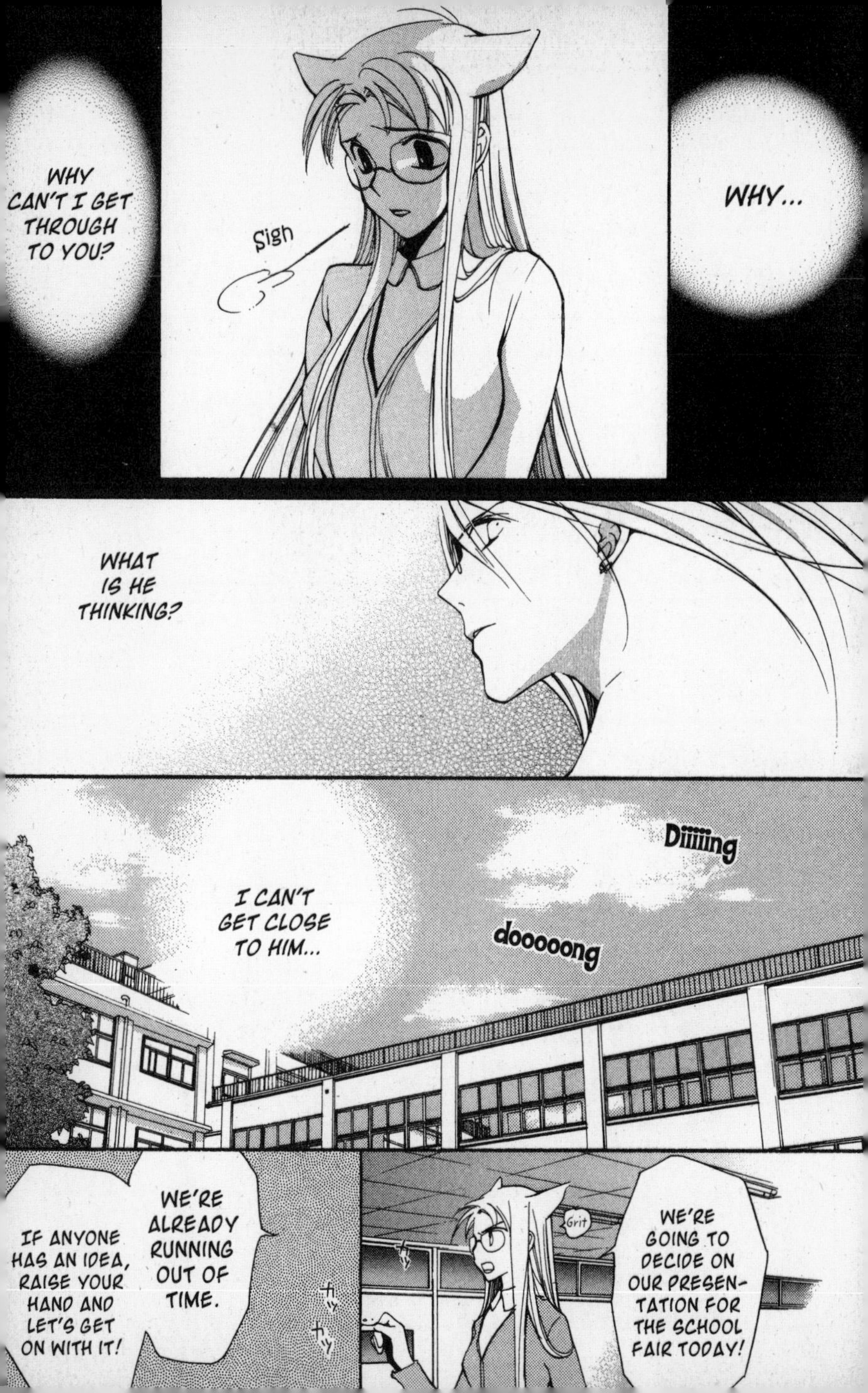
WHY...
WHY CAN'T I GET THROUGH TO YOU?
Sigh
WHAT IS HE THINKING?
Diiiiing
doooooong
I CAN'T GET CLOSE TO HIM...
WE'RE GOING TO DECIDE ON OUR PRESEN-TATION FOR THE SCHOOL FAIR TODAY!
Grit
WE'RE ALREADY RUNNING OUT OF TIME.
IF ANYONE HAS AN IDEA, RAISE YOUR HAND AND LET'S GET ON WITH IT!

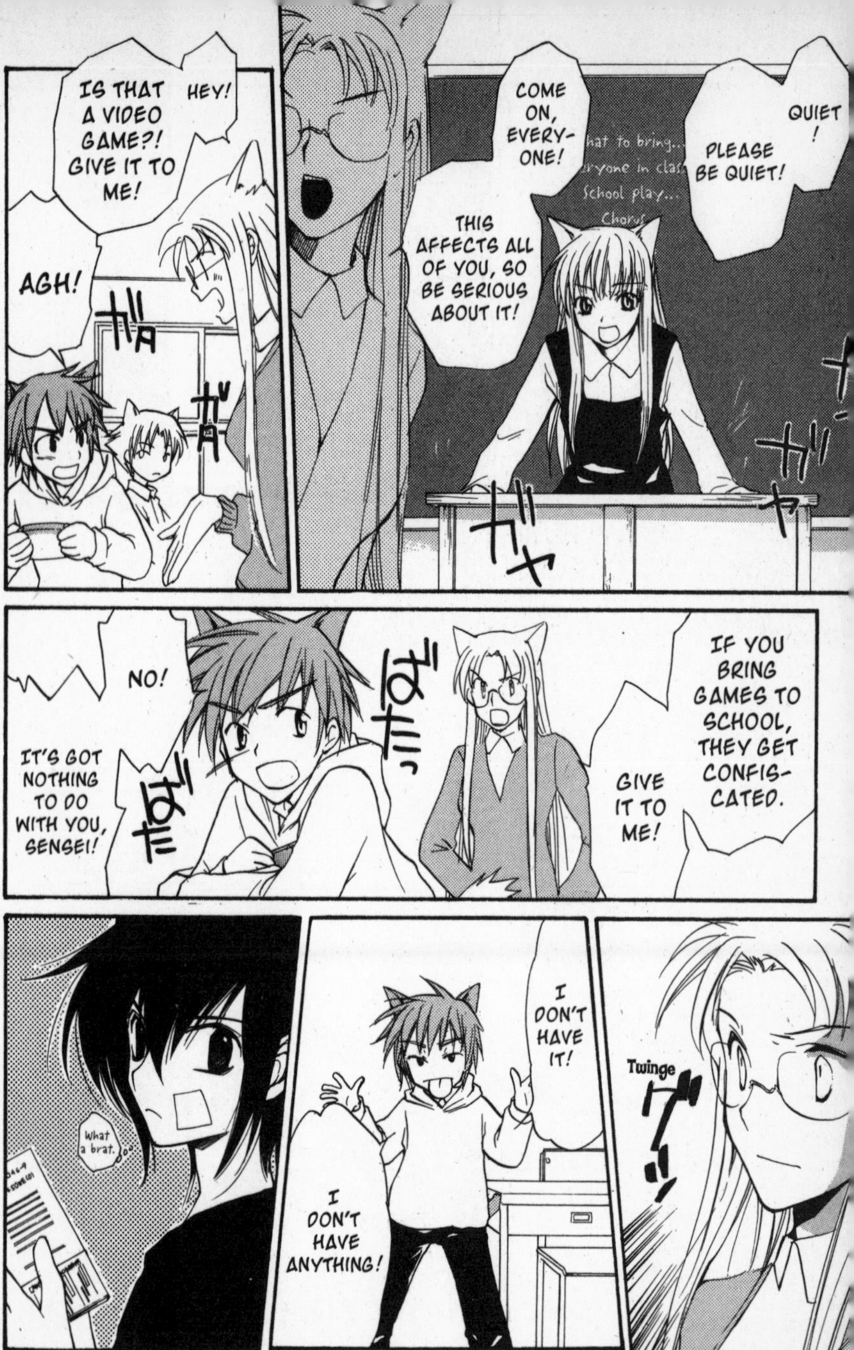
QUIET!
PLEASE BE QUIET!
COME ON, EVERYONE!
THIS AFFECTS ALL OF YOU, SO BE SERIOUS ABOUT IT!
ガヤ
ガヤ
HEY!
IS THAT A VIDEO GAME?! GIVE IT TO ME!
AGH!
ガタ
ガタ
IF YOU BRING GAMES TO SCHOOL, THEY GET CONFISCATED.
GIVE IT TO ME!
ばたっ
NO!
ばた
IT'S GOT NOTHING TO DO WITH YOU, SENSEI!
Twinge
I DON'T HAVE IT!
I DON'T HAVE ANYTHING!
What a brat.

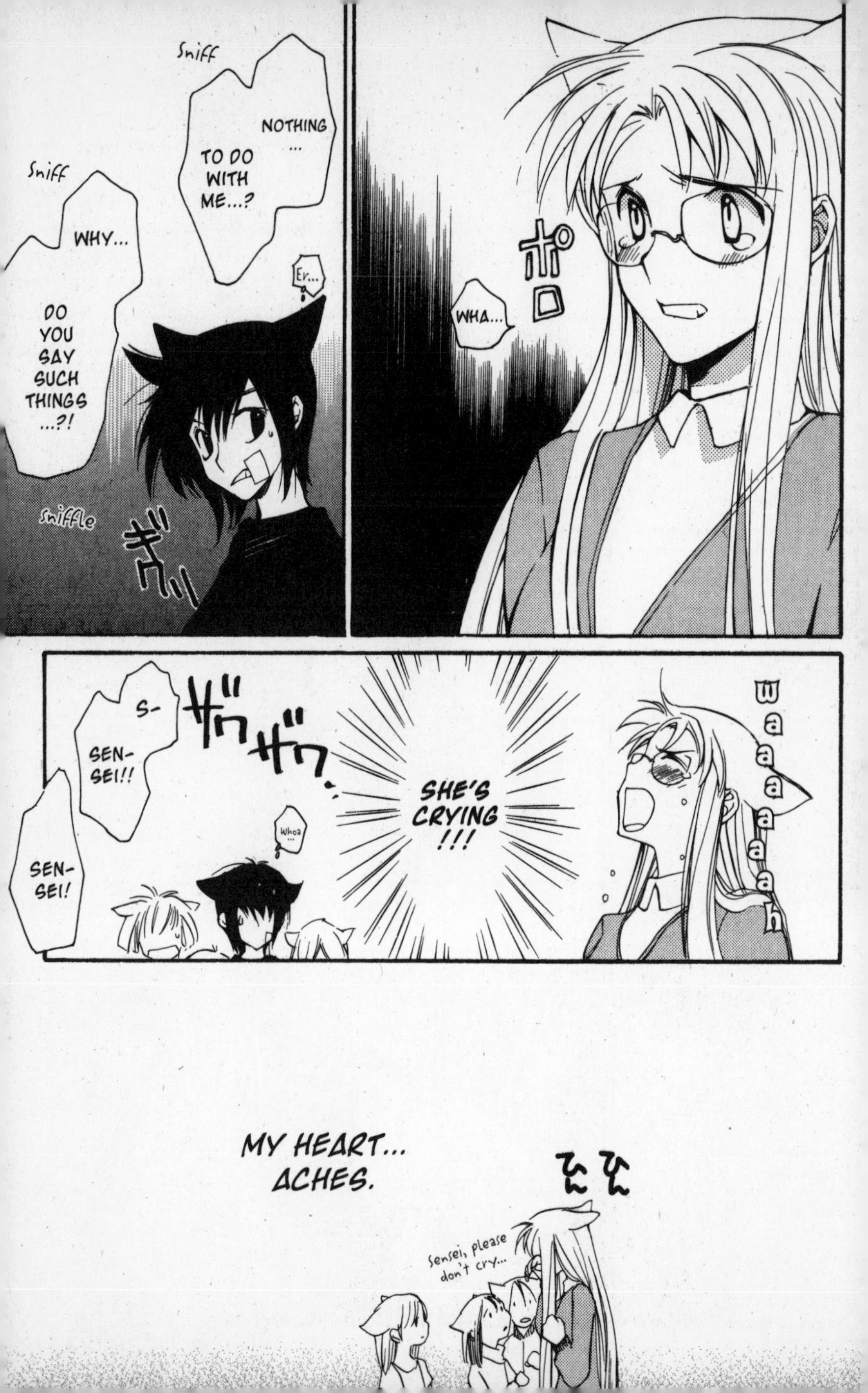
ポロ
WHA...
Sniff
NOTHING...
TO DO WITH ME...?
Sniff
WHY...
DO YOU SAY SUCH THINGS...?!
Er...
sniffle
ギクッ
Waaaaaaah
SHE'S CRYING!!!
Whoa...
ザワザワ
S-
SEN-SEI!!
SEN-SEI!
MY HEART... ACHES.
ひんひん
Sensei, please don't cry...

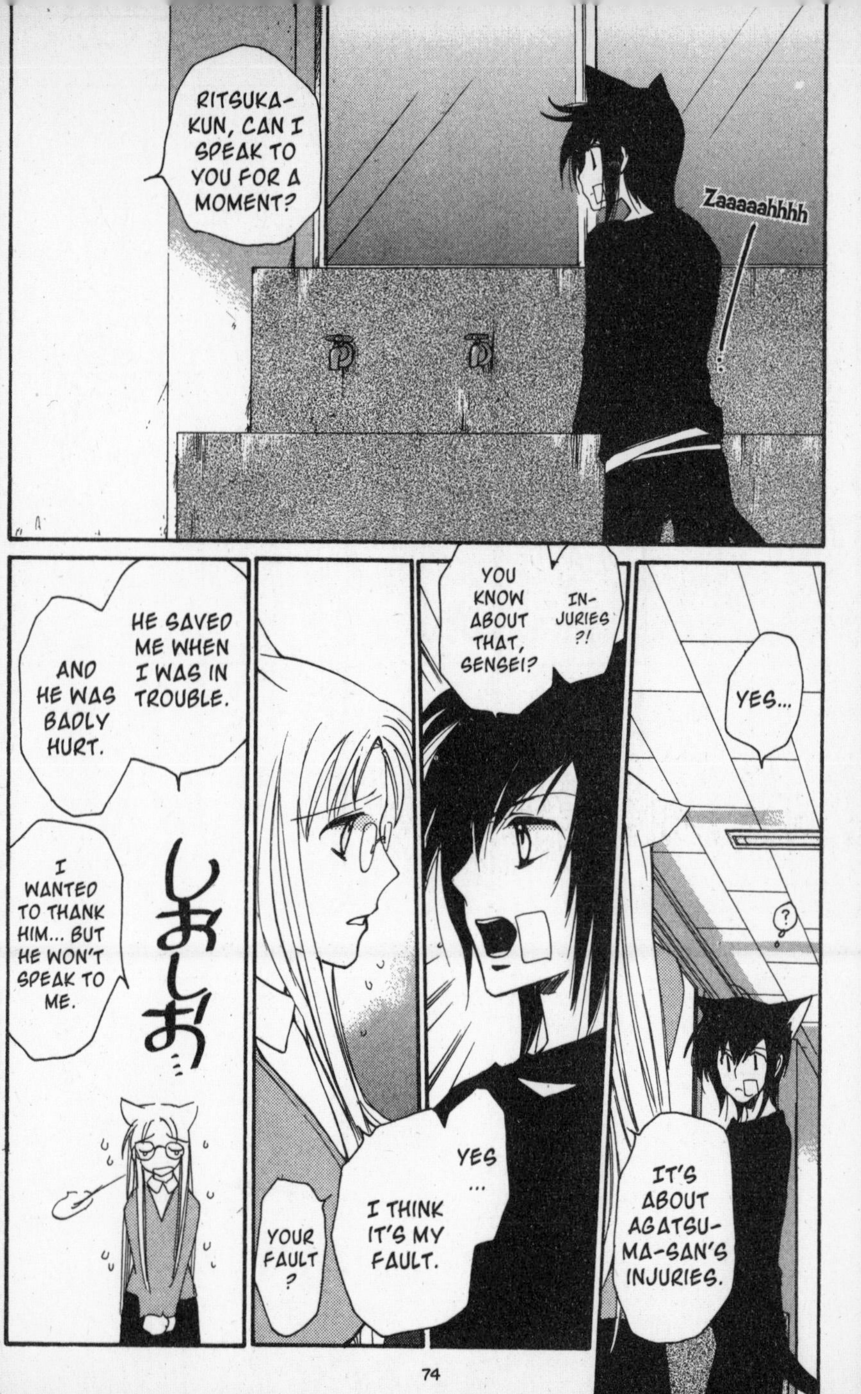
RITSUKA-KUN, CAN I SPEAK TO YOU FOR A MOMENT?
Zaaaaahhhh
YES...
?
IT'S ABOUT AGATSUMA-SAN'S INJURIES.
INJURIES?!
YOU KNOW ABOUT THAT, SENSEI?
YES ...
I THINK IT'S MY FAULT.
YOUR FAULT?
HE SAVED ME WHEN I WAS IN TROUBLE.
AND HE WAS BADLY HURT.
I WANTED TO THANK HIM... BUT HE WON'T SPEAK TO ME.
しおしお…

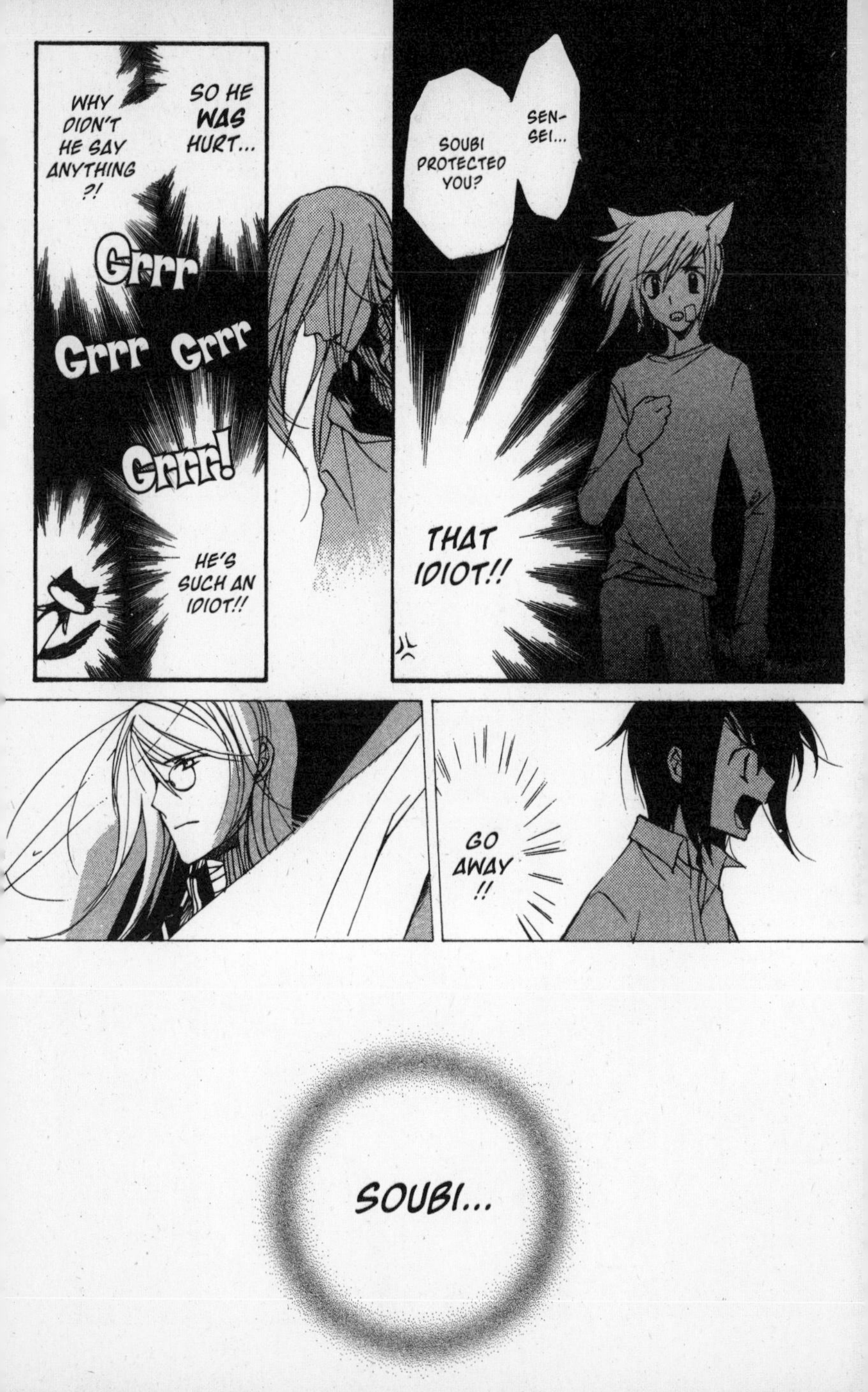
SEN-SEI...
SOUBI PROTECTED YOU?
THAT IDIOT!!
SO HE WAS HURT...
WHY DIDN'T HE SAY ANYTHING ?!
Grrr
Grrr Grrr
Grrr!
HE'S SUCH AN IDIOT!!
GO AWAY !!
SOUBI...

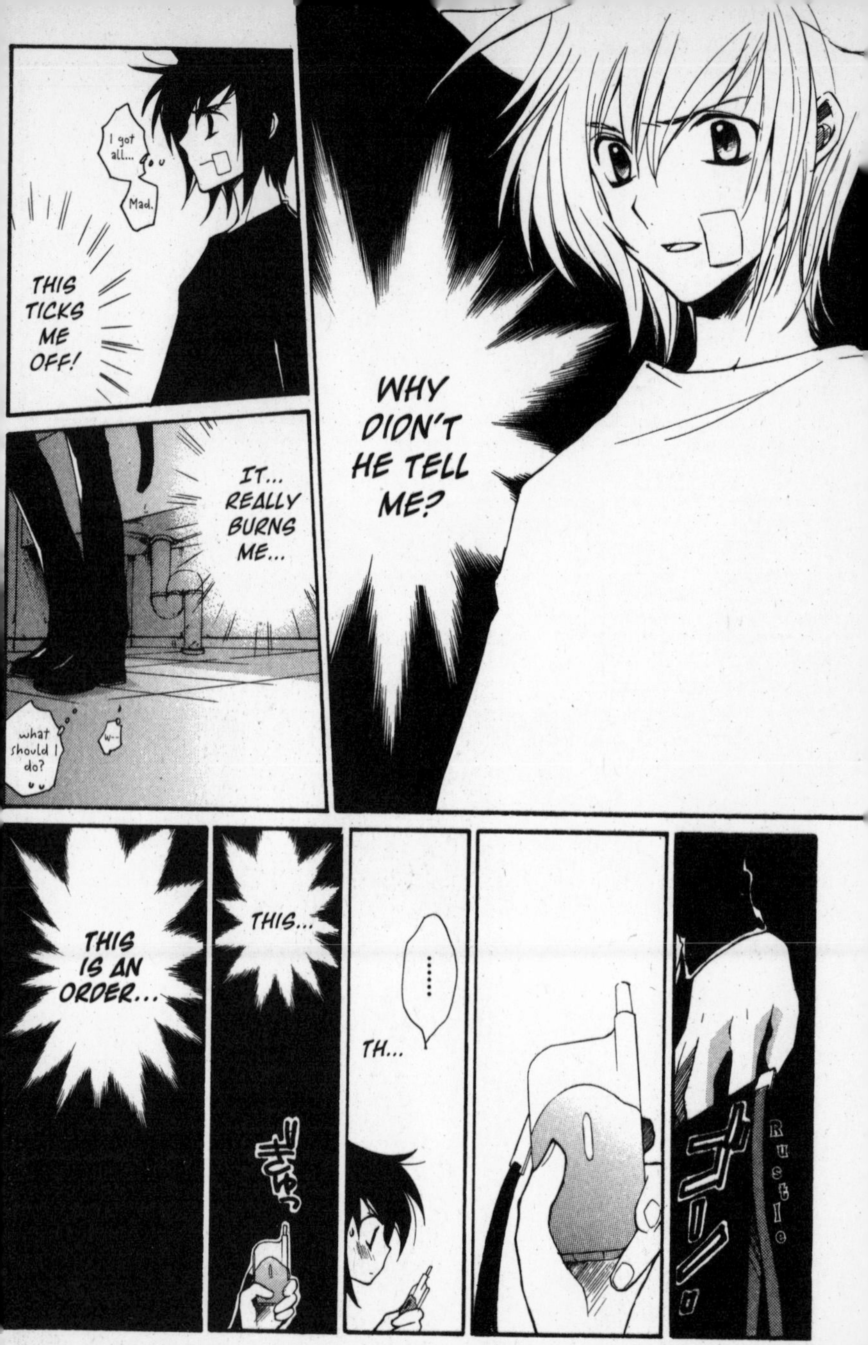
WHY DIDN'T HE TELL ME?
I got all...
Mad.
THIS TICKS ME OFF!
IT... REALLY BURNS ME...
what should I do?
w--
Rustle
......
TH...
THIS...
THIS IS AN ORDER...

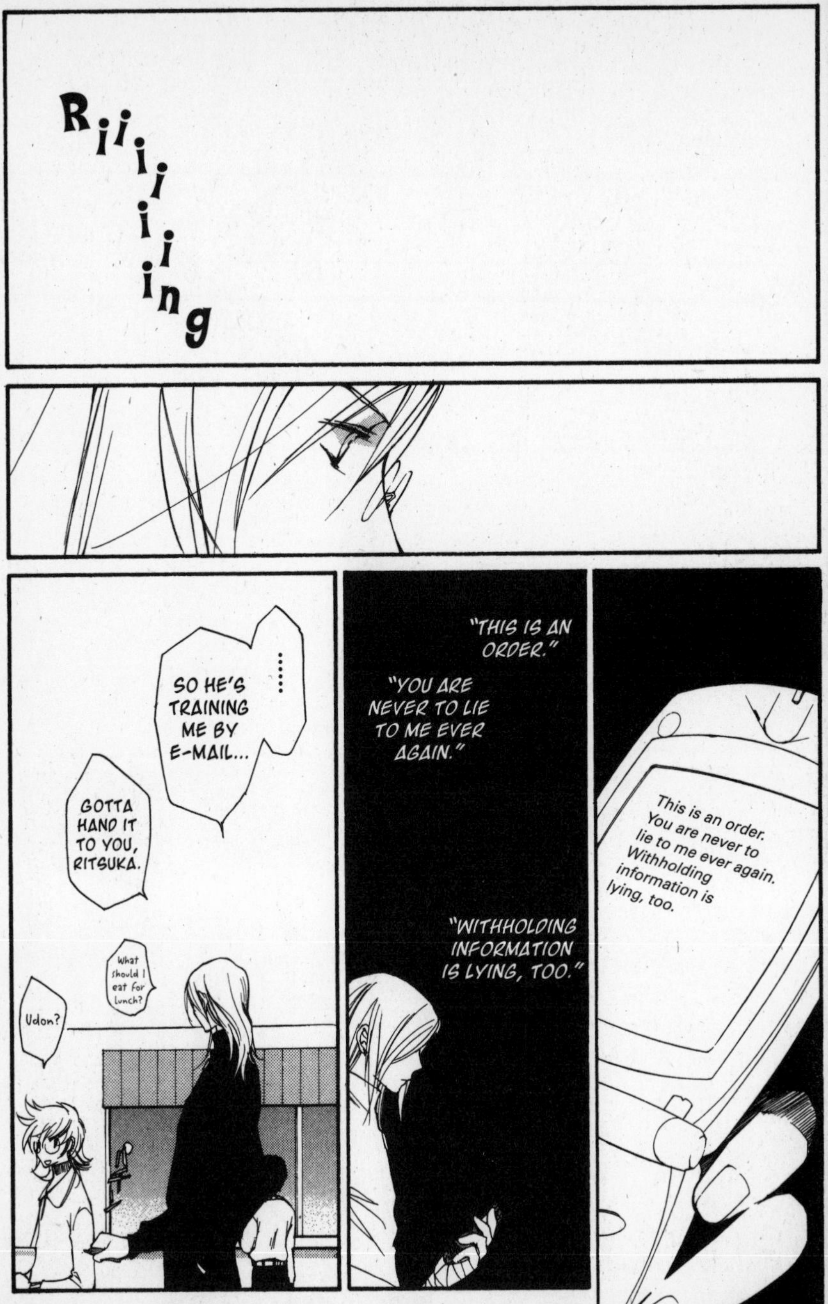
Riiiiiiing
This is an order. You are never to lie to me ever again. Withholding information is lying, too.
"THIS IS AN ORDER."
"YOU ARE NEVER TO LIE TO ME EVER AGAIN."
"WITHHOLDING INFORMATION IS LYING, TOO."
......
SO HE'S TRAINING ME BY E-MAIL...
GOTTA HAND IT TO YOU, RITSUKA.
What should I eat for lunch?
Udon?

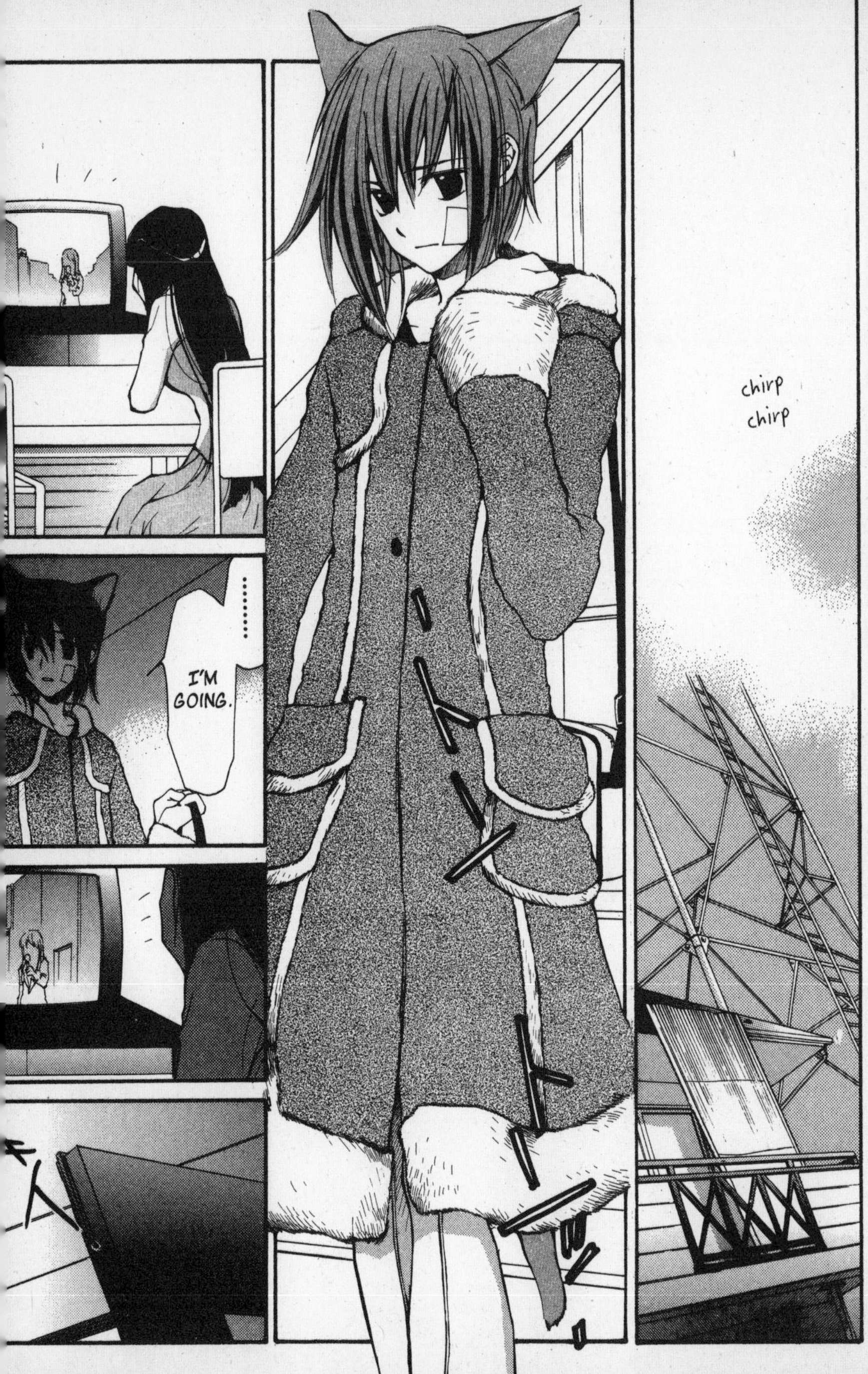
chirp
chirp
……
I'M GOING.

The Volume of the Absolute Toy Master II
Chapter 9

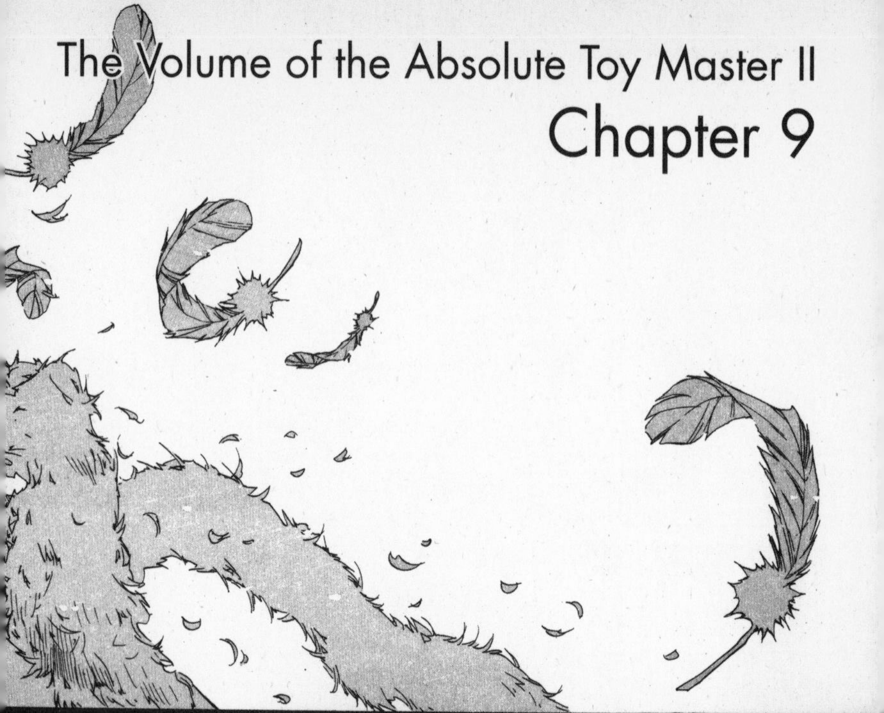

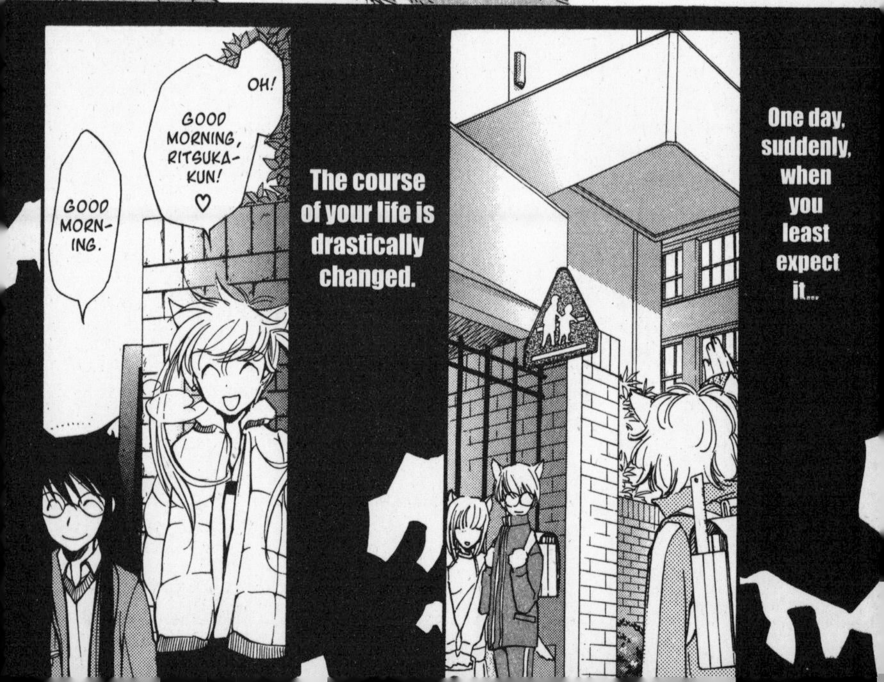
One day, suddenly, when you least expect it...
The course of your life is drastically changed.
OH!
GOOD MORNING, RITSUKA-KUN! ♡
GOOD MORNING.

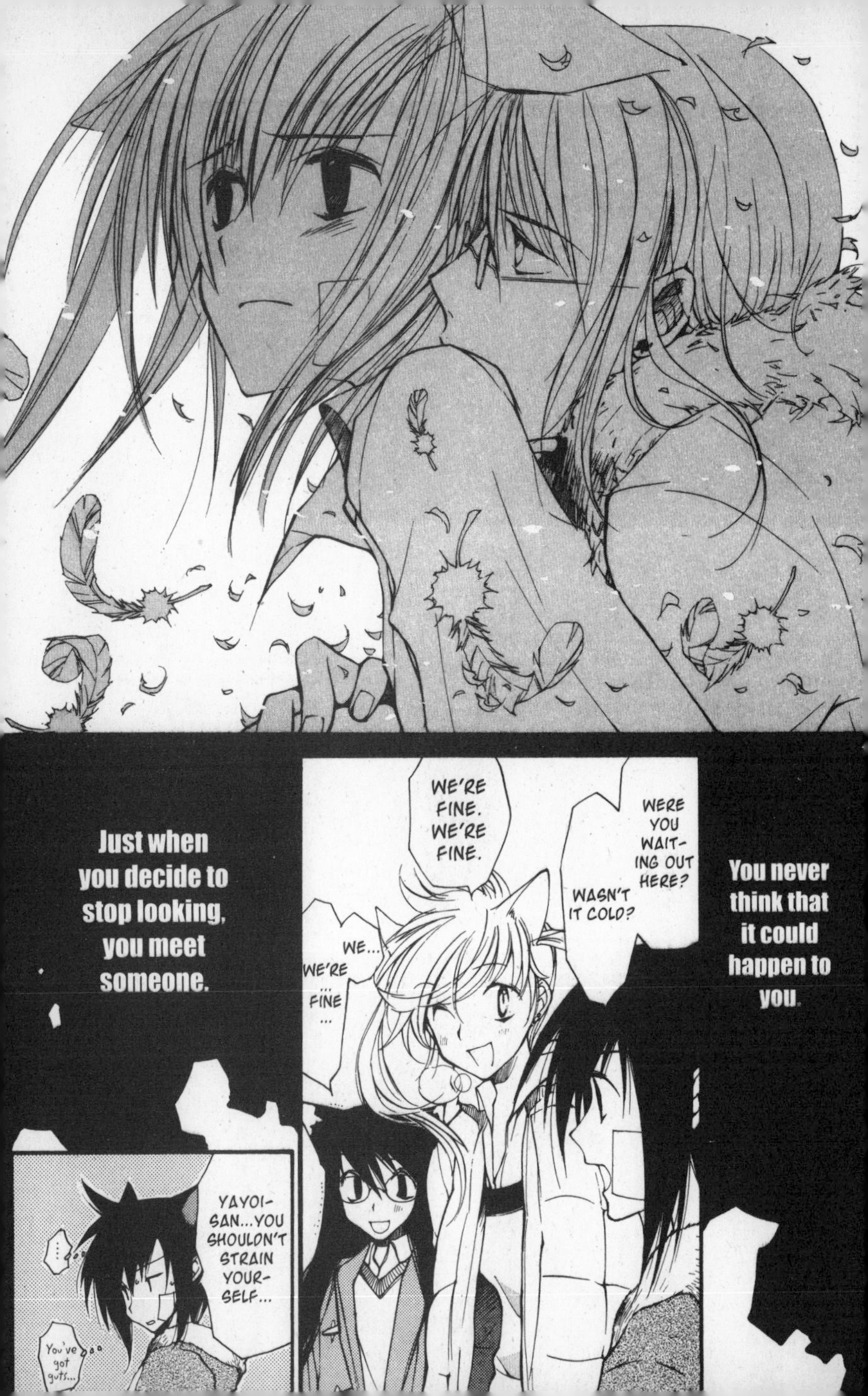
You never think that it could happen to you.
WERE YOU WAIT-ING OUT HERE?
WASN'T IT COLD?
WE'RE FINE. WE'RE FINE.
WE... WE'RE ... FINE ...
Just when you decide to stop looking, you meet someone.
YAYOI-SAN...YOU SHOULDN'T STRAIN YOUR-SELF...
...
You've got guts...

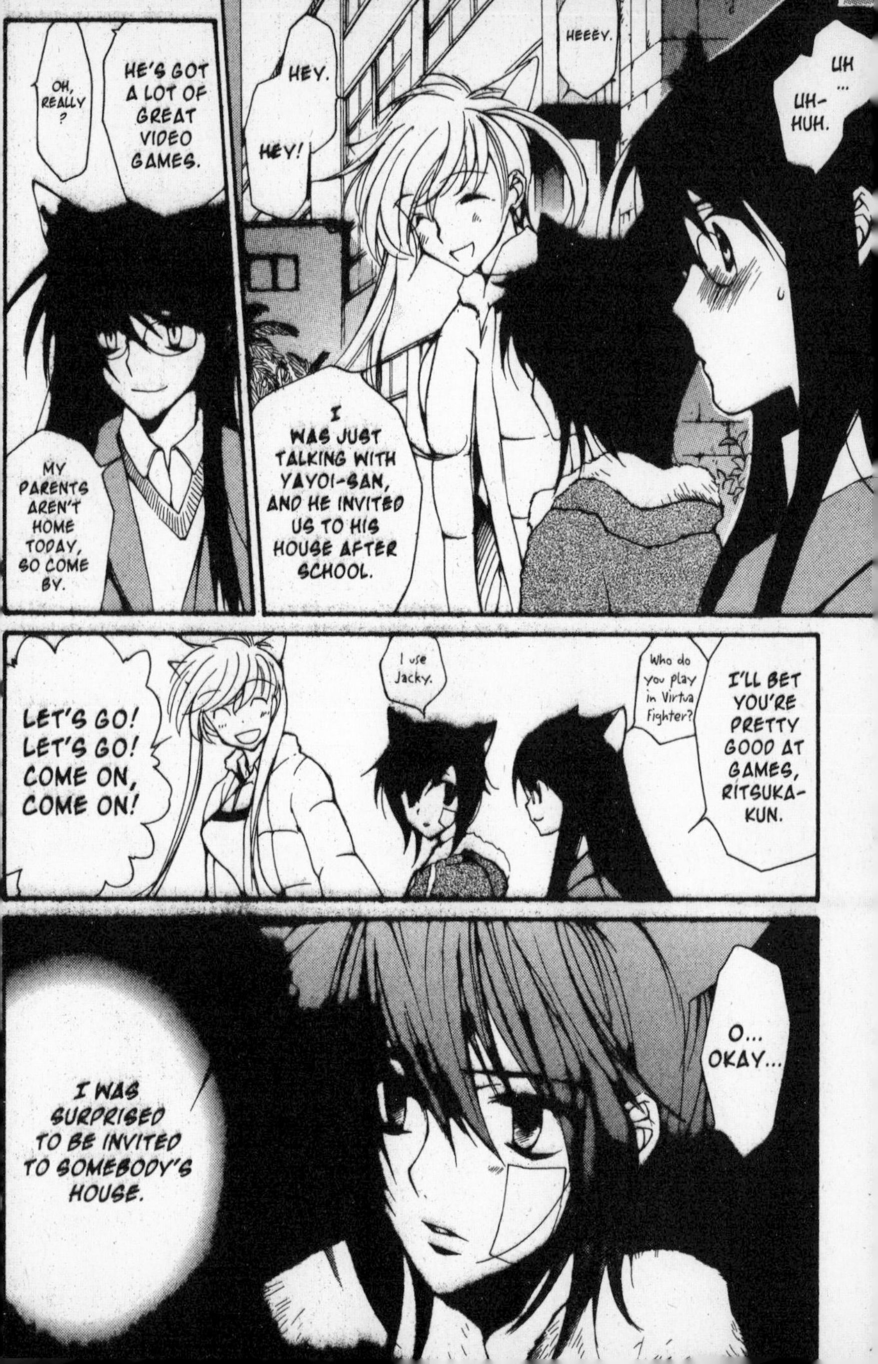
UH ... UH-HUH.
HEEEY.
HEY.
HEY!
I WAS JUST TALKING WITH YAYOI-SAN, AND HE INVITED US TO HIS HOUSE AFTER SCHOOL.
HE'S GOT A LOT OF GREAT VIDEO GAMES.
OH, REALLY?
MY PARENTS AREN'T HOME TODAY, SO COME BY.
I'LL BET YOU'RE PRETTY GOOD AT GAMES, RITSUKA-KUN.
Who do you play in Virtua Fighter?
I use Jacky.
LET'S GO! LET'S GO! COME ON, COME ON!
O... OKAY...
I WAS SURPRISED TO BE INVITED TO SOMEBODY'S HOUSE.

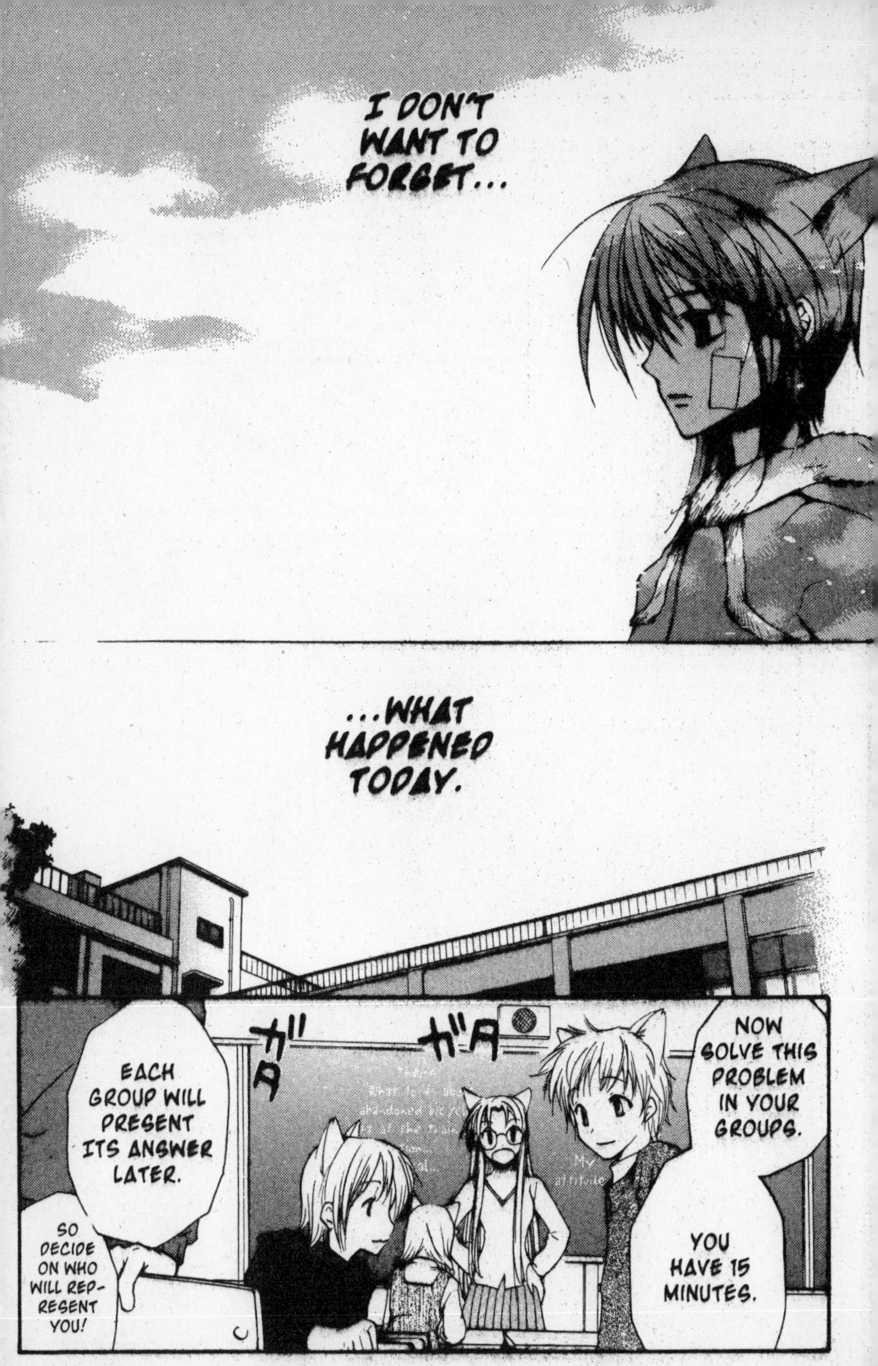
I DON'T WANT TO FORGET...
...WHAT HAPPENED TODAY.
NOW SOLVE THIS PROBLEM IN YOUR GROUPS.
YOU HAVE 15 MINUTES.
ガラ
ガラ
EACH GROUP WILL PRESENT ITS ANSWER LATER.
SO DECIDE ON WHO WILL REP-RESENT YOU!

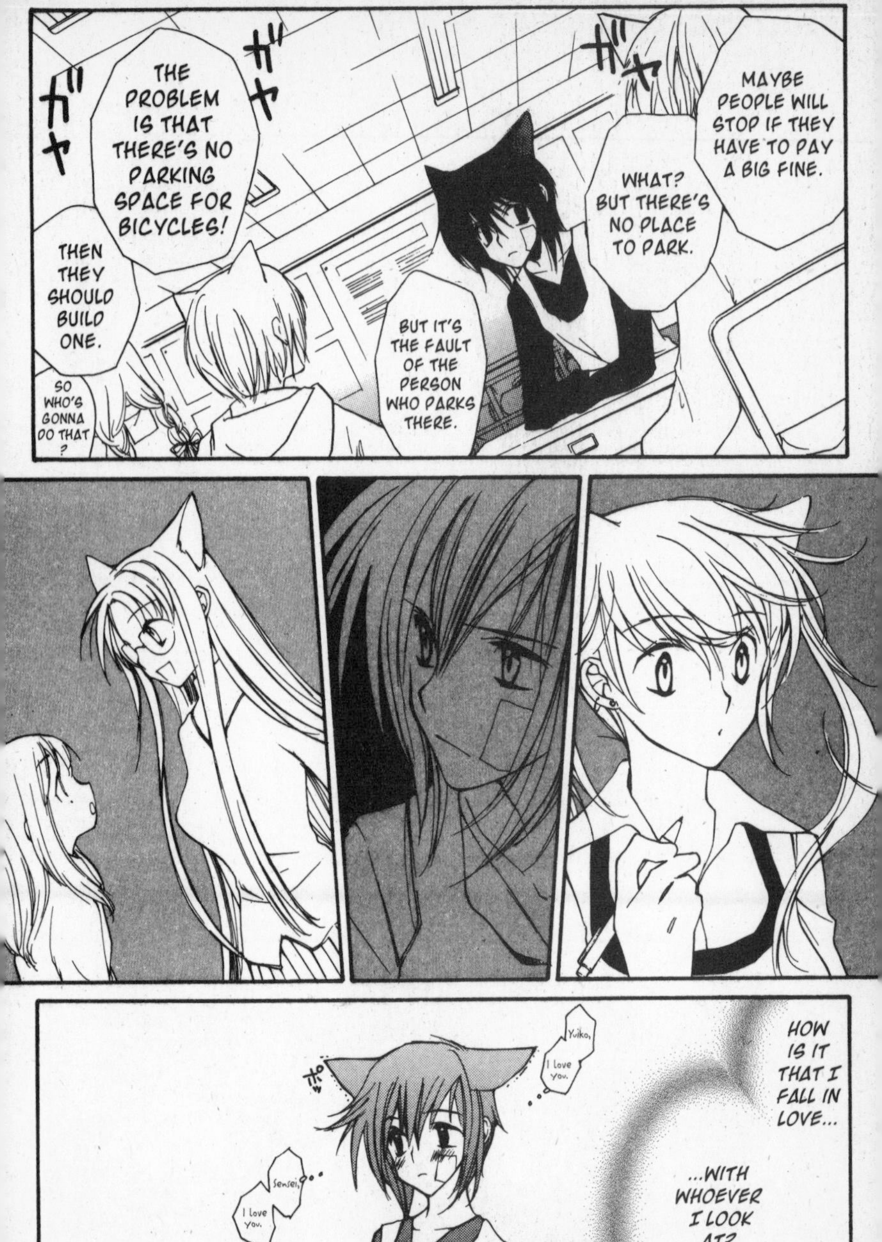
ガヤ
MAYBE PEOPLE WILL STOP IF THEY HAVE TO PAY A BIG FINE.
WHAT? BUT THERE'S NO PLACE TO PARK.
BUT IT'S THE FAULT OF THE PERSON WHO PARKS THERE.
ガヤ
THE PROBLEM IS THAT THERE'S NO PARKING SPACE FOR BICYCLES!
ガヤ
THEN THEY SHOULD BUILD ONE.
SO WHO'S GONNA DO THAT?
HOW IS IT THAT I FALL IN LOVE...
Yuiko, I love you.
Sensei, I love you.
...WITH WHOEVER I LOOK AT?

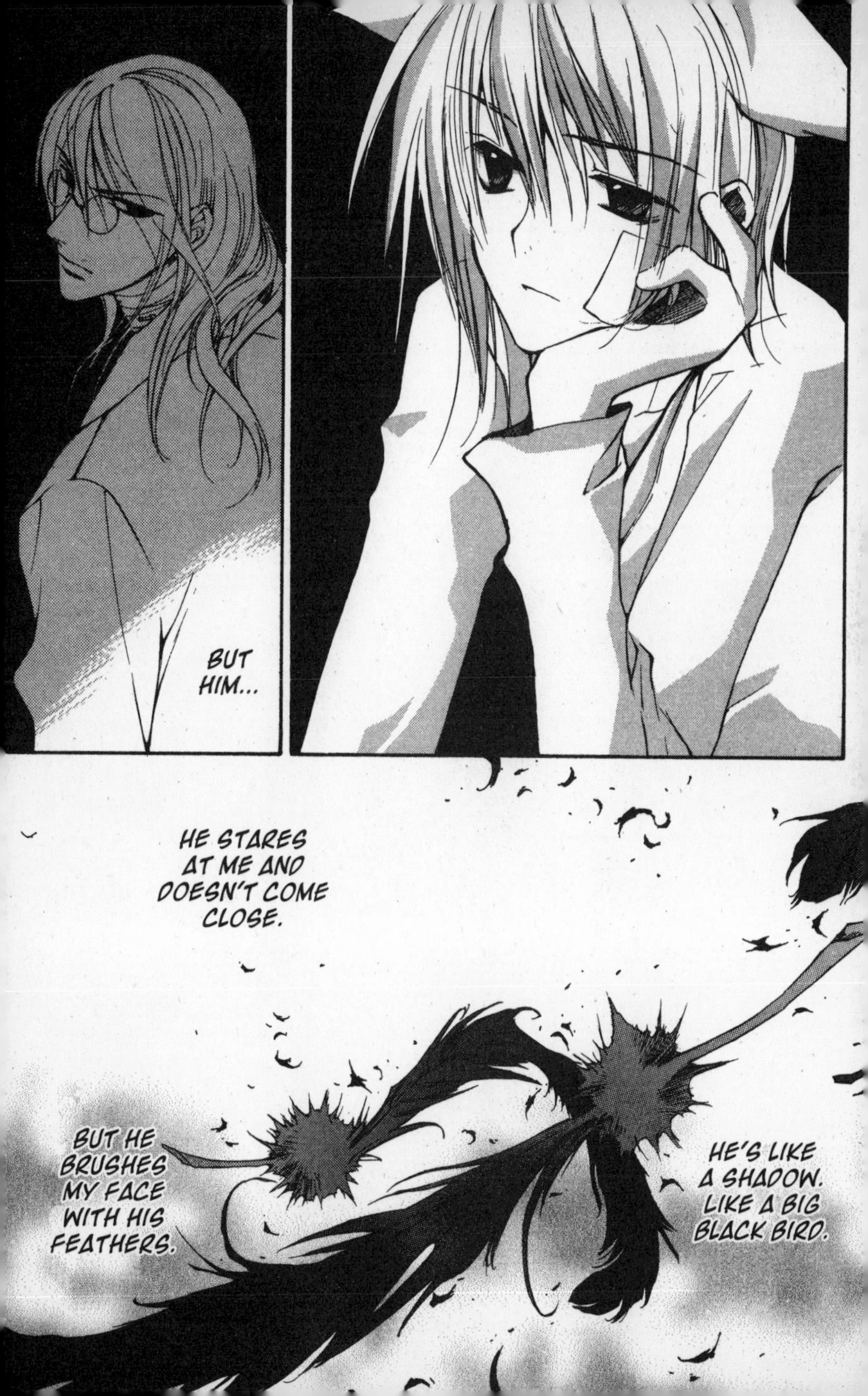
BUT HIM...
HE STARES AT ME AND DOESN'T COME CLOSE.
HE'S LIKE A SHADOW. LIKE A BIG BLACK BIRD.
BUT HE BRUSHES MY FACE WITH HIS FEATHERS.

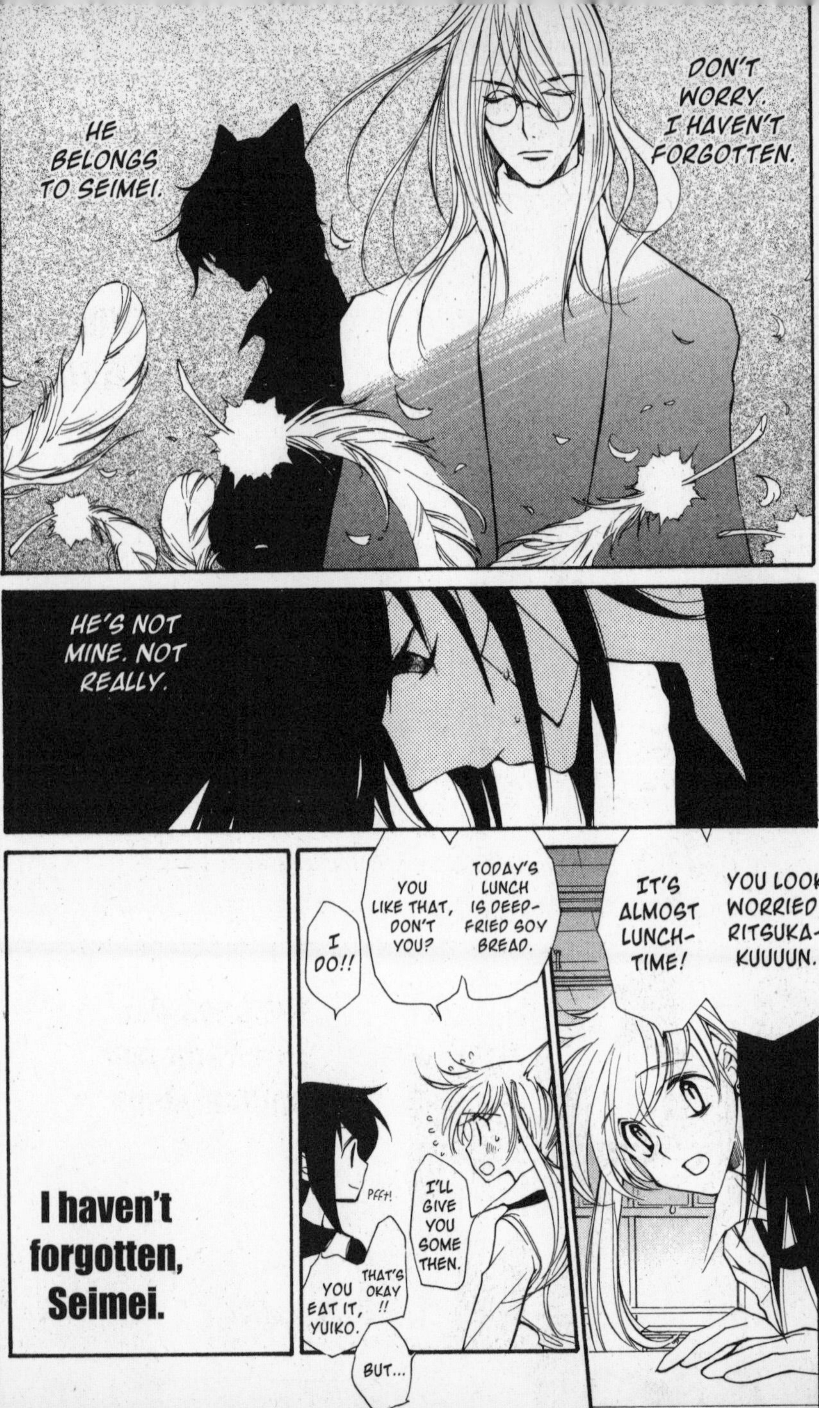
DON'T WORRY. I HAVEN'T FORGOTTEN.
HE BELONGS TO SEIMEI.
HE'S NOT MINE. NOT REALLY.
YOU LOOK WORRIED, RITSUKA-KUUUUN.
IT'S ALMOST LUNCH-TIME!
TODAY'S LUNCH IS DEEP-FRIED SOY BREAD.
YOU LIKE THAT, DON'T YOU?
I DO!!
I'LL GIVE YOU SOME THEN.
PFFT!
THAT'S OKAY!!
YOU EAT IT, YUIKO.
BUT...
I haven't forgotten, Seimei.

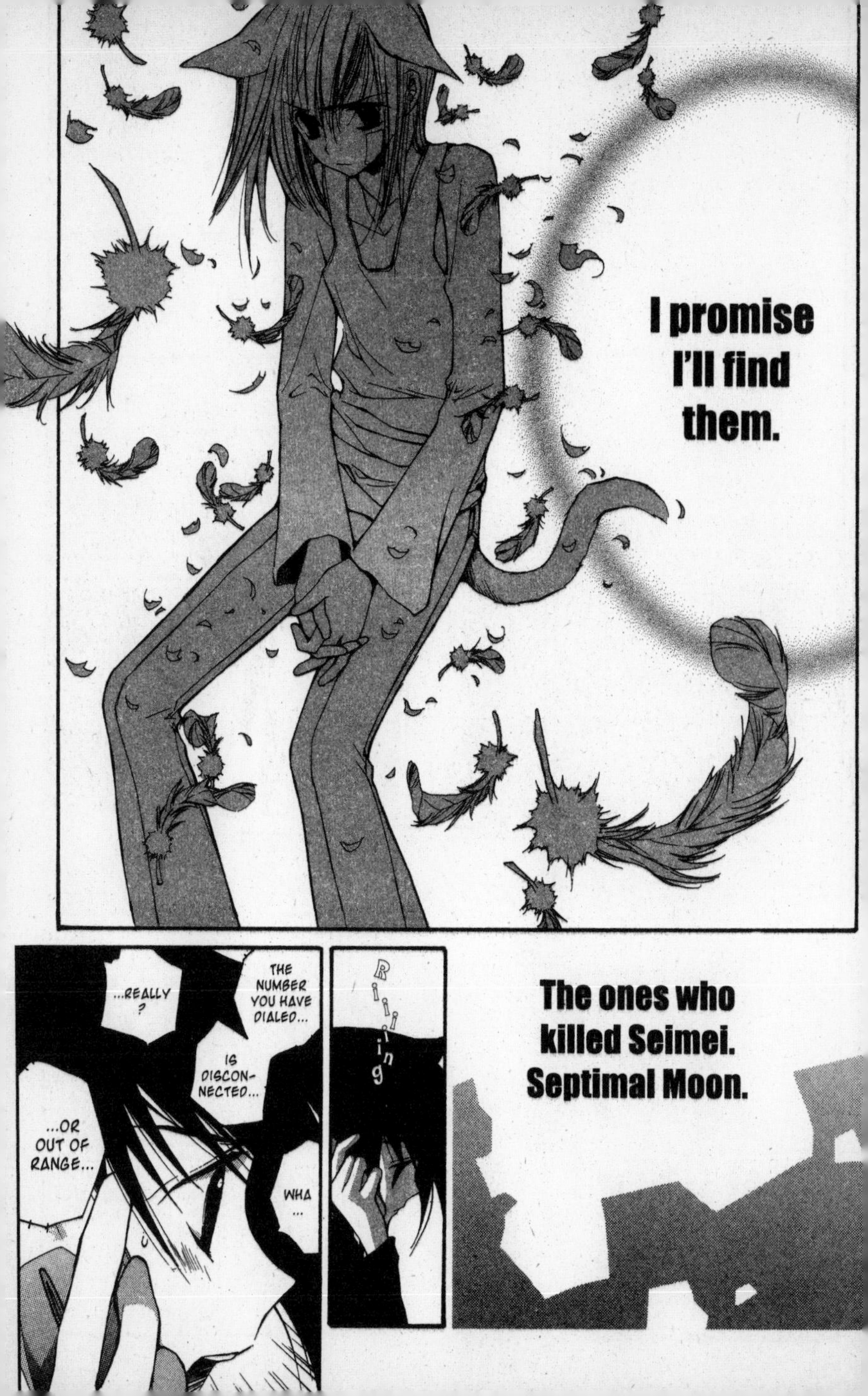
I promise I'll find them.
The ones who killed Seimei. Septimal Moon.
Riiiiing
THE NUMBER YOU HAVE DIALED...
...REALLY?
IS DISCON-NECTED...
...OR OUT OF RANGE...
WHA...

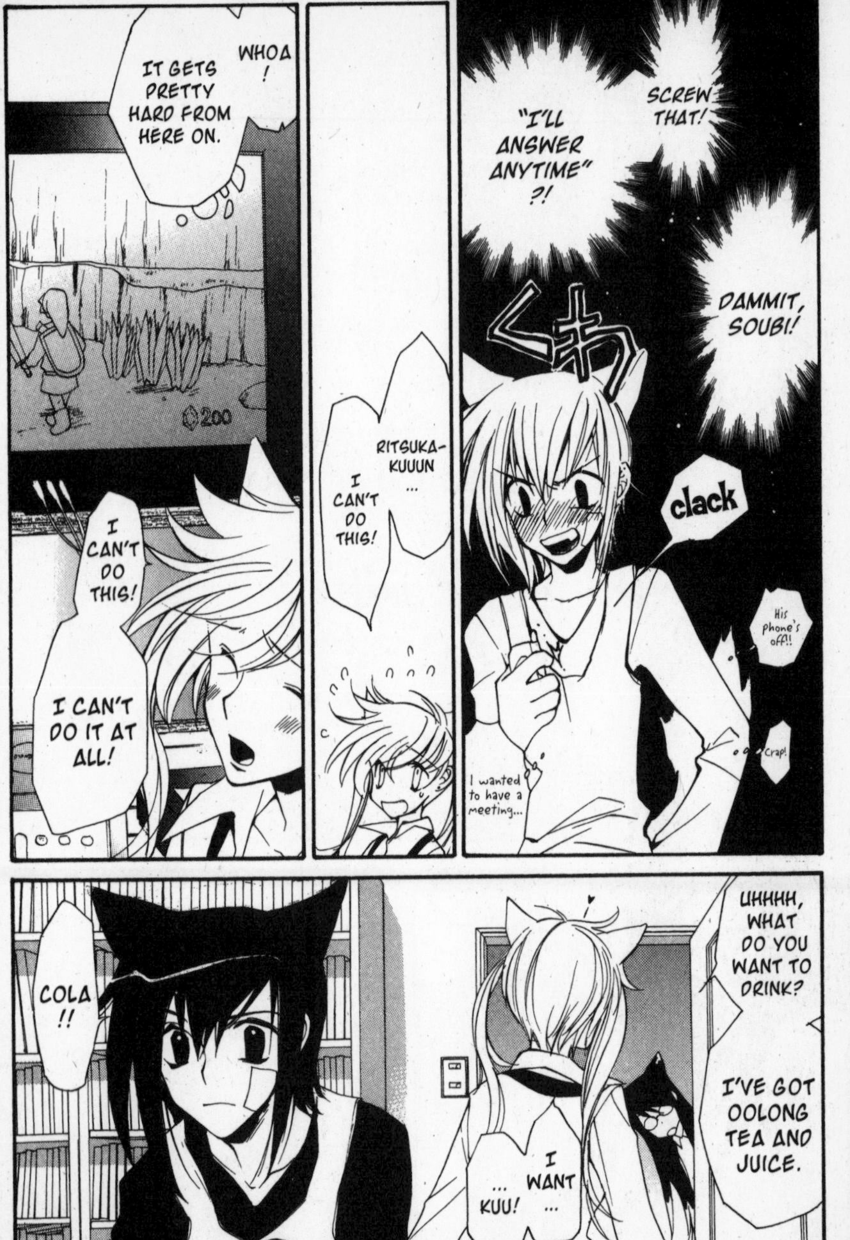
SCREW THAT!
DAMMIT, SOUBI!
"I'LL ANSWER ANYTIME" ?!
clack
His phone's off!!
Crap!
I wanted to have a meeting...
RITSUKA-KUUUN ...
I CAN'T DO THIS!
WHOA !
IT GETS PRETTY HARD FROM HERE ON.
I CAN'T DO THIS!
I CAN'T DO IT AT ALL!
UHHHH, WHAT DO YOU WANT TO DRINK?
I'VE GOT OOLONG TEA AND JUICE.
I WANT ...
... KUU!
COLA !!

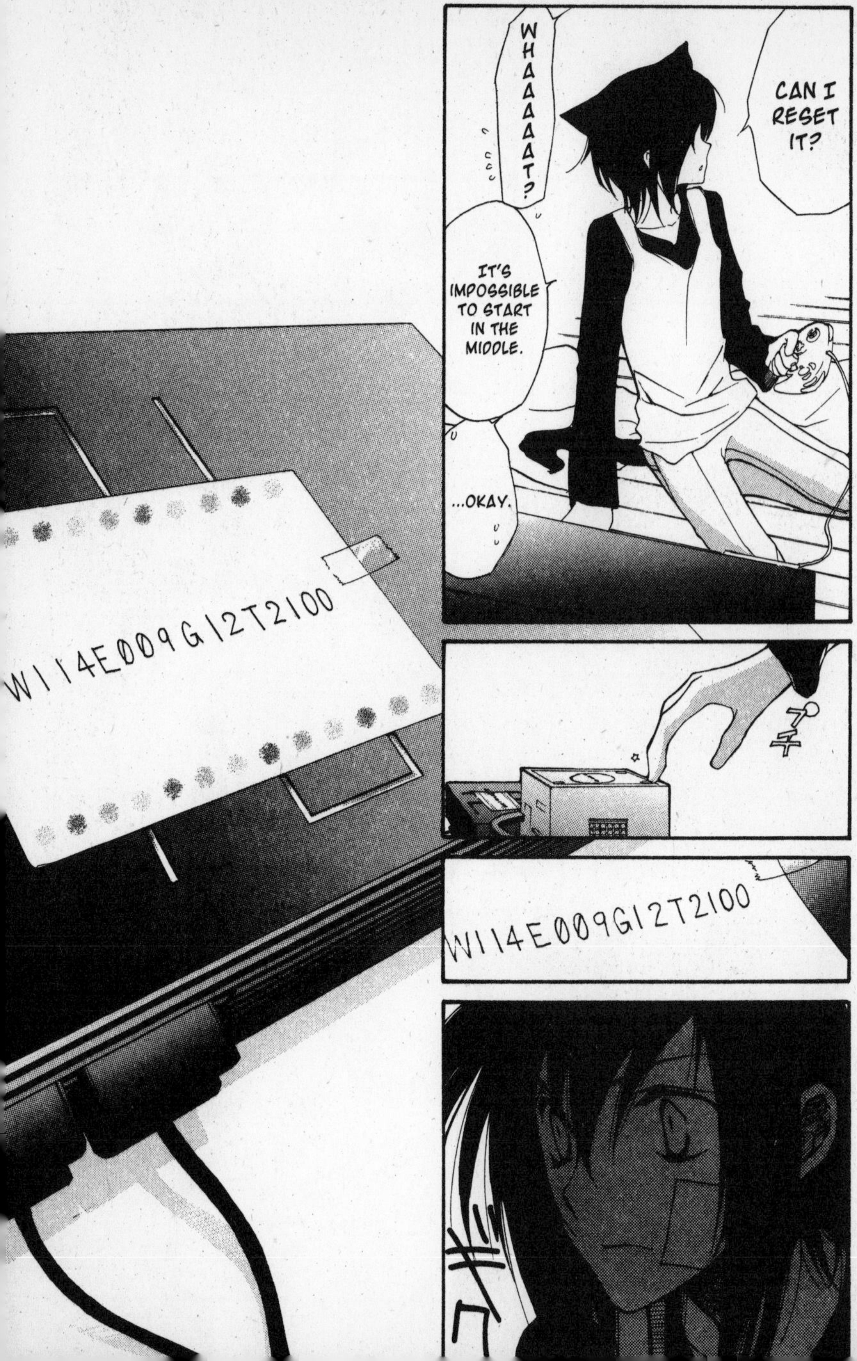
CAN I RESET IT?
WHAAAAAAAT?
IT'S IMPOSSIBLE TO START IN THE MIDDLE.
...OKAY.
W114E009G12T2100
W114E009G12T2100

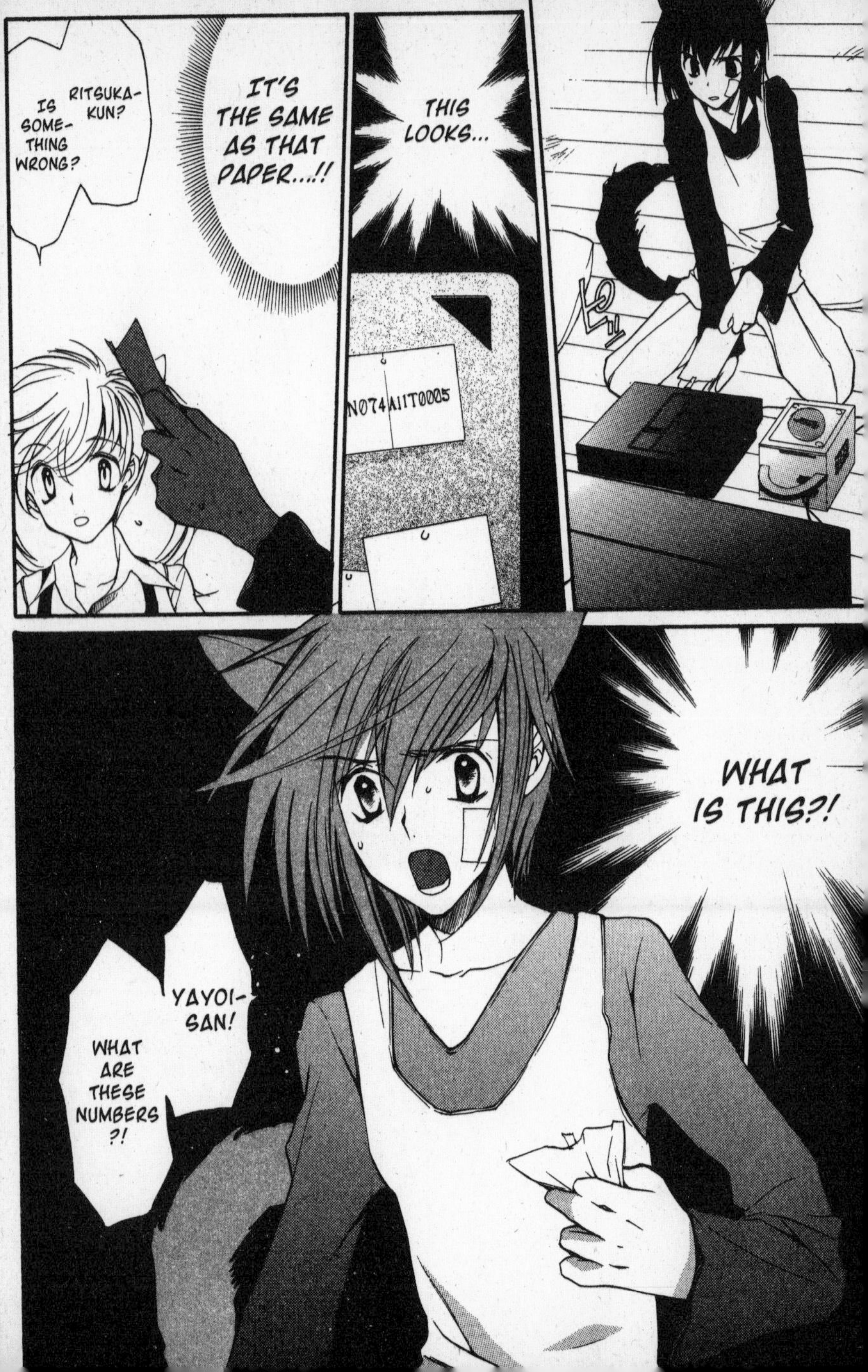
THIS LOOKS...
N074A11T0005
IT'S THE SAME AS THAT PAPER...!!
RITSUKA-KUN? IS SOMETHING WRONG?
WHAT IS THIS?!
YAYOI-SAN!
WHAT ARE THESE NUMBERS?!

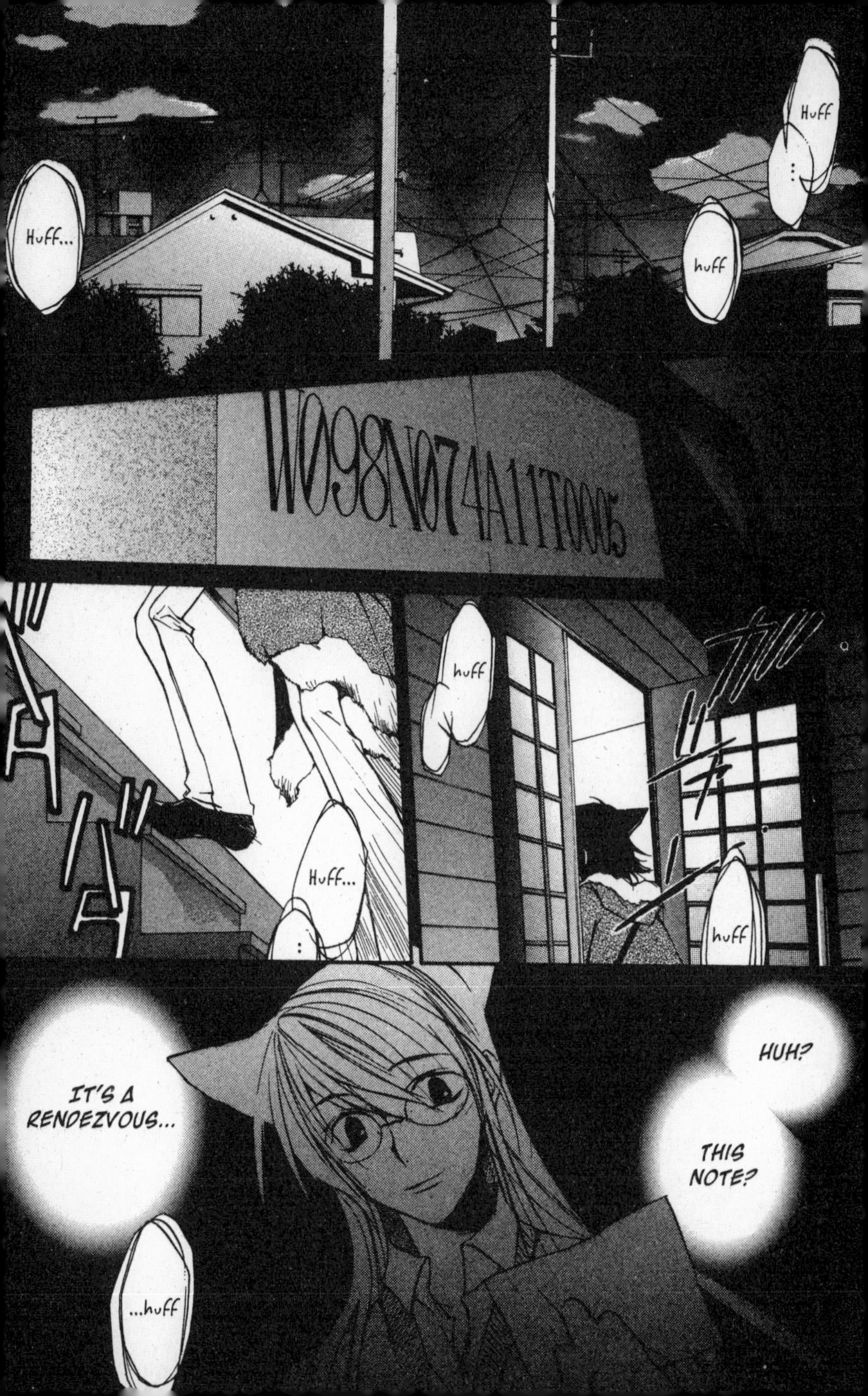

Huff
huff
Huff...
W098N074A11T0005
huff
huff
Huff...
HUH?
THIS NOTE?
IT'S A RENDEZVOUS...
...huff

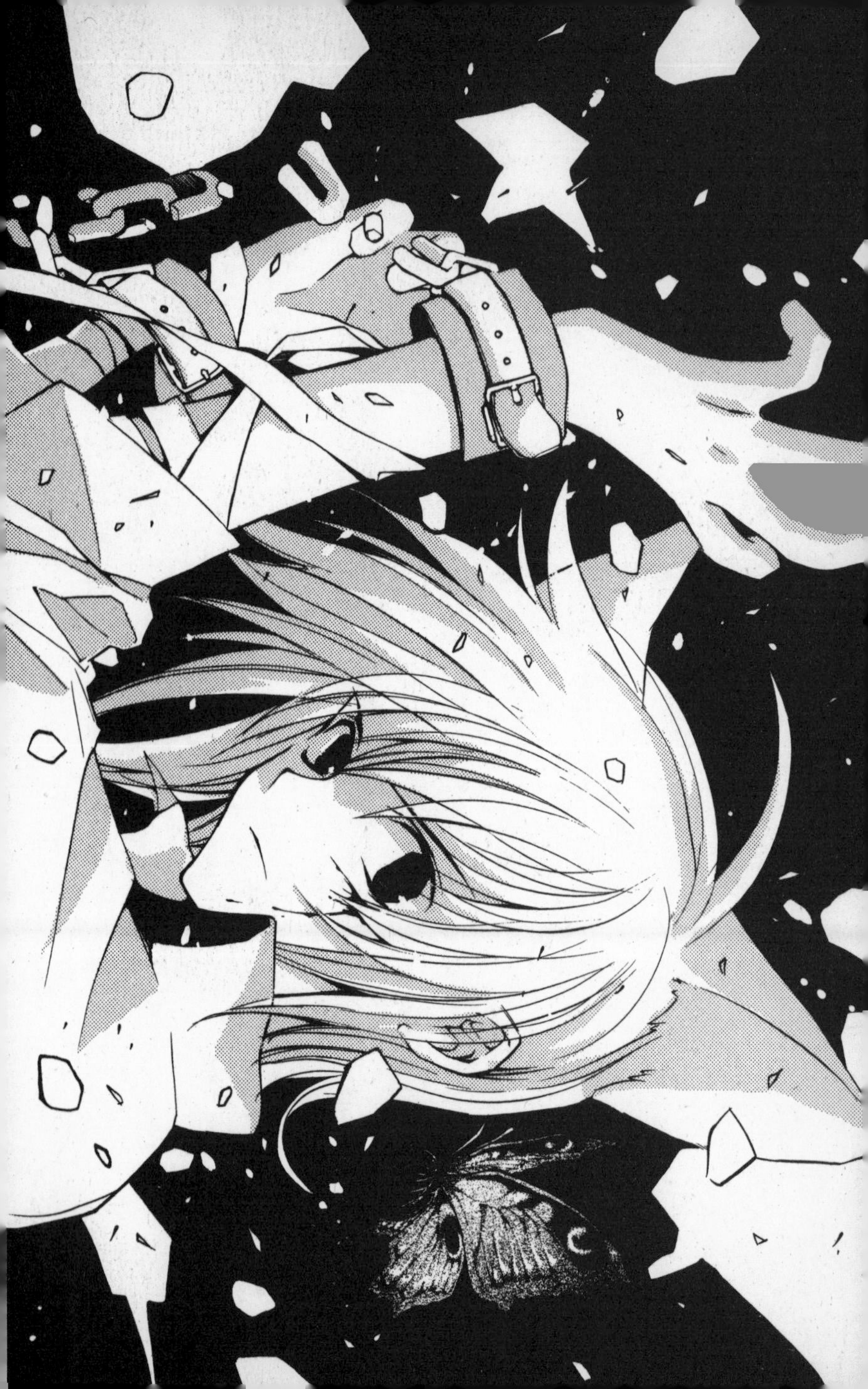

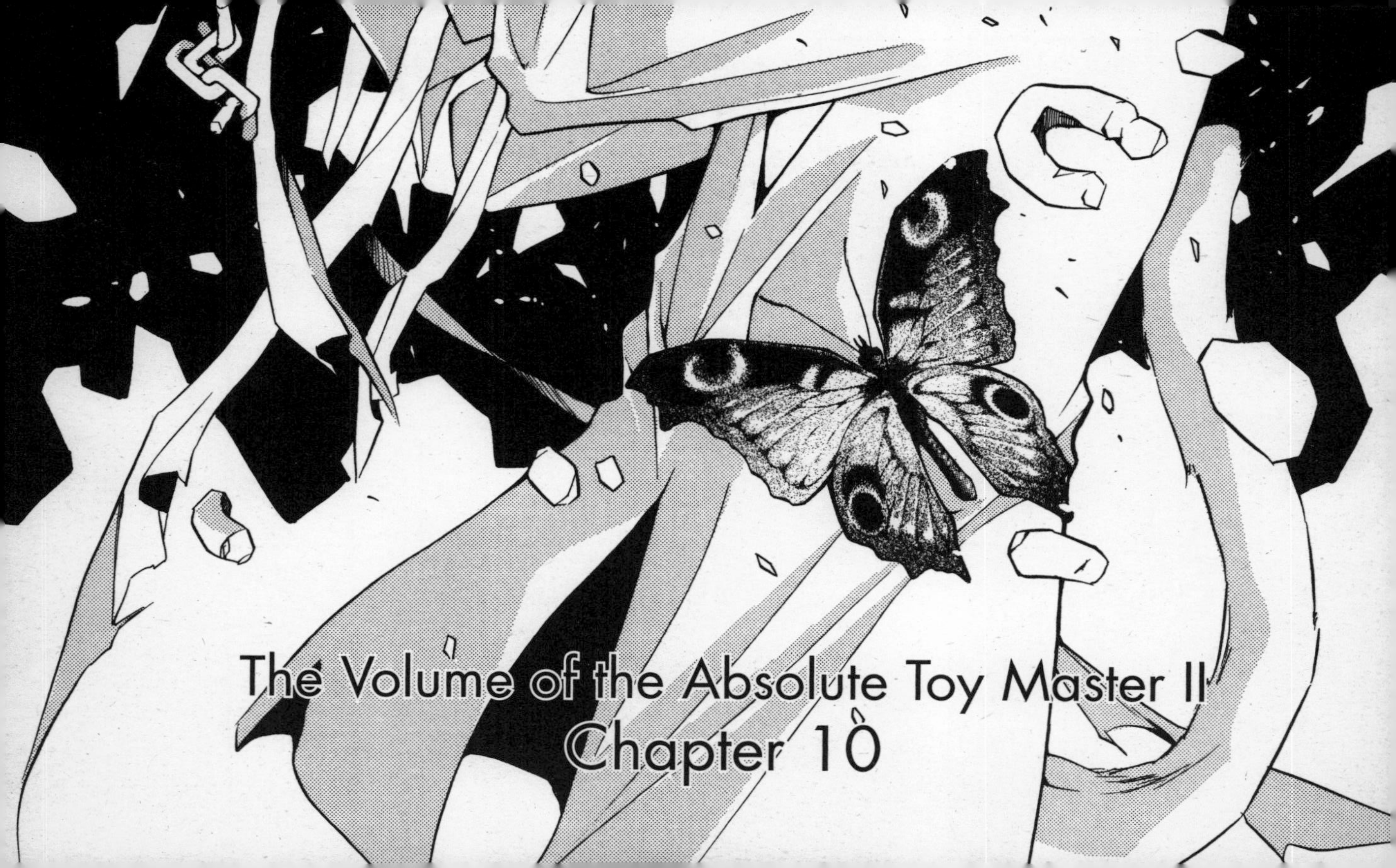
The Volume of the Absolute Toy Master II
Chapter 10

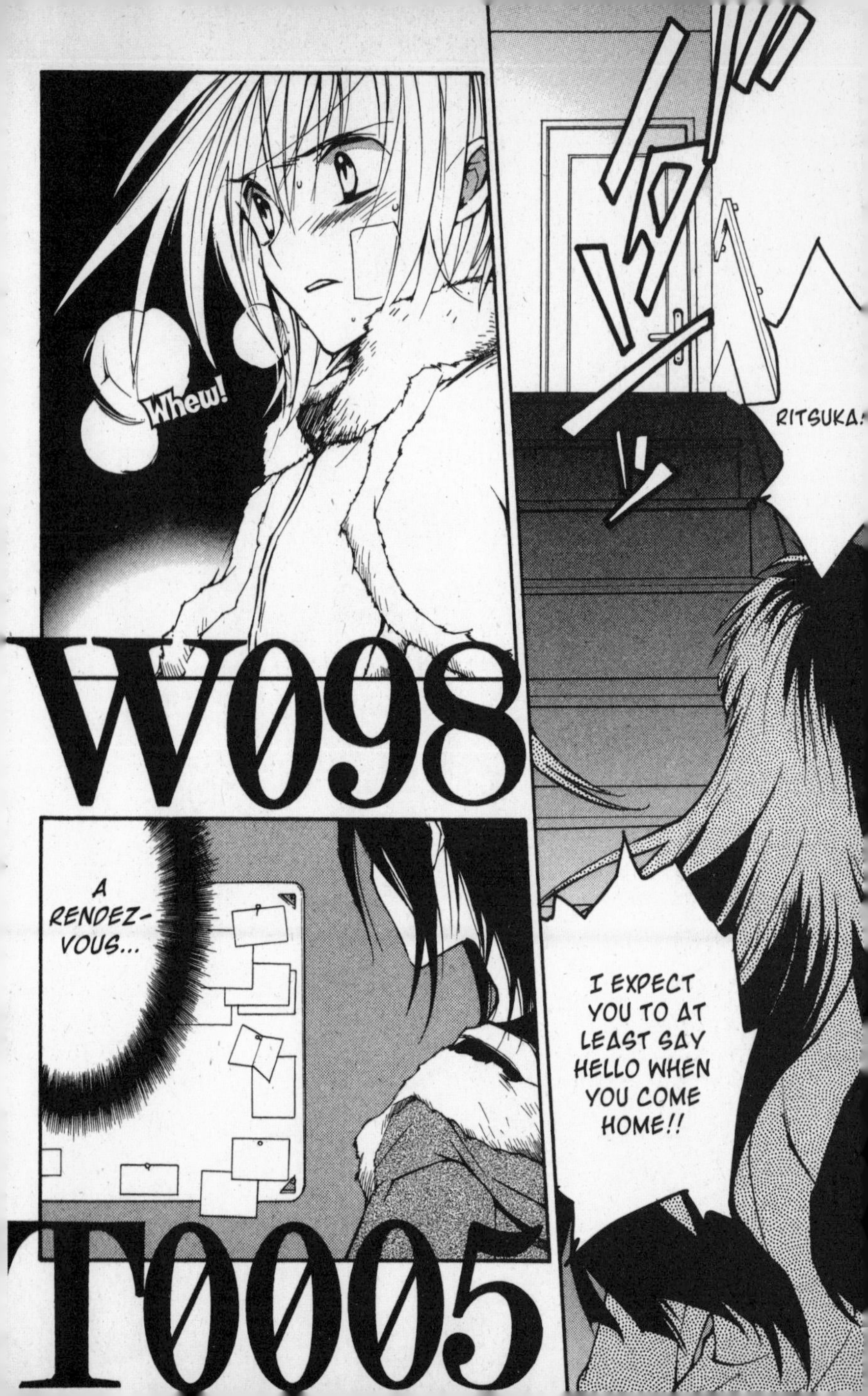
RITSUKA!
I EXPECT YOU TO AT LEAST SAY HELLO WHEN YOU COME HOME!!
Whew!
W098
A RENDEZ-VOUS...
T0005

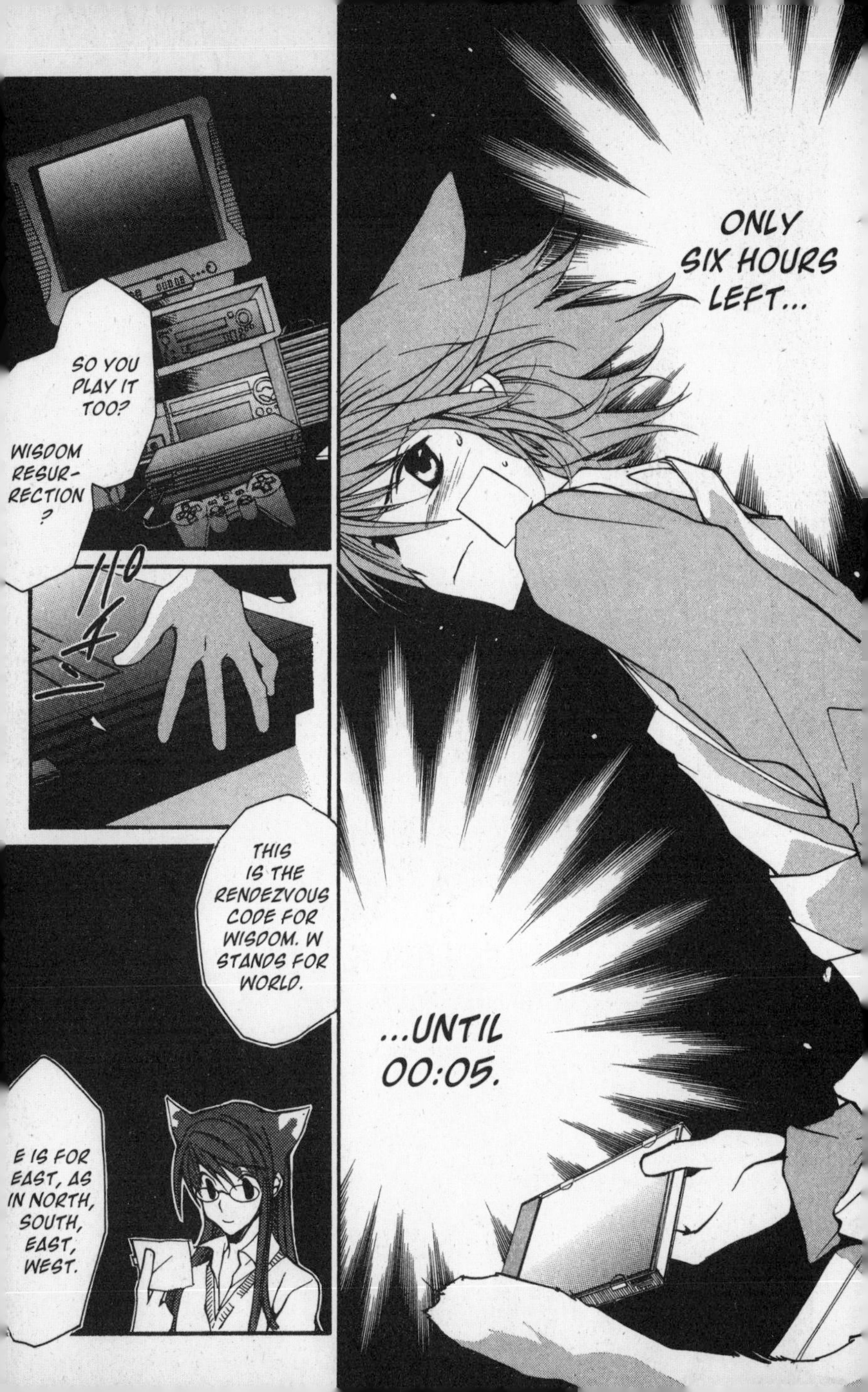
ONLY SIX HOURS LEFT...
...UNTIL 00:05.
SO YOU PLAY IT TOO?
WISDOM RESUR-RECTION?
THIS IS THE RENDEZVOUS CODE FOR WISDOM. W STANDS FOR WORLD.
E IS FOR EAST, AS IN NORTH, SOUTH, EAST, WEST.

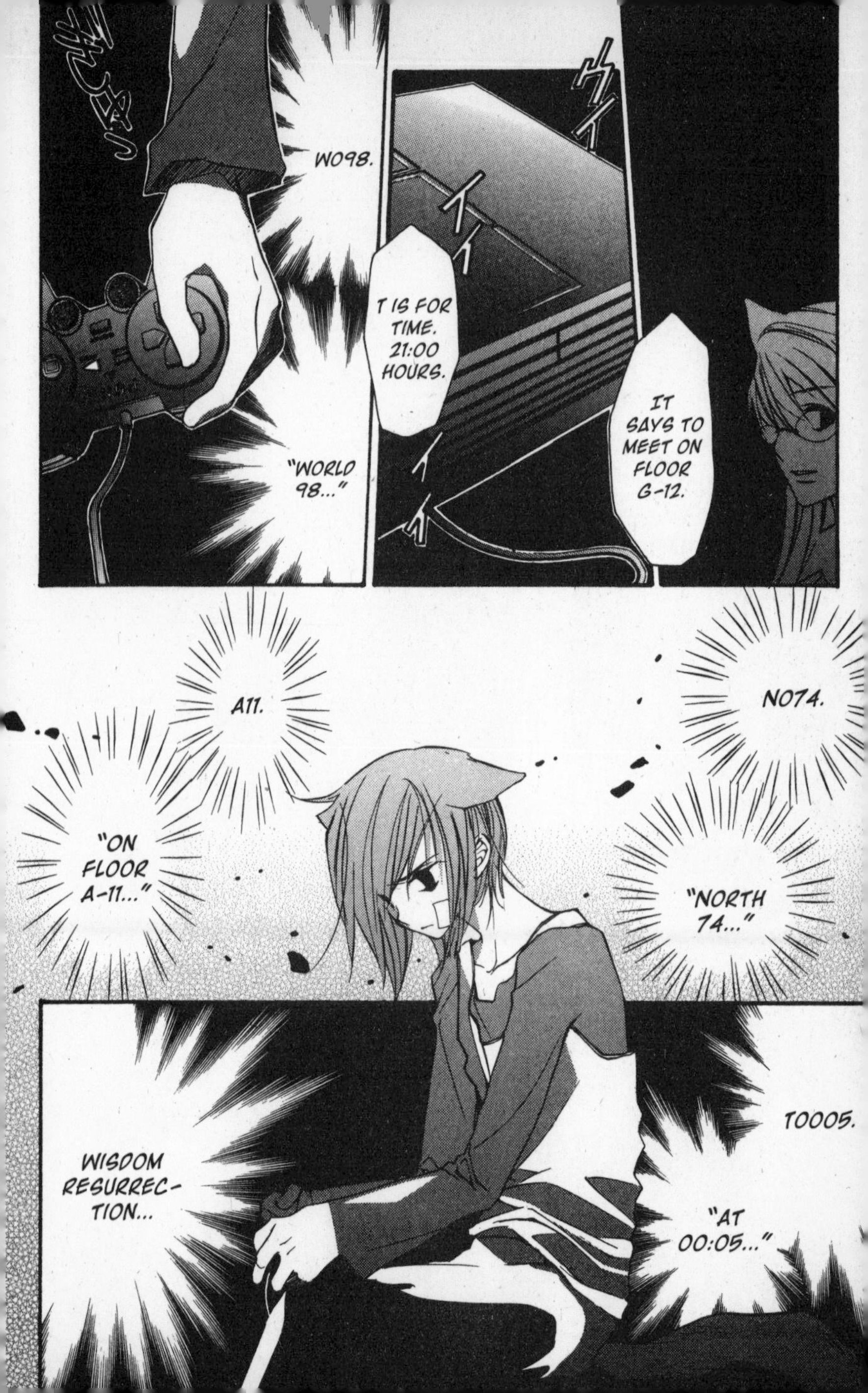
IT SAYS TO MEET ON FLOOR G-12.
T IS FOR TIME. 21:00 HOURS.
W098.
"WORLD 98..."
N074.
"NORTH 74..."
A11.
"ON FLOOR A-11..."
T0005.
"AT 00:05..."
WISDOM RESURREC-TION...

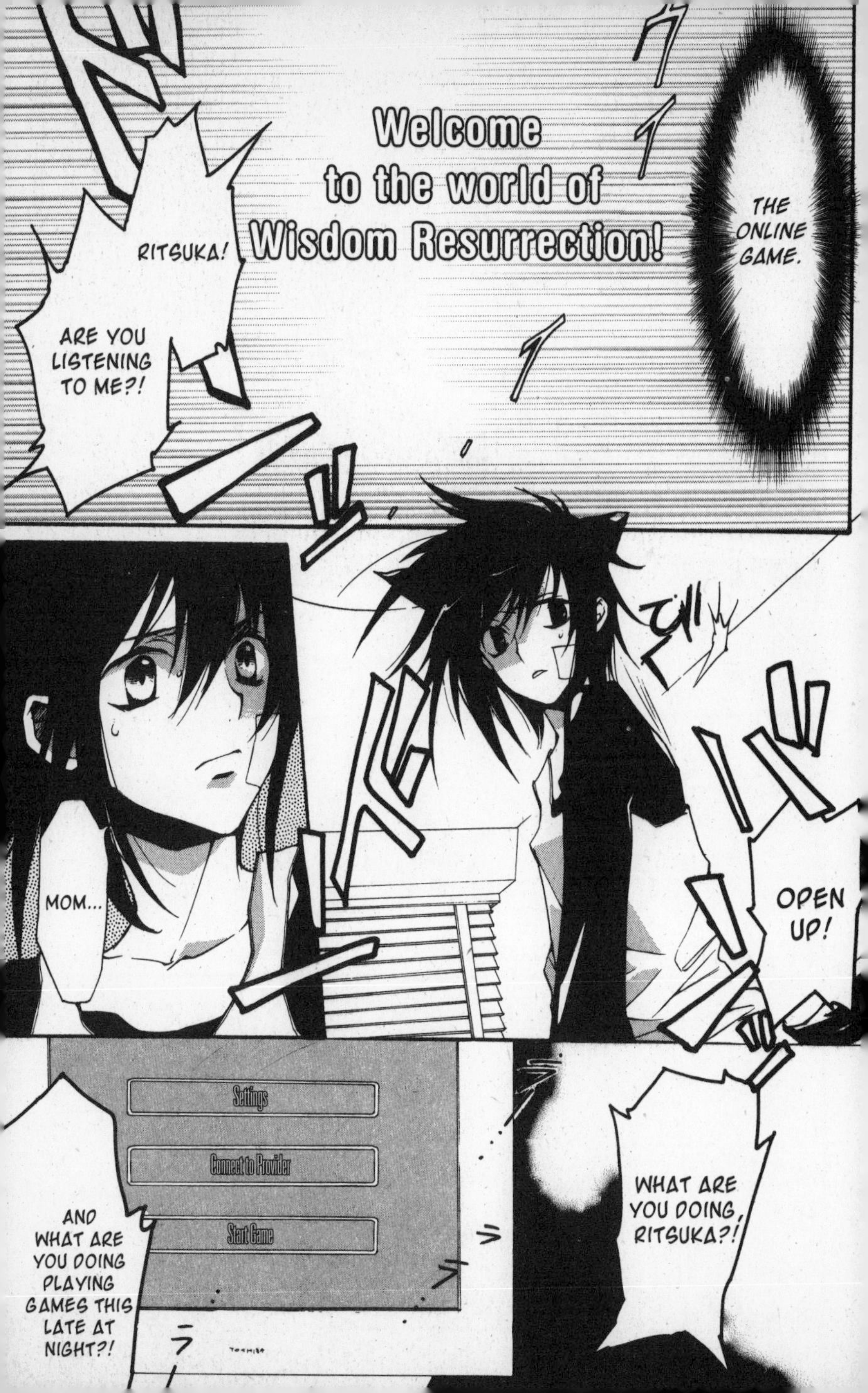
THE ONLINE GAME.
Welcome to the world of Wisdom Resurrection!
RITSUKA!
ARE YOU LISTENING TO ME?!
OPEN UP!
MOM...
WHAT ARE YOU DOING, RITSUKA?!
Settings
Connect to Provider
Start Game
AND WHAT ARE YOU DOING PLAYING GAMES THIS LATE AT NIGHT?!

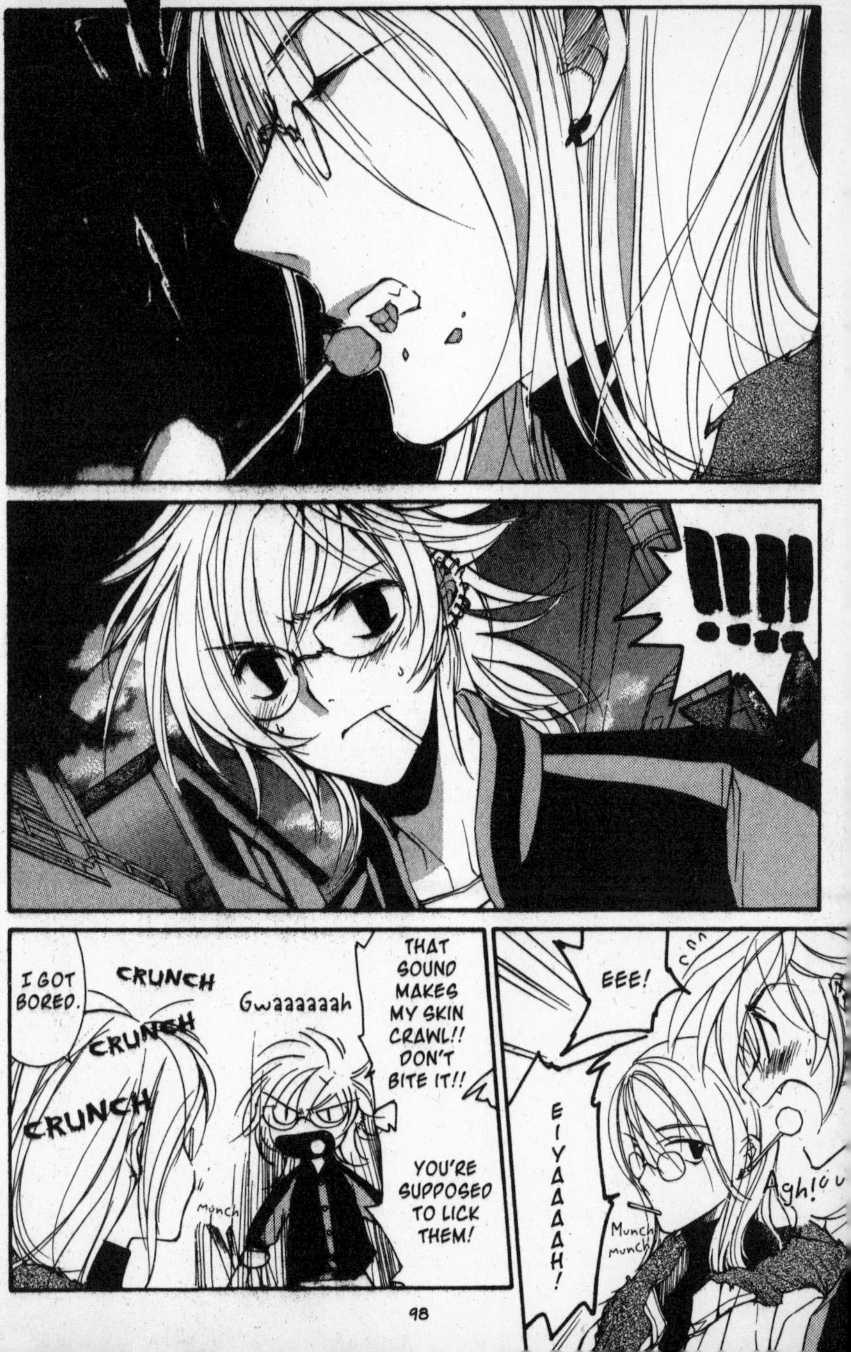
!!!!
EEE!
Agh!
EIYAAAAAH!
Munch munch
THAT SOUND MAKES MY SKIN CRAWL!! DON'T BITE IT!!
Gwaaaaaah
CRUNCH
I GOT BORED.
CRUNCH
CRUNCH
YOU'RE SUPPOSED TO LICK THEM!
Munch

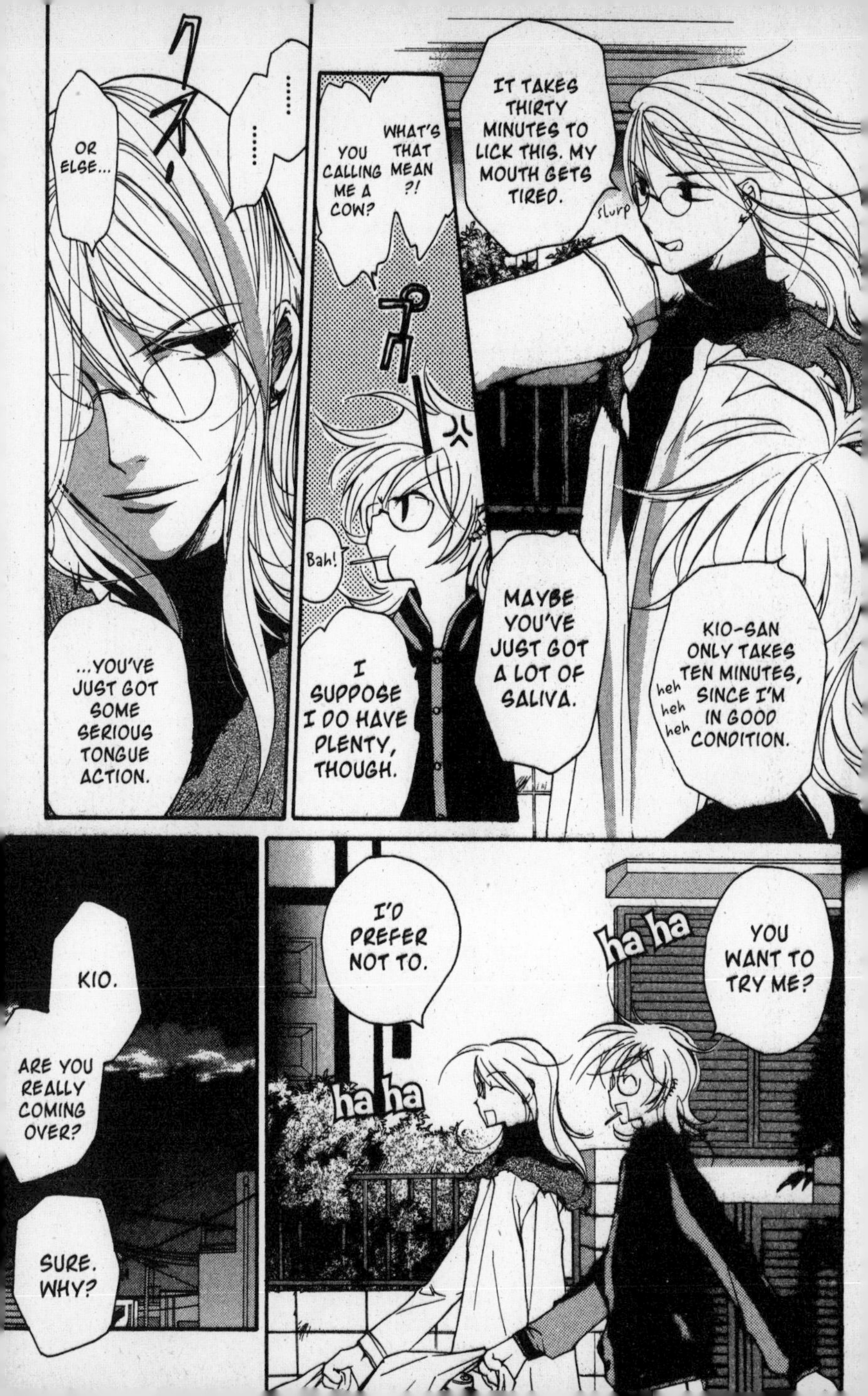
IT TAKES THIRTY MINUTES TO LICK THIS. MY MOUTH GETS TIRED.
slurp
KIO-SAN ONLY TAKES TEN MINUTES, SINCE I'M IN GOOD CONDITION.
heh heh heh
MAYBE YOU'VE JUST GOT A LOT OF SALIVA.
WHAT'S THAT MEAN ?!
YOU CALLING ME A COW?
Bah!
I SUPPOSE I DO HAVE PLENTY, THOUGH.
......
OR ELSE...
...YOU'VE JUST GOT SOME SERIOUS TONGUE ACTION.
YOU WANT TO TRY ME?
ha ha
I'D PREFER NOT TO.
ha ha
KIO.
ARE YOU REALLY COMING OVER?
SURE. WHY?

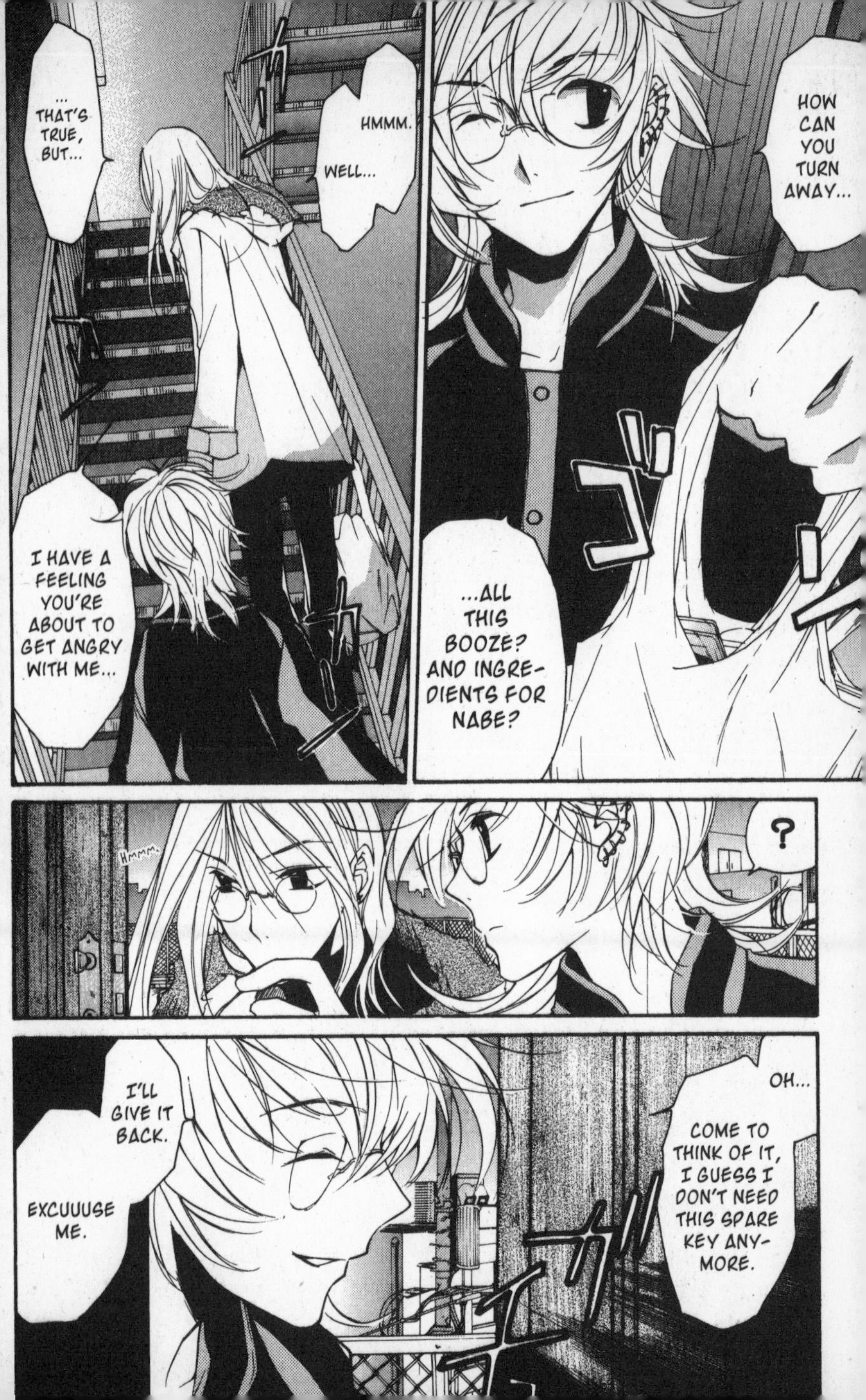
HOW CAN YOU TURN AWAY...
...ALL THIS BOOZE? AND INGREDIENTS FOR NABE?
HMMM.
WELL...
...THAT'S TRUE, BUT...
I HAVE A FEELING YOU'RE ABOUT TO GET ANGRY WITH ME...
?
HMMM.
OH...
COME TO THINK OF IT, I GUESS I DON'T NEED THIS SPARE KEY ANYMORE.
I'LL GIVE IT BACK.
EXCUUUSE ME.

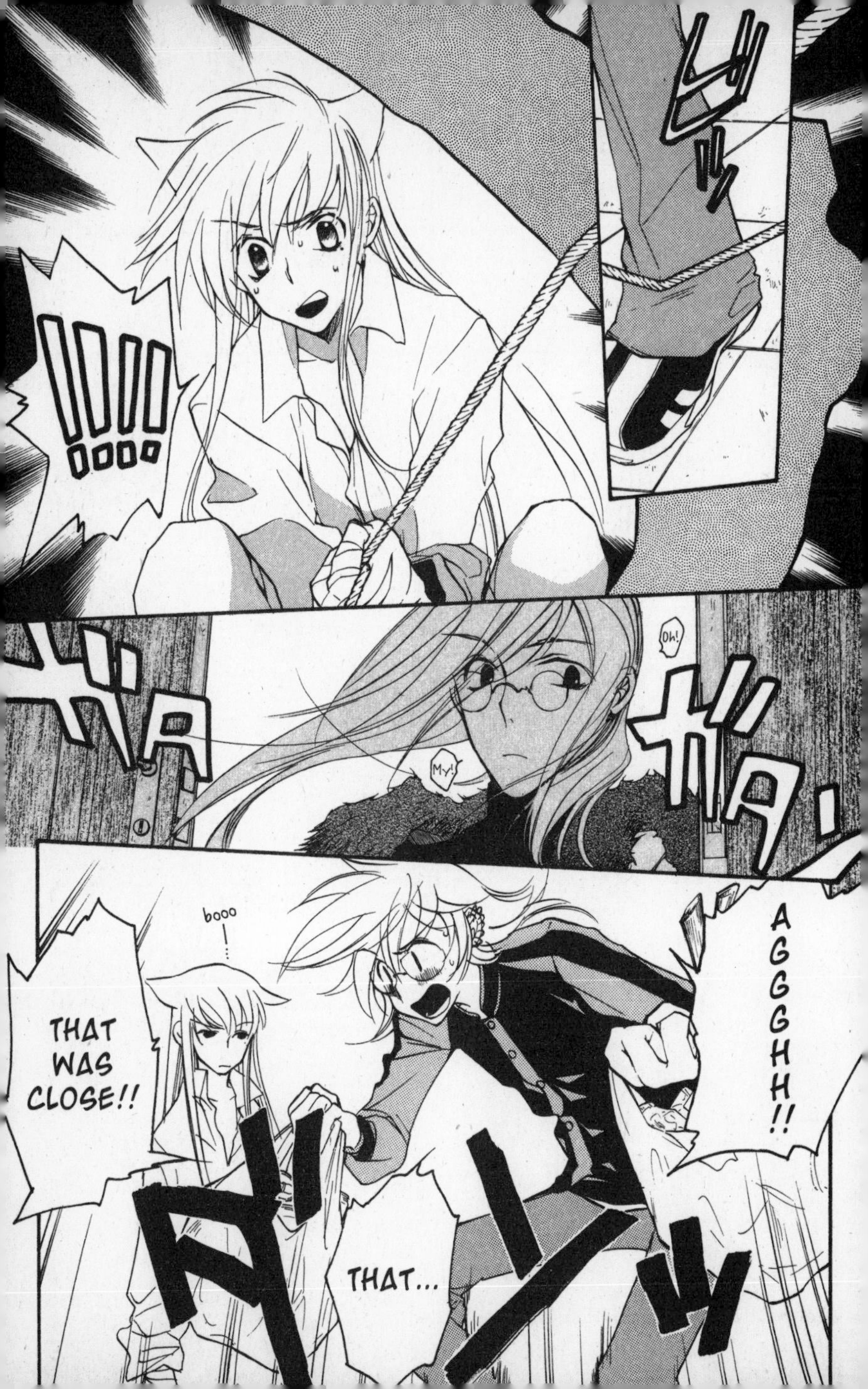
Oh!
My!
AGGGGHH!!
booo...
THAT WAS CLOSE!!
THAT...

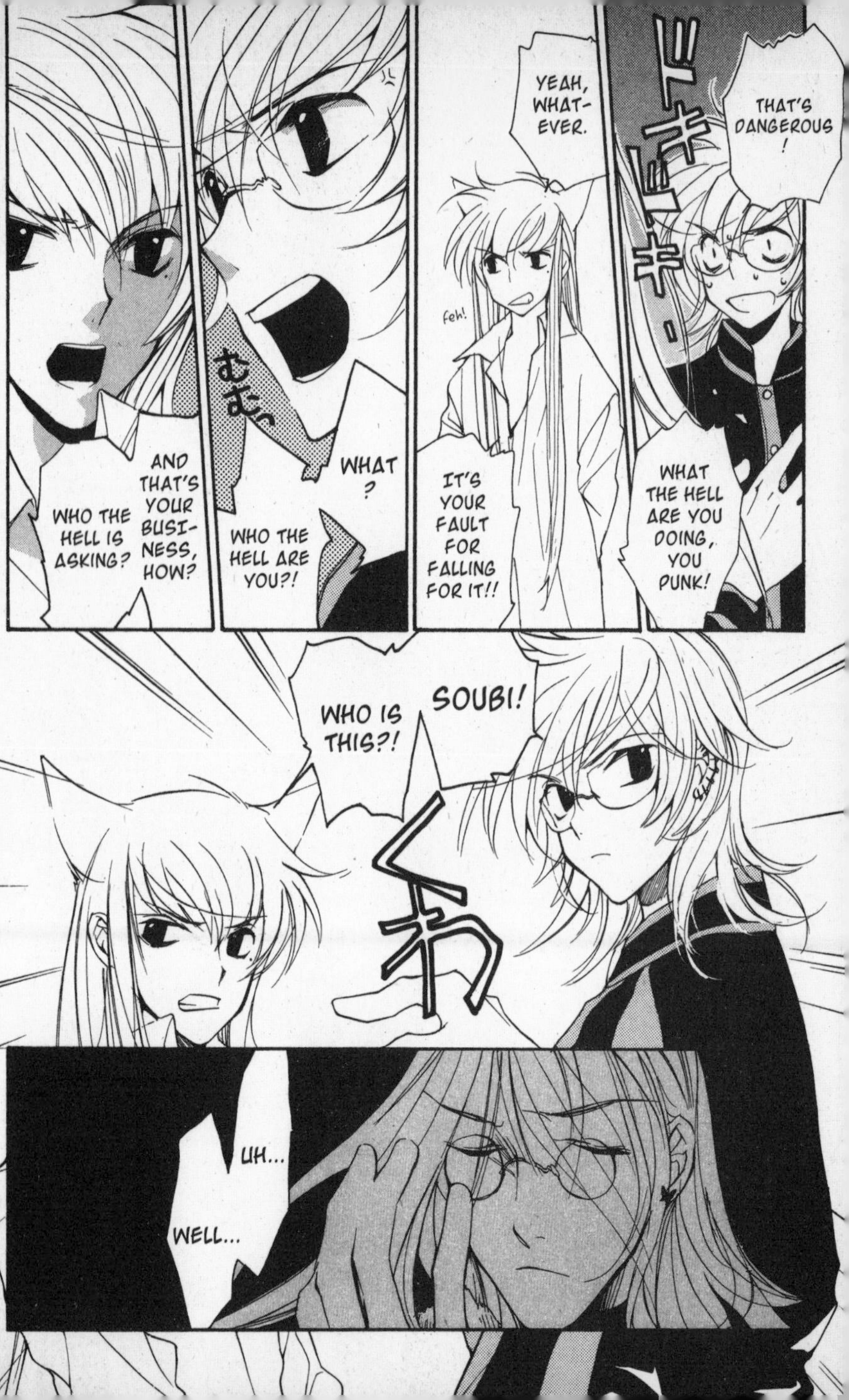

THAT'S DANGEROUS!
ドキドキ
WHAT THE HELL ARE YOU DOING, YOU PUNK!
YEAH, WHATEVER.
feh!
IT'S YOUR FAULT FOR FALLING FOR IT!!
WHAT?
WHO THE HELL ARE YOU?!
AND THAT'S YOUR BUSINESS, HOW?
WHO THE HELL IS ASKING?
SOUBI!
WHO IS THIS?!
UH...
WELL...

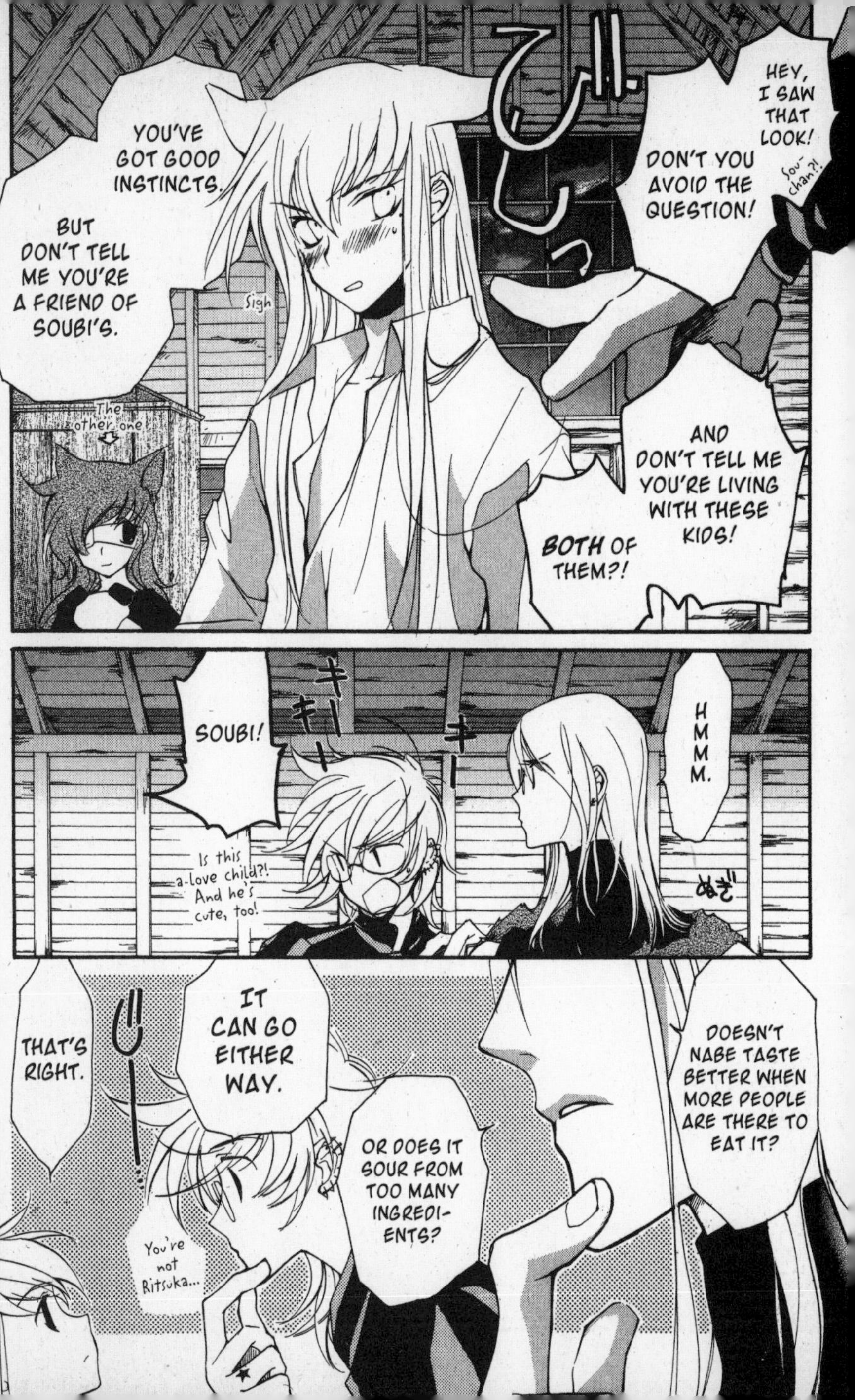
HEY, I SAW THAT LOOK!
Sou-chan?!
DON'T YOU AVOID THE QUESTION!
AND DON'T TELL ME YOU'RE LIVING WITH THESE KIDS!
BOTH OF THEM?!
YOU'VE GOT GOOD INSTINCTS.
BUT DON'T TELL ME YOU'RE A FRIEND OF SOUBI'S.
Sigh
The other one
HMMM.
Is this a love child?! And he's cute, too!
SOUBI!
DOESN'T NABE TASTE BETTER WHEN MORE PEOPLE ARE THERE TO EAT IT?
OR DOES IT SOUR FROM TOO MANY INGREDI-ENTS?
IT CAN GO EITHER WAY.
THAT'S RIGHT.
You're not Ritsuka...

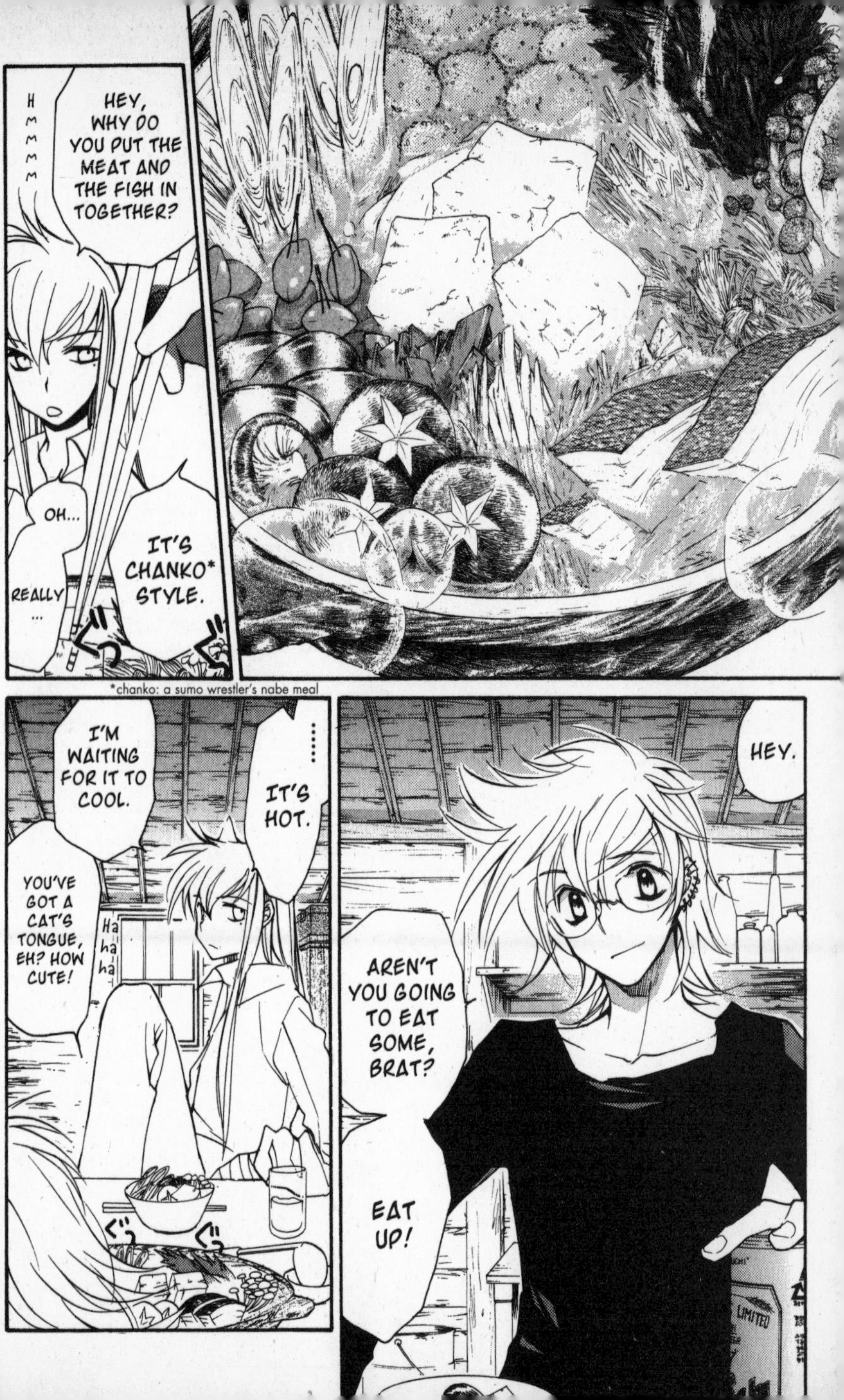
HEY, WHY DO YOU PUT THE MEAT AND THE FISH IN TOGETHER?
HMMMM
IT'S CHANKO* STYLE.
OH...
REALLY...
......
IT'S HOT.
I'M WAITING FOR IT TO COOL.
Ha ha ha
YOU'VE GOT A CAT'S TONGUE, EH? HOW CUTE!
HEY.
AREN'T YOU GOING TO EAT SOME, BRAT?
EAT UP!

*chanko: a sumo wrestler's nabe meal

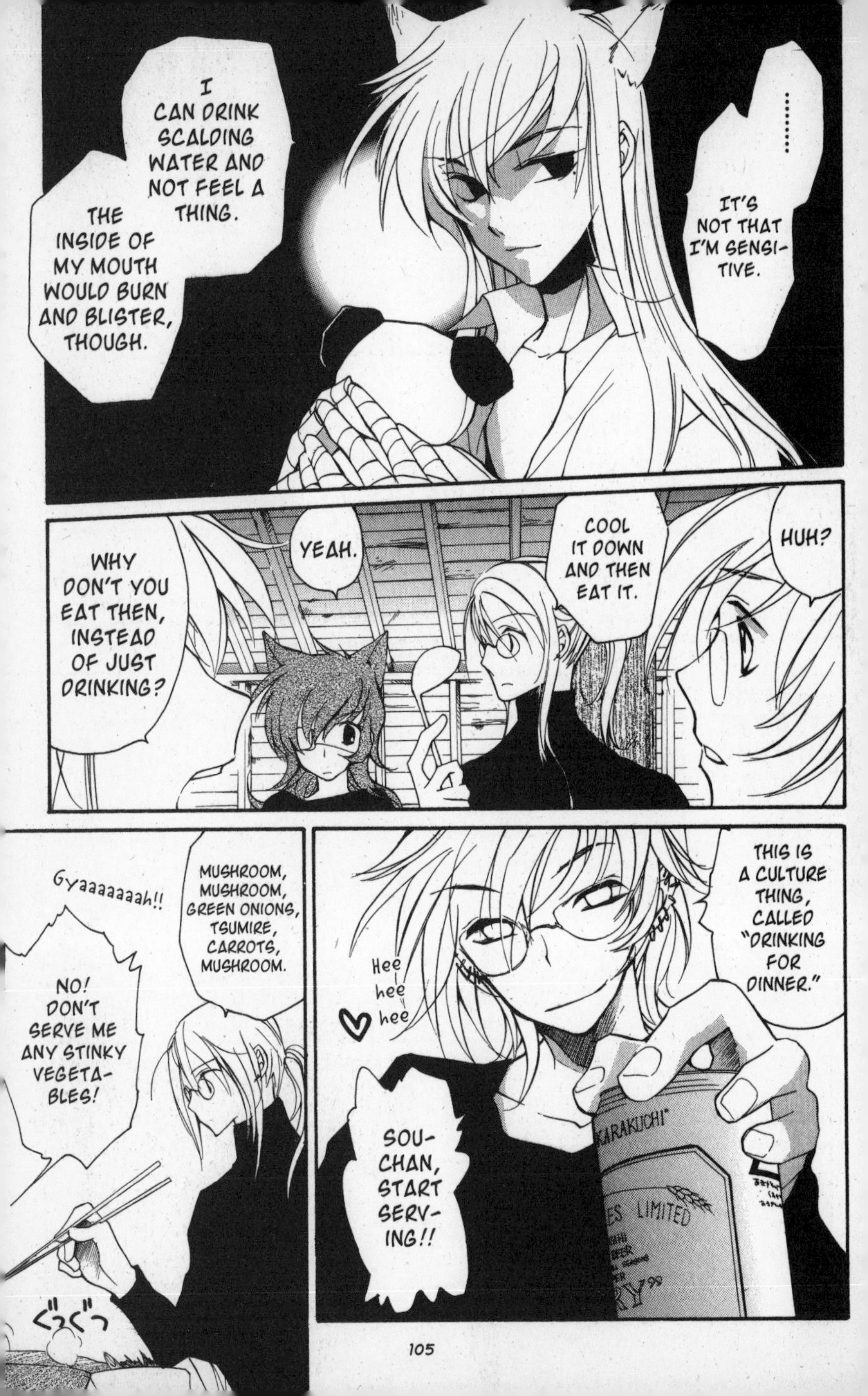
......
IT'S NOT THAT I'M SENSI-TIVE.
I CAN DRINK SCALDING WATER AND NOT FEEL A THING.
THE INSIDE OF MY MOUTH WOULD BURN AND BLISTER, THOUGH.
HUH?
COOL IT DOWN AND THEN EAT IT.
YEAH.
WHY DON'T YOU EAT THEN, INSTEAD OF JUST DRINKING?
THIS IS A CULTURE THING, CALLED "DRINKING FOR DINNER."
Hee hee hee
SOU-CHAN, START SERV-ING!!
"KARAKUCHI"
MUSHROOM, MUSHROOM, GREEN ONIONS, TSUMIRE, CARROTS, MUSHROOM.
Gyaaaaaaah!!
NO! DON'T SERVE ME ANY STINKY VEGETA-BLES!
ぐつぐつ

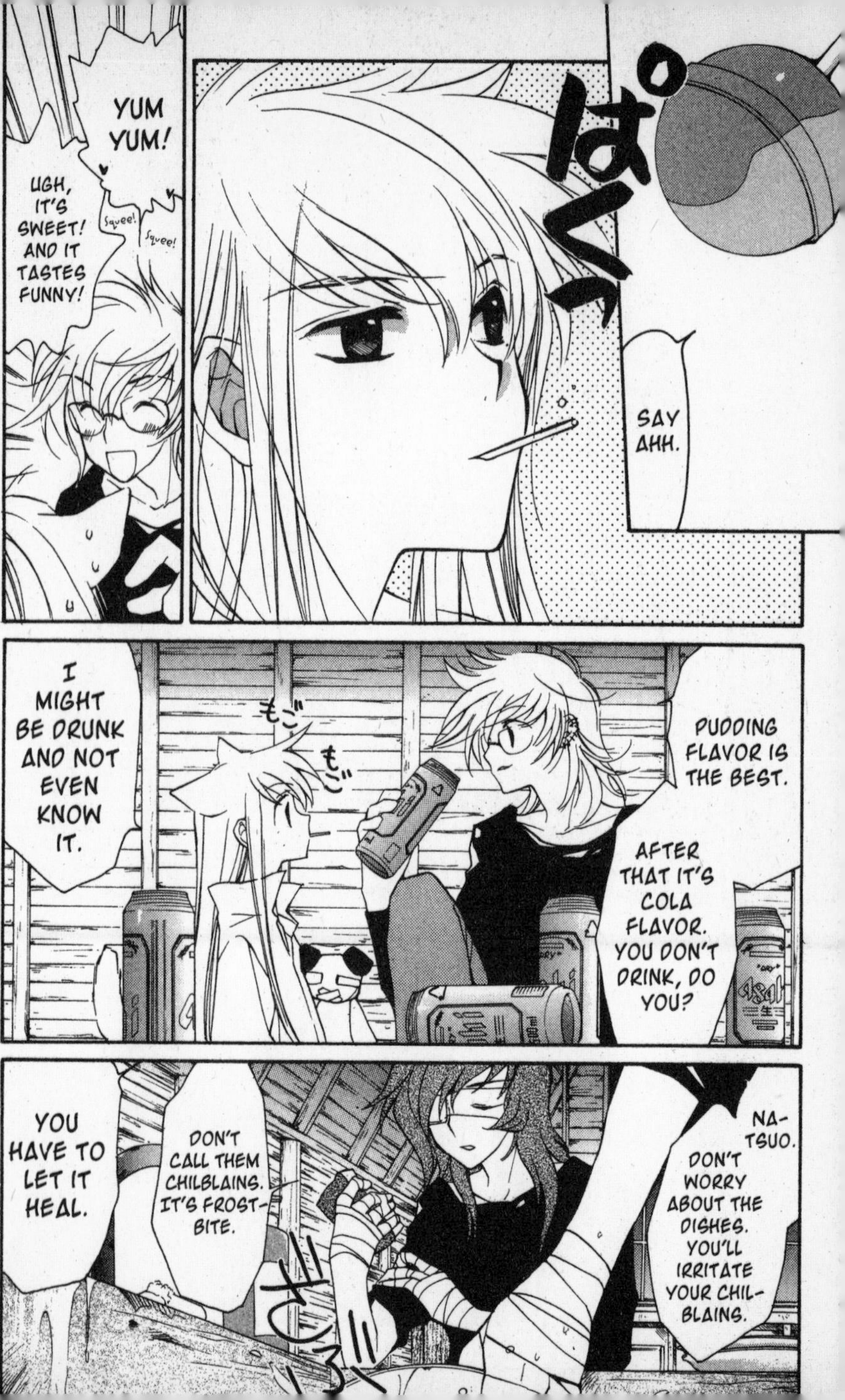
ぱく
SAY AHH.
YUM YUM!
UGH, IT'S SWEET! AND IT TASTES FUNNY!
Squee!
Squee!
PUDDING FLAVOR IS THE BEST.
AFTER THAT IT'S COLA FLAVOR. YOU DON'T DRINK, DO YOU?
もご
もご
I MIGHT BE DRUNK AND NOT EVEN KNOW IT.
NATSUO. DON'T WORRY ABOUT THE DISHES. YOU'LL IRRITATE YOUR CHILBLAINS.
DON'T CALL THEM CHILBLAINS. IT'S FROSTBITE.
YOU HAVE TO LET IT HEAL.

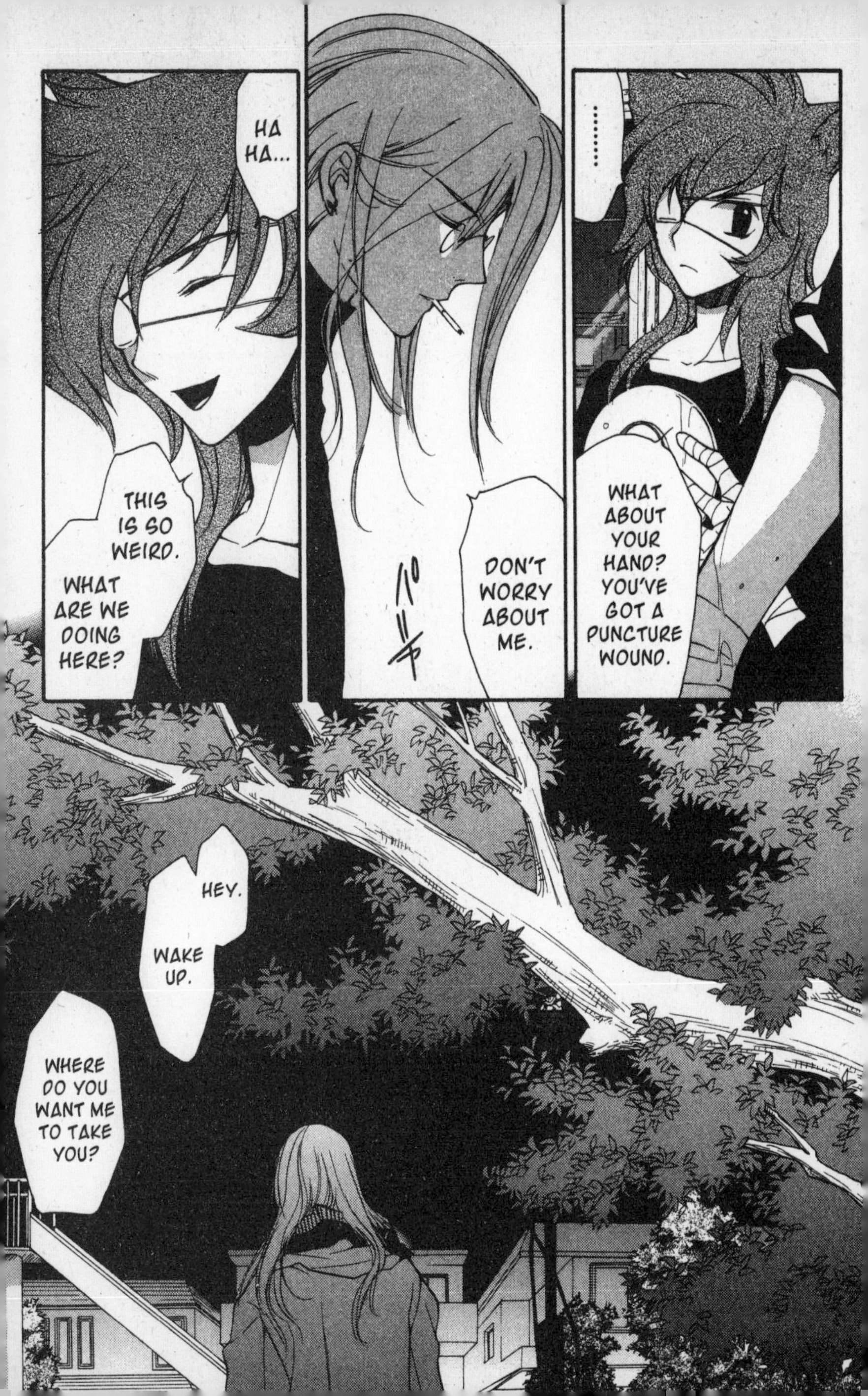
......
WHAT ABOUT YOUR HAND? YOU'VE GOT A PUNCTURE WOUND.
DON'T WORRY ABOUT ME.
HA HA...
THIS IS SO WEIRD.
WHAT ARE WE DOING HERE?
HEY.
WAKE UP.
WHERE DO YOU WANT ME TO TAKE YOU?

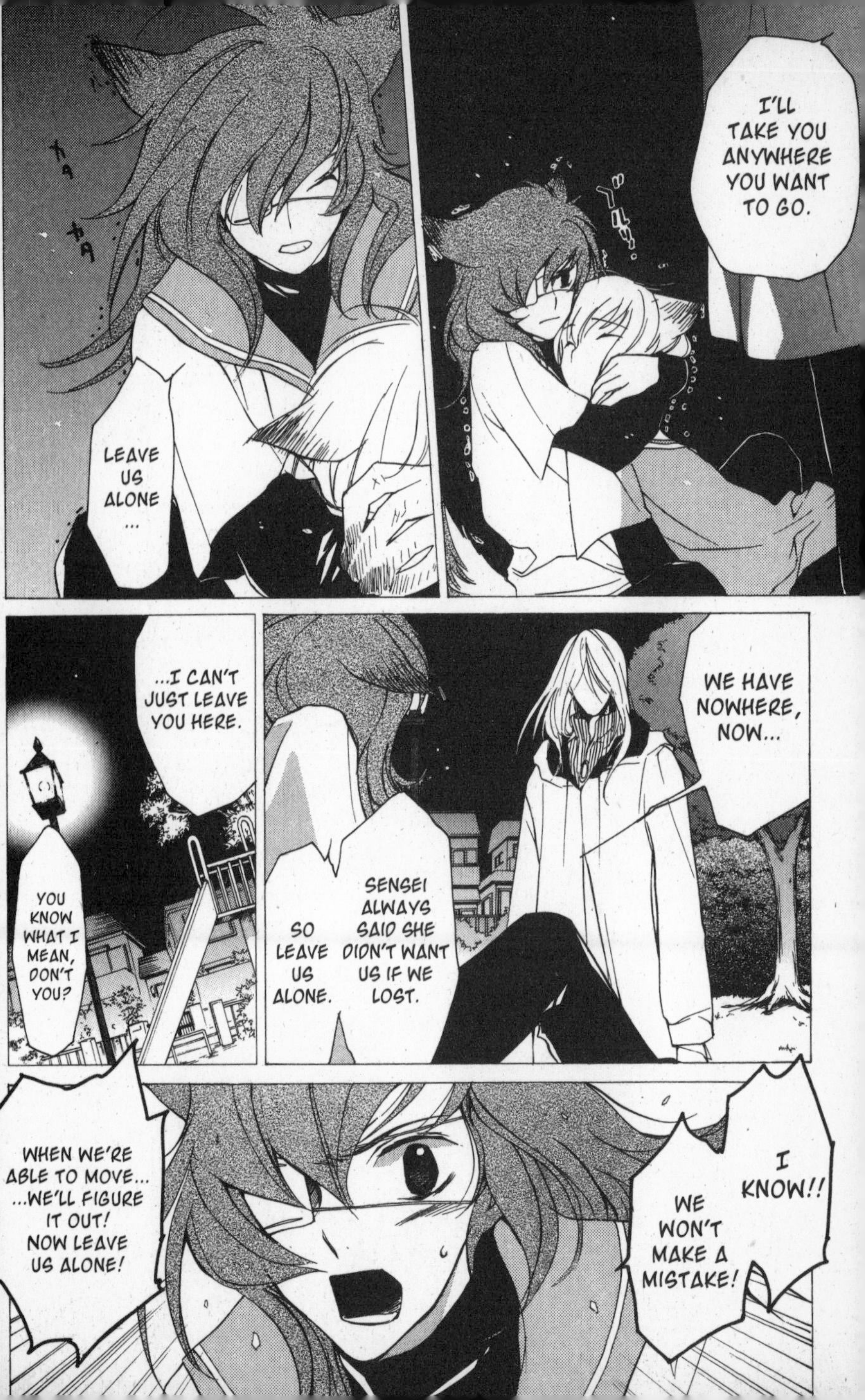
I'LL TAKE YOU ANYWHERE YOU WANT TO GO.
LEAVE US ALONE ...
WE HAVE NOWHERE, NOW...
SENSEI ALWAYS SAID SHE DIDN'T WANT US IF WE LOST.
SO LEAVE US ALONE.
...I CAN'T JUST LEAVE YOU HERE.
YOU KNOW WHAT I MEAN, DON'T YOU?
I KNOW!!
WE WON'T MAKE A MISTAKE!
WHEN WE'RE ABLE TO MOVE... ...WE'LL FIGURE IT OUT! NOW LEAVE US ALONE!

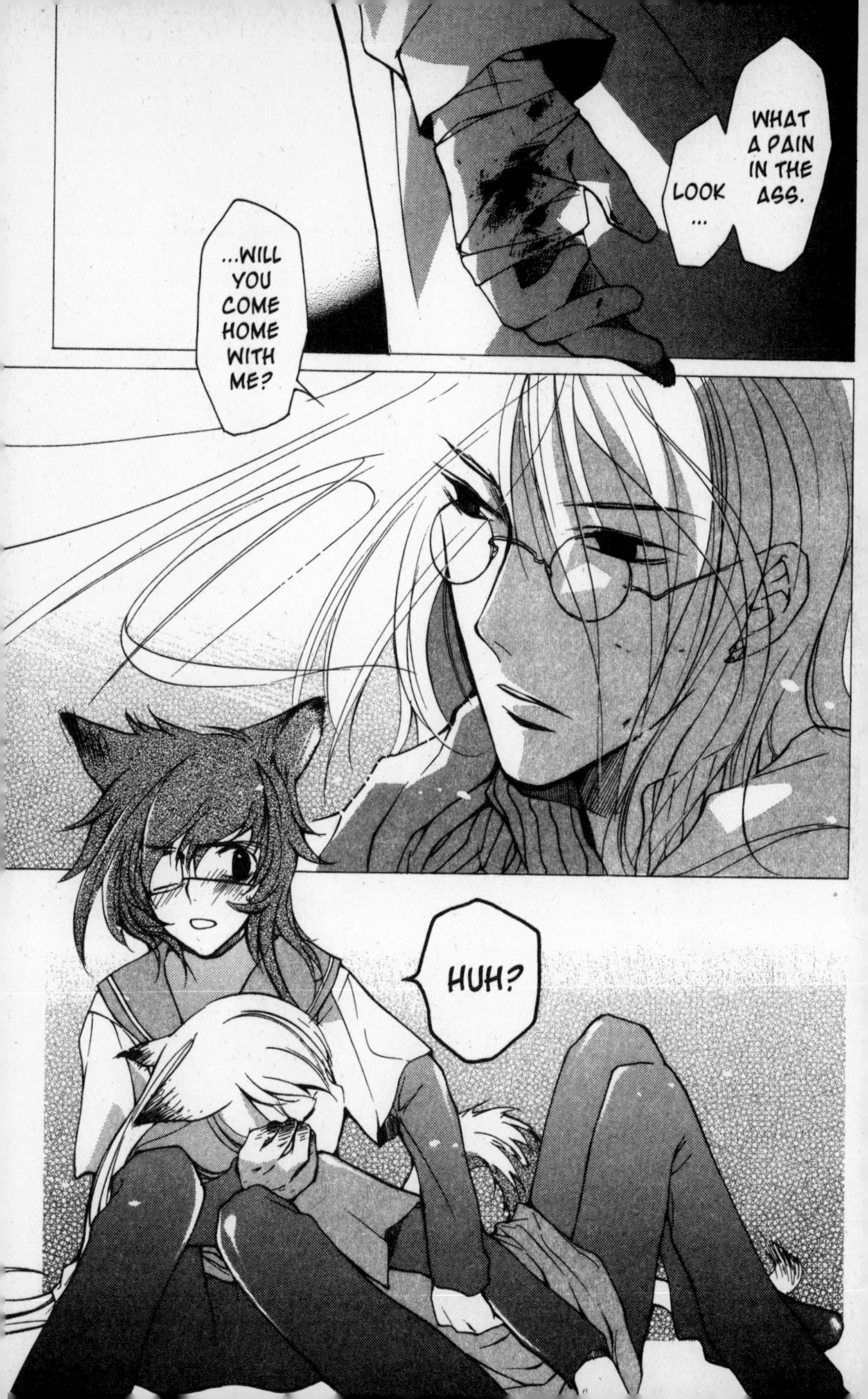
WHAT A PAIN IN THE ASS.
LOOK ...
...WILL YOU COME HOME WITH ME?
HUH?

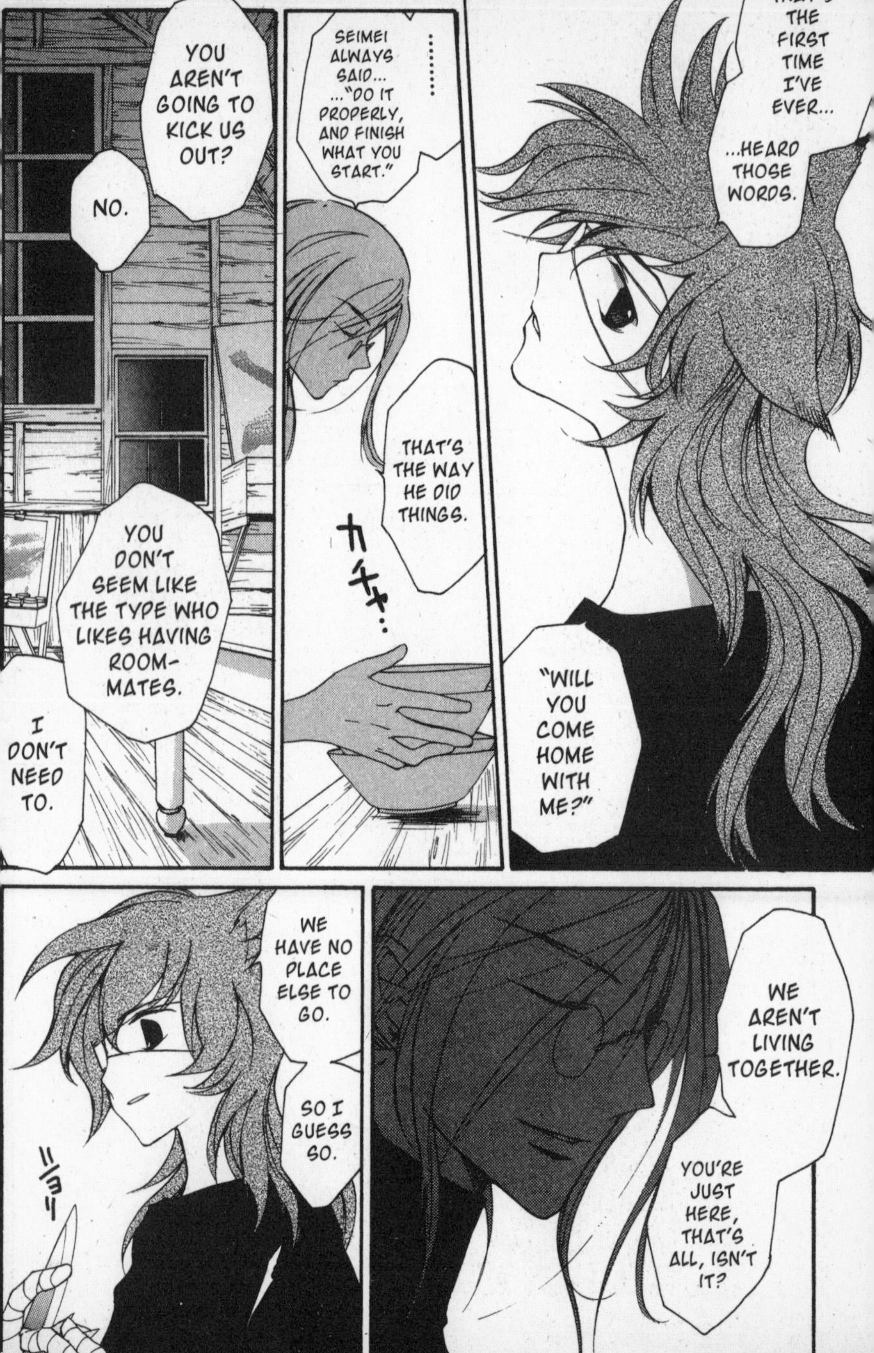
THAT'S THE FIRST TIME I'VE EVER...
...HEARD THOSE WORDS.
"WILL YOU COME HOME WITH ME?"
......
SEIMEI ALWAYS SAID... ..."DO IT PROPERLY, AND FINISH WHAT YOU START."
THAT'S THE WAY HE DID THINGS.
カチャ...
YOU AREN'T GOING TO KICK US OUT?
NO.
YOU DON'T SEEM LIKE THE TYPE WHO LIKES HAVING ROOM-MATES.
I DON'T NEED TO.
WE AREN'T LIVING TOGETHER.
YOU'RE JUST HERE, THAT'S ALL, ISN'T IT?
WE HAVE NO PLACE ELSE TO GO.
SO I GUESS SO.

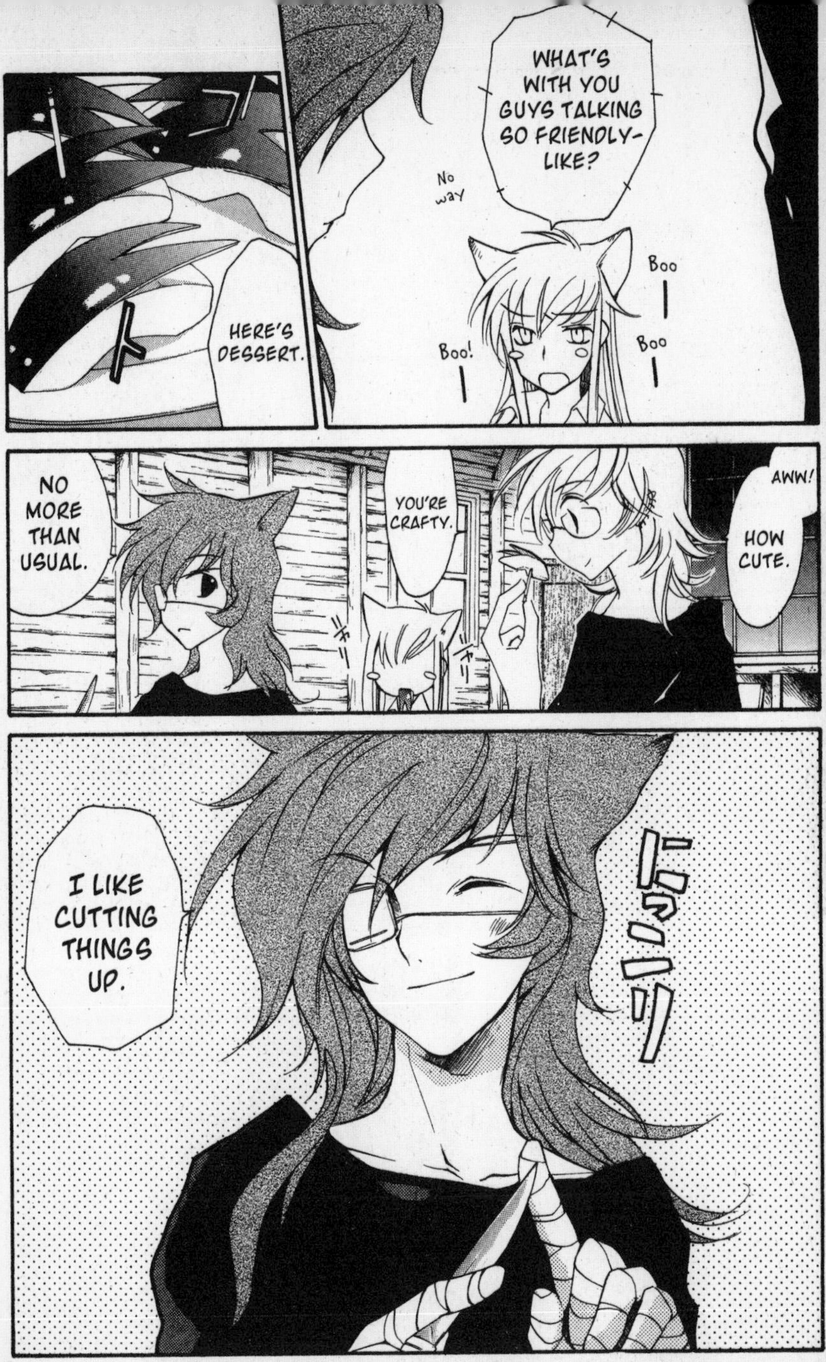
WHAT'S WITH YOU GUYS TALKING SO FRIENDLY-LIKE?
No way
Boo
Boo
Boo!
HERE'S DESSERT.
AWW!
HOW CUTE.
YOU'RE CRAFTY.
NO MORE THAN USUAL.
I LIKE CUTTING THINGS UP.

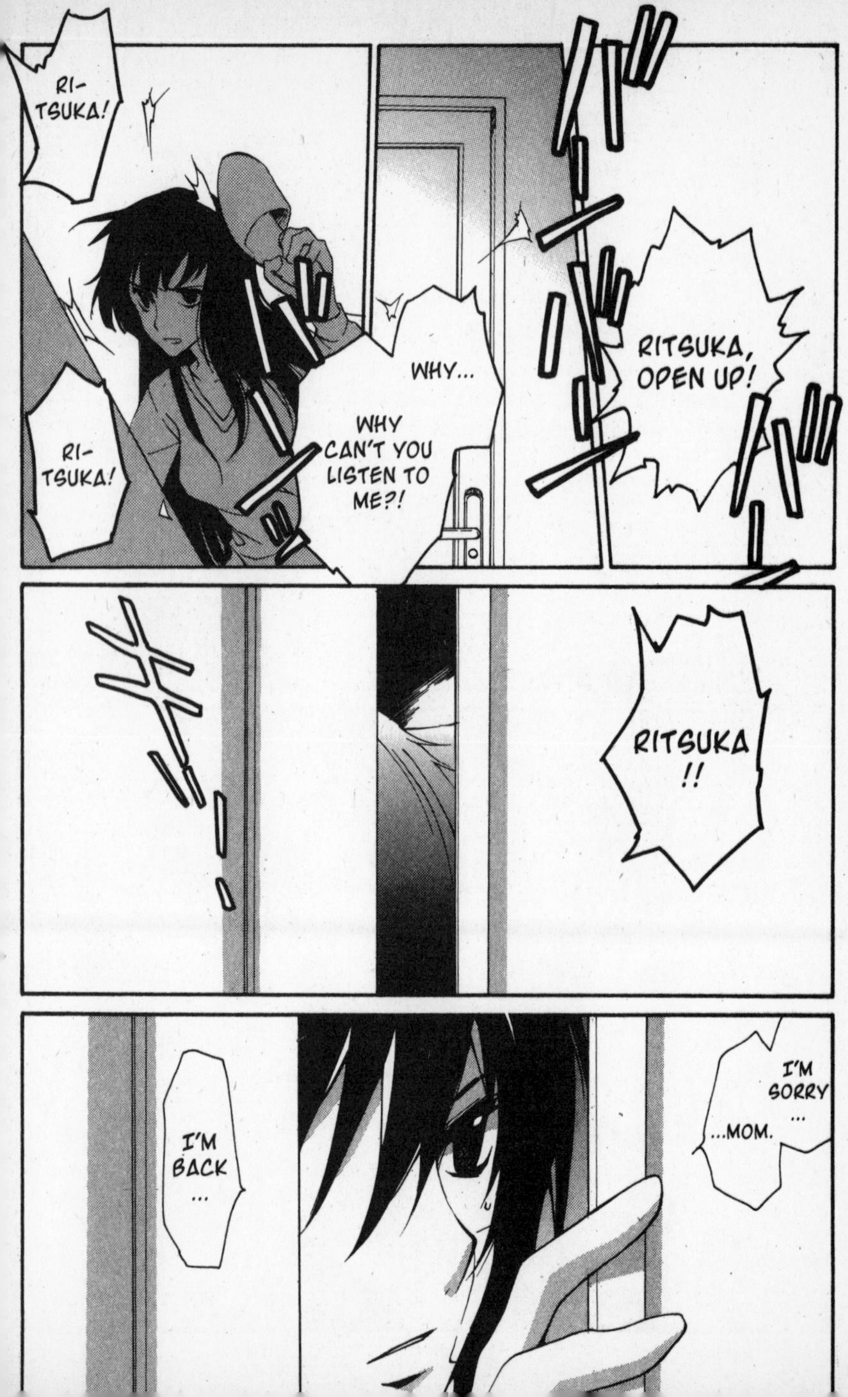
RITSUKA, OPEN UP!
WHY...
WHY CAN'T YOU LISTEN TO ME?!
RI-TSUKA!
RI-TSUKA!
RITSUKA !!
I'M SORRY ...
...MOM.
I'M BACK ...

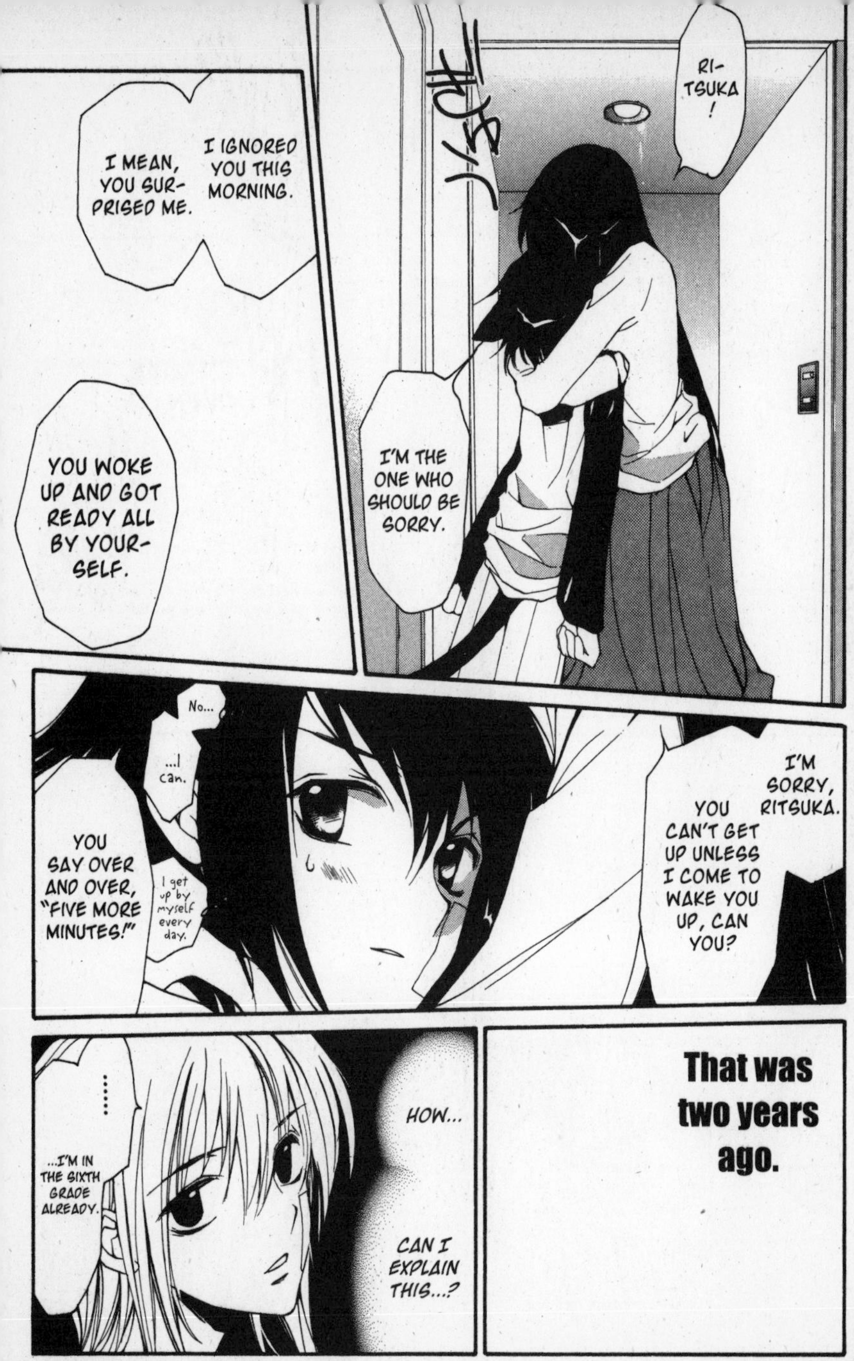
RI-TSUKA!
I'M THE ONE WHO SHOULD BE SORRY.
I IGNORED YOU THIS MORNING.
I MEAN, YOU SURPRISED ME.
YOU WOKE UP AND GOT READY ALL BY YOURSELF.
I'M SORRY, RITSUKA.
YOU CAN'T GET UP UNLESS I COME TO WAKE YOU UP, CAN YOU?
No...
...I can.
I get up by myself every day.
YOU SAY OVER AND OVER, "FIVE MORE MINUTES!"
That was two years ago.
HOW...
CAN I EXPLAIN THIS...?
......
...I'M IN THE SIXTH GRADE ALREADY.

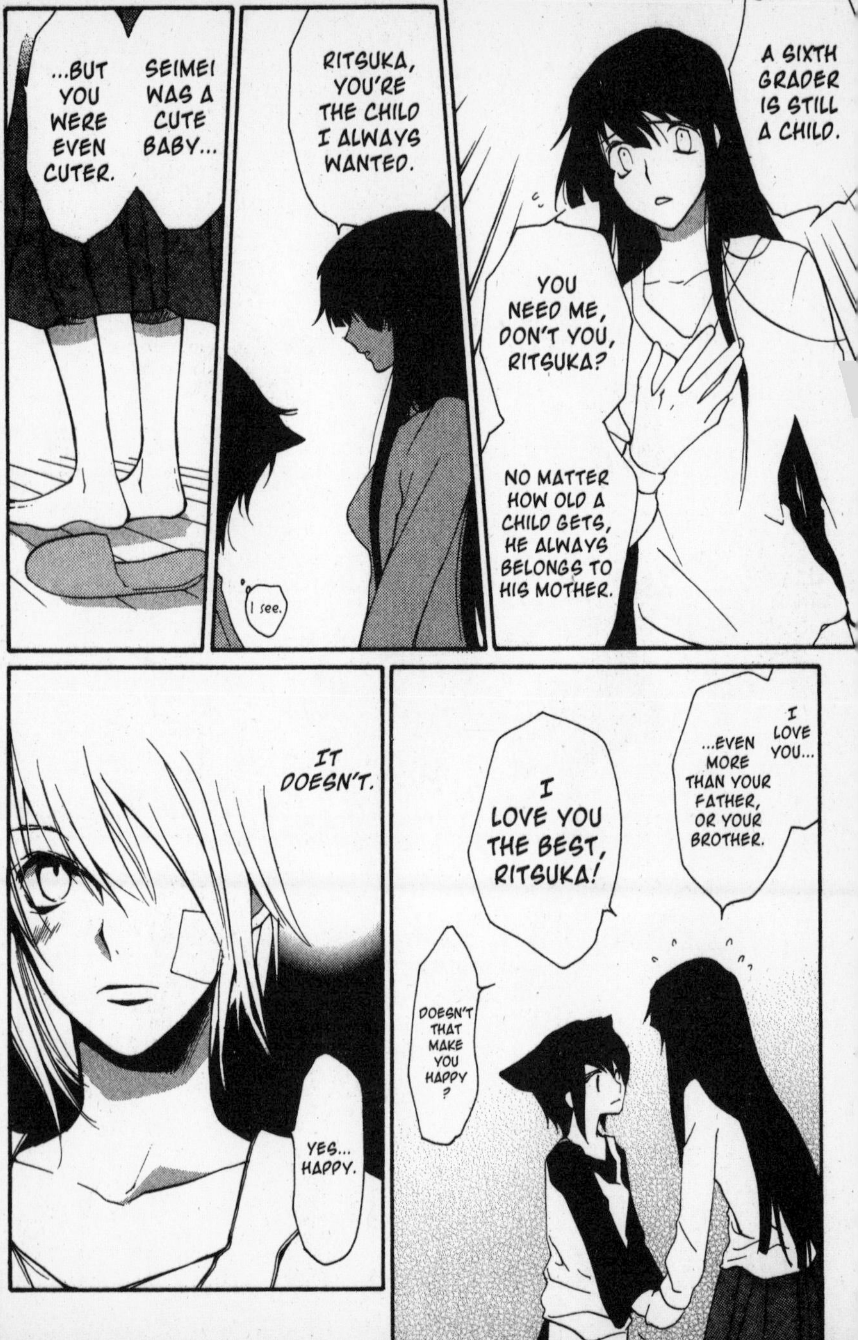
A SIXTH GRADER IS STILL A CHILD.
YOU NEED ME, DON'T YOU, RITSUKA?
NO MATTER HOW OLD A CHILD GETS, HE ALWAYS BELONGS TO HIS MOTHER.
RITSUKA, YOU'RE THE CHILD I ALWAYS WANTED.
I see.
SEIMEI WAS A CUTE BABY...
...BUT YOU WERE EVEN CUTER.
I LOVE YOU...
...EVEN MORE THAN YOUR FATHER, OR YOUR BROTHER.
I LOVE YOU THE BEST, RITSUKA!
DOESN'T THAT MAKE YOU HAPPY?
IT DOESN'T.
YES... HAPPY.

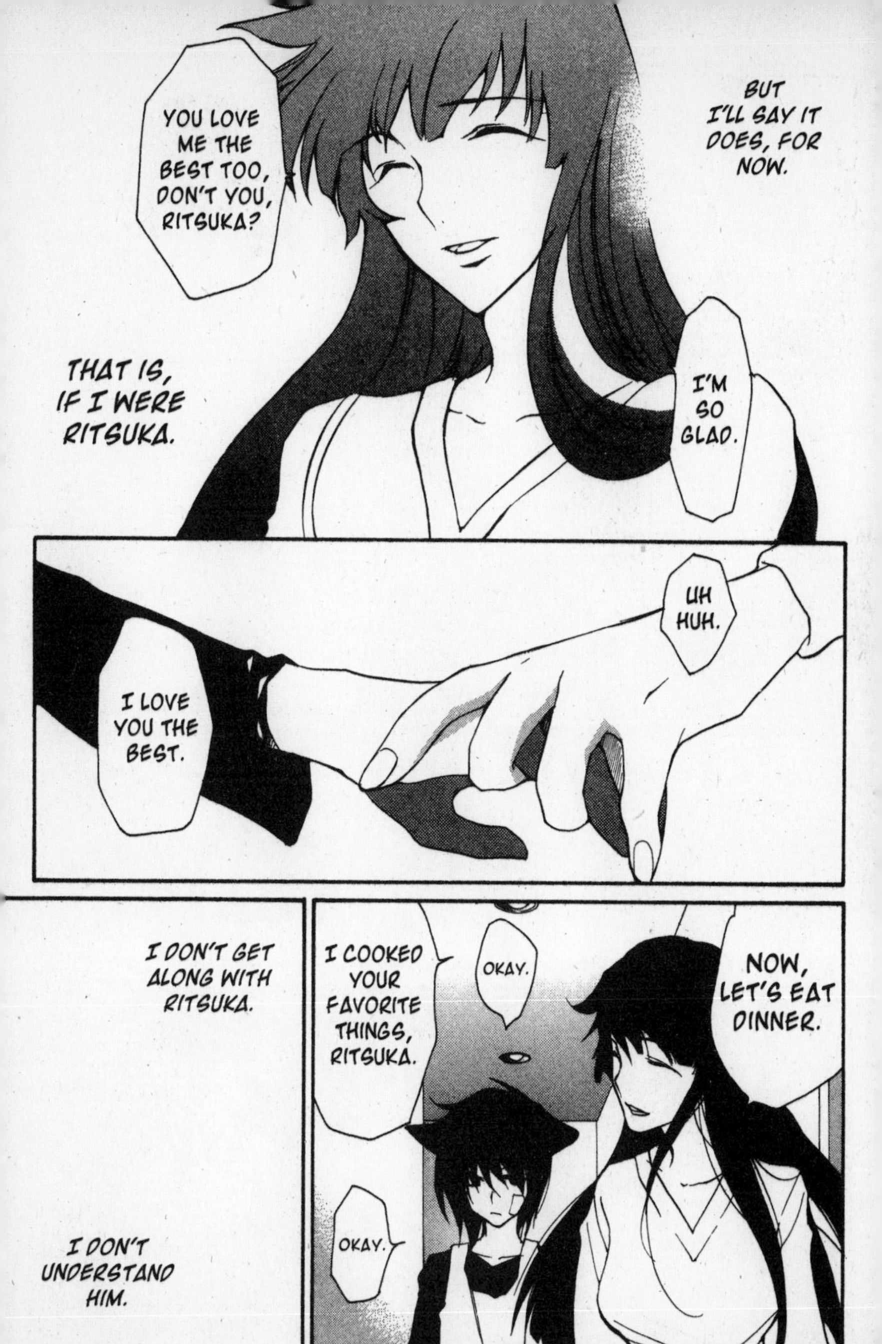
BUT I'LL SAY IT DOES, FOR NOW.
YOU LOVE ME THE BEST TOO, DON'T YOU, RITSUKA?
I'M SO GLAD.
THAT IS, IF I WERE RITSUKA.
UH HUH.
I LOVE YOU THE BEST.
NOW, LET'S EAT DINNER.
OKAY.
I COOKED YOUR FAVORITE THINGS, RITSUKA.
OKAY.
I DON'T GET ALONG WITH RITSUKA.
I DON'T UNDERSTAND HIM.

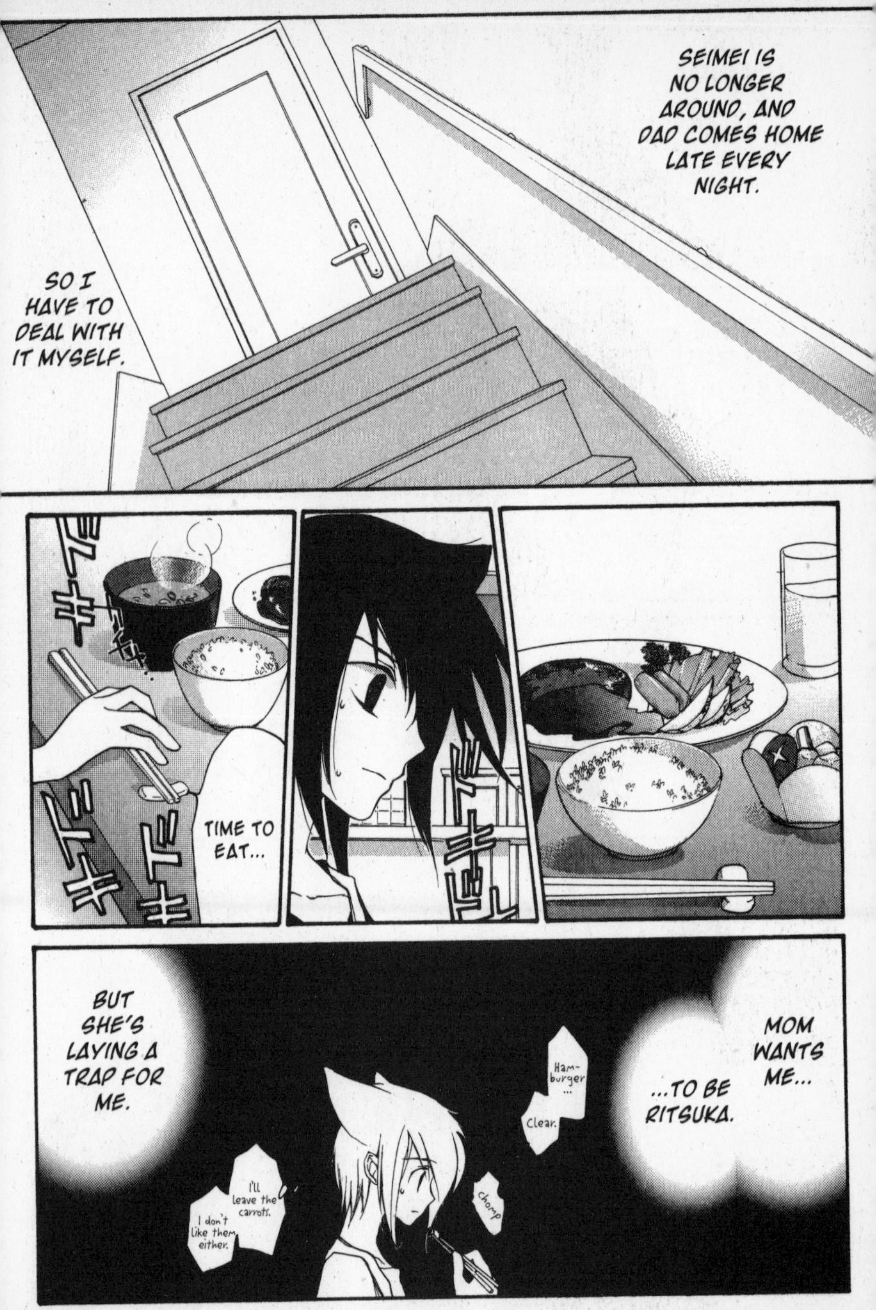
SEIMEI IS NO LONGER AROUND, AND DAD COMES HOME LATE EVERY NIGHT.
SO I HAVE TO DEAL WITH IT MYSELF.
TIME TO EAT...
MOM WANTS ME...
...TO BE RITSUKA.
Ham-burger...
Clear.
chomp
I'll leave the carrots.
I don't like them either.
BUT SHE'S LAYING A TRAP FOR ME.

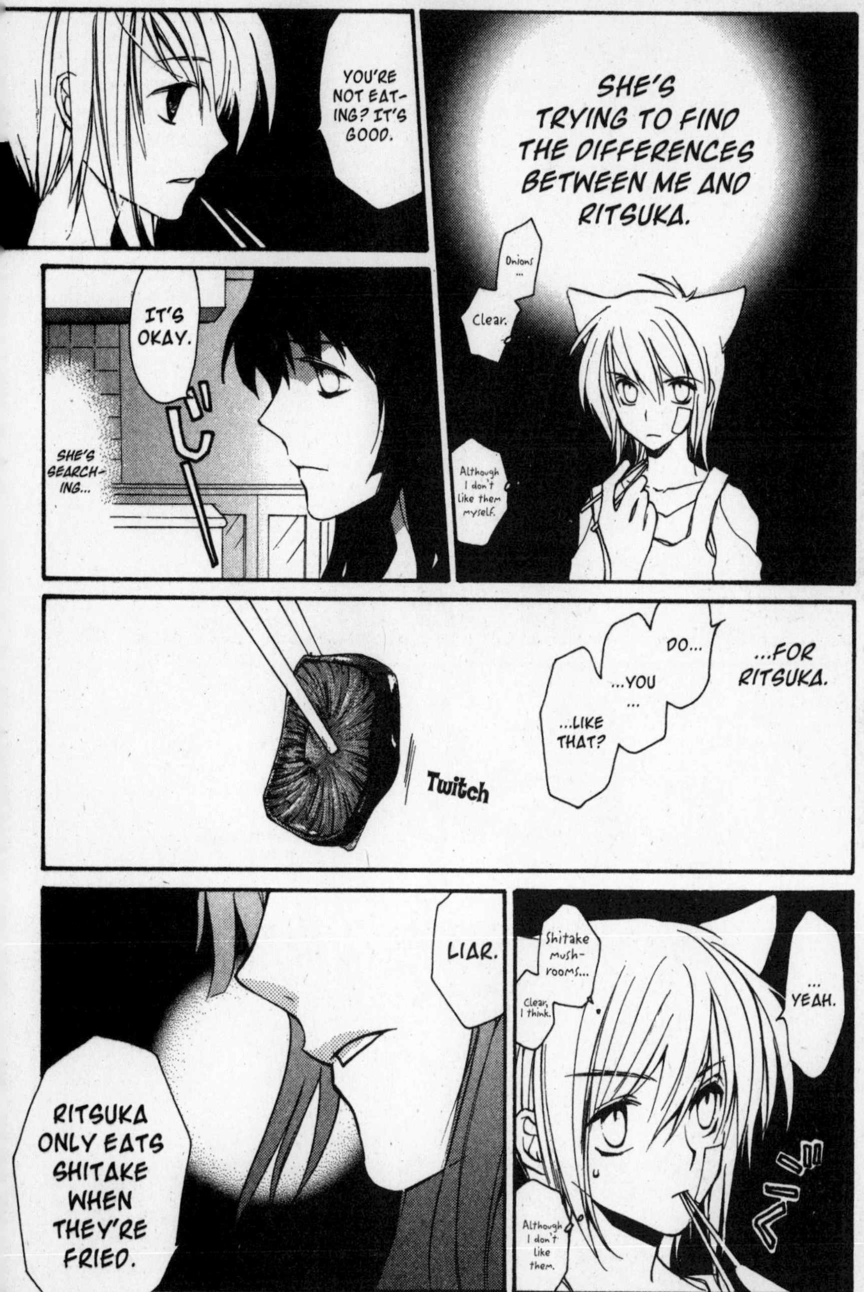
SHE'S TRYING TO FIND THE DIFFERENCES BETWEEN ME AND RITSUKA.
Onions ...
Clear.
Although I don't like them myself.
YOU'RE NOT EATING? IT'S GOOD.
IT'S OKAY.
SHE'S SEARCHING...
...FOR RITSUKA.
DO...
...YOU ...
...LIKE THAT?
Twitch
... YEAH.
Shitake mush-rooms...
Clear, I think.
Although I don't like them.
LIAR.
RITSUKA ONLY EATS SHITAKE WHEN THEY'RE FRIED.

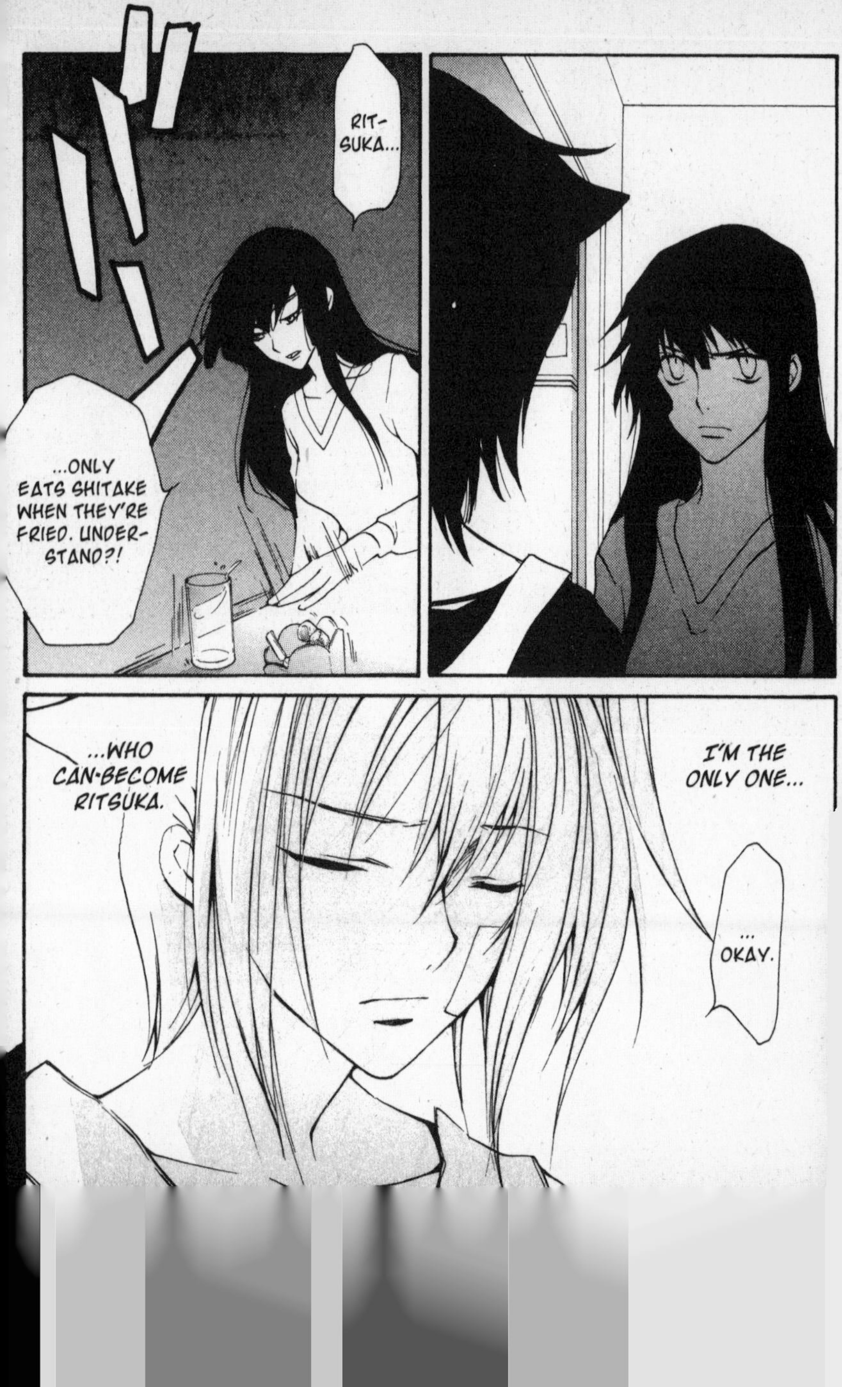
RIT-SUKA...
...ONLY EATS SHITAKE WHEN THEY'RE FRIED. UNDER-STAND?!
I'M THE ONLY ONE...
...WHO CAN·BECOME RITSUKA.
...OKAY.

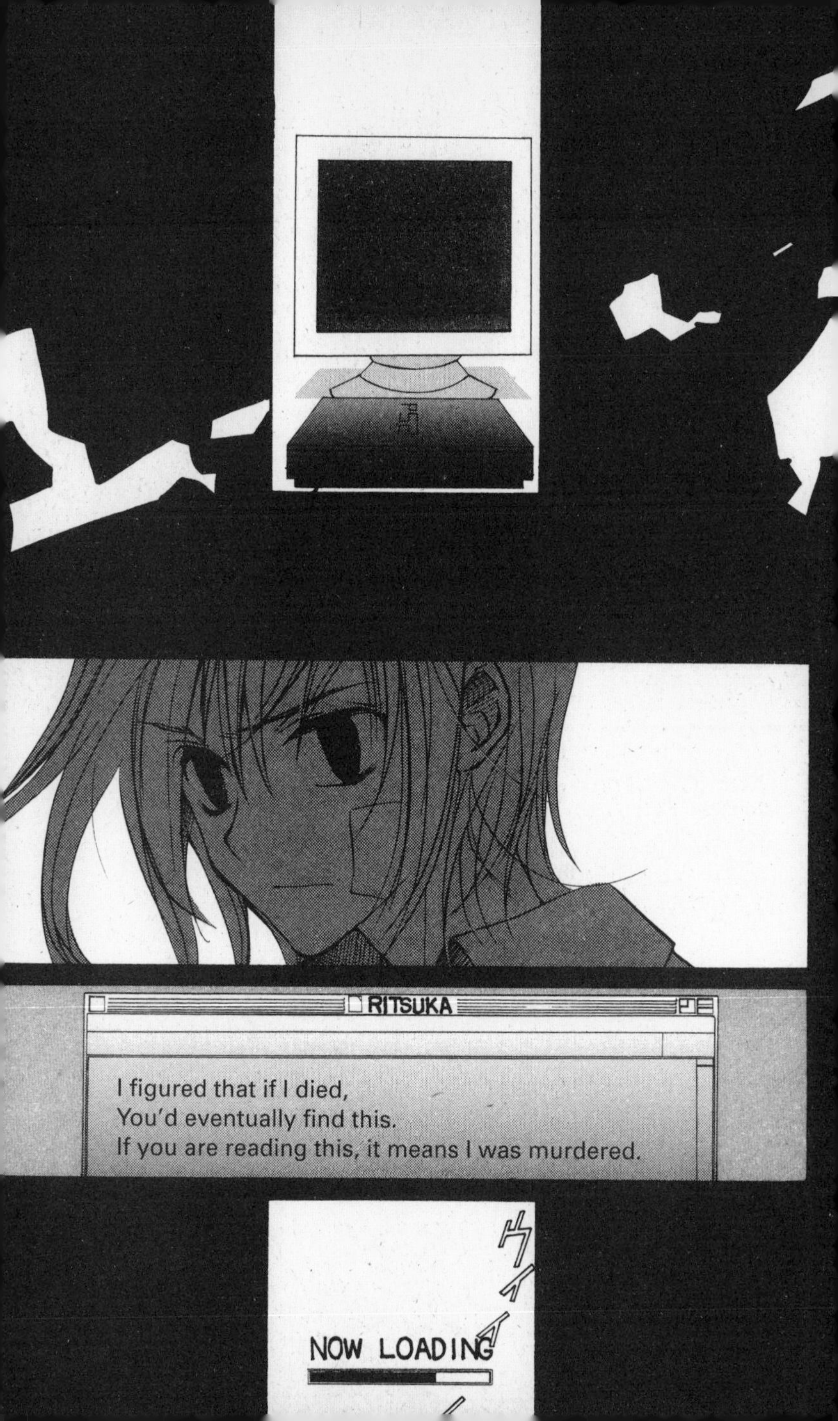
RITSUKA
I figured that if I died,
You'd eventually find this.
If you are reading this, it means I was murdered.
NOW LOADING
ウイィ

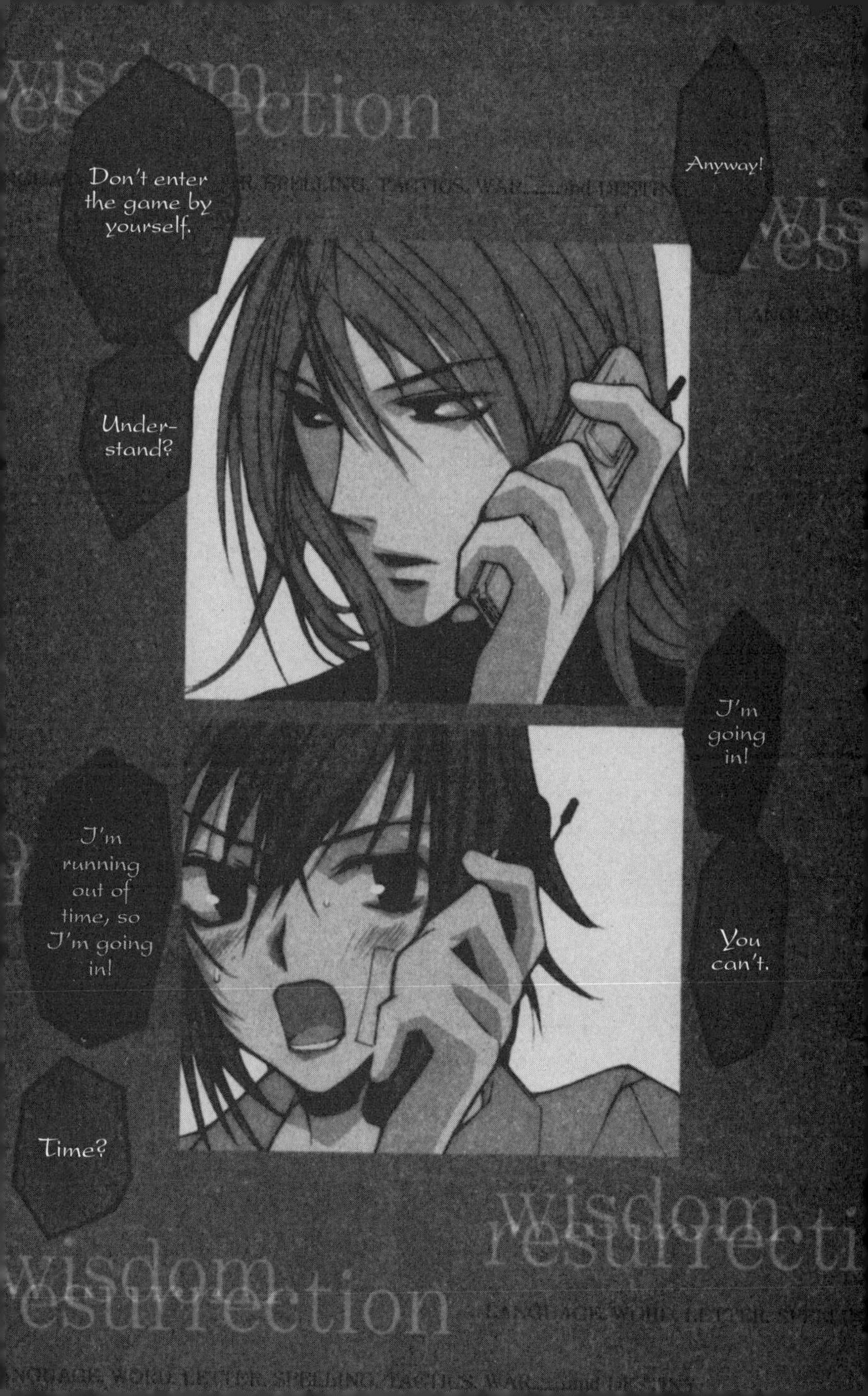
Anyway!
Don't enter the game by yourself.
Under-stand?
I'm going in!
You can't.
I'm running out of time, so I'm going in!
Time?

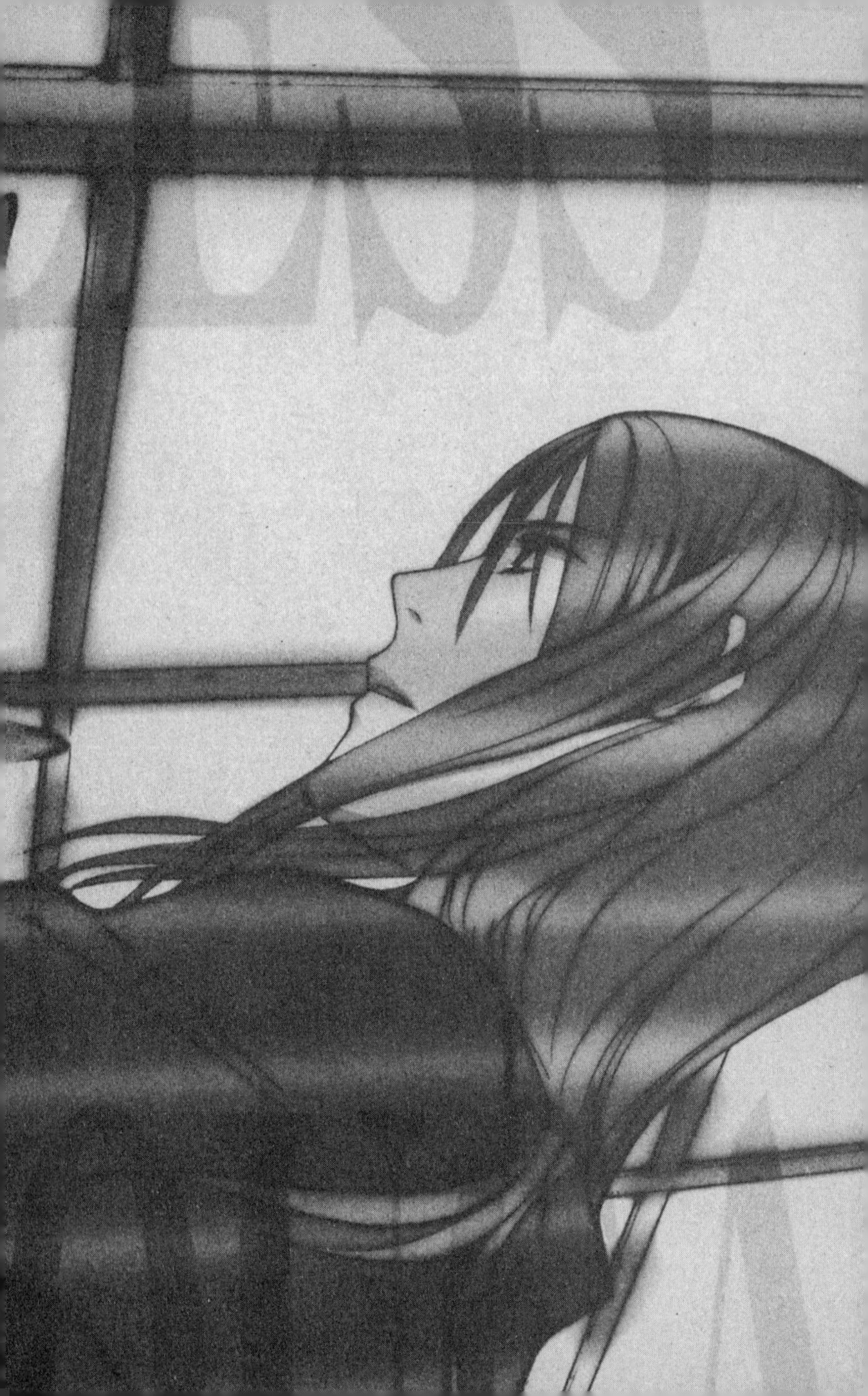

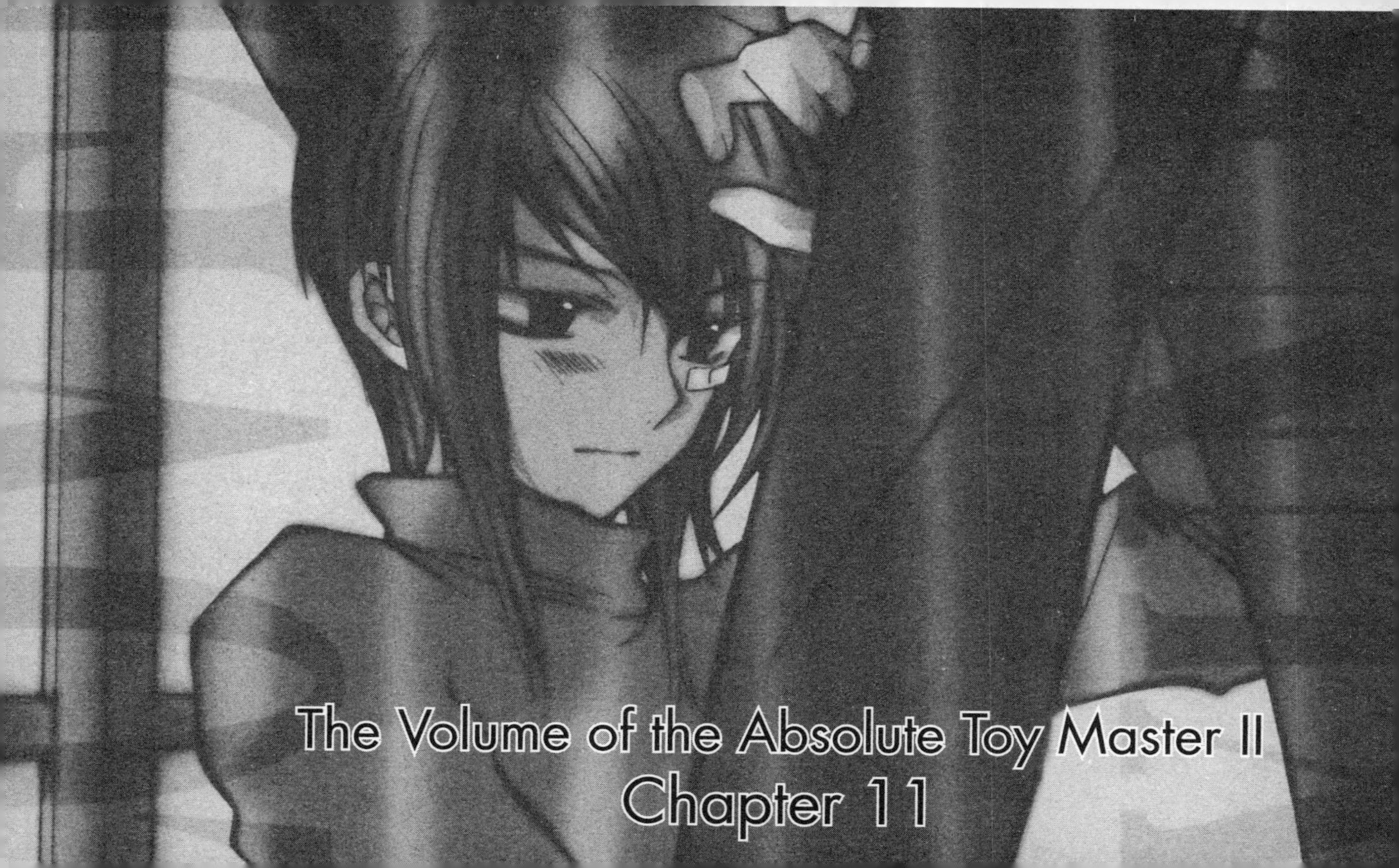
The Volume of the Absolute Toy Master II
Chapter 11

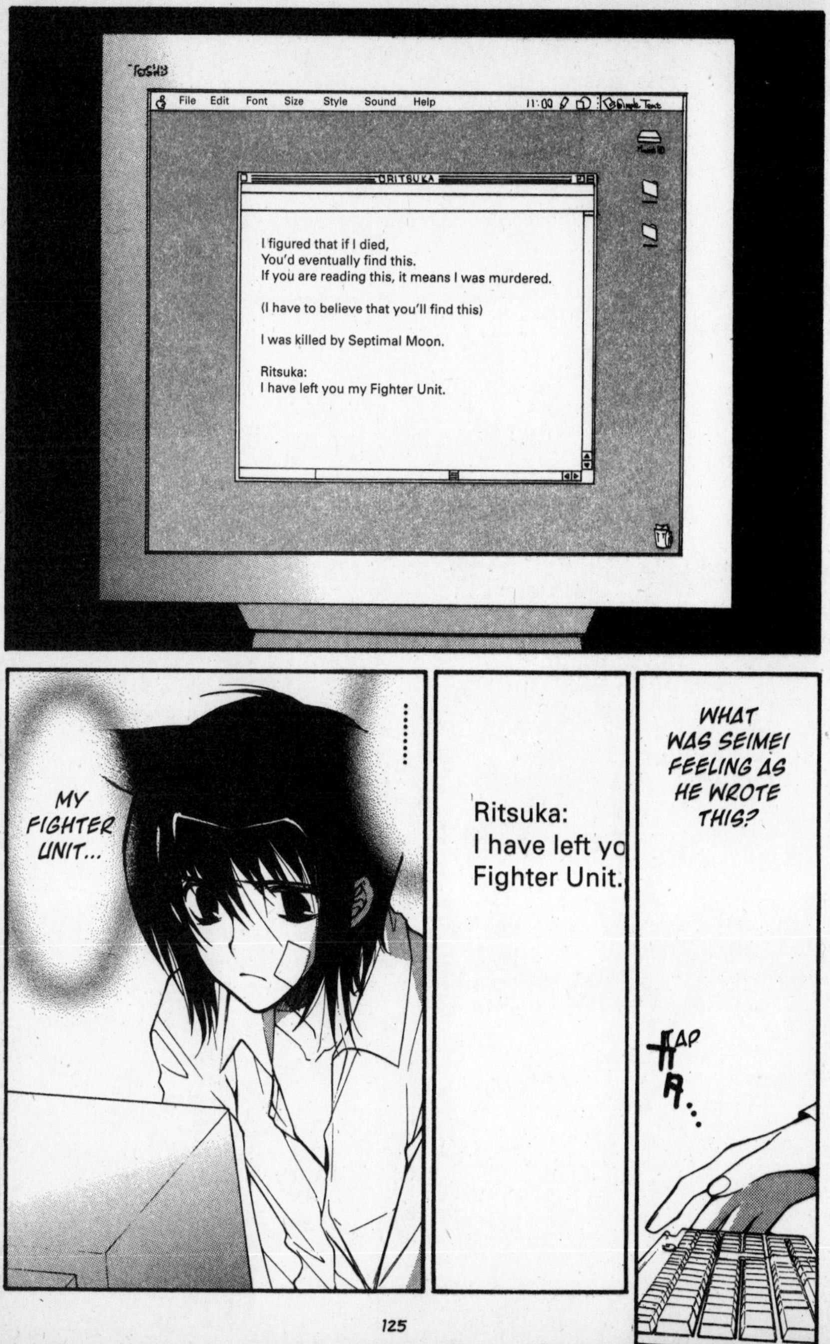
File Edit Font Size Style Sound Help
11:00
Simple Text
RITSUKA
I figured that if I died,
You'd eventually find this.
If you are reading this, it means I was murdered.
(I have to believe that you'll find this)
I was killed by Septimal Moon.
Ritsuka:
I have left you my Fighter Unit.
WHAT WAS SEIMEI FEELING AS HE WROTE THIS?
TAP
TA...
Ritsuka:
I have left yo
Fighter Unit.
......
MY FIGHTER UNIT...

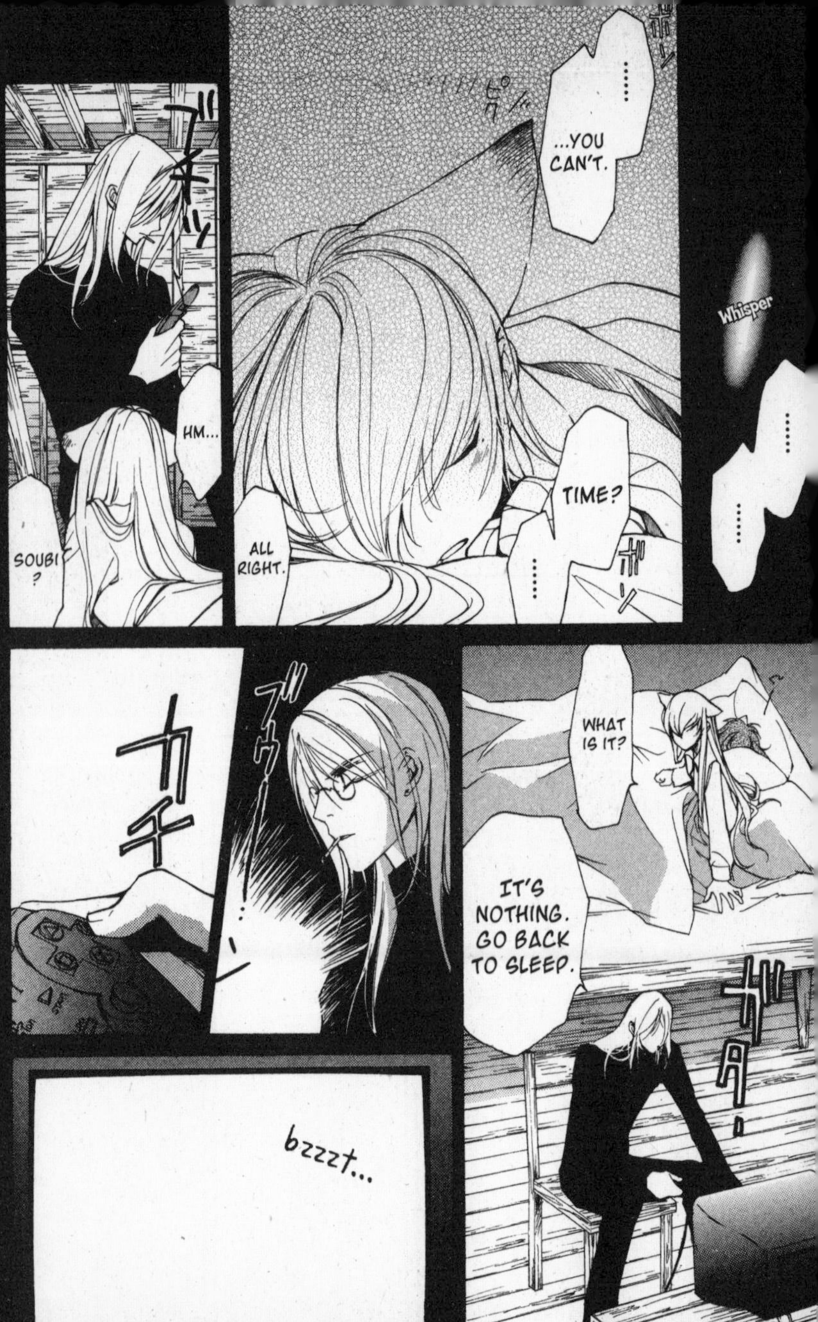

Whisper
......
......
......
...YOU CAN'T.
TIME?
......
ALL RIGHT.
HM...
SOUBI?
WHAT IS IT?
IT'S NOTHING. GO BACK TO SLEEP.
bzzzt...

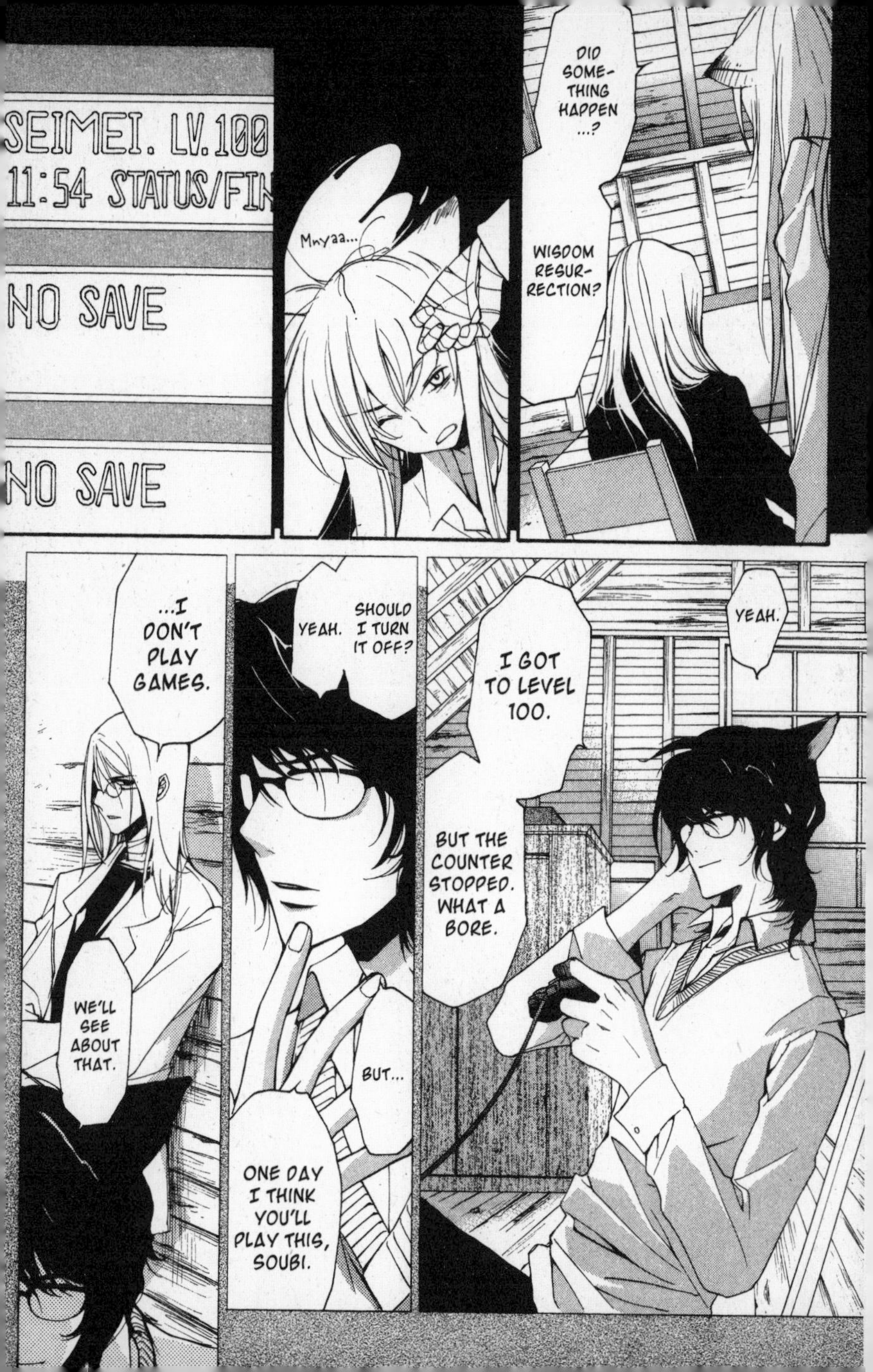
DID SOMETHING HAPPEN ...?
WISDOM RESURRECTION?
Mnyaa...
SEIMEI. LV.100
11:54 STATUS/FIN
NO SAVE
NO SAVE
YEAH.
I GOT TO LEVEL 100.
BUT THE COUNTER STOPPED. WHAT A BORE.
SHOULD I TURN IT OFF?
YEAH.
BUT...
ONE DAY I THINK YOU'LL PLAY THIS, SOUBI.
...I DON'T PLAY GAMES.
WE'LL SEE ABOUT THAT.

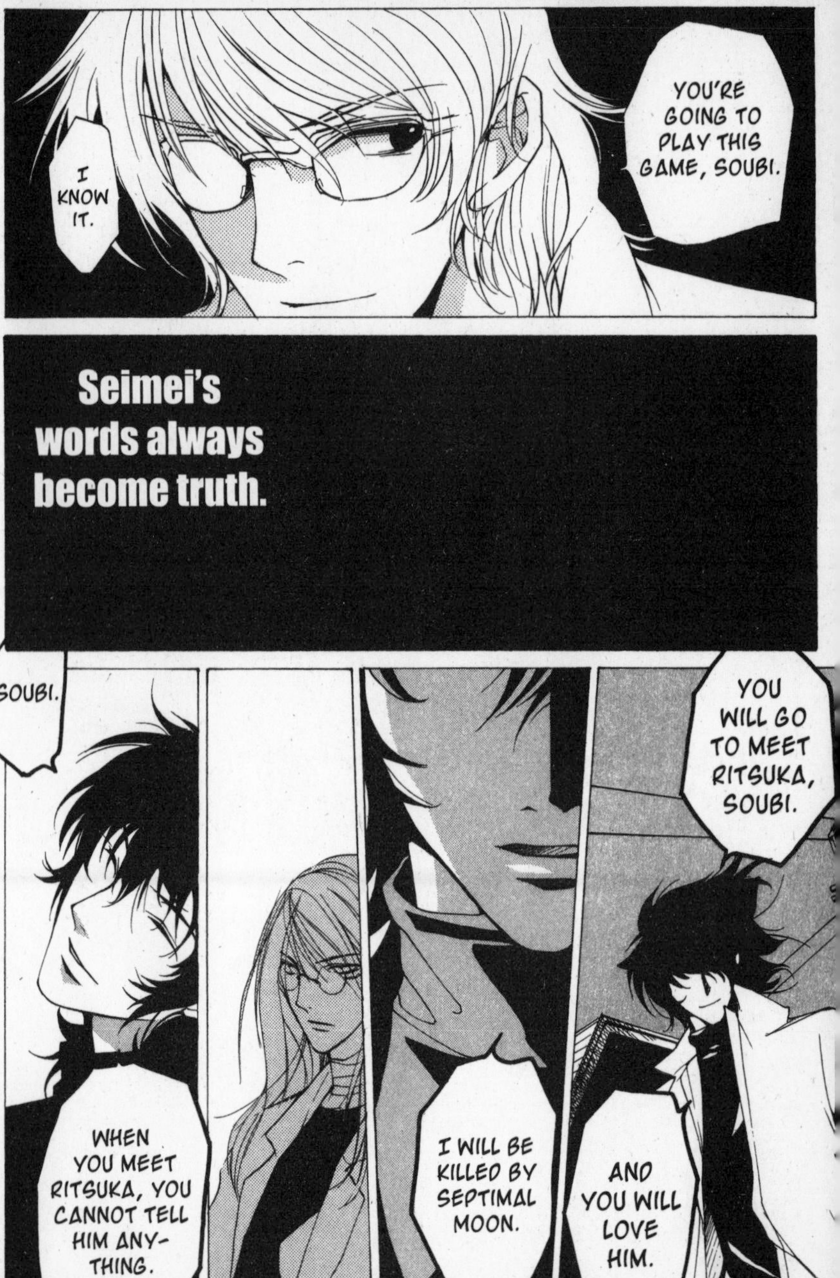
YOU'RE GOING TO PLAY THIS GAME, SOUBI.
I KNOW IT.
Seimei's words always become truth.
YOU WILL GO TO MEET RITSUKA, SOUBI.
AND YOU WILL LOVE HIM.
I WILL BE KILLED BY SEPTIMAL MOON.
SOUBI.
WHEN YOU MEET RITSUKA, YOU CANNOT TELL HIM ANY-THING.

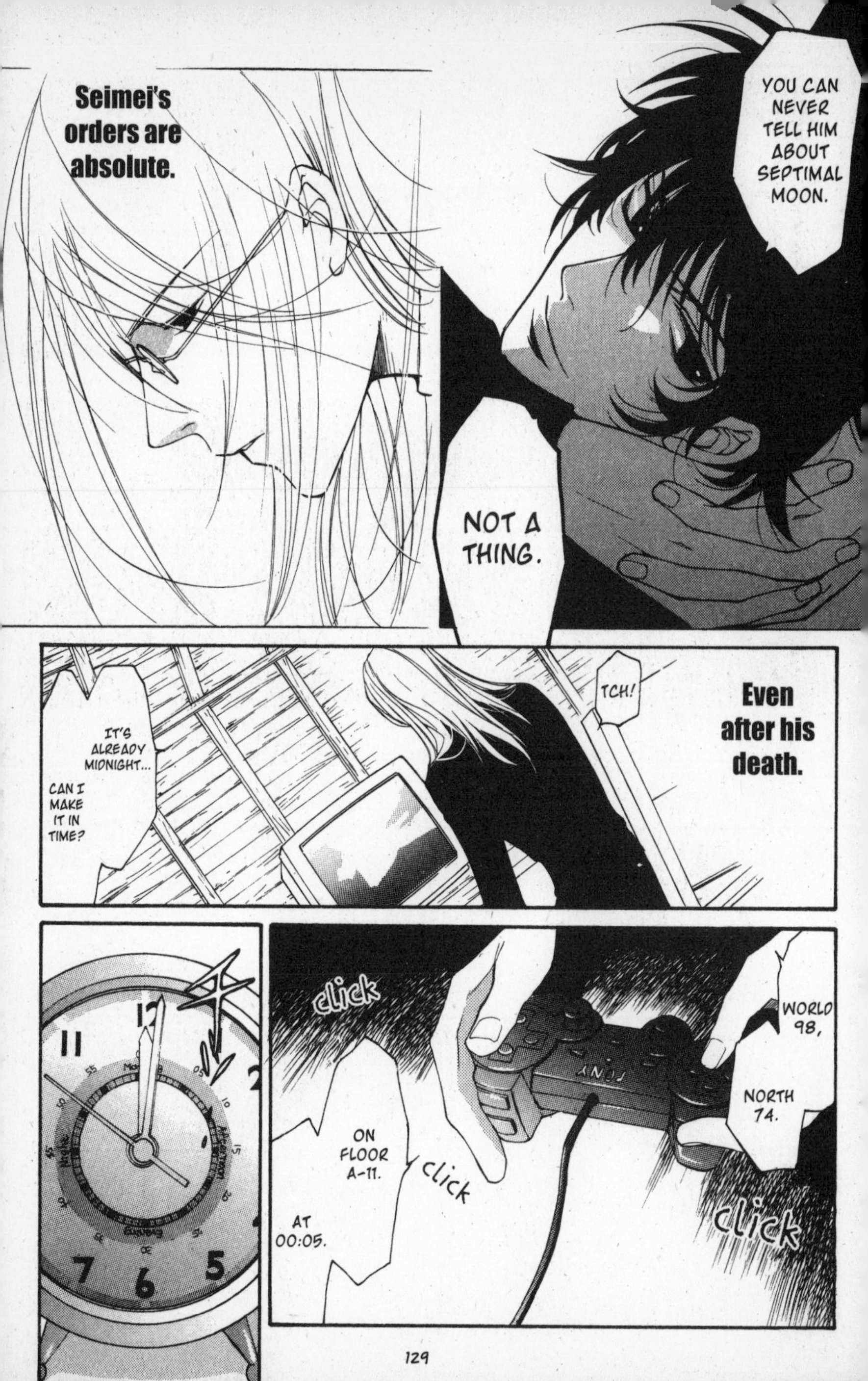
YOU CAN NEVER TELL HIM ABOUT SEPTIMAL MOON.
NOT A THING.
Seimei's orders are absolute.
Even after his death.
TCH!
IT'S ALREADY MIDNIGHT...
CAN I MAKE IT IN TIME?
WORLD 98,
NORTH 74.
click
ON FLOOR A-11.
click
AT 00:05.
click

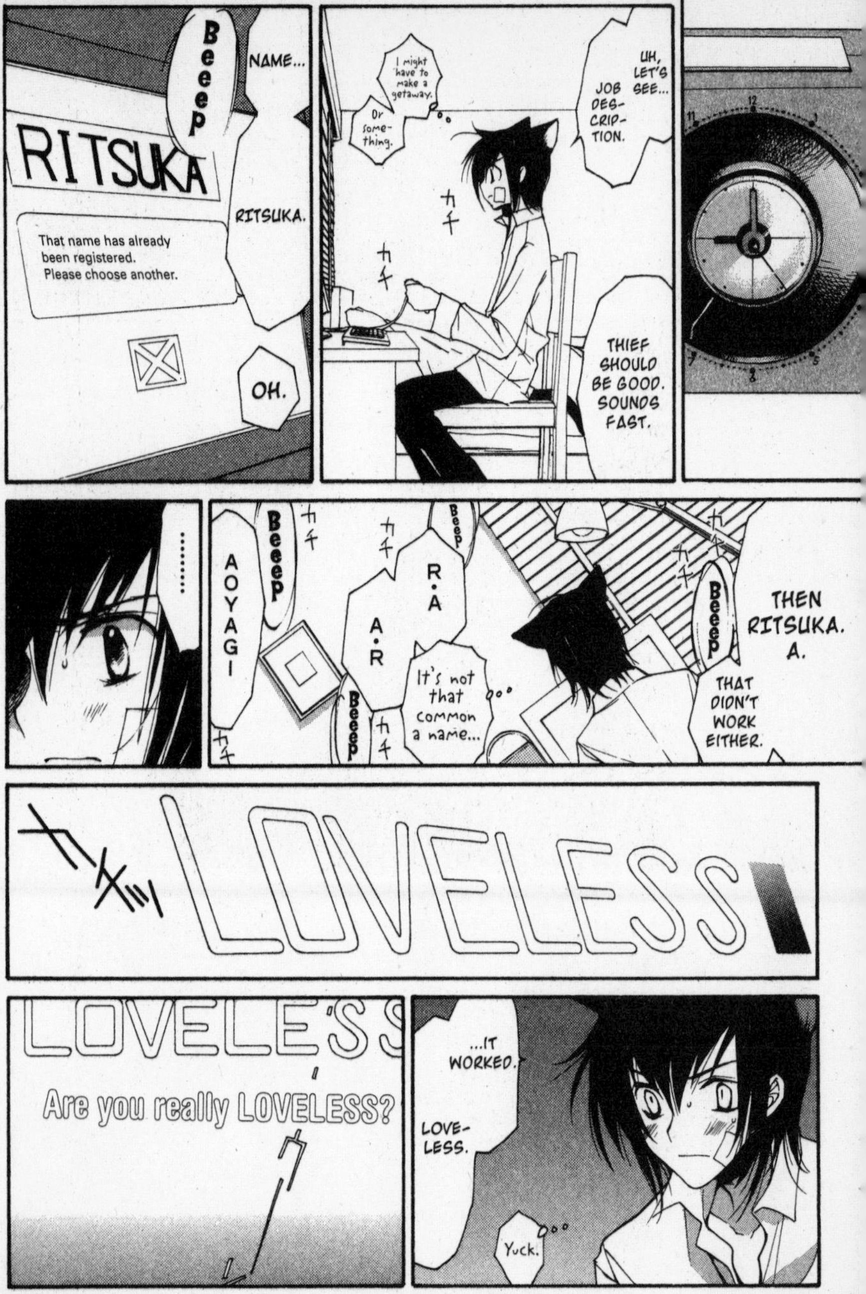
UH, LET'S SEE... JOB DESCRIPTION.
I might have to make a getaway.
Or something.
カチ
カチ
THIEF SHOULD BE GOOD. SOUNDS FAST.
Beeep
NAME...
RITSUKA
RITSUKA.
That name has already been registered. Please choose another.
OH.
THEN RITSUKA. A.
Beeep
THAT DIDN'T WORK EITHER.
Beep
R•A
カチ
A•R
It's not that common a name...
Beeep
カチ
Beeep
AOYAGI
カチ
......
LOVELESS
LOVELESS
...IT WORKED.
LOVE-LESS.
Yuck.
LOVELESS
Are you really LOVELESS?

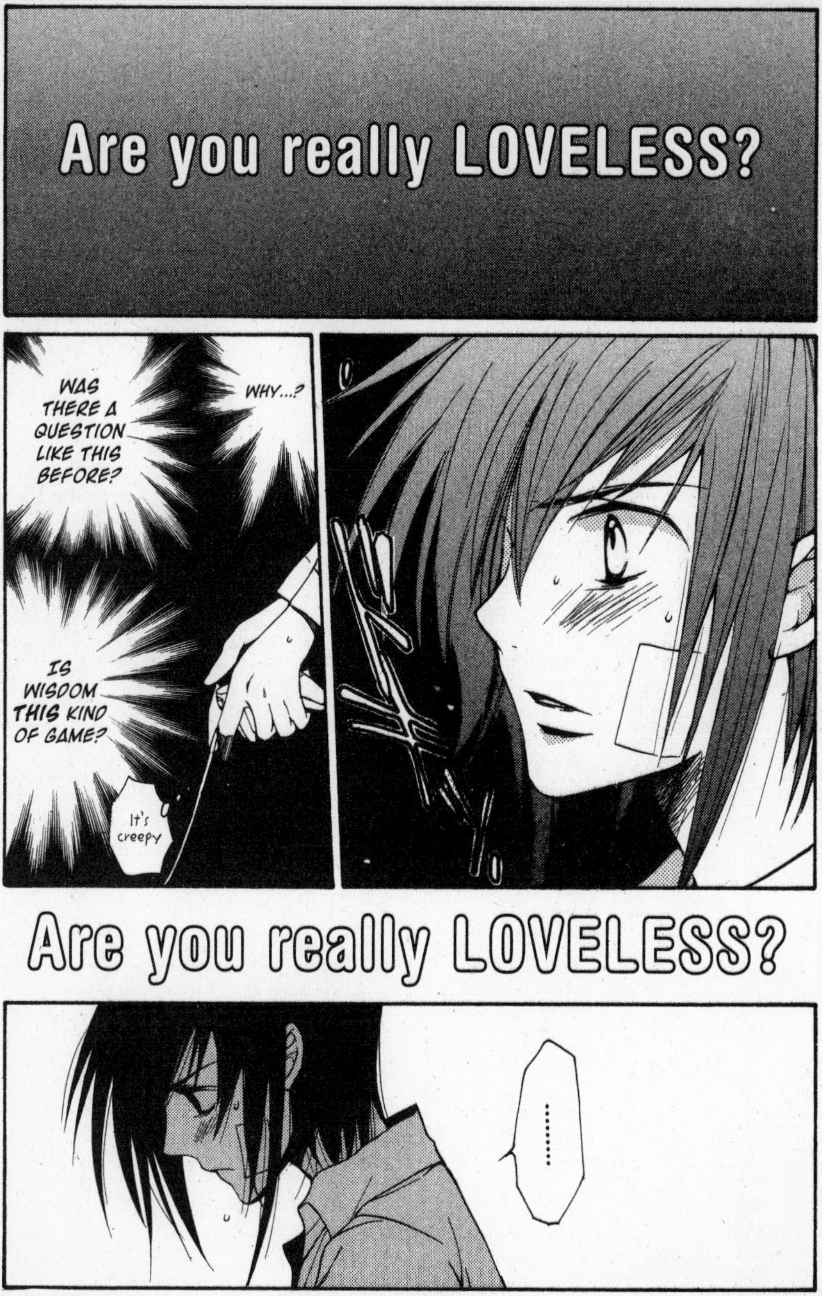
Are you really LOVELESS?
WHY...?
WAS THERE A QUESTION LIKE THIS BEFORE?
IS WISDOM THIS KIND OF GAME?
It's creepy
Are you really LOVELESS?
......

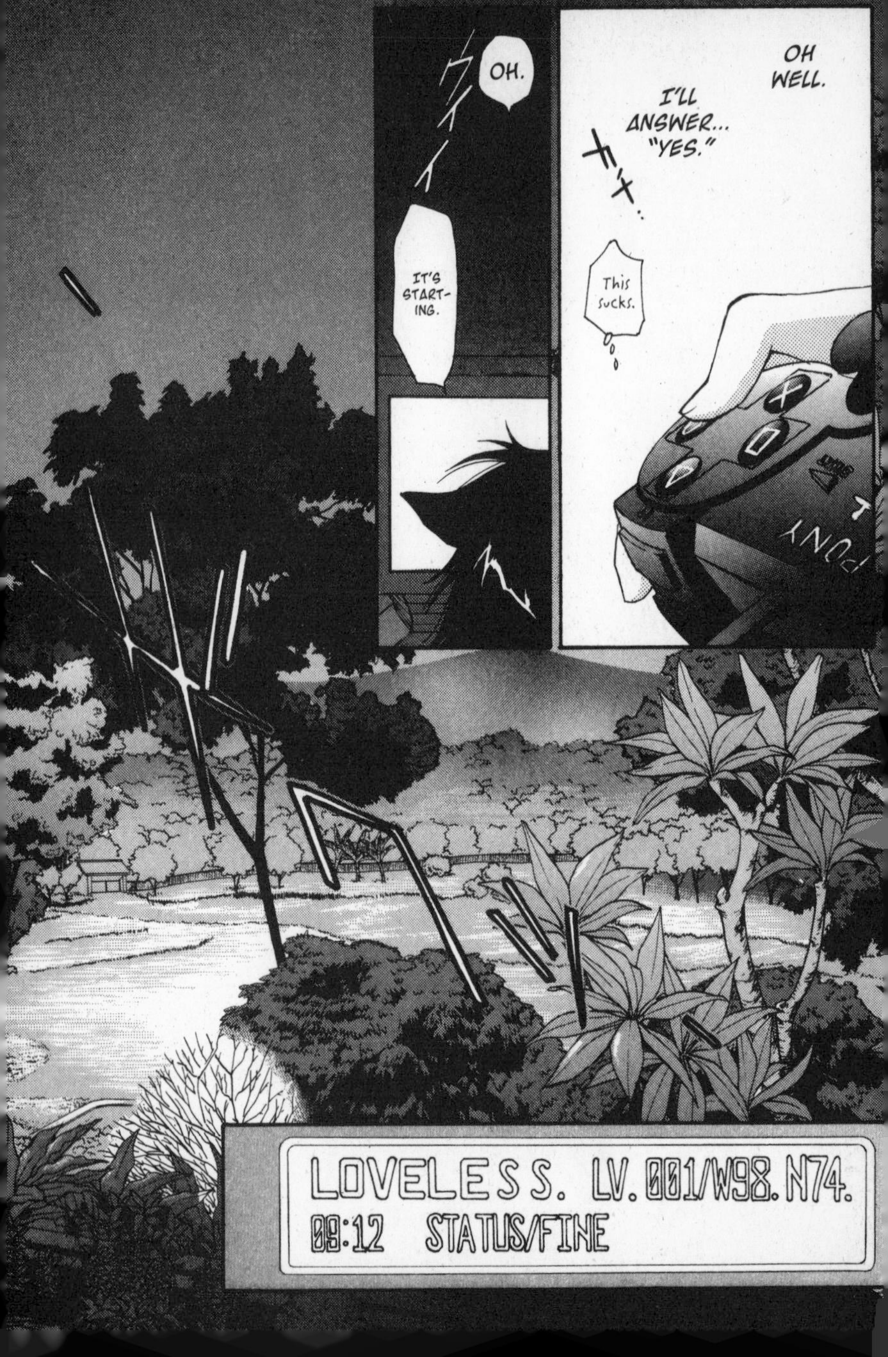
OH WELL.
I'LL ANSWER... "YES."
This sucks.
OH.
IT'S START-ING.
LOVELESS. LV.001/W98.N74.
09:12 STATUS/FINE

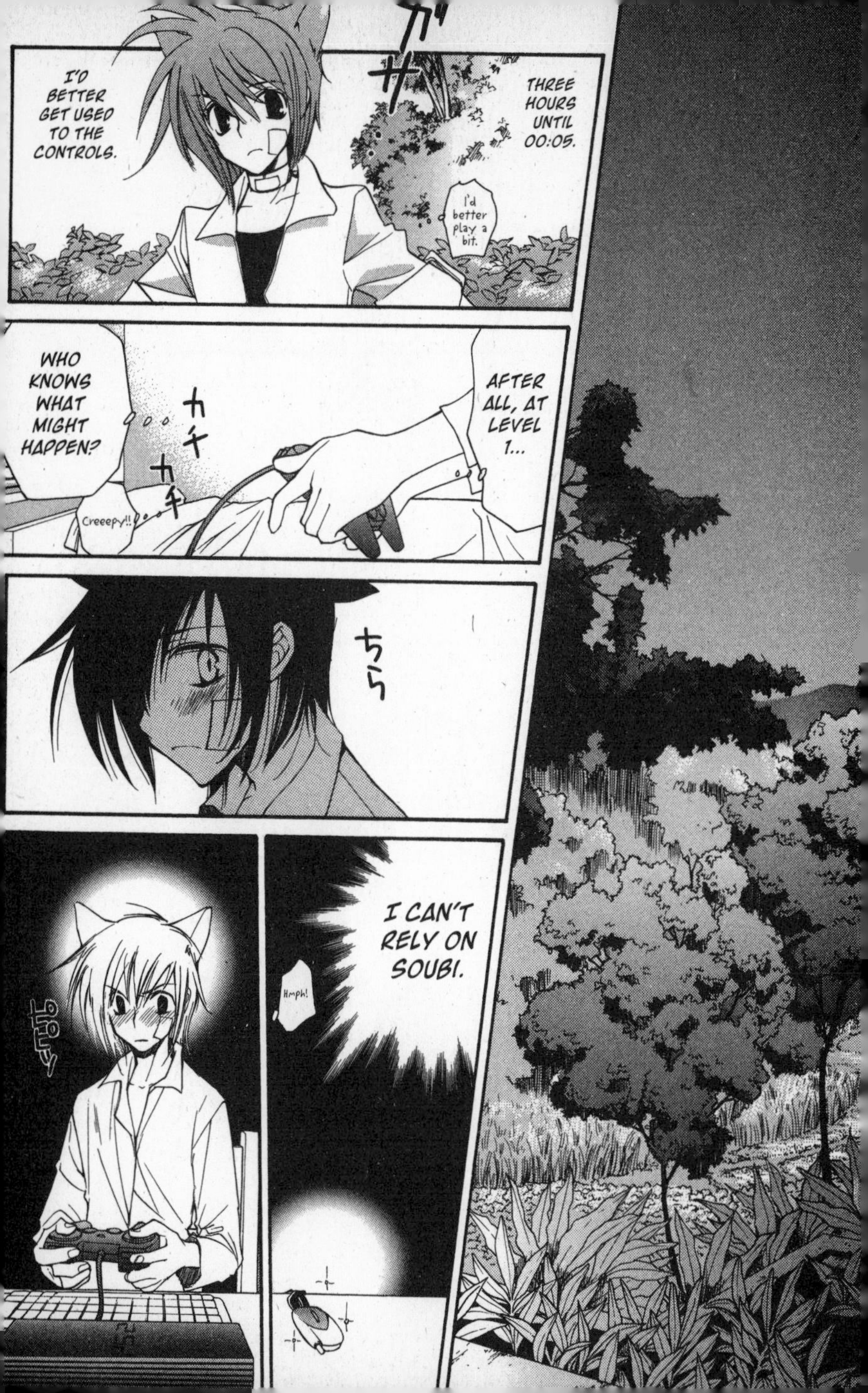
ガサ
THREE HOURS UNTIL 00:05.
I'd better play a bit.
I'D BETTER GET USED TO THE CONTROLS.
AFTER ALL, AT LEVEL 1...
カチ
カチ
WHO KNOWS WHAT MIGHT HAPPEN?
Creeepy!!
ちら
I CAN'T RELY ON SOUBI.
Hmph!

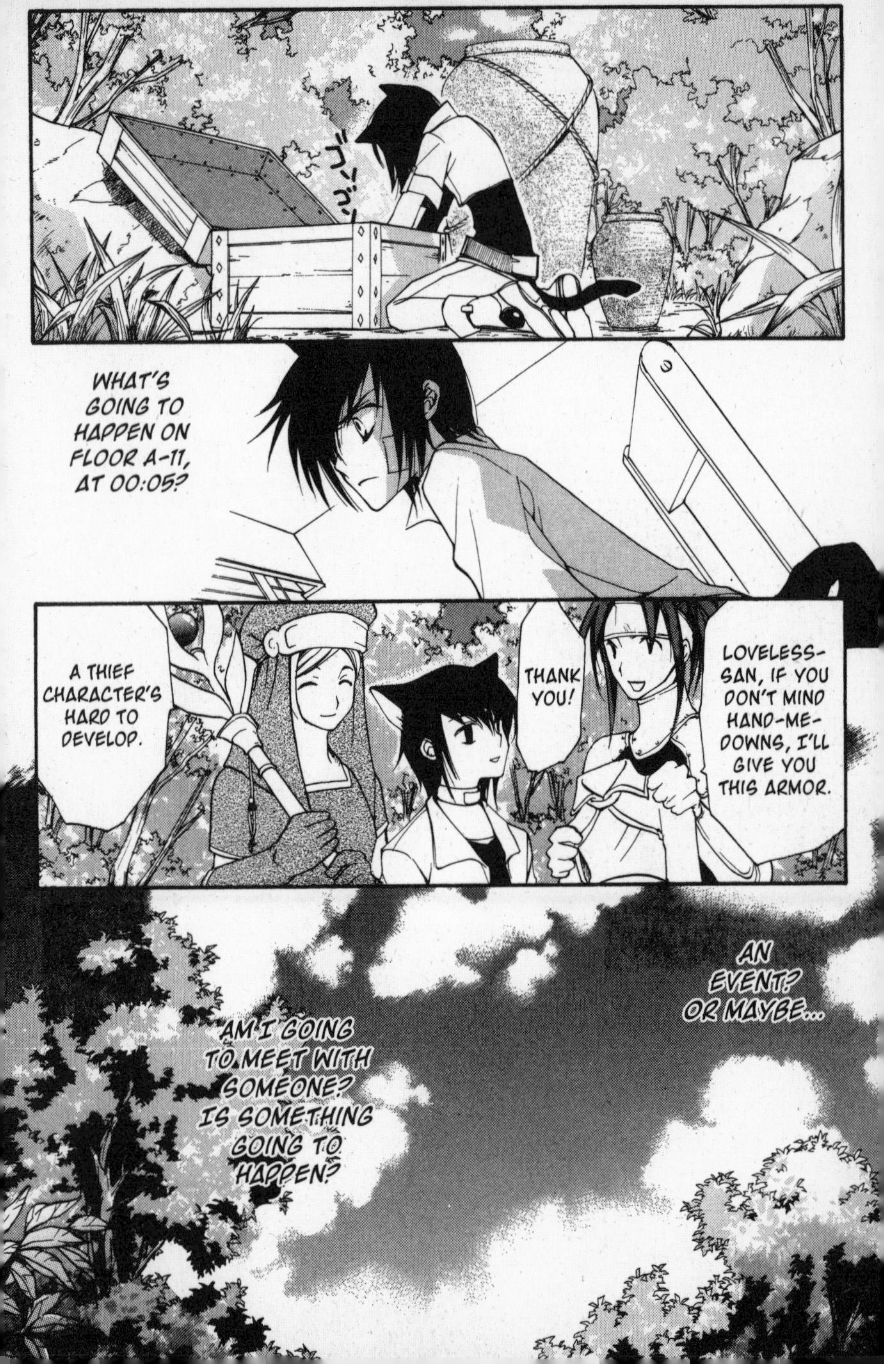
ゴソゴソ
WHAT'S GOING TO HAPPEN ON FLOOR A-11, AT 00:05?
LOVELESS-SAN, IF YOU DON'T MIND HAND-ME-DOWNS, I'LL GIVE YOU THIS ARMOR.
THANK YOU!
A THIEF CHARACTER'S HARD TO DEVELOP.
AN EVENT? OR MAYBE...
AM I GOING TO MEET WITH SOMEONE? IS SOMETHING GOING TO HAPPEN?

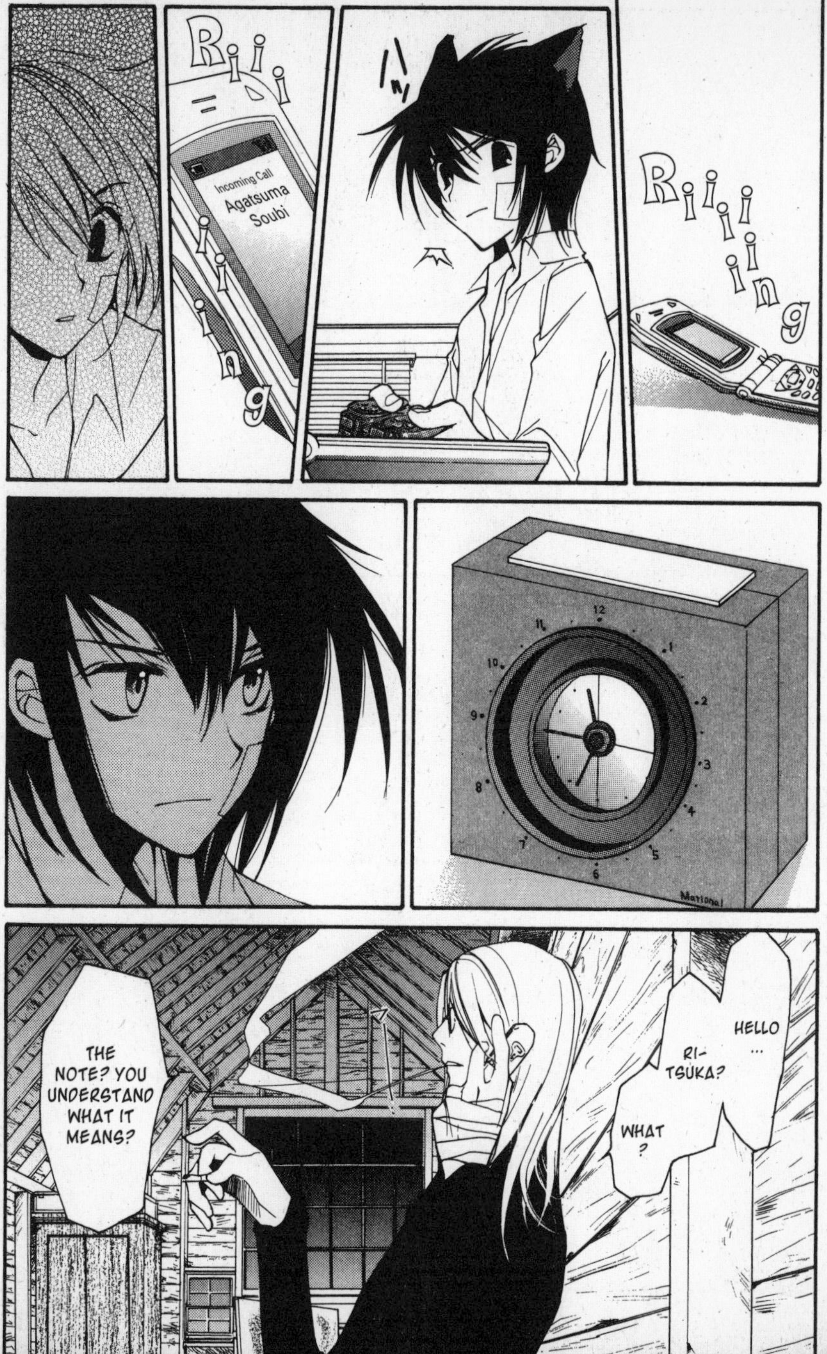
Riiiiiing
Incoming Call
Agatsuma Soubi
Riiiiiing
HELLO ...
RI-TSUKA?
WHAT ?
THE NOTE? YOU UNDERSTAND WHAT IT MEANS?

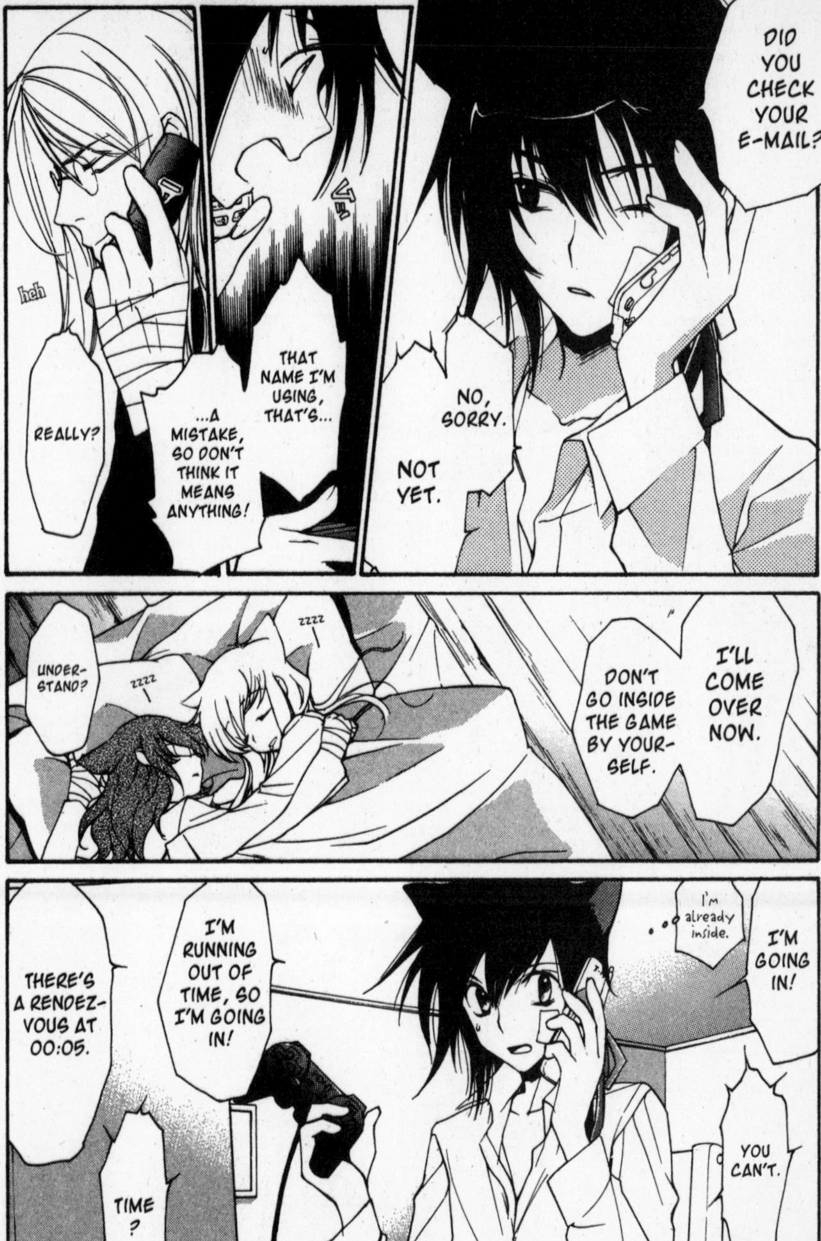
DID YOU CHECK YOUR E-MAIL?
NO, SORRY.
NOT YET.
THAT NAME I'M USING, THAT'S...
...A MISTAKE, SO DON'T THINK IT MEANS ANYTHING!
heh
REALLY?
I'LL COME OVER NOW.
DON'T GO INSIDE THE GAME BY YOURSELF.
zzzz
zzzz
UNDER-STAND?
...I'm already inside.
I'M GOING IN!
YOU CAN'T.
I'M RUNNING OUT OF TIME, SO I'M GOING IN!
THERE'S A RENDEZ-VOUS AT 00:05.
TIME?

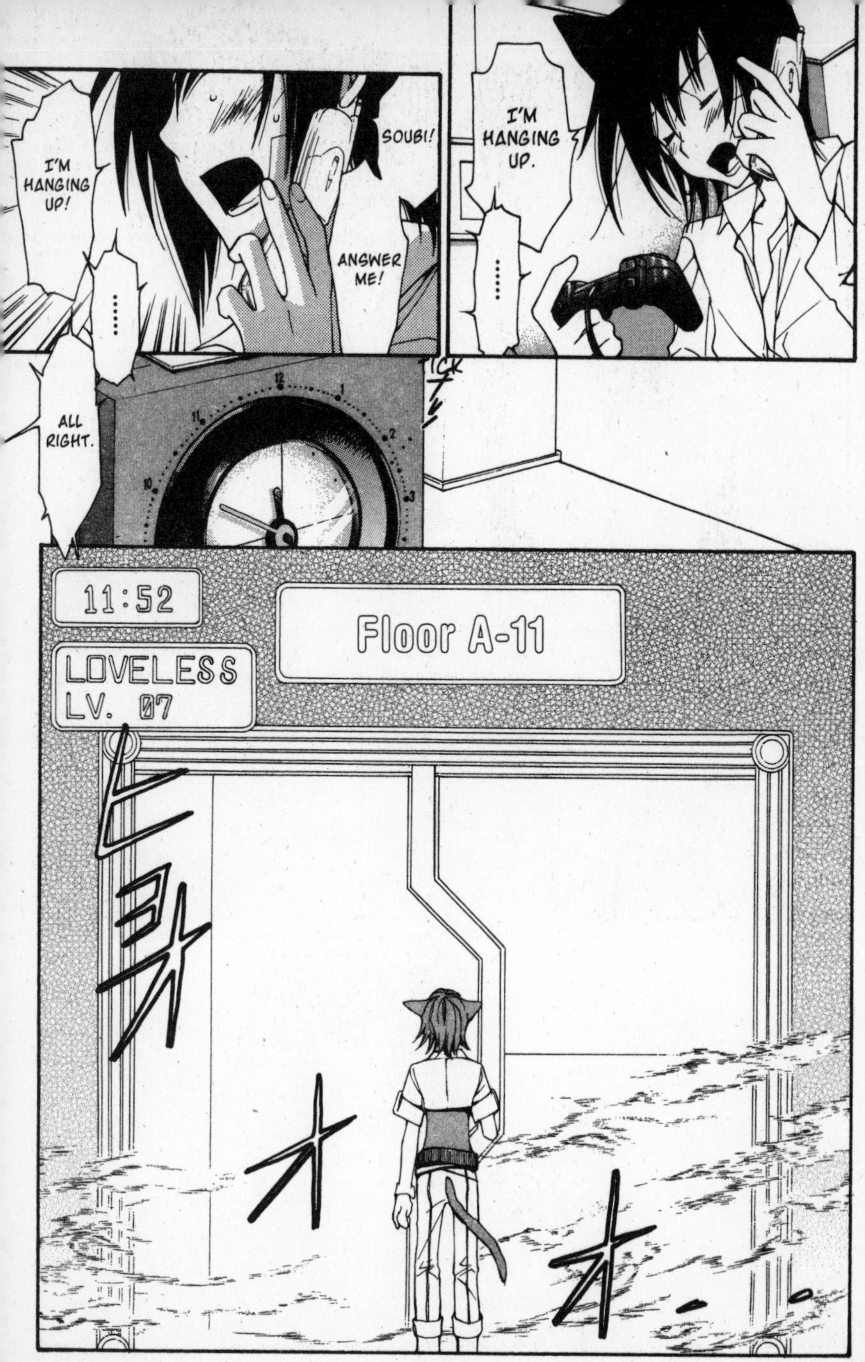
I'M HANGING UP.
......
SOUBI!
ANSWER ME!
I'M HANGING UP!
......
TICK
ALL RIGHT.
11:52
Floor A-11
LOVELESS
LV. 07
ヒョオ
オオ

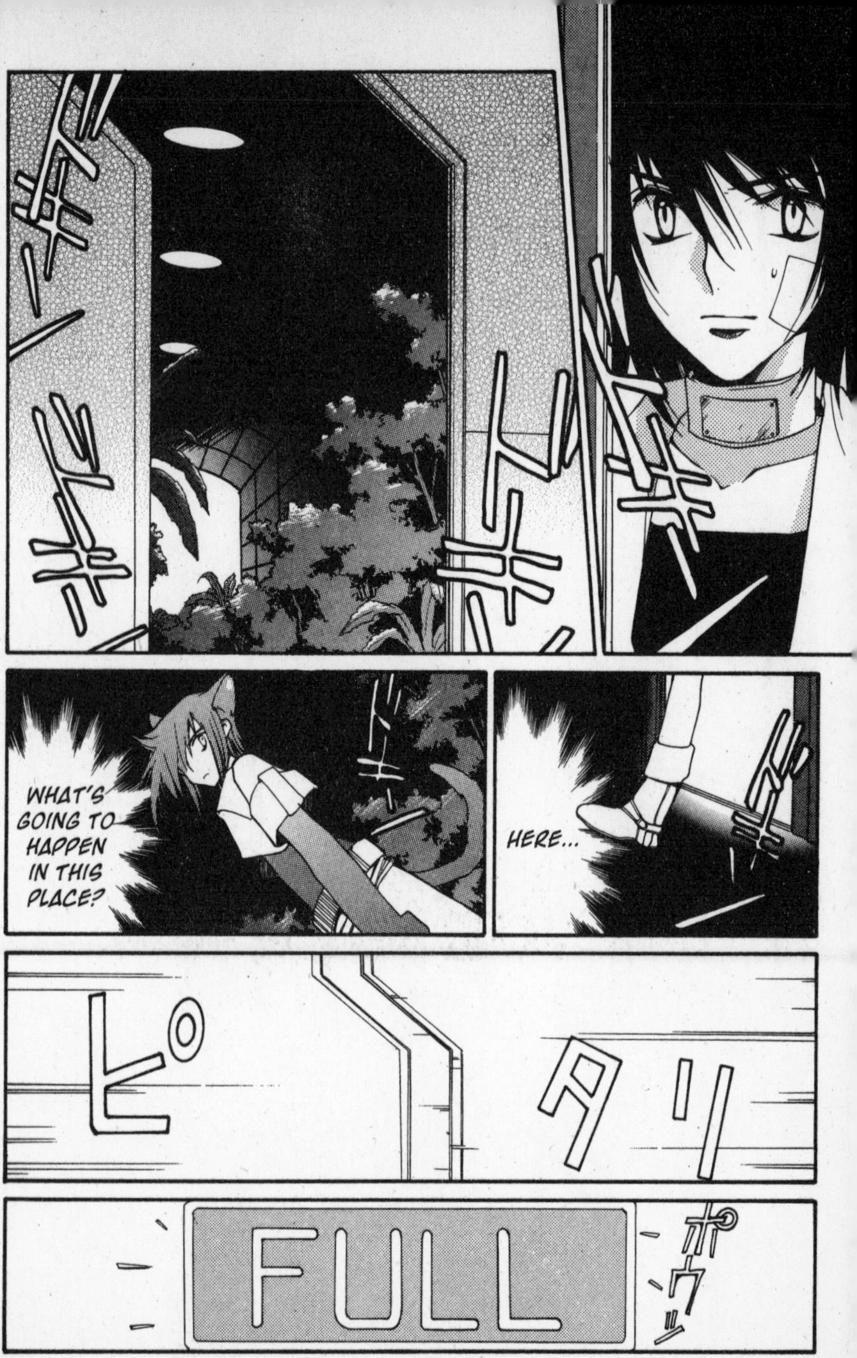
HERE...
WHAT'S GOING TO HAPPEN IN THIS PLACE?
ピタリ
FULL

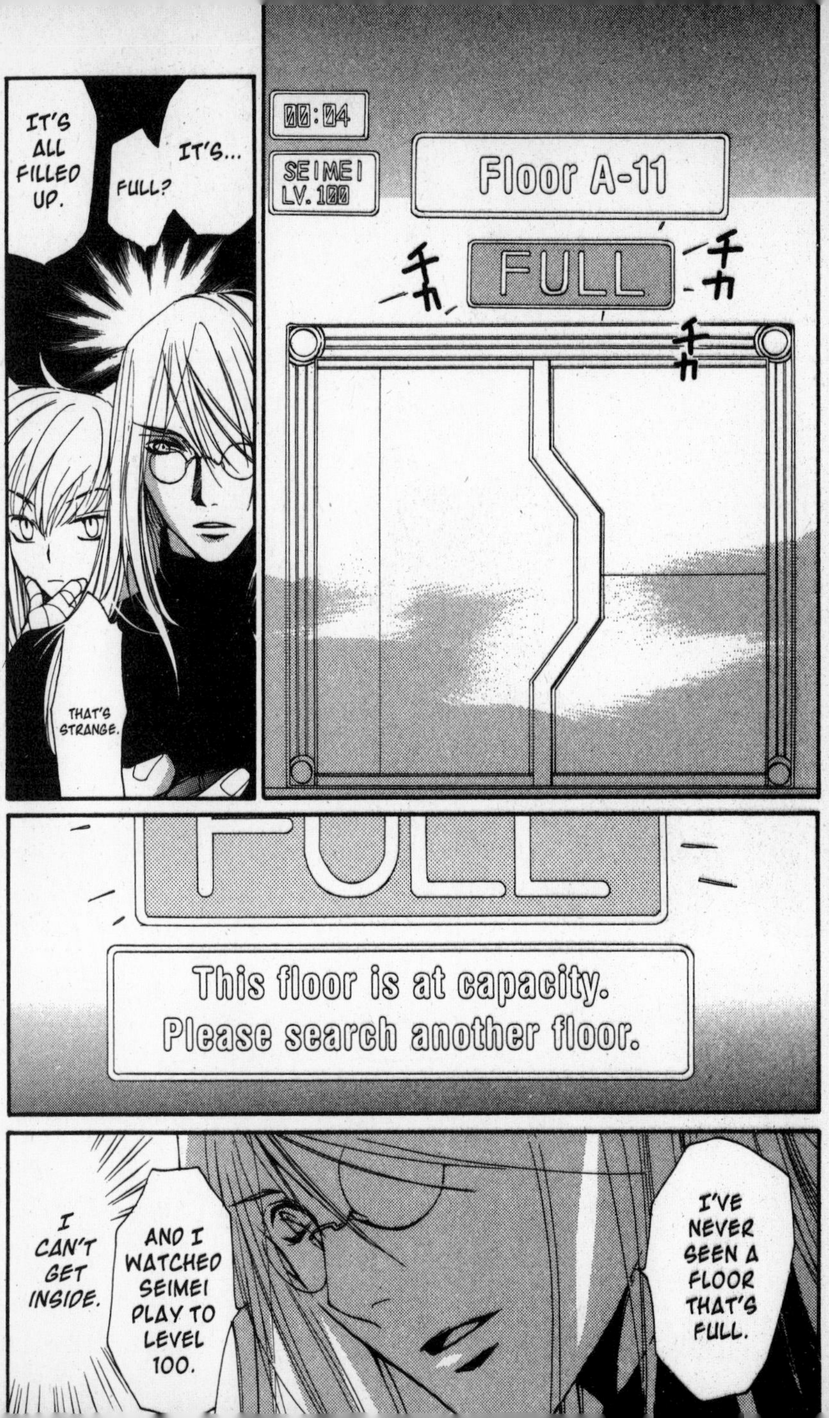
00:04
SEIMEI LV. 100
Floor A-11
FULL
チカ
チカ
チカ
IT'S... FULL?
IT'S ALL FILLED UP.
THAT'S STRANGE.
FULL
This floor is at capacity. Please search another floor.
I'VE NEVER SEEN A FLOOR THAT'S FULL.
AND I WATCHED SEIMEI PLAY TO LEVEL 100.
I CAN'T GET INSIDE.

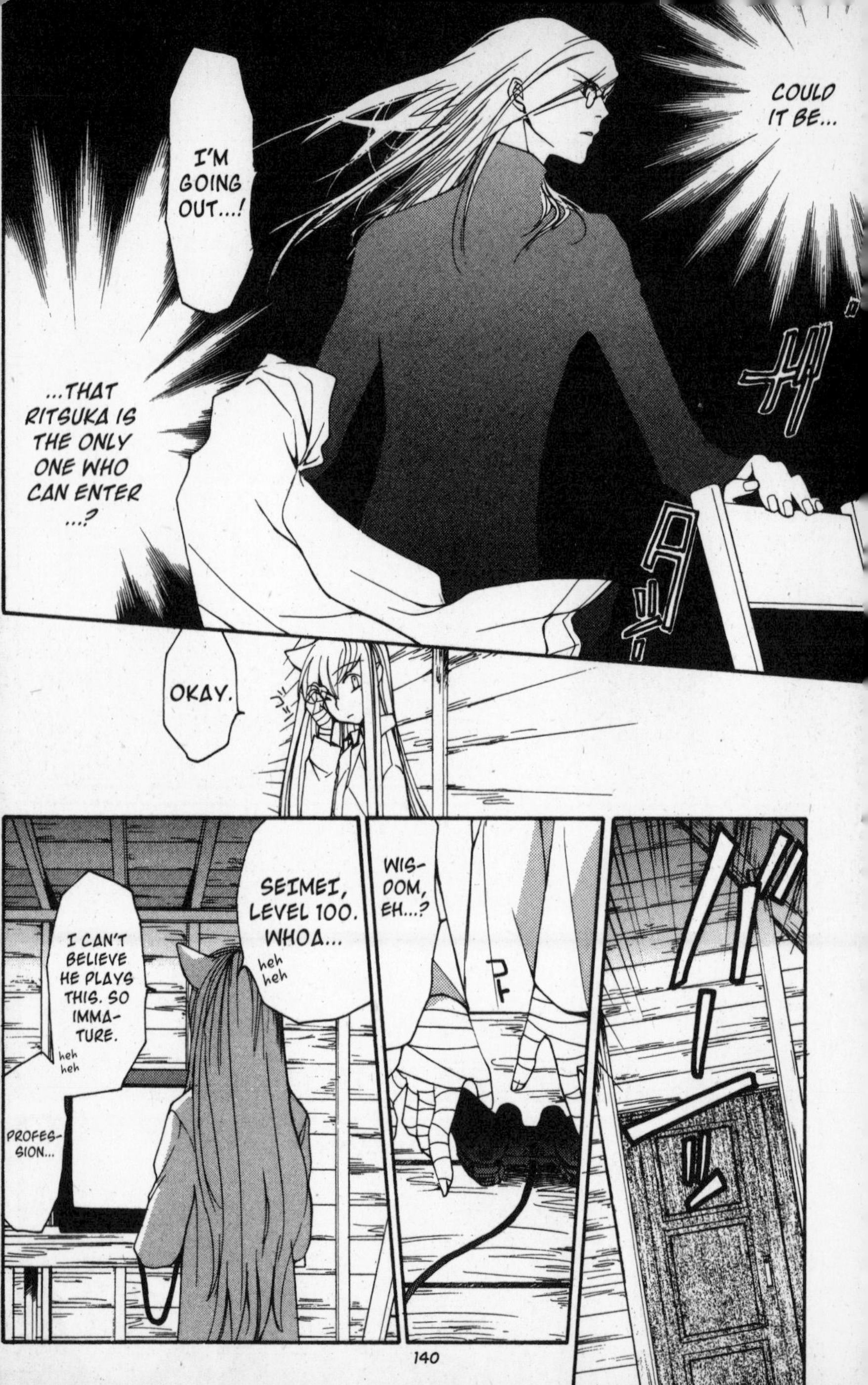
COULD IT BE...
I'M GOING OUT...!
...THAT RITSUKA IS THE ONLY ONE WHO CAN ENTER ...?
OKAY.
WIS-DOOM, EH...?
SEIMEI, LEVEL 100. WHOA...
heh heh
I CAN'T BELIEVE HE PLAYS THIS. SO IMMA-TURE.
heh heh
PROFES-SION...

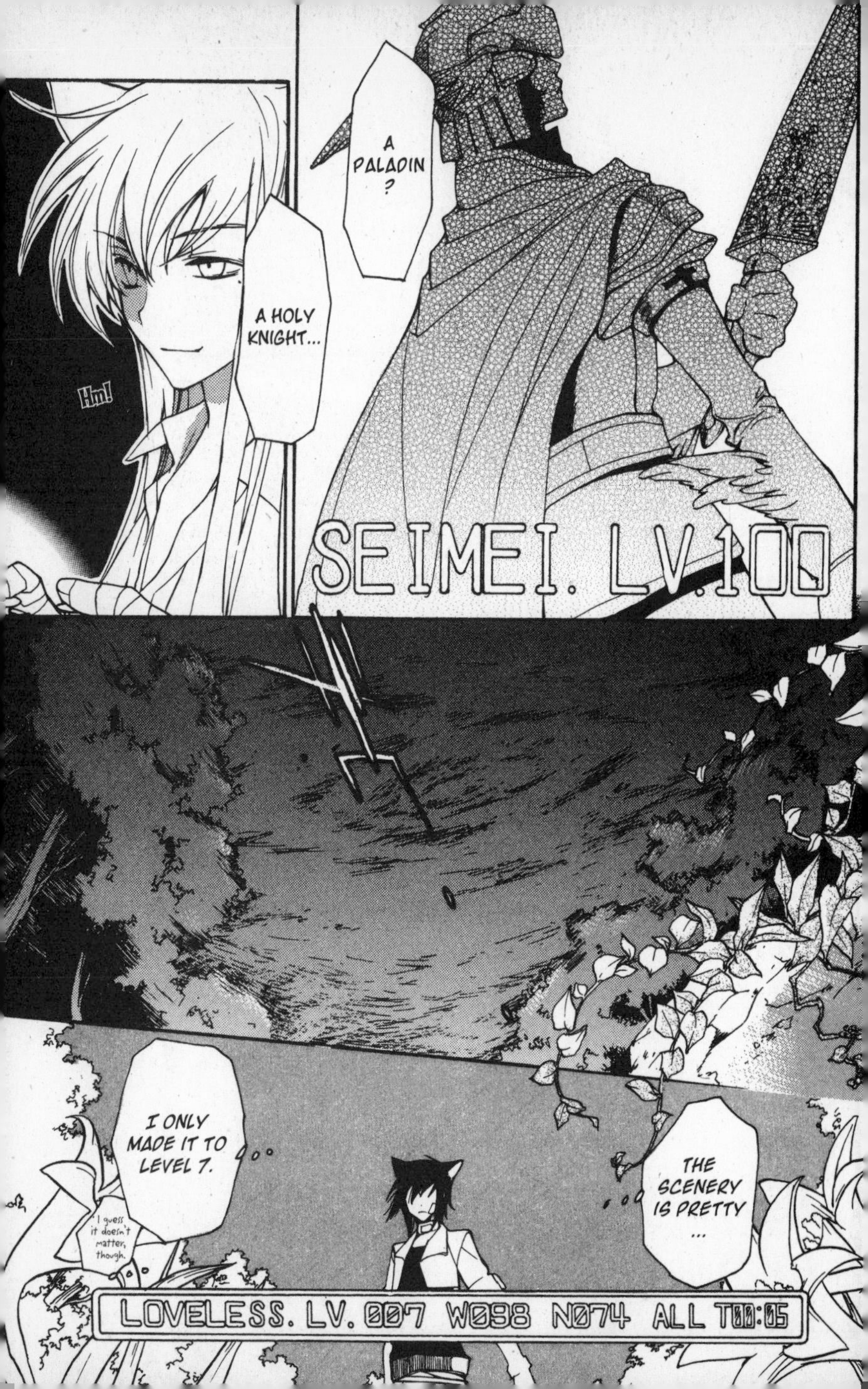
A PALADIN ?
SEIMEI. LV.100
A HOLY KNIGHT...
Hm!
THE SCENERY IS PRETTY ...
I ONLY MADE IT TO LEVEL 7.
I guess it doesn't matter, though.
LOVELESS. LV. 007 W098 N074 ALL T00:05

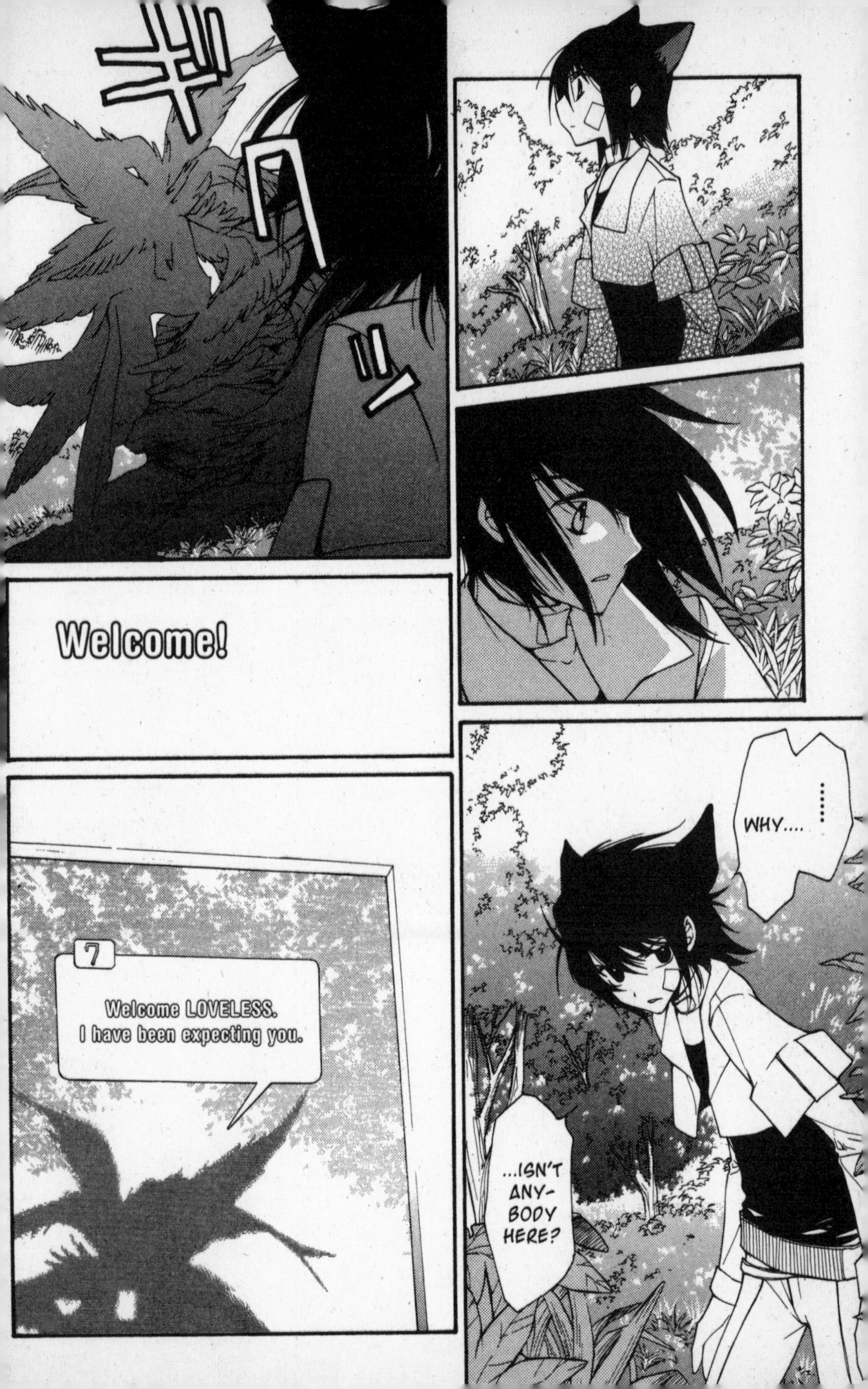
ギロッ
Welcome!
WHY....
......
...ISN'T ANY-BODY HERE?
7
Welcome LOVELESS. I have been expecting you.

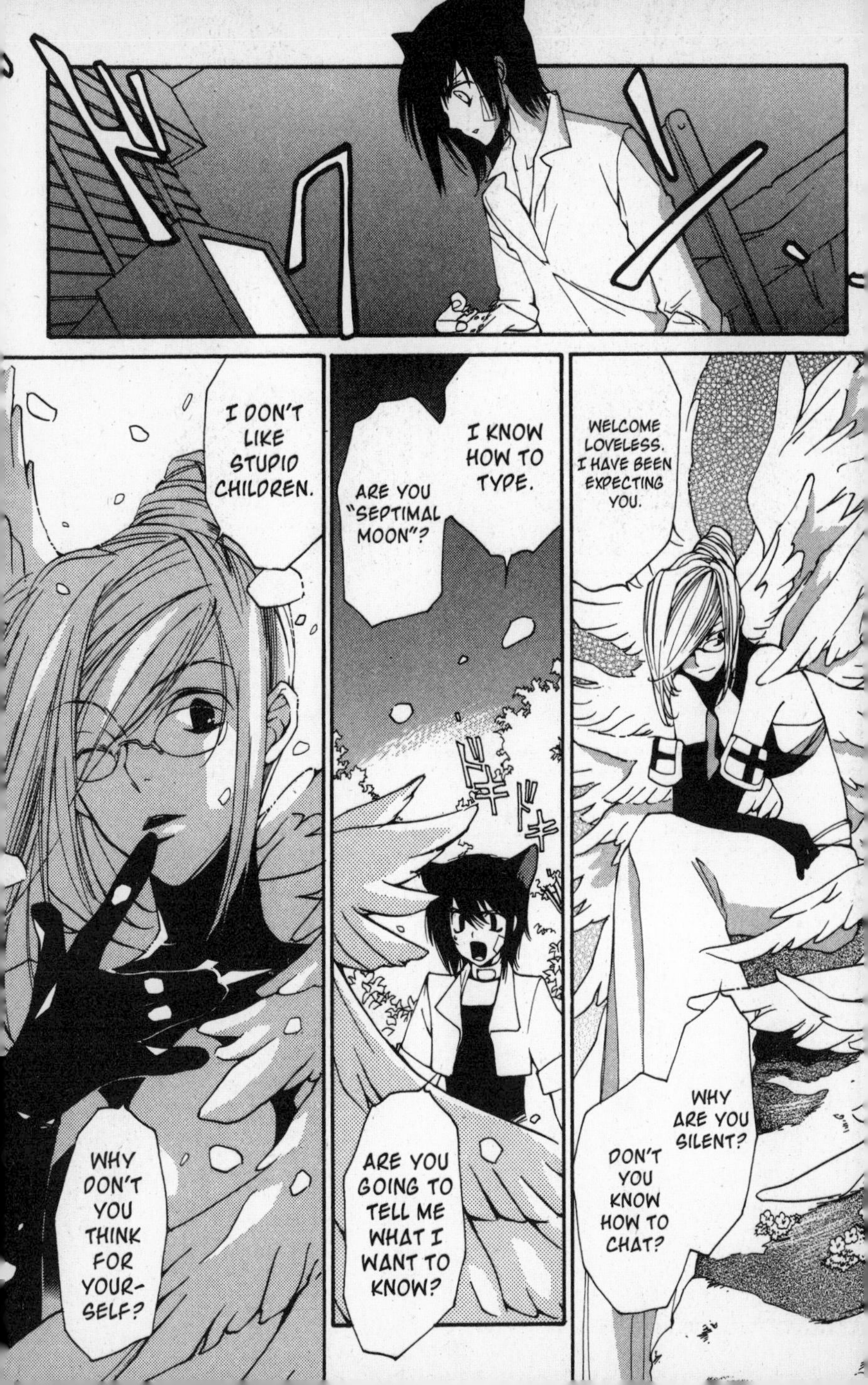
WELCOME LOVELESS. I HAVE BEEN EXPECTING YOU.
WHY ARE YOU SILENT?
DON'T YOU KNOW HOW TO CHAT?
I KNOW HOW TO TYPE.
ARE YOU "SEPTIMAL MOON"?
ARE YOU GOING TO TELL ME WHAT I WANT TO KNOW?
I DON'T LIKE STUPID CHILDREN.
WHY DON'T YOU THINK FOR YOUR-SELF?

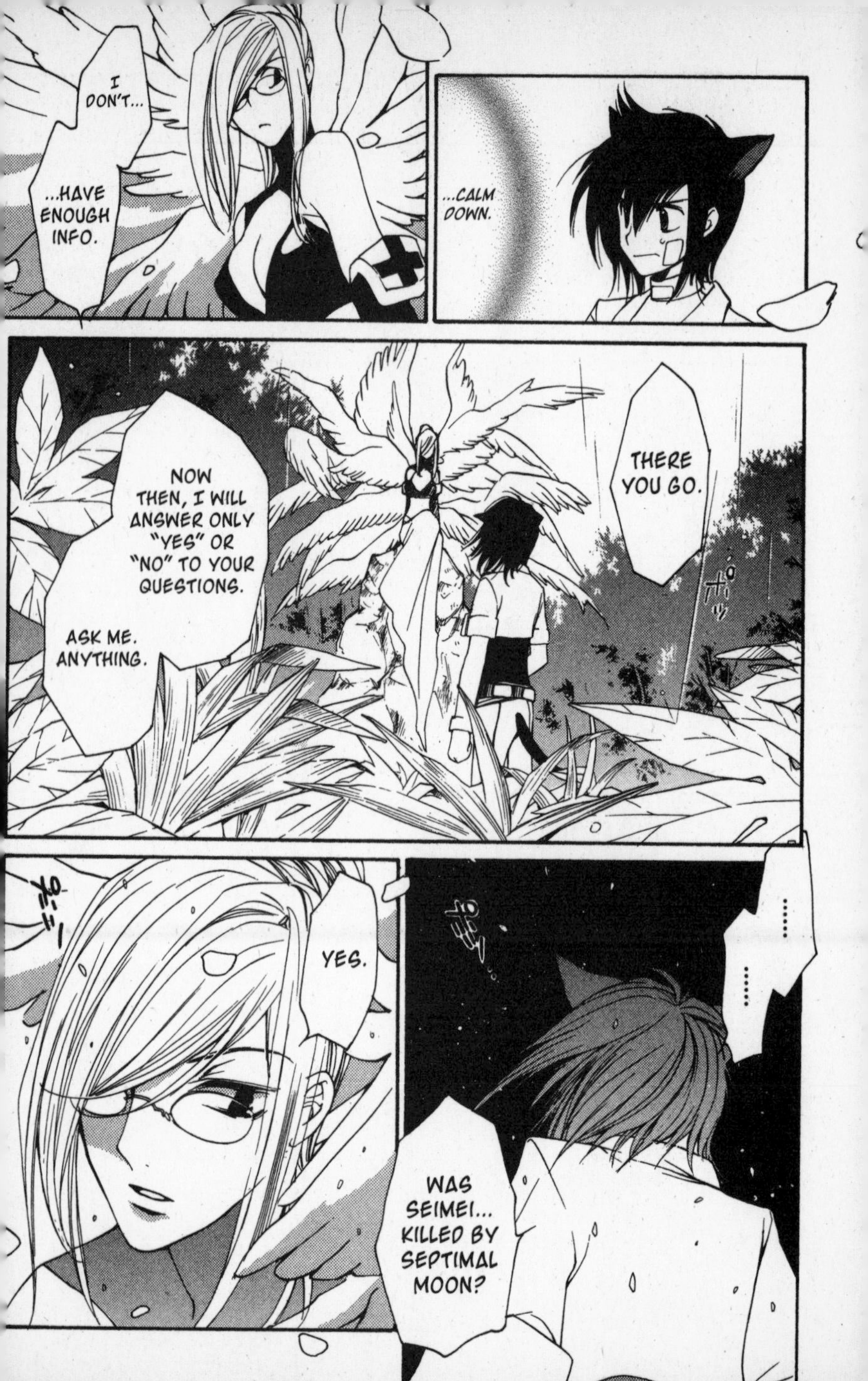
...CALM DOWN.
I DON'T...
...HAVE ENOUGH INFO.
THERE YOU GO.
NOW THEN, I WILL ANSWER ONLY "YES" OR "NO" TO YOUR QUESTIONS.
ASK ME. ANYTHING.
......
......
WAS SEIMEI... KILLED BY SEPTIMAL MOON?
YES.

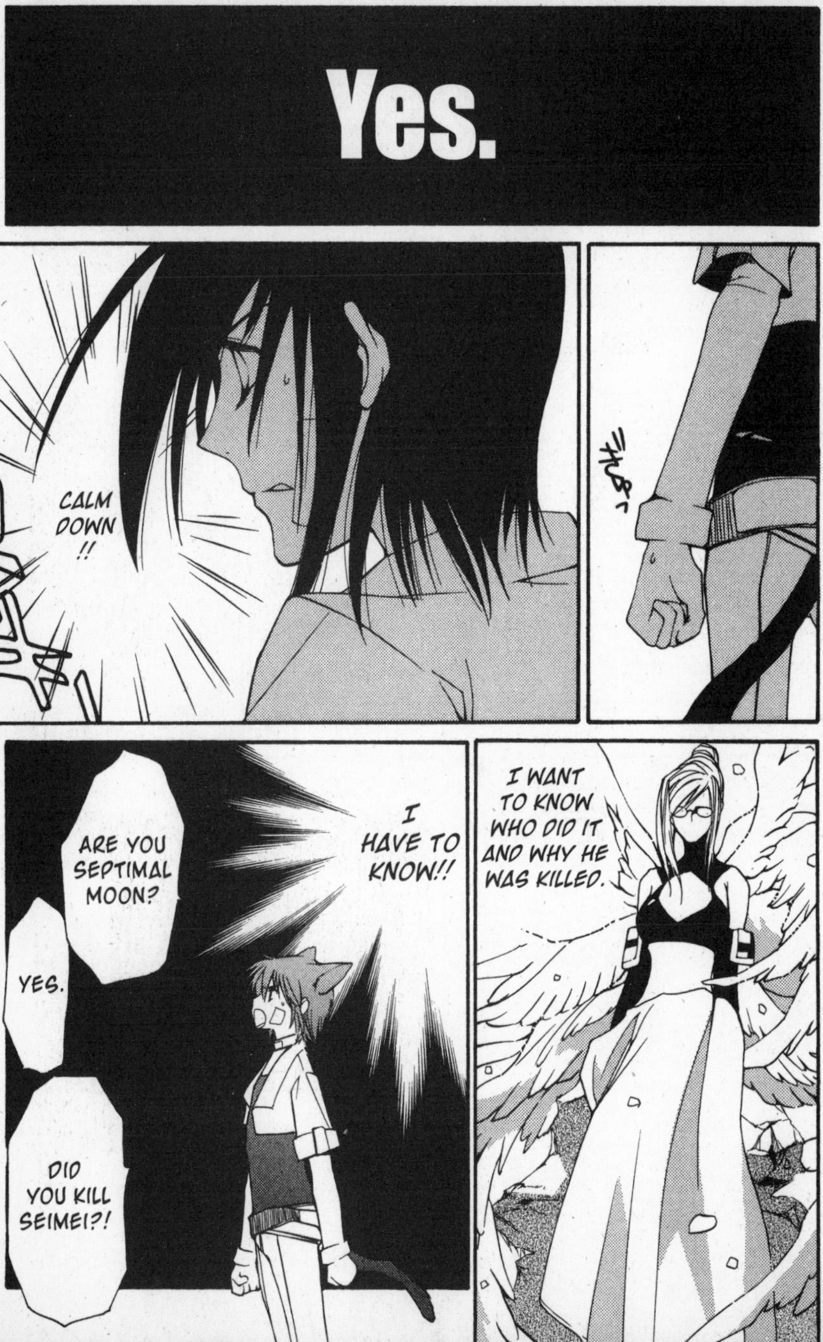
Yes.
CALM DOWN !!
I WANT TO KNOW WHO DID IT AND WHY HE WAS KILLED.
I HAVE TO KNOW!!
ARE YOU SEPTIMAL MOON?
YES.
DID YOU KILL SEIMEI?!

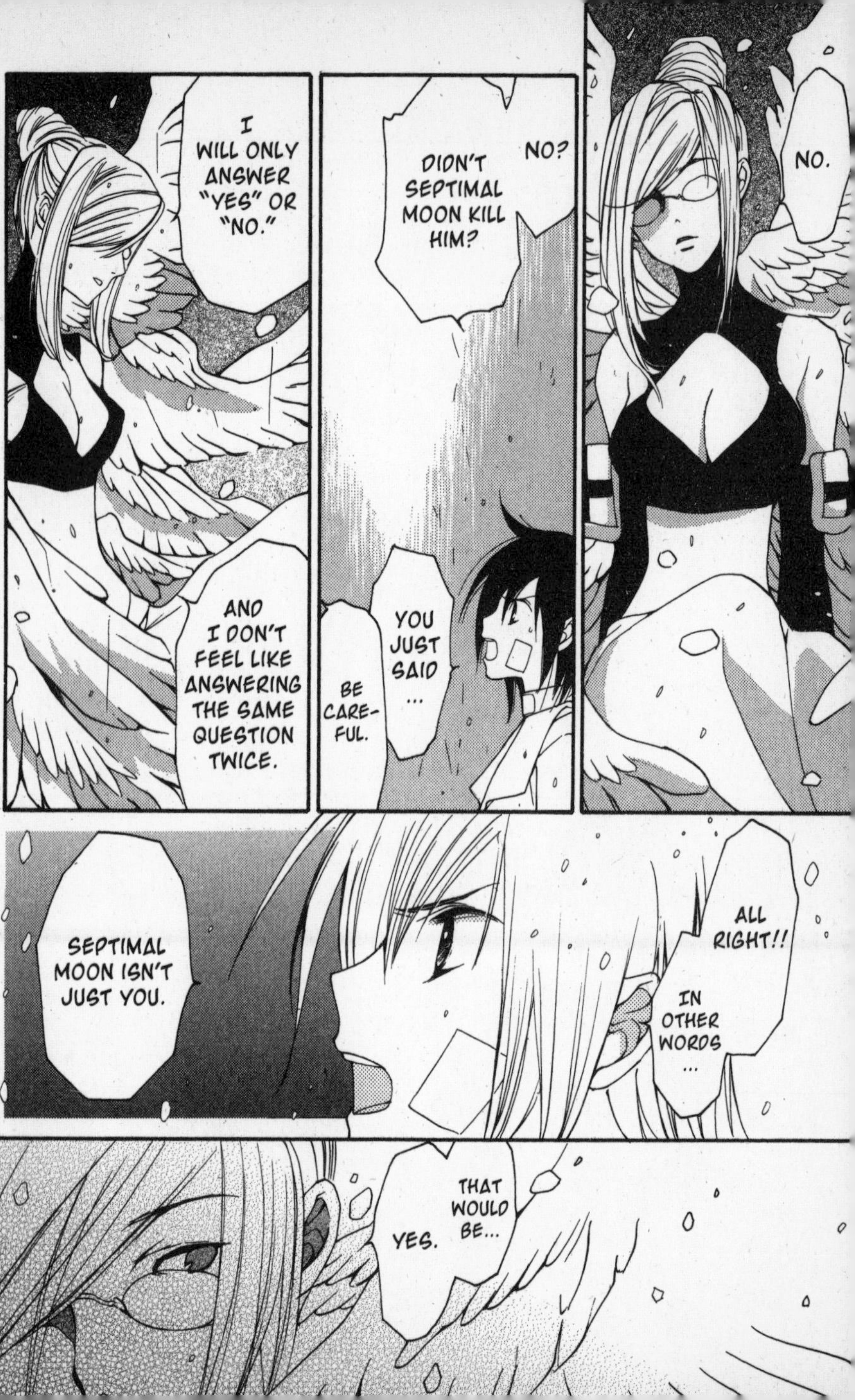
NO.
NO?
DIDN'T SEPTIMAL MOON KILL HIM?
YOU JUST SAID ...
BE CARE-FUL.
I WILL ONLY ANSWER "YES" OR "NO."
AND I DON'T FEEL LIKE ANSWERING THE SAME QUESTION TWICE.
ALL RIGHT!!
IN OTHER WORDS ...
SEPTIMAL MOON ISN'T JUST YOU.
THAT WOULD BE...
YES.

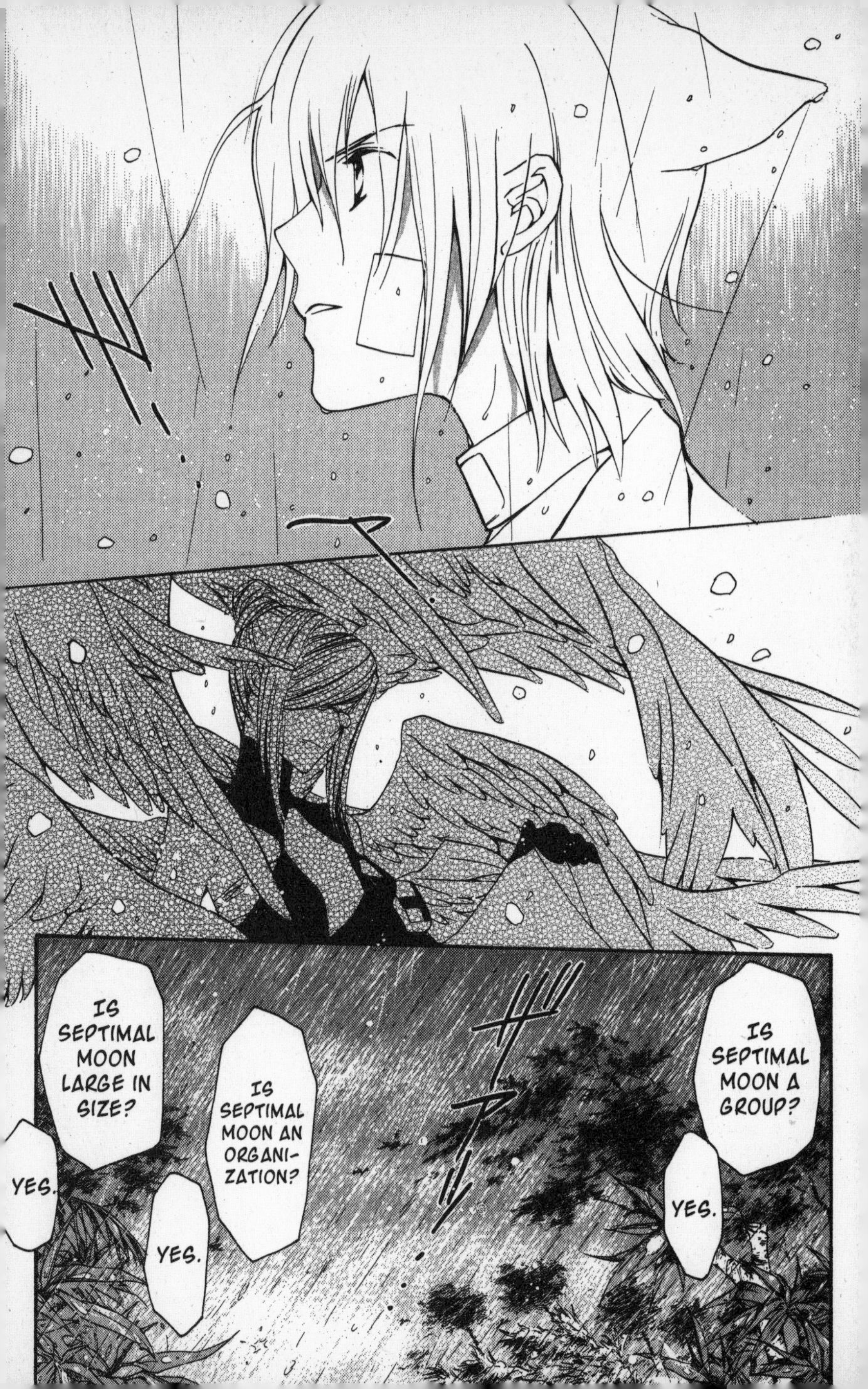
IS SEPTIMAL MOON A GROUP?
YES.
IS SEPTIMAL MOON AN ORGANI-ZATION?
YES.
IS SEPTIMAL MOON LARGE IN SIZE?
YES.

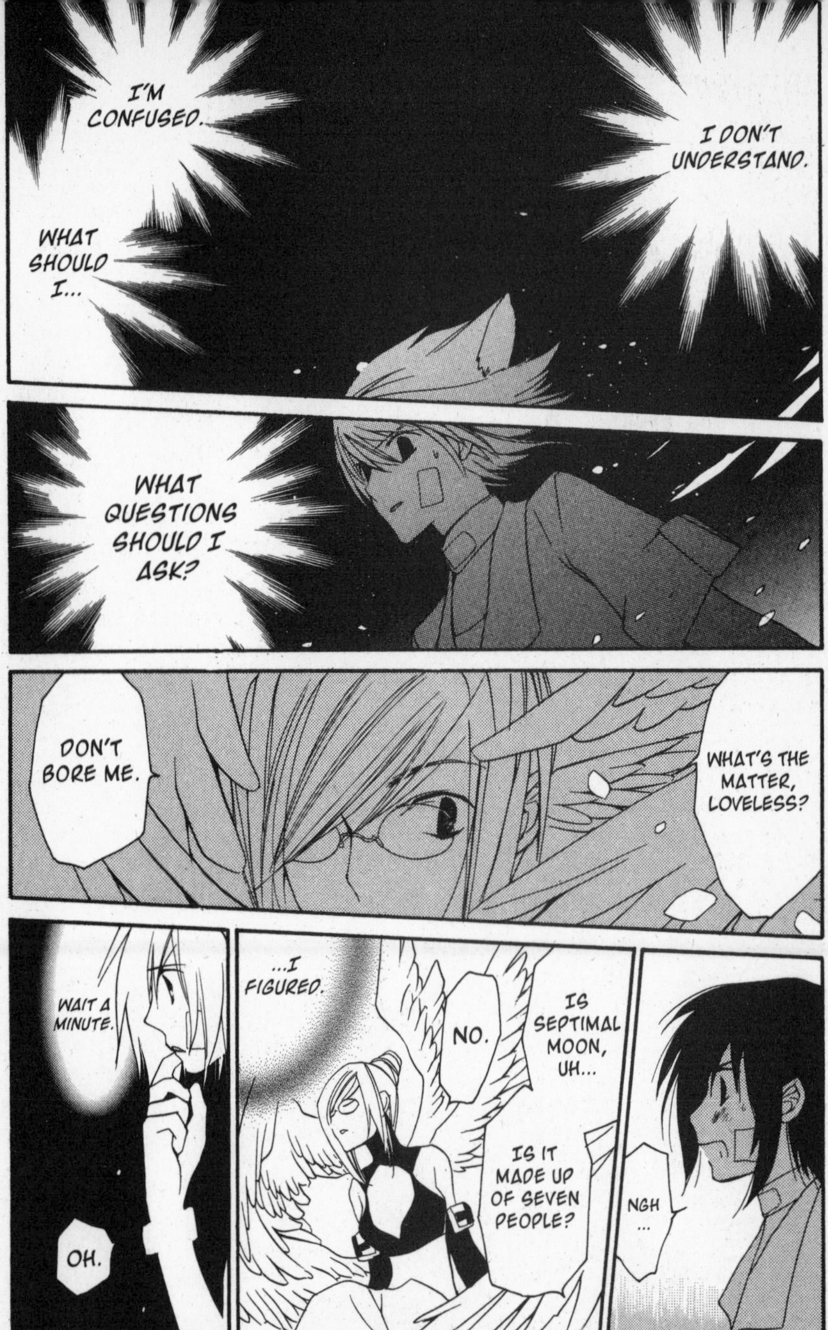
I DON'T UNDERSTAND.
I'M CONFUSED.
WHAT SHOULD I...
WHAT QUESTIONS SHOULD I ASK?
WHAT'S THE MATTER, LOVELESS?
DON'T BORE ME.
NGH...
IS SEPTIMAL MOON, UH...
IS IT MADE UP OF SEVEN PEOPLE?
NO.
...I FIGURED.
WAIT A MINUTE.
OH.

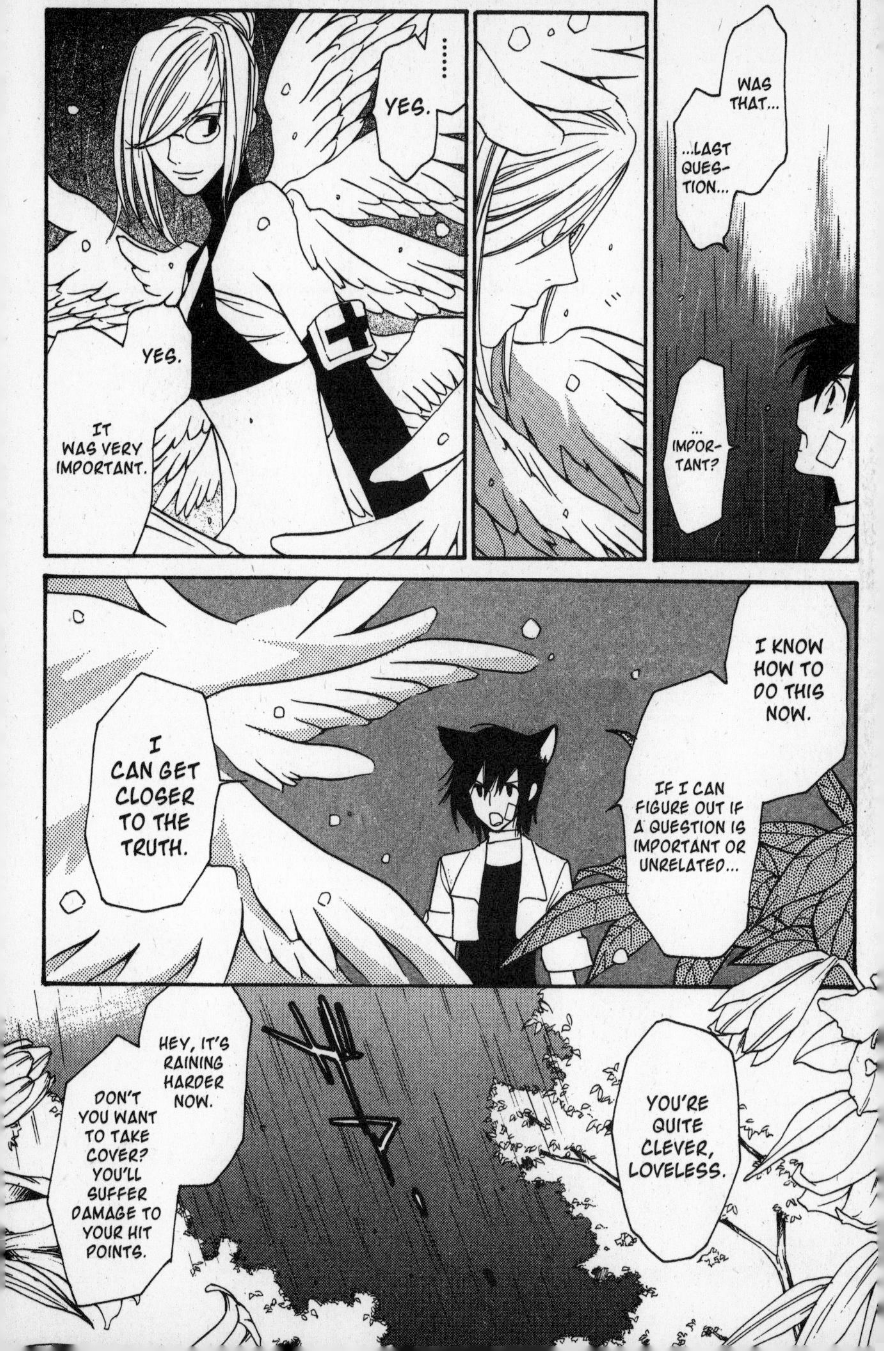
WAS THAT... ...LAST QUESTION...
...IMPORTANT?
......
YES.
YES.
IT WAS VERY IMPORTANT.
I KNOW HOW TO DO THIS NOW.
IF I CAN FIGURE OUT IF A QUESTION IS IMPORTANT OR UNRELATED...
I CAN GET CLOSER TO THE TRUTH.
YOU'RE QUITE CLEVER, LOVELESS.
HEY, IT'S RAINING HARDER NOW.
DON'T YOU WANT TO TAKE COVER? YOU'LL SUFFER DAMAGE TO YOUR HIT POINTS.

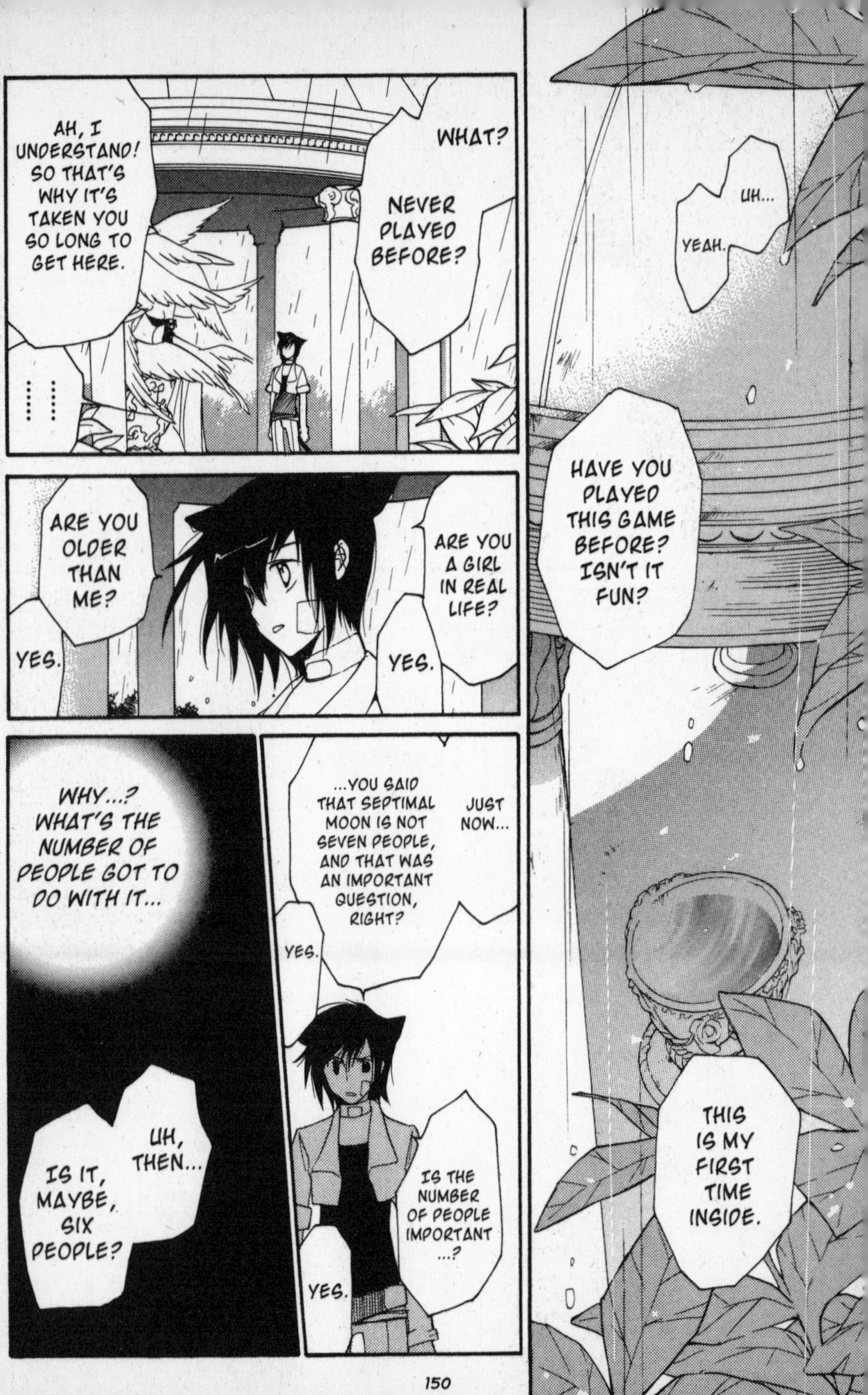
UH...
YEAH.
HAVE YOU PLAYED THIS GAME BEFORE? ISN'T IT FUN?
THIS IS MY FIRST TIME INSIDE.
WHAT?
NEVER PLAYED BEFORE?
AH, I UNDERSTAND! SO THAT'S WHY IT'S TAKEN YOU SO LONG TO GET HERE.
......
ARE YOU A GIRL IN REAL LIFE?
YES.
ARE YOU OLDER THAN ME?
YES.
JUST NOW...
...YOU SAID THAT SEPTIMAL MOON IS NOT SEVEN PEOPLE, AND THAT WAS AN IMPORTANT QUESTION, RIGHT?
YES.
IS THE NUMBER OF PEOPLE IMPORTANT ...?
YES.
WHY...? WHAT'S THE NUMBER OF PEOPLE GOT TO DO WITH IT...
UH, THEN...
IS IT, MAYBE, SIX PEOPLE?

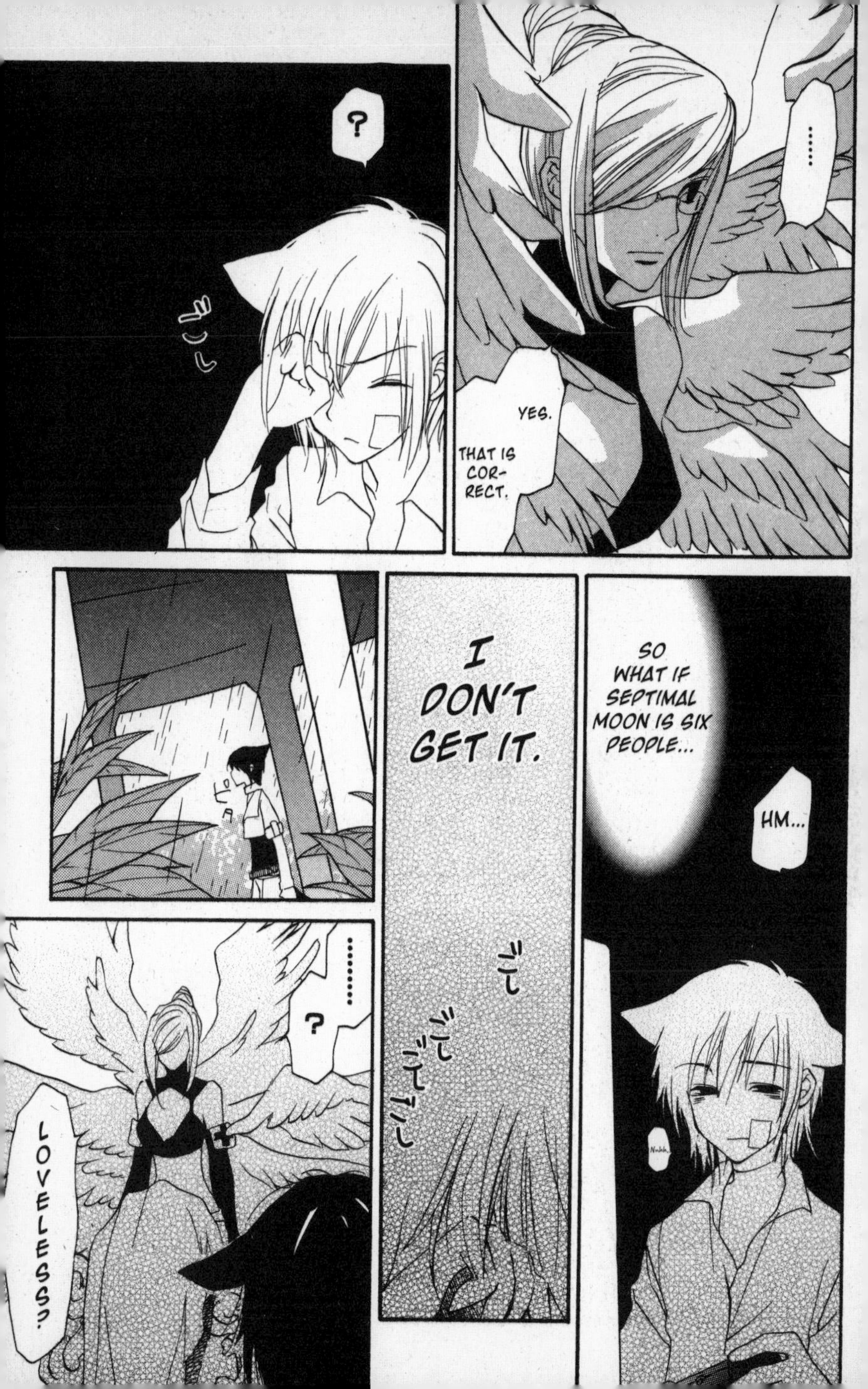
......
YES.
THAT IS COR-RECT.
?
SO WHAT IF SEPTIMAL MOON IS SIX PEOPLE...
HM...
I DON'T GET IT.
....
?
LOVELESS?

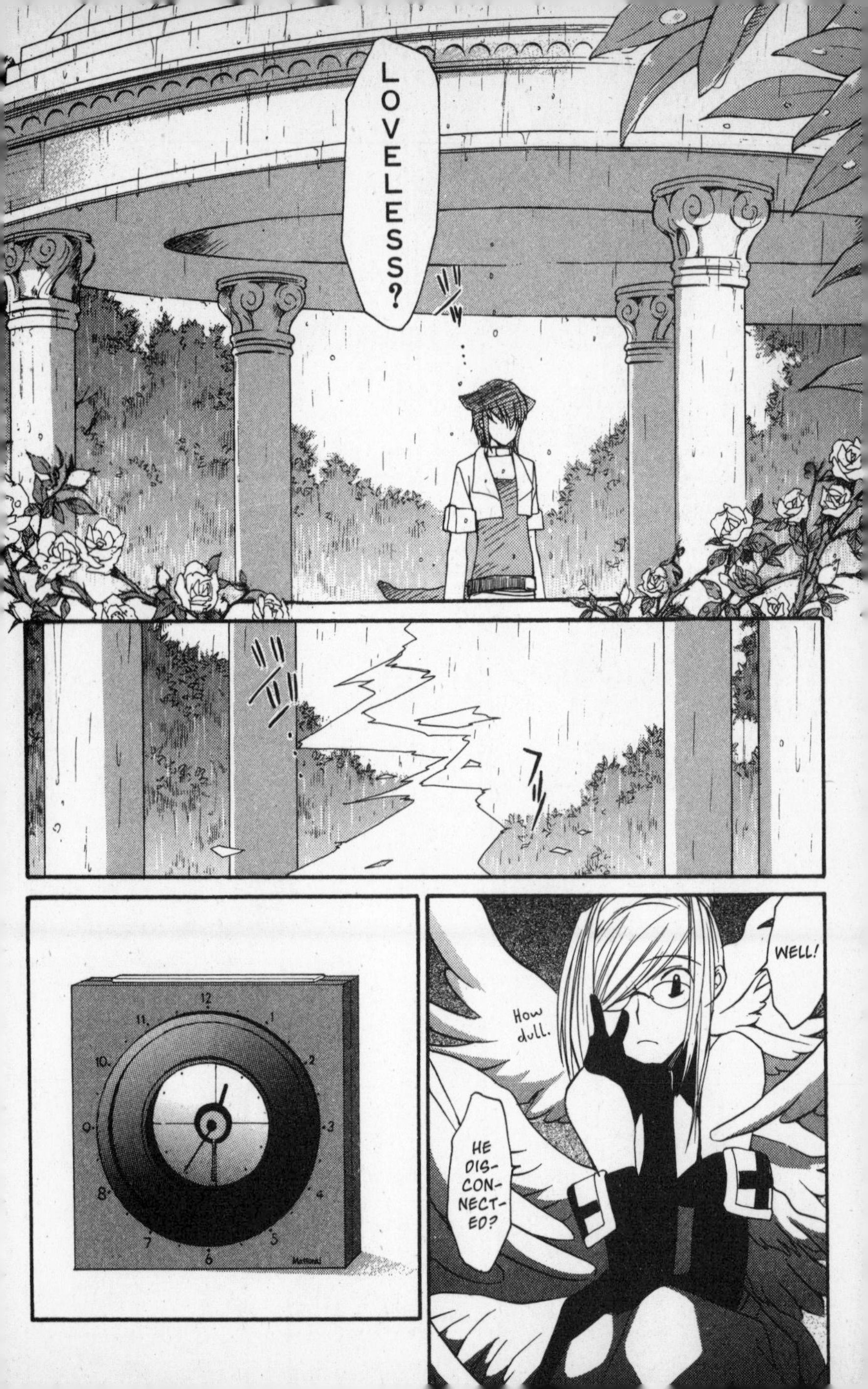
LOVELESS?
WELL!
How dull.
HE DISCONNECTED?

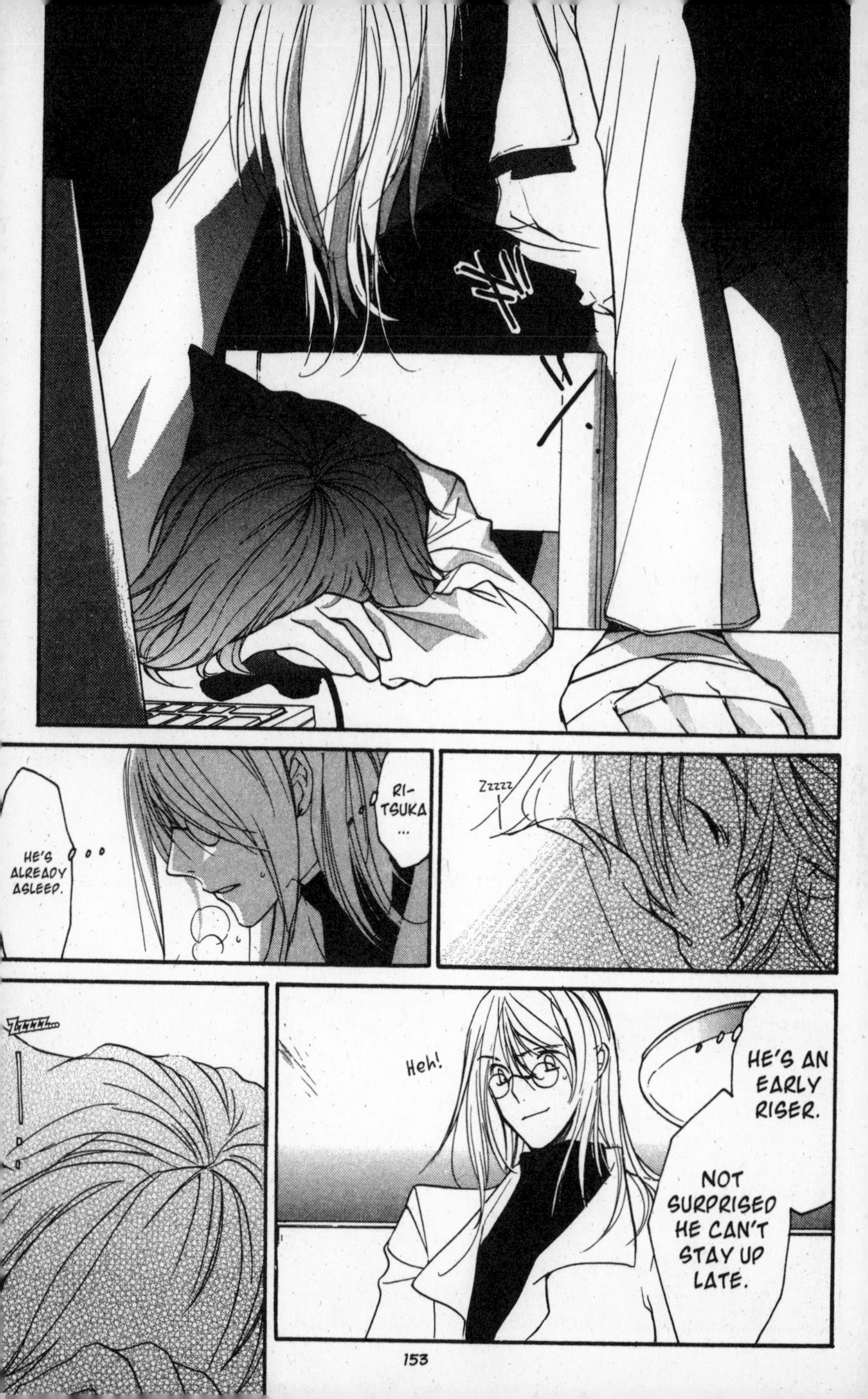
RI-TSUKA ...
HE'S ALREADY ASLEEP.
Zzzzz
HE'S AN EARLY RISER.
NOT SURPRISED HE CAN'T STAY UP LATE.
Heh!
Zzzzz...

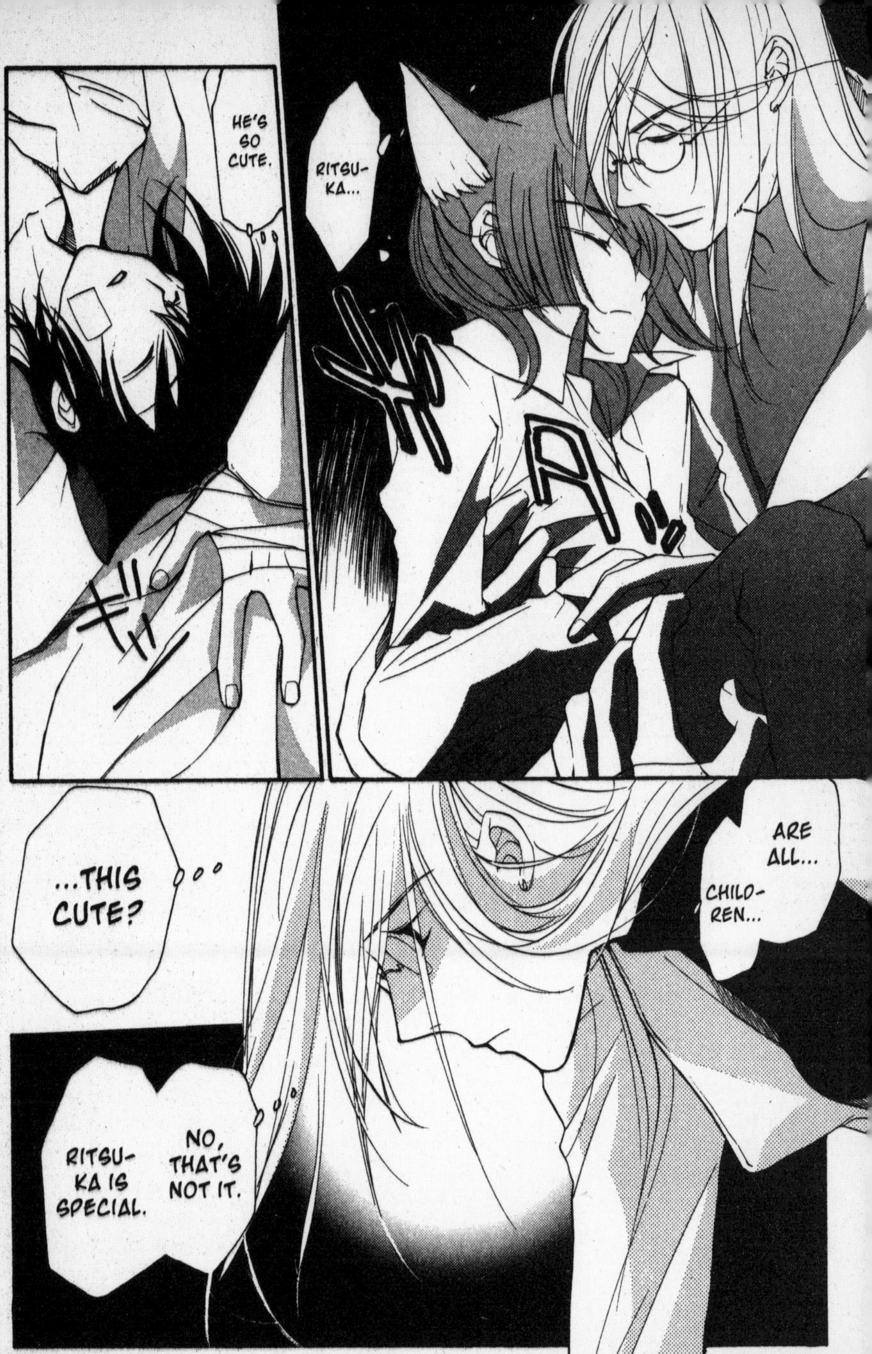
RITSU-KA...
HE'S SO CUTE.
ARE ALL... CHILD-REN...
...THIS CUTE?
NO, THAT'S NOT IT.
RITSU-KA IS SPECIAL.

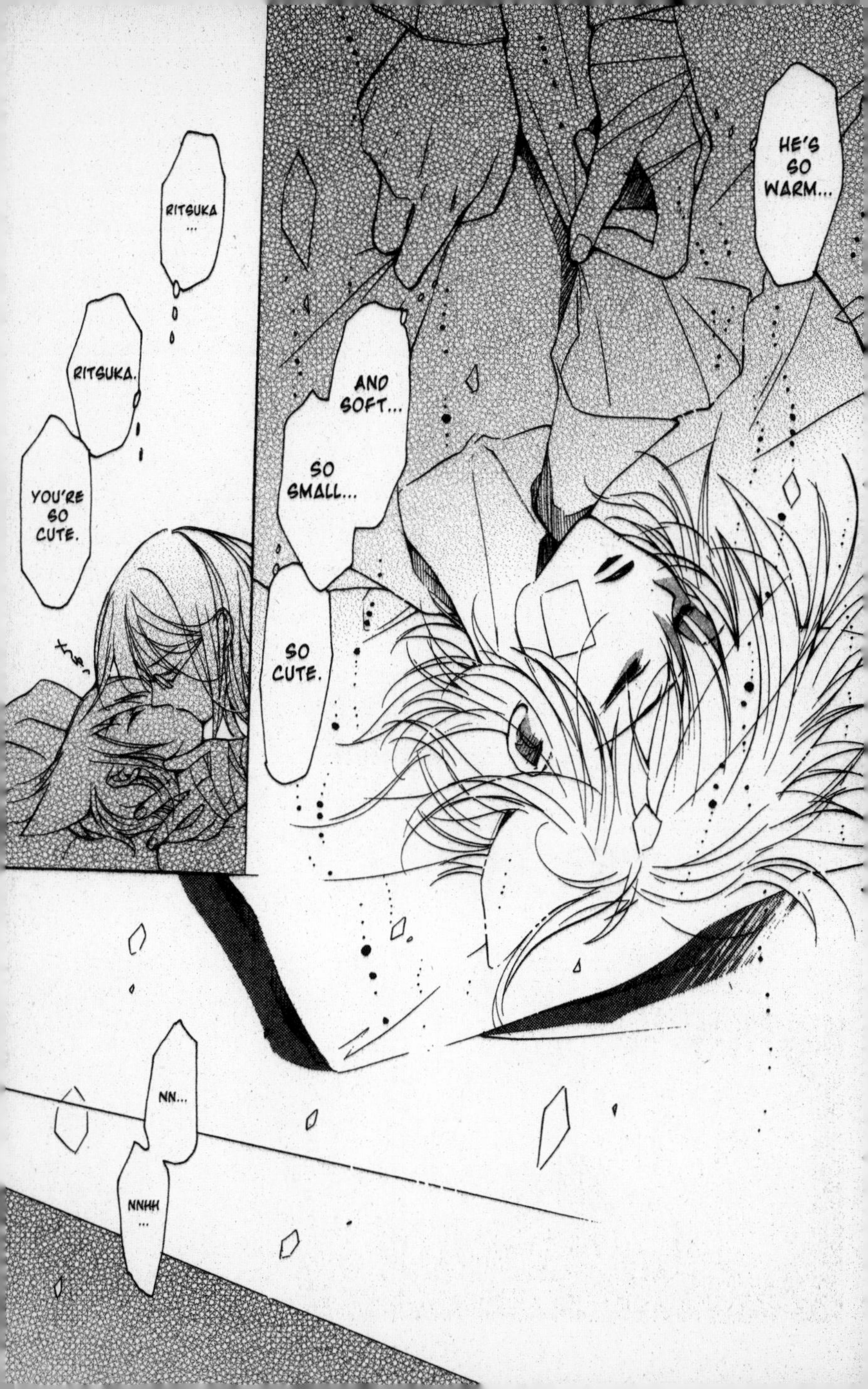

HE'S SO WARM...
AND SOFT...
SO SMALL...
SO CUTE.
RITSUKA...
RITSUKA.
YOU'RE SO CUTE.
NN...
NNHH...

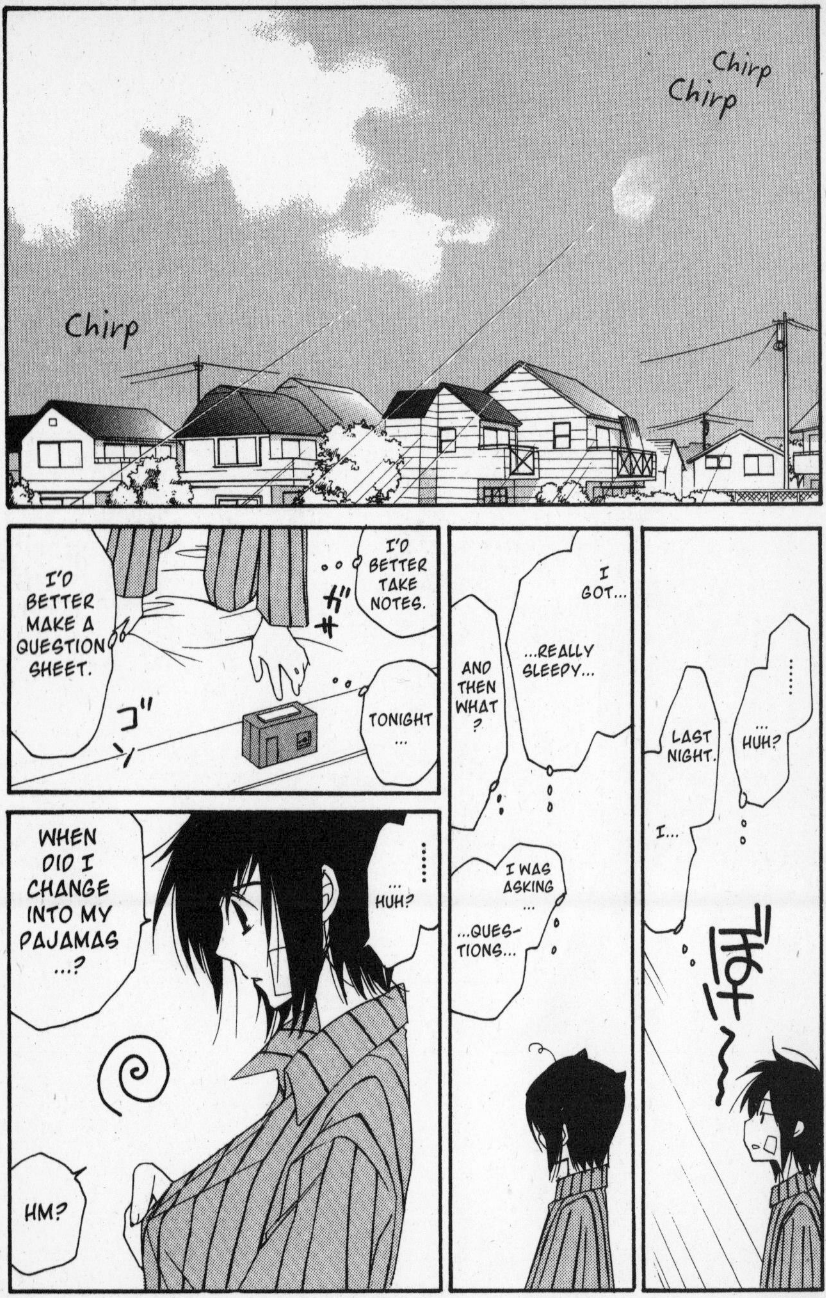
Chirp
Chirp
Chirp
......
... HUH?
LAST NIGHT.
I...
ぽけ〜
I GOT...
...REALLY SLEEPY...
AND THEN WHAT?
I WAS ASKING... ...QUES-TIONS...
I'D BETTER TAKE NOTES.
ガ
TONIGHT...
I'D BETTER MAKE A QUESTION SHEET.
ゴン
......
... HUH?
WHEN DID I CHANGE INTO MY PAJAMAS...?
HM?

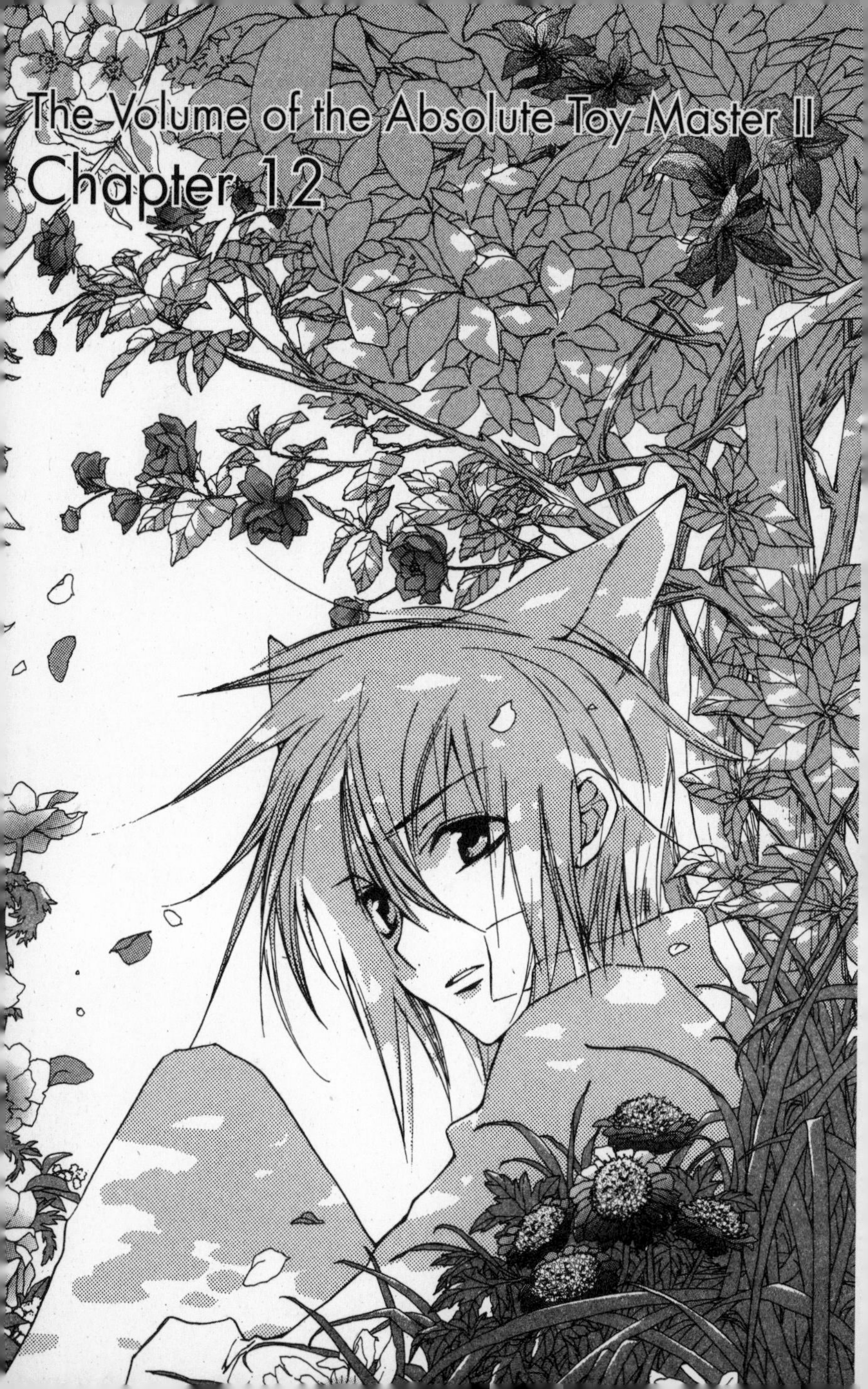
The Volume of the Absolute Toy Master II
Chapter 12

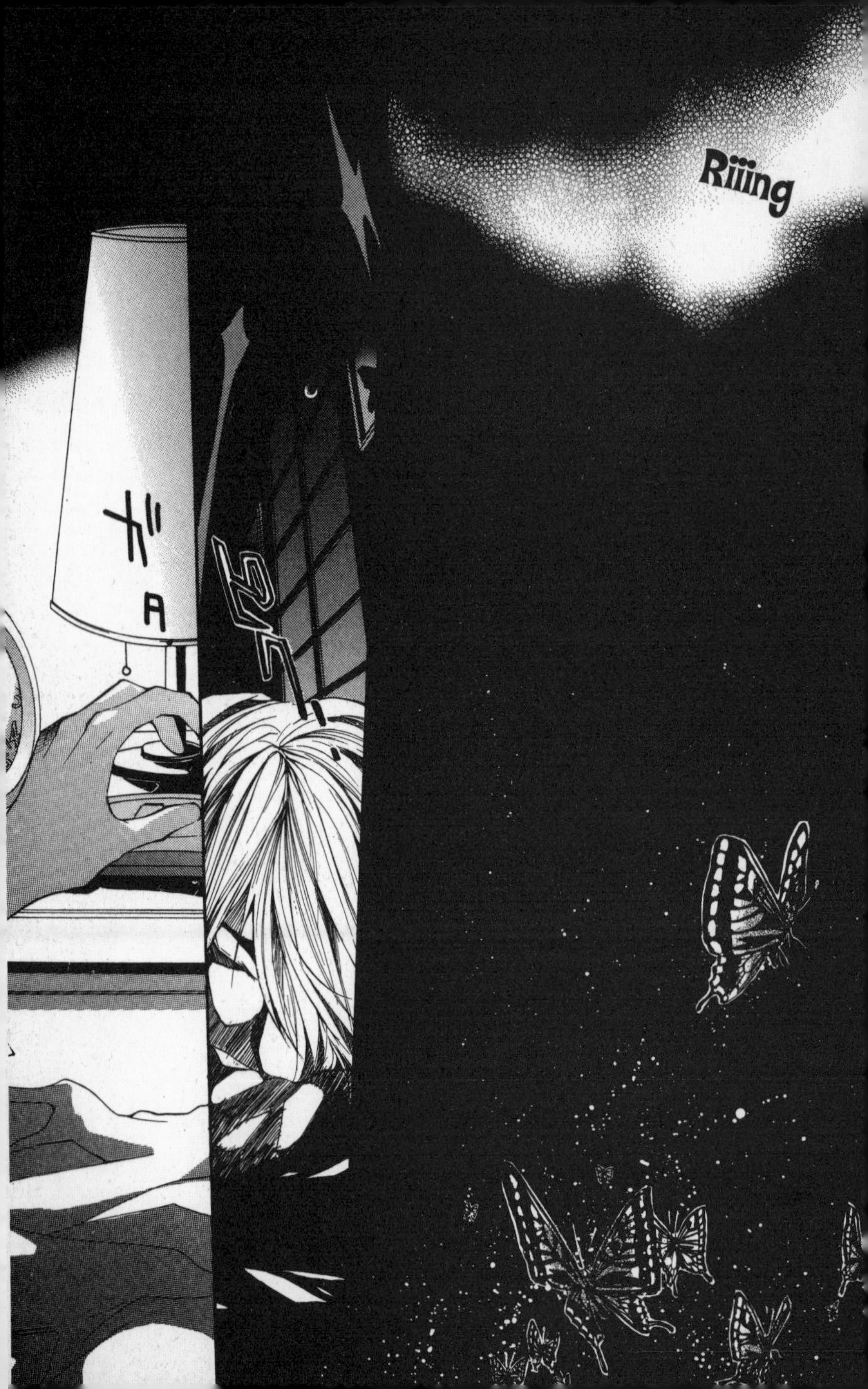
Riiing
ガ
A

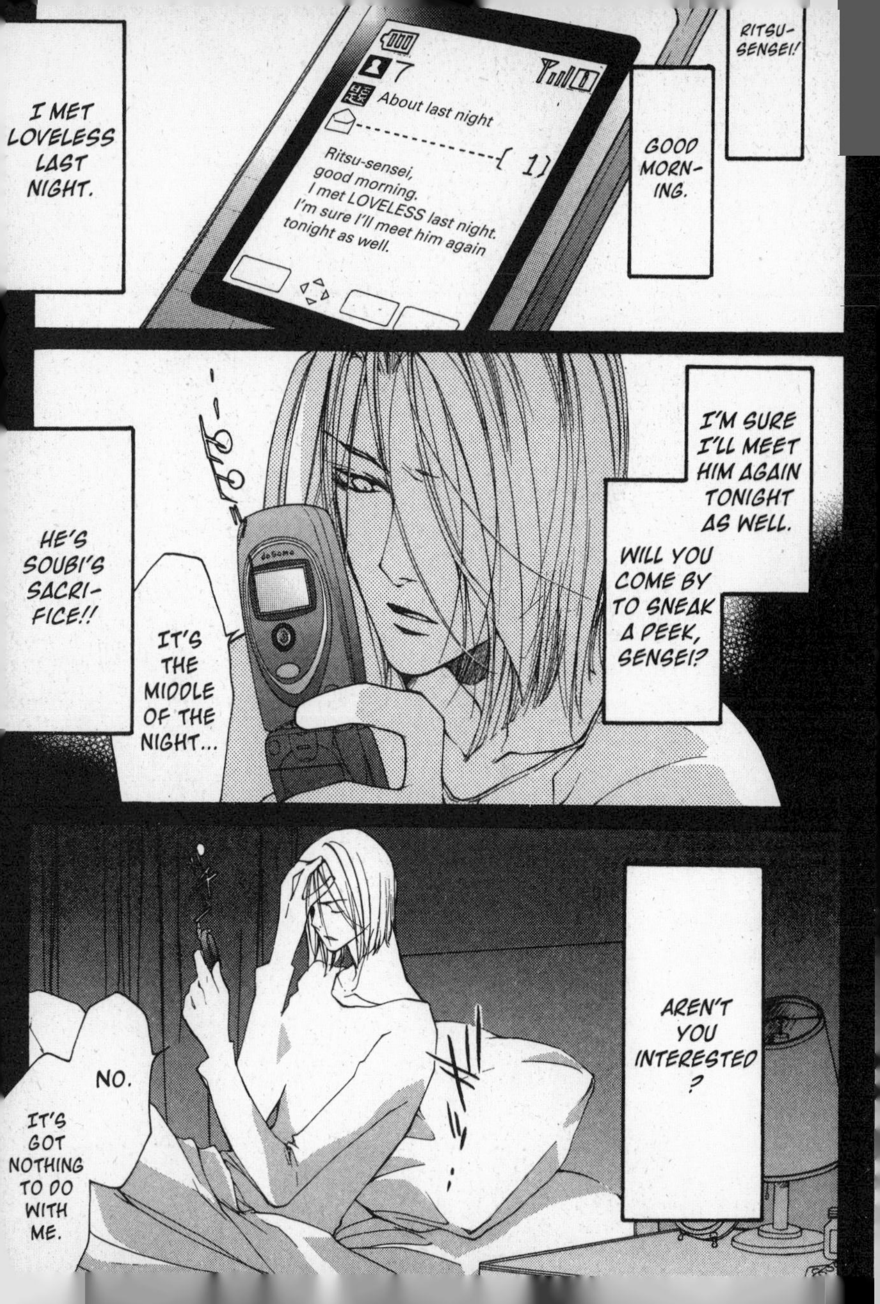
RITSU-SENSEI!
GOOD MORNING.
7
About last night
1
Ritsu-sensei, good morning. I met LOVELESS last night. I'm sure I'll meet him again tonight as well.
I MET LOVELESS LAST NIGHT.
I'M SURE I'LL MEET HIM AGAIN TONIGHT AS WELL.
WILL YOU COME BY TO SNEAK A PEEK, SENSEI?
HE'S SOUBI'S SACRIFICE!!
IT'S THE MIDDLE OF THE NIGHT...
AREN'T YOU INTERESTED?
NO.
IT'S GOT NOTHING TO DO WITH ME.

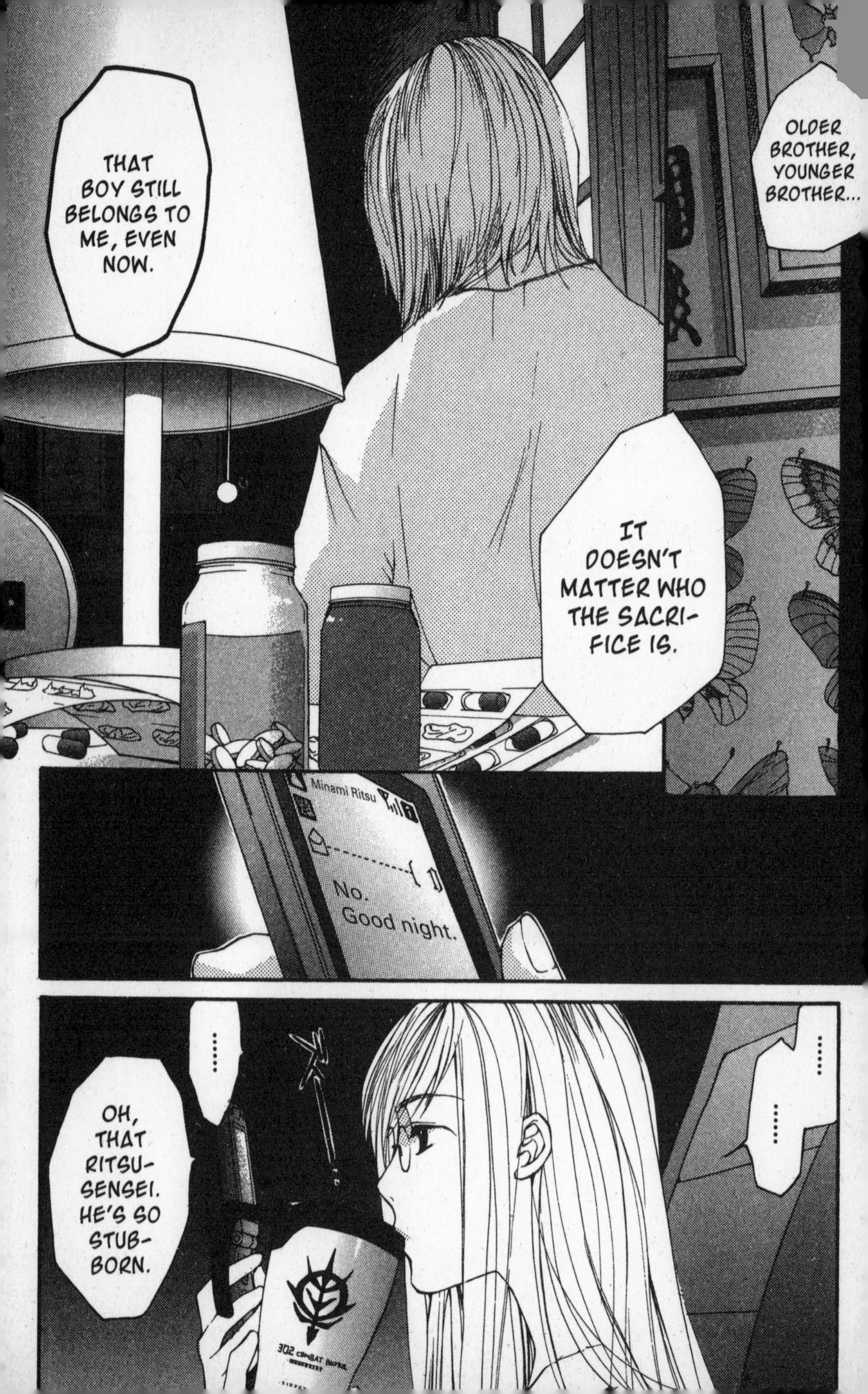
OLDER BROTHER, YOUNGER BROTHER...
IT DOESN'T MATTER WHO THE SACRIFICE IS.
THAT BOY STILL BELONGS TO ME, EVEN NOW.
Minami Ritsu
No.
Good night.
......
......
......
OH, THAT RITSU-SENSEI. HE'S SO STUBBORN.
302 COMBAT PATROL

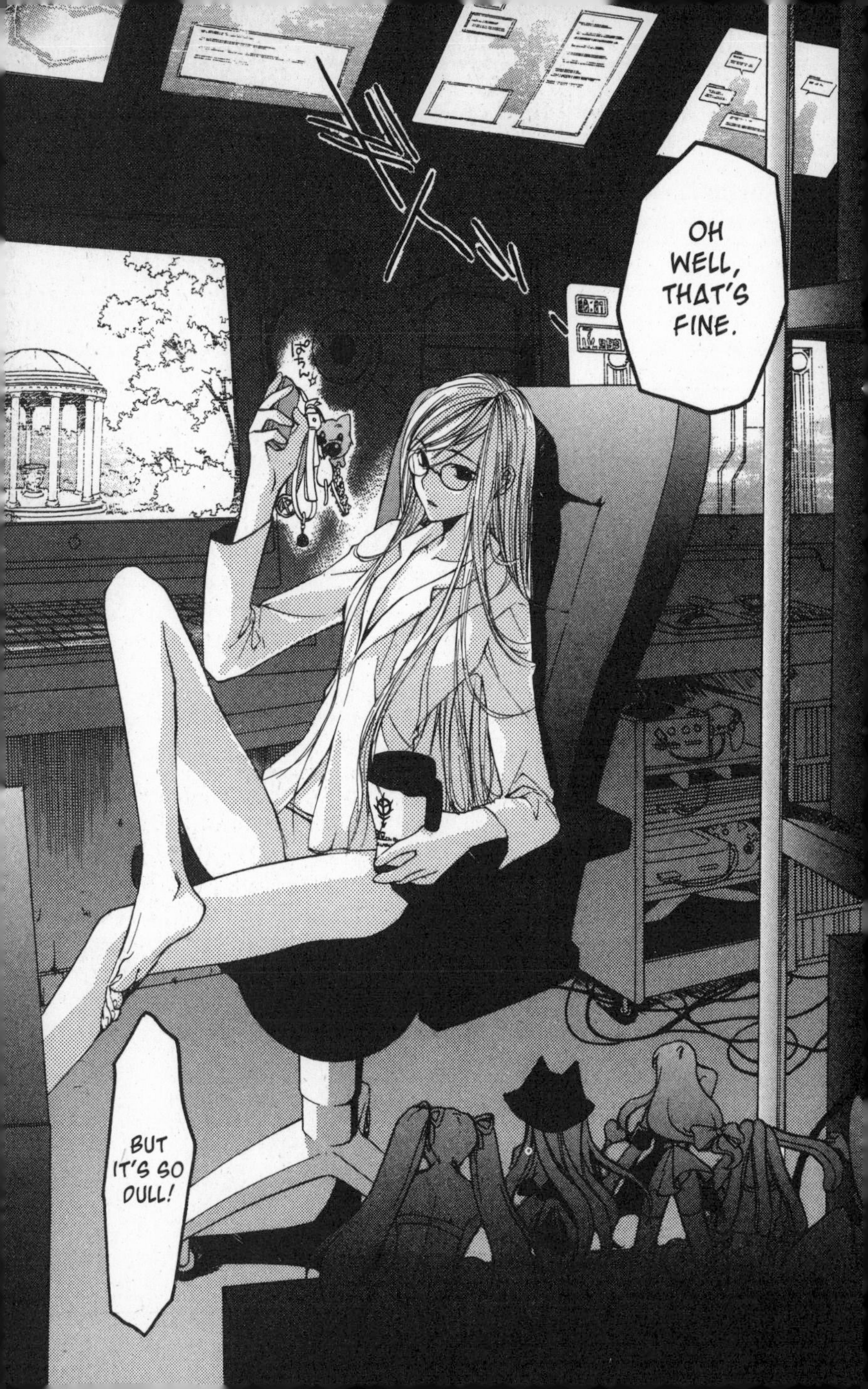
OH WELL, THAT'S FINE.
BUT IT'S SO DULL!

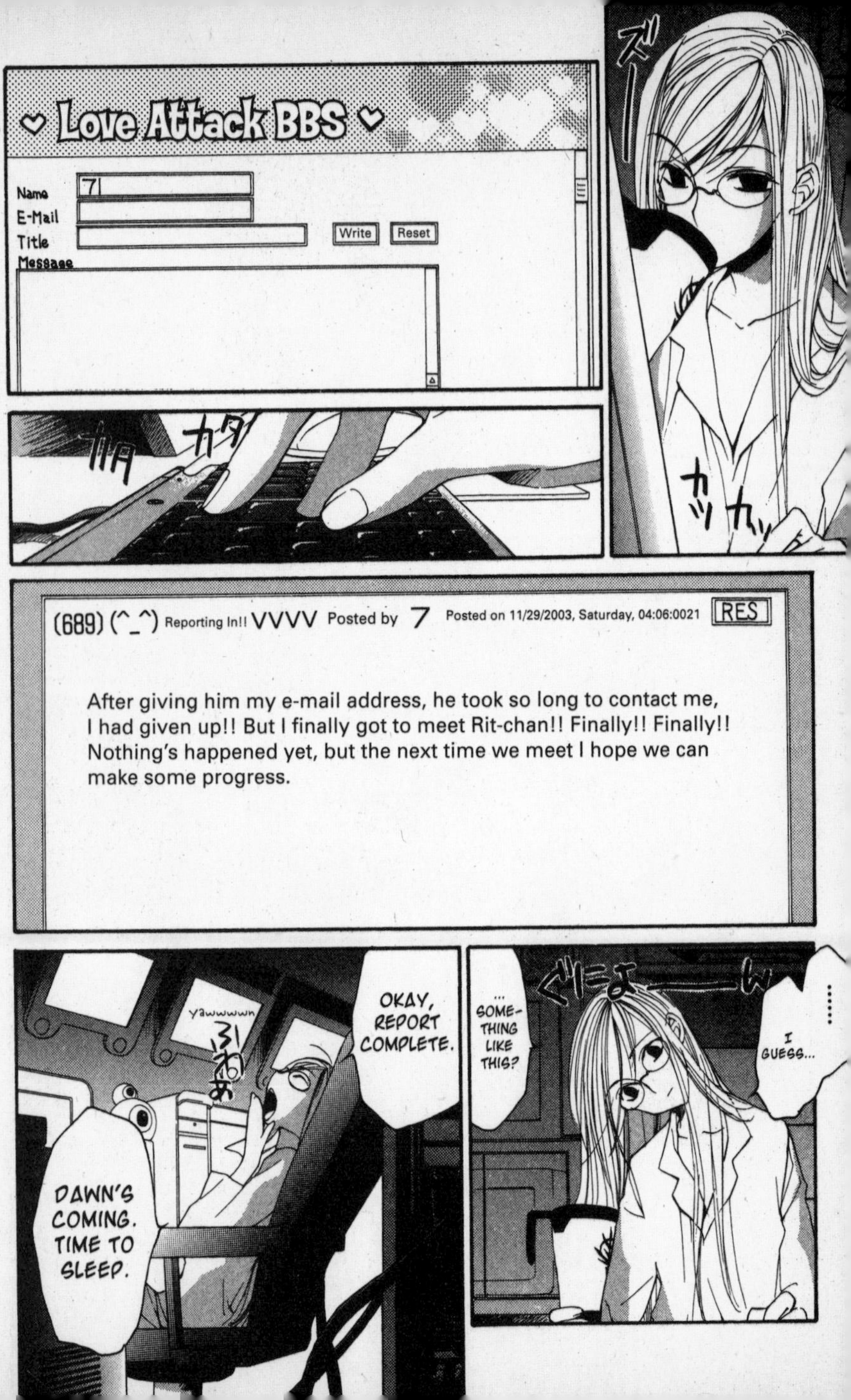
ズー
カッカッ
Love Attack BBS
Name 7
E-Mail
Title
Message
Write
Reset
カタ カタ
(689) (^_^) Reporting In!! VVVV Posted by 7 Posted on 11/29/2003, Saturday, 04:06:0021
RES
After giving him my e-mail address, he took so long to contact me, I had given up!! But I finally got to meet Rit-chan!! Finally!! Finally!! Nothing's happened yet, but the next time we meet I hope we can make some progress.
...... I GUESS...
ぐにょーん
... SOMETHING LIKE THIS?
OKAY, REPORT COMPLETE.
yawwwwn
ふわあ
DAWN'S COMING. TIME TO SLEEP.

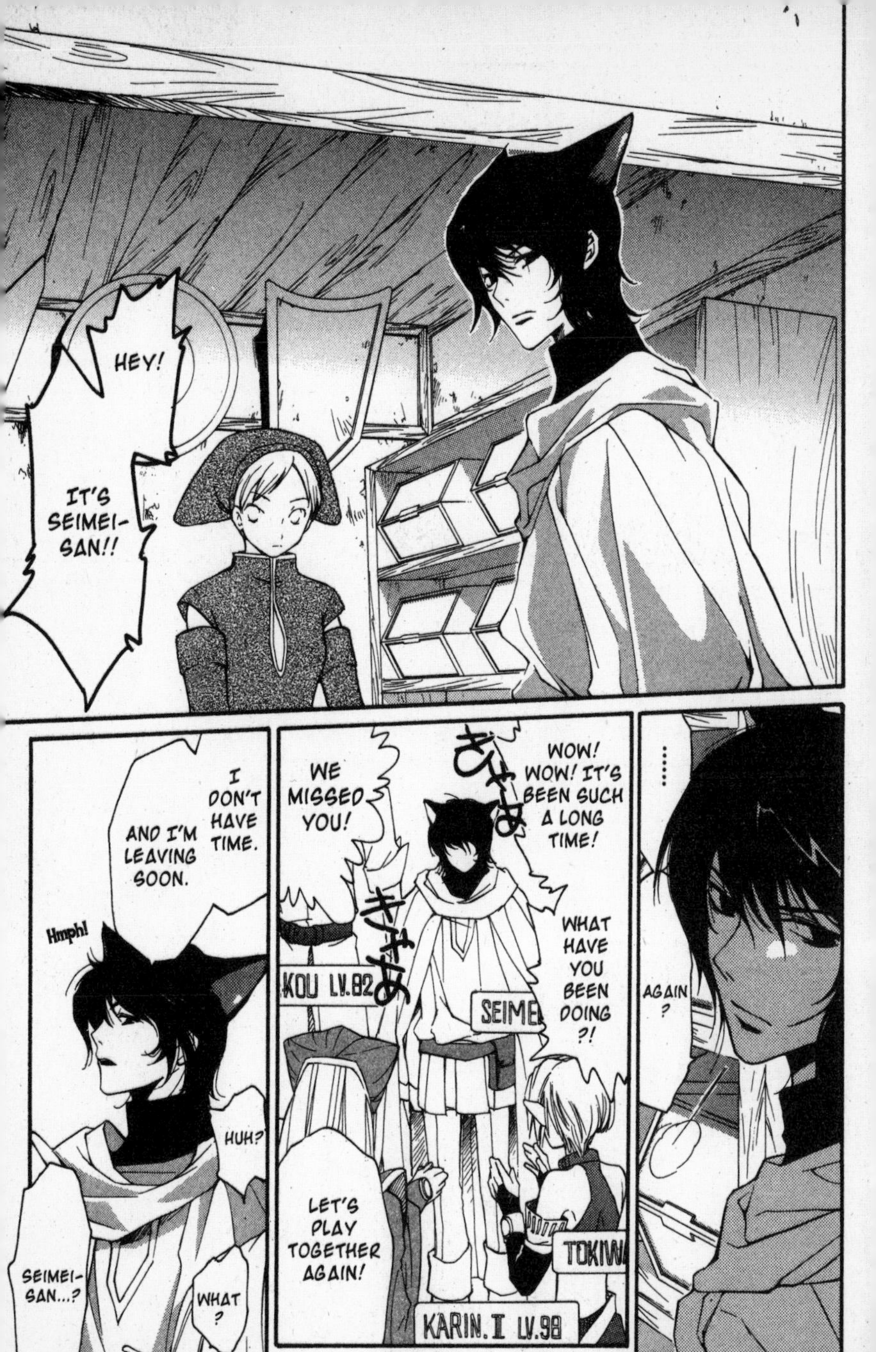
HEY!
IT'S SEIMEI-SAN!!
......
AGAIN?
きゃあ
WOW! WOW! IT'S BEEN SUCH A LONG TIME!
WE MISSED YOU!
きゃあ
KOU LV.82
SEIME
WHAT HAVE YOU BEEN DOING?!
TOKIW
LET'S PLAY TOGETHER AGAIN!
KARIN.II LV.98
I DON'T HAVE TIME.
AND I'M LEAVING SOON.
Hmph!
HUH?
SEIMEI-SAN...?
WHAT?

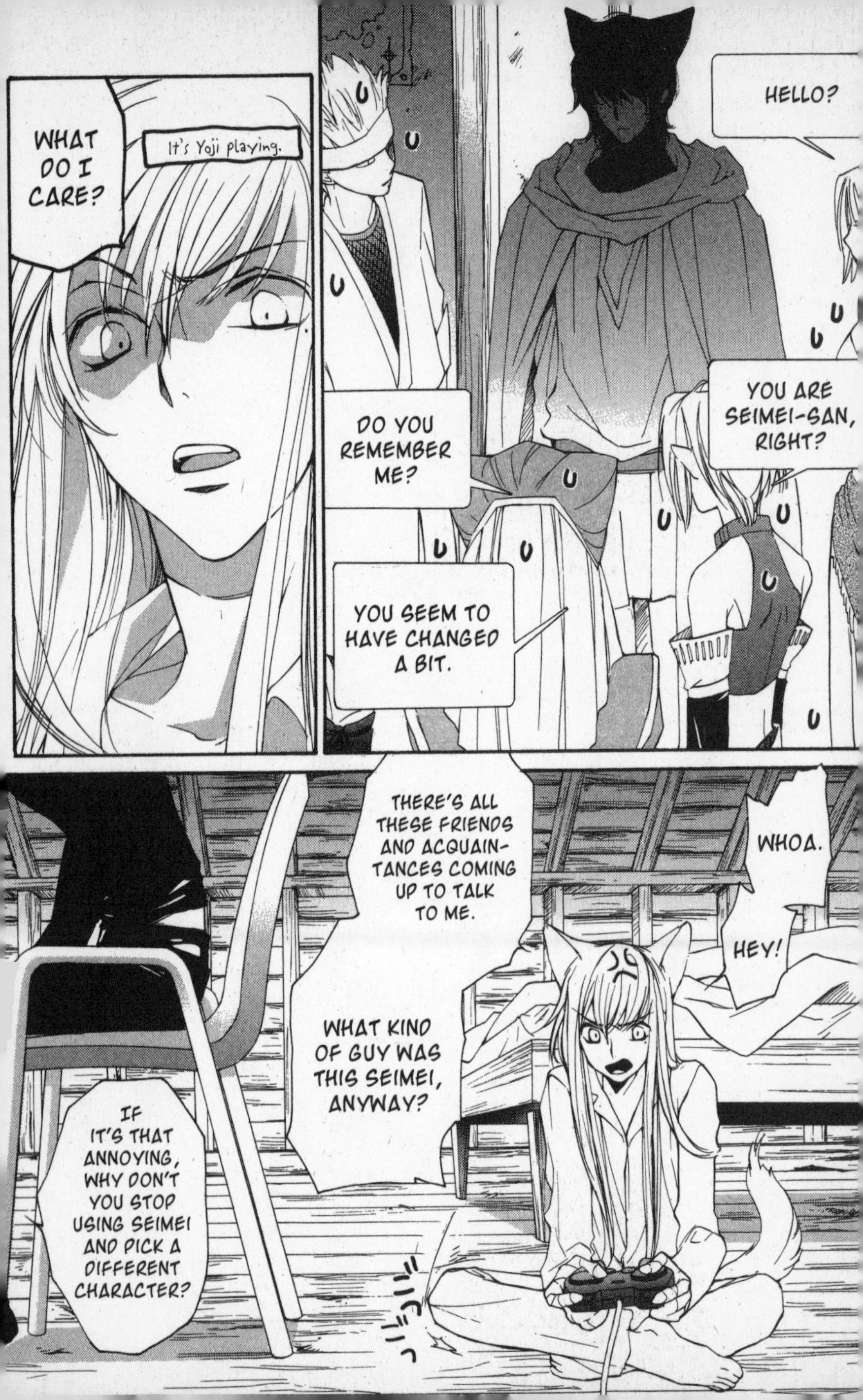
HELLO?
YOU ARE SEIMEI-SAN, RIGHT?
DO YOU REMEMBER ME?
YOU SEEM TO HAVE CHANGED A BIT.
It's Yoji playing.
WHAT DO I CARE?
WHOA.
HEY!
THERE'S ALL THESE FRIENDS AND ACQUAIN-TANCES COMING UP TO TALK TO ME.
WHAT KIND OF GUY WAS THIS SEIMEI, ANYWAY?
IF IT'S THAT ANNOYING, WHY DON'T YOU STOP USING SEIMEI AND PICK A DIFFERENT CHARACTER?

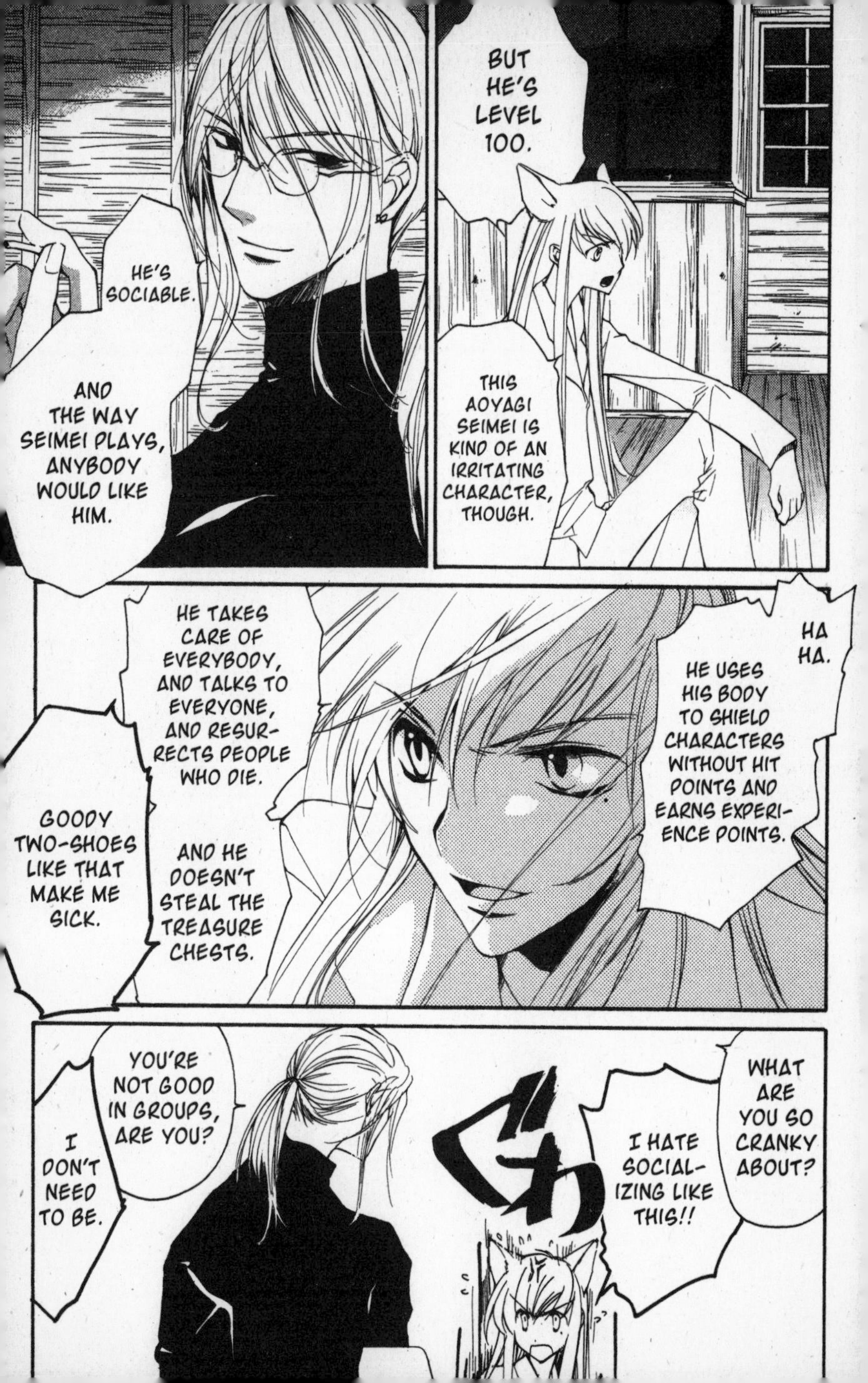

BUT HE'S LEVEL 100.
THIS AOYAGI SEIMEI IS KIND OF AN IRRITATING CHARACTER, THOUGH.
HE'S SOCIABLE.
AND THE WAY SEIMEI PLAYS, ANYBODY WOULD LIKE HIM.
HA HA.
HE USES HIS BODY TO SHIELD CHARACTERS WITHOUT HIT POINTS AND EARNS EXPERIENCE POINTS.
HE TAKES CARE OF EVERYBODY, AND TALKS TO EVERYONE, AND RESURRECTS PEOPLE WHO DIE.
AND HE DOESN'T STEAL THE TREASURE CHESTS.
GOODY TWO-SHOES LIKE THAT MAKE ME SICK.
WHAT ARE YOU SO CRANKY ABOUT?
I HATE SOCIALIZING LIKE THIS!!
YOU'RE NOT GOOD IN GROUPS, ARE YOU?
I DON'T NEED TO BE.

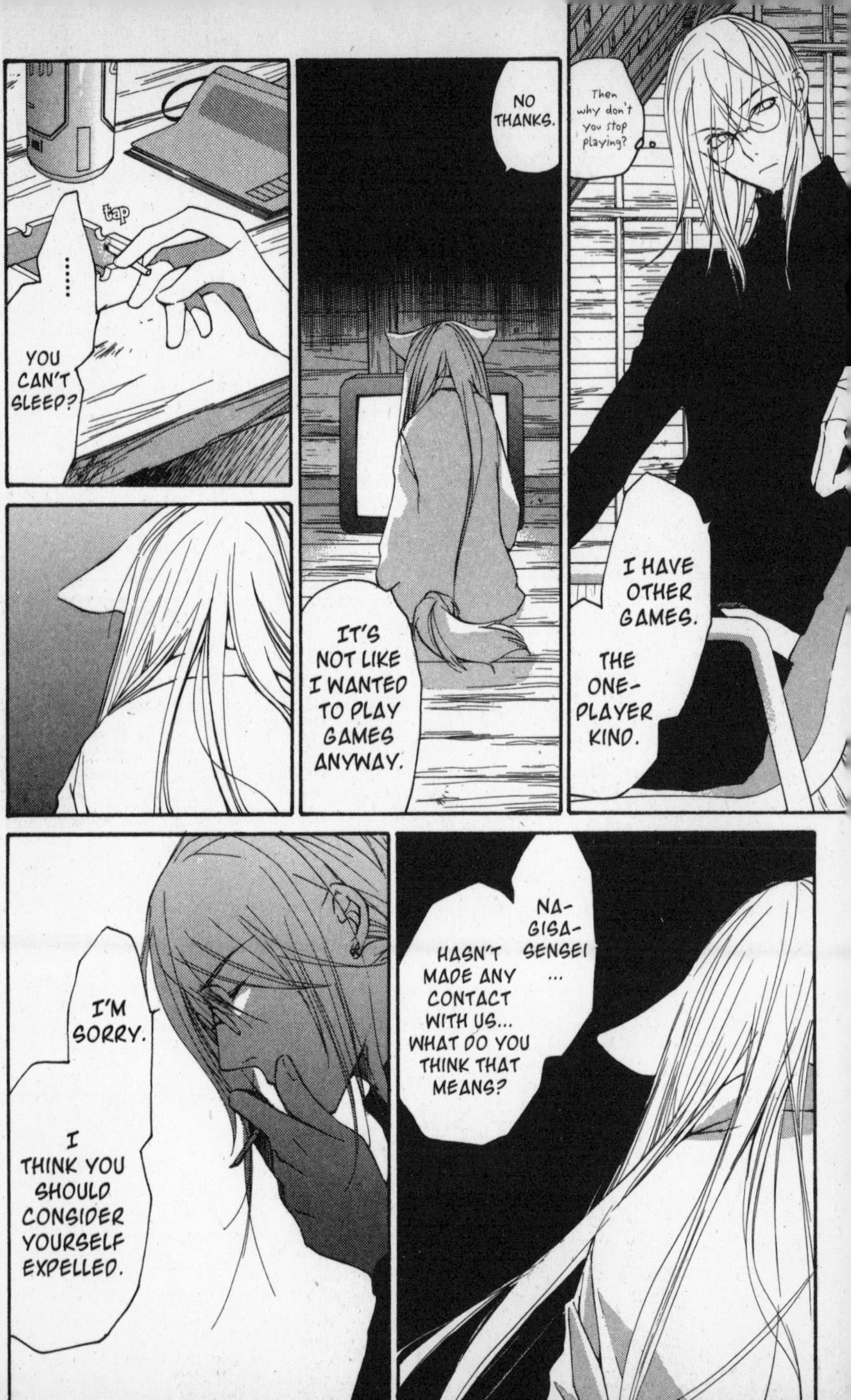
Then why don't you stop playing?
I HAVE OTHER GAMES.
THE ONE-PLAYER KIND.
NO THANKS.
IT'S NOT LIKE I WANTED TO PLAY GAMES ANYWAY.
tap
......
YOU CAN'T SLEEP?
NAGISA-SENSEI...
HASN'T MADE ANY CONTACT WITH US... WHAT DO YOU THINK THAT MEANS?
I'M SORRY.
I THINK YOU SHOULD CONSIDER YOURSELF EXPELLED.

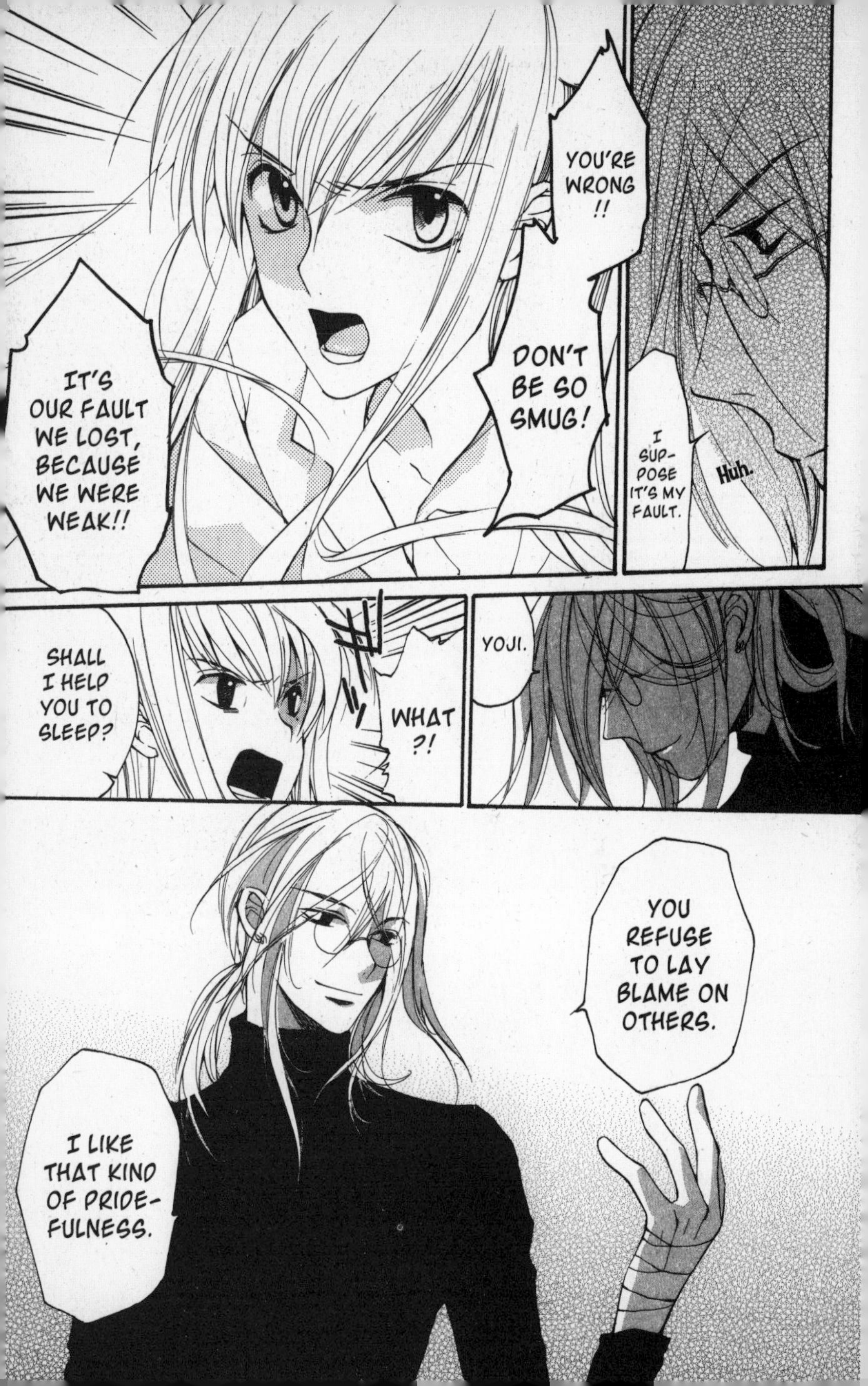
Huh.
I SUPPOSE IT'S MY FAULT.
YOU'RE WRONG!!
DON'T BE SO SMUG!
IT'S OUR FAULT WE LOST, BECAUSE WE WERE WEAK!!
YOJI.
WHAT?!
SHALL I HELP YOU TO SLEEP?
YOU REFUSE TO LAY BLAME ON OTHERS.
I LIKE THAT KIND OF PRIDE-FULNESS.

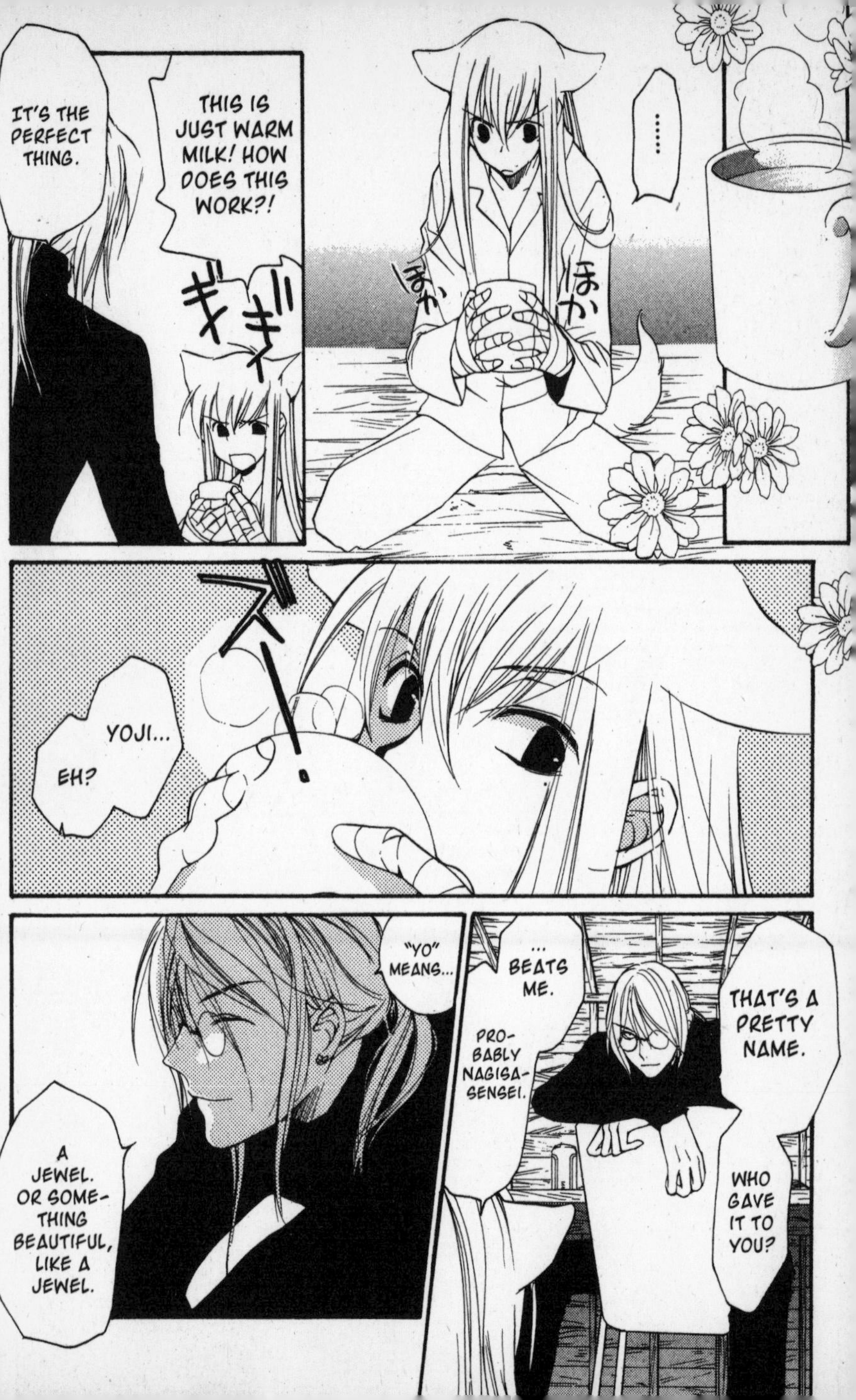
......
ほか ほか
THIS IS JUST WARM MILK! HOW DOES THIS WORK?!
IT'S THE PERFECT THING.
YOJI...
EH?
THAT'S A PRETTY NAME.
WHO GAVE IT TO YOU?
... BEATS ME.
PRO-BABLY NAGISA-SENSEI.
"YO" MEANS...
A JEWEL. OR SOME-THING BEAUTIFUL, LIKE A JEWEL.

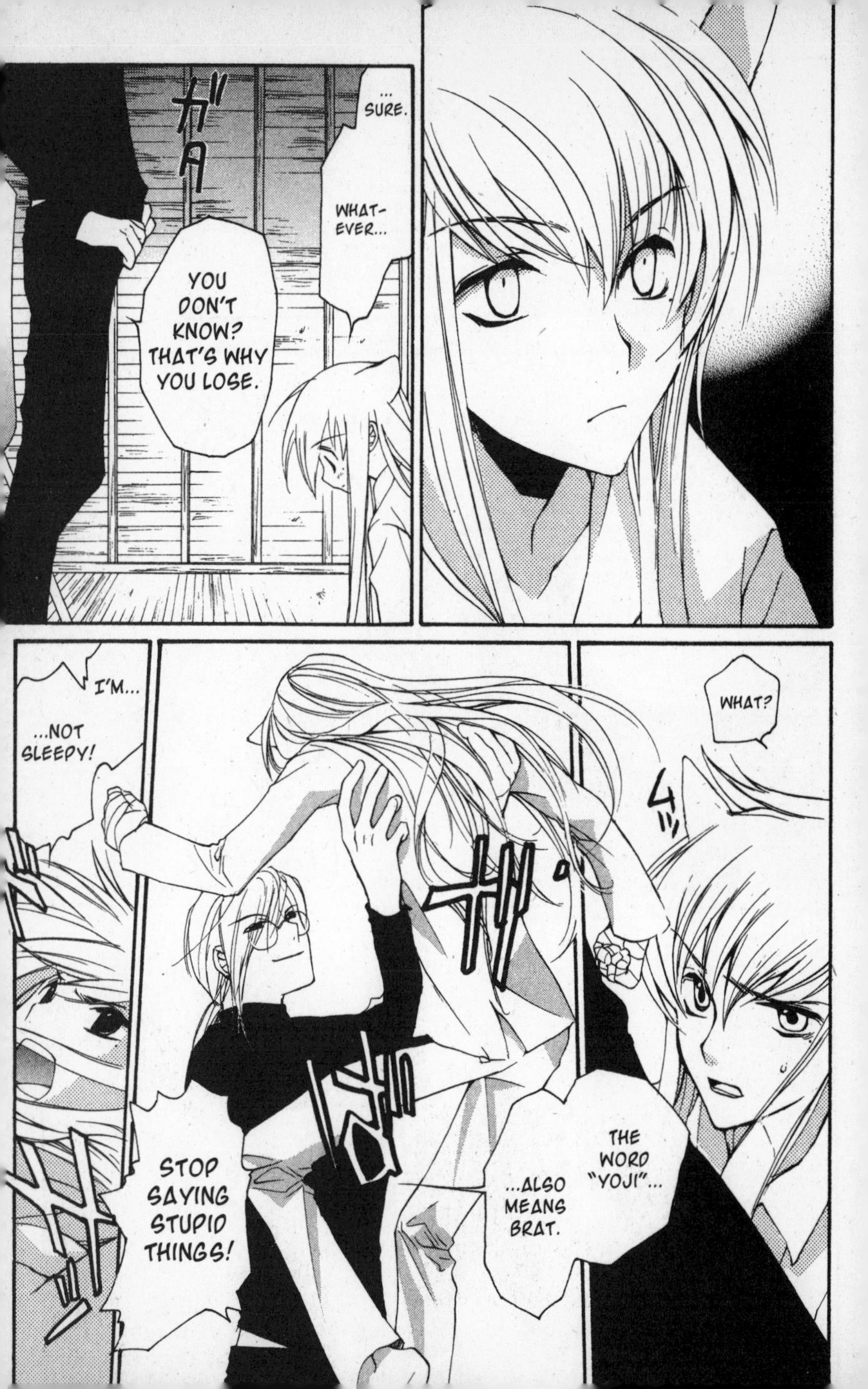
...SURE.
WHAT-EVER...
YOU DON'T KNOW? THAT'S WHY YOU LOSE.
WHAT?
THE WORD "YOJI"...
...ALSO MEANS BRAT.
STOP SAYING STUPID THINGS!
I'M...
...NOT SLEEPY!

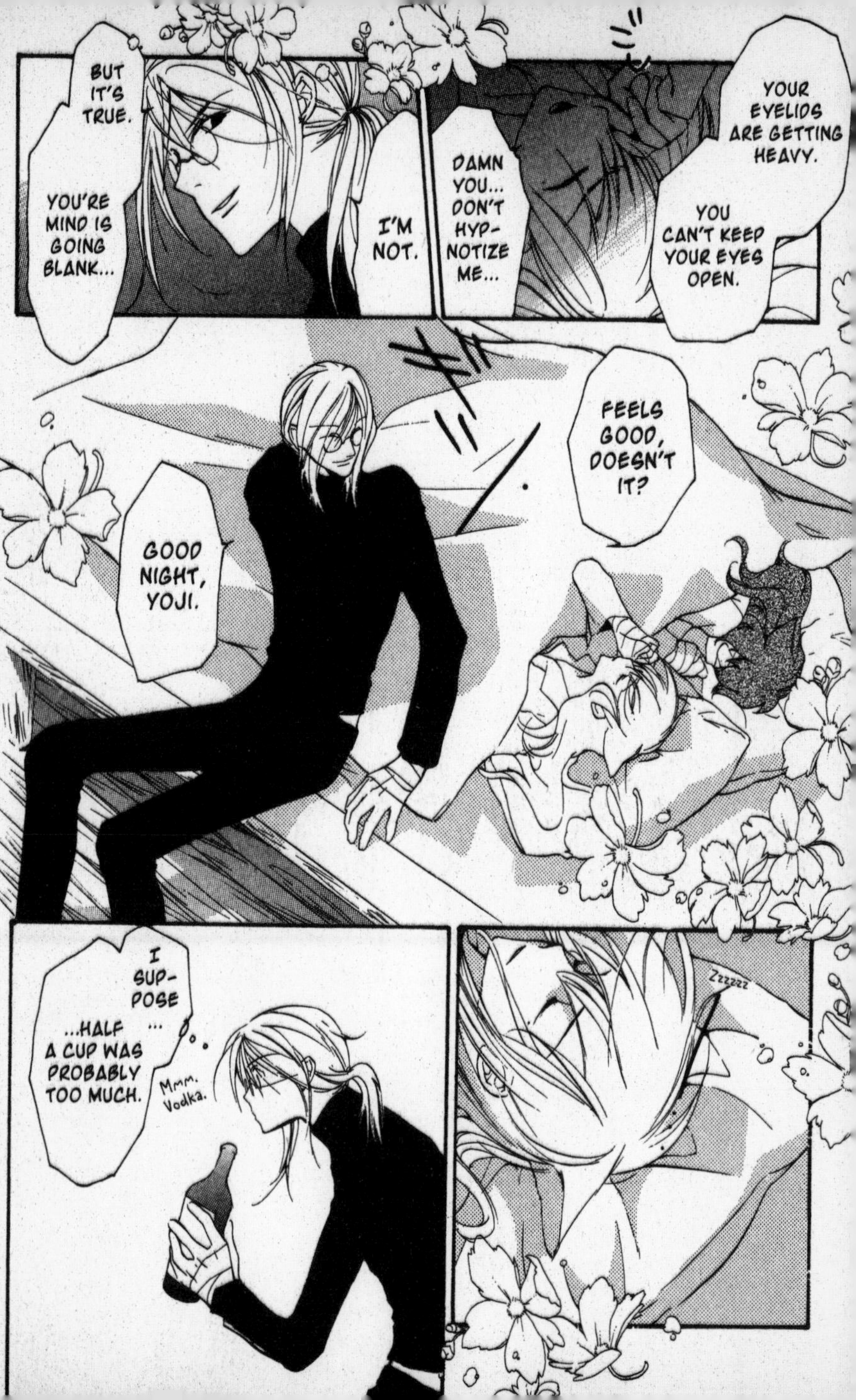
YOUR EYELIDS ARE GETTING HEAVY.
YOU CAN'T KEEP YOUR EYES OPEN.
DAMN YOU... DON'T HYP-NOTIZE ME...
I'M NOT.
BUT IT'S TRUE.
YOU'RE MIND IS GOING BLANK...
FEELS GOOD, DOESN'T IT?
GOOD NIGHT, YOJI.
Zzzzzz
I SUP-POSE ...
...HALF A CUP WAS PROBABLY TOO MUCH.
Mmm. Vodka.

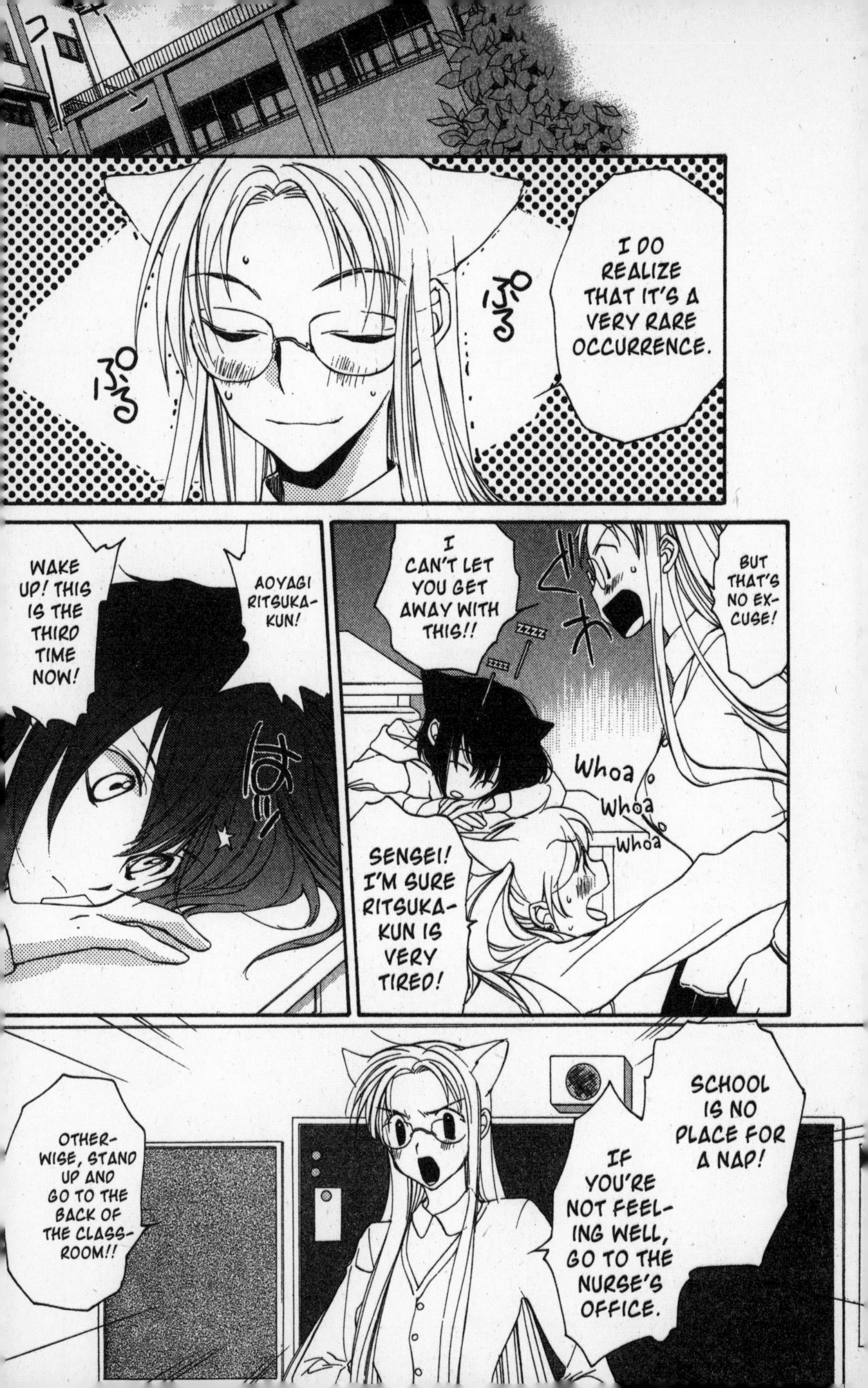
I DO REALIZE THAT IT'S A VERY RARE OCCURRENCE.
BUT THAT'S NO EX-CUSE!
I CAN'T LET YOU GET AWAY WITH THIS!!
Whoa
Whoa
Whoa
SENSEI! I'M SURE RITSUKA-KUN IS VERY TIRED!
AOYAGI RITSUKA-KUN!
WAKE UP! THIS IS THE THIRD TIME NOW!
SCHOOL IS NO PLACE FOR A NAP!
IF YOU'RE NOT FEEL-ING WELL, GO TO THE NURSE'S OFFICE.
OTHER-WISE, STAND UP AND GO TO THE BACK OF THE CLASS-ROOM!!

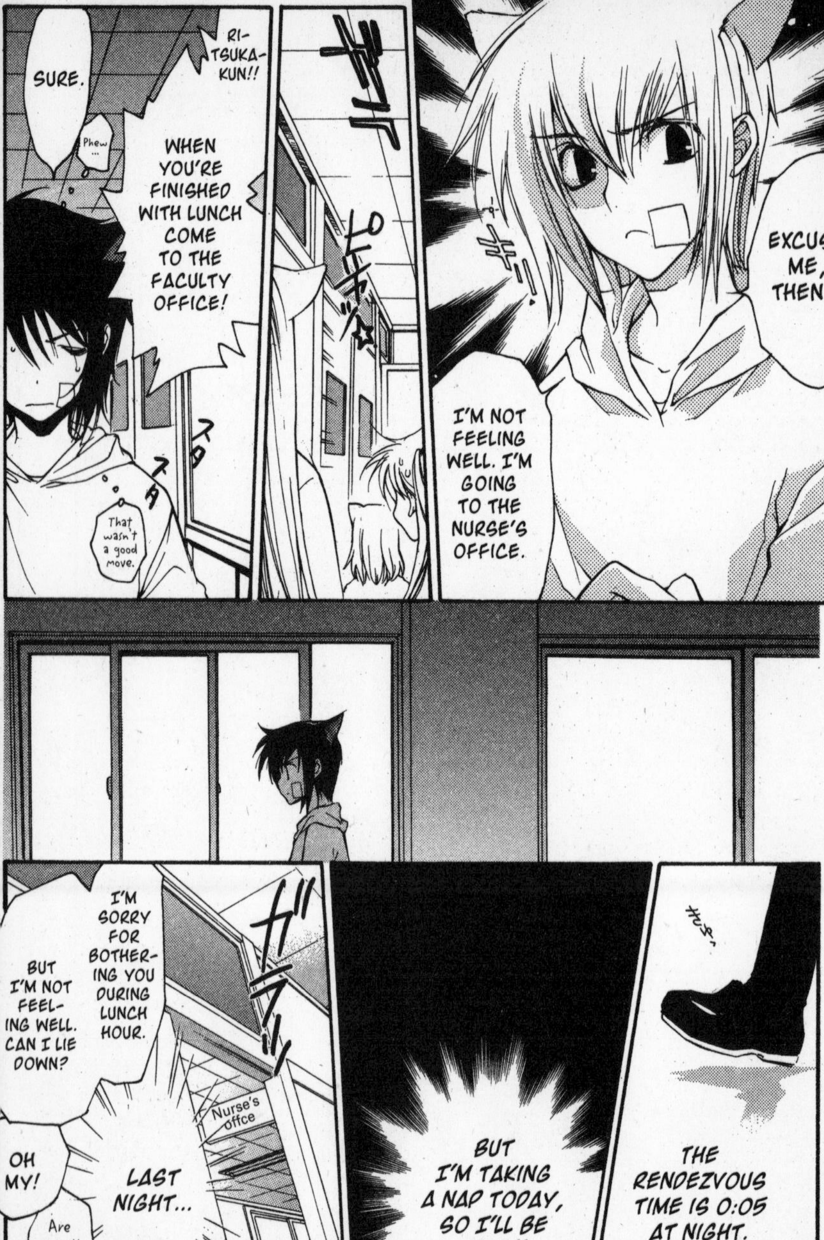
EXCUSE ME, THEN...
I'M NOT FEELING WELL. I'M GOING TO THE NURSE'S OFFICE.
RI-TSUKA-KUN!!
WHEN YOU'RE FINISHED WITH LUNCH COME TO THE FACULTY OFFICE!
SURE.
Phew...
That wasn't a good move.
THE RENDEZVOUS TIME IS 0:05 AT NIGHT.
BUT I'M TAKING A NAP TODAY, SO I'LL BE FINE!!
Nurse's offce
I'M SORRY FOR BOTHERING YOU DURING LUNCH HOUR.
BUT I'M NOT FEELING WELL. CAN I LIE DOWN?
LAST NIGHT...
OH MY!
Are you all right?

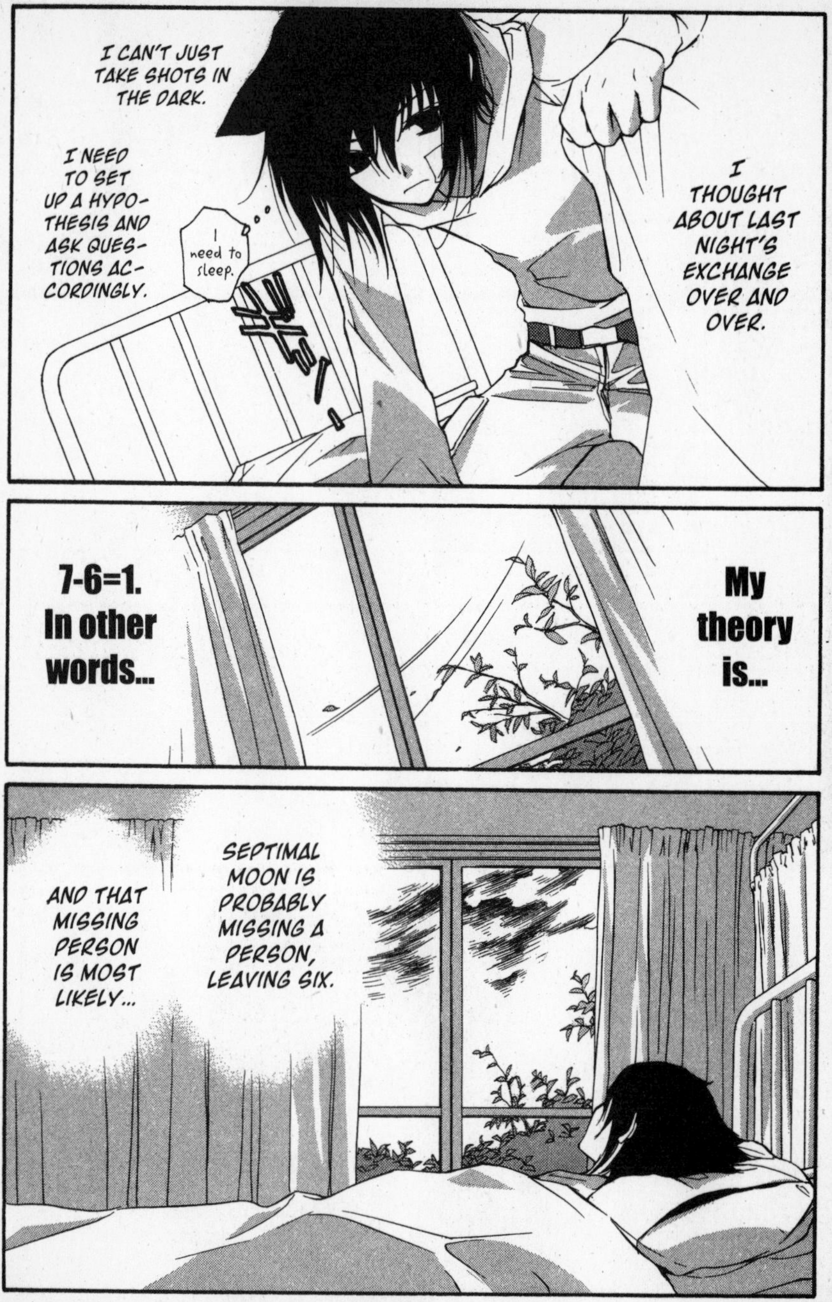
I THOUGHT ABOUT LAST NIGHT'S EXCHANGE OVER AND OVER.
I CAN'T JUST TAKE SHOTS IN THE DARK.
I NEED TO SET UP A HYPOTHESIS AND ASK QUESTIONS ACCORDINGLY.
I need to sleep.
My theory is...
7-6=1. In other words...
SEPTIMAL MOON IS PROBABLY MISSING A PERSON, LEAVING SIX.
AND THAT MISSING PERSON IS MOST LIKELY...

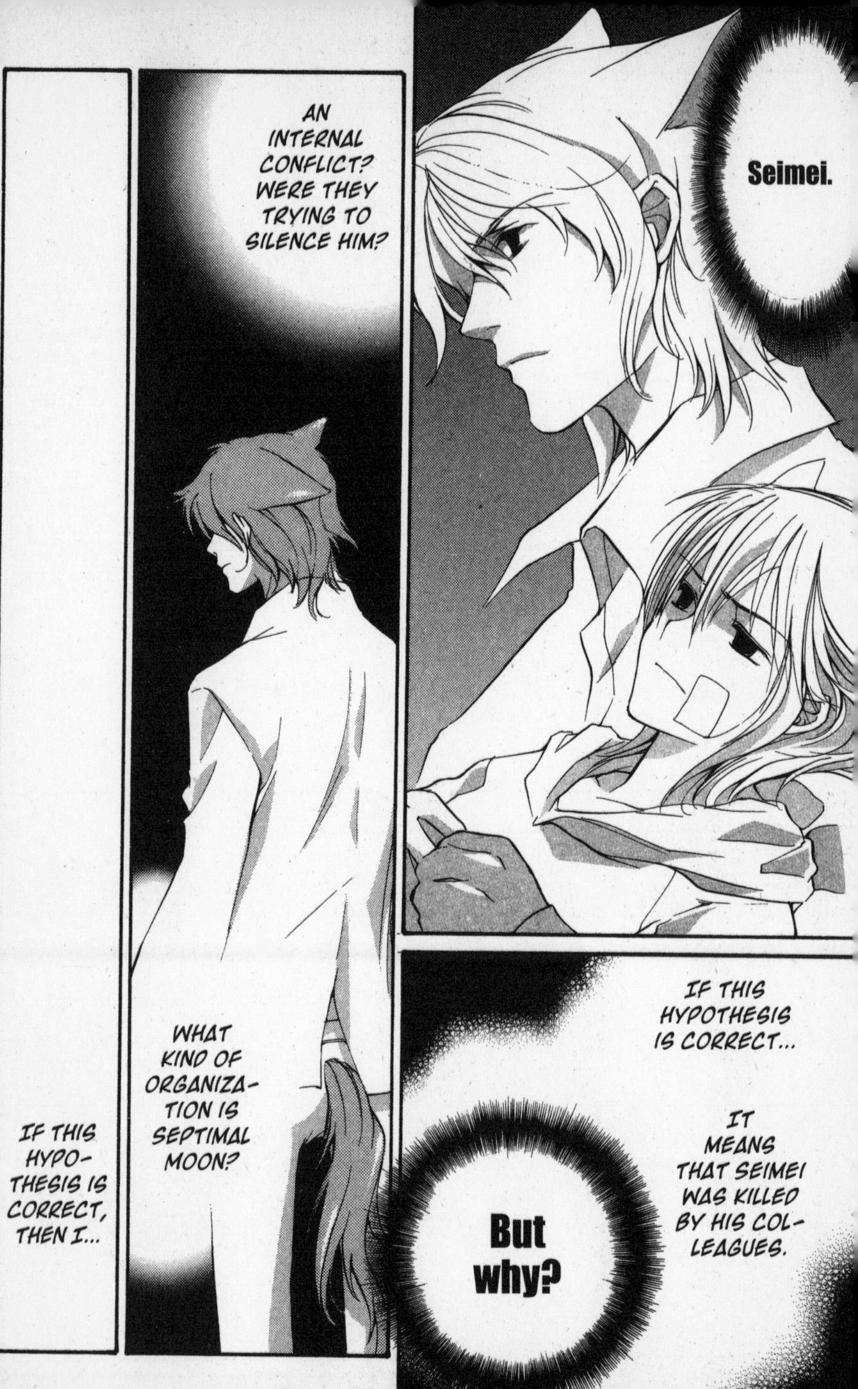
Seimei.
AN INTERNAL CONFLICT? WERE THEY TRYING TO SILENCE HIM?
IF THIS HYPOTHESIS IS CORRECT...
IT MEANS THAT SEIMEI WAS KILLED BY HIS COL-LEAGUES.
But why?
WHAT KIND OF ORGANIZA-TION IS SEPTIMAL MOON?
IF THIS HYPO-THESIS IS CORRECT, THEN I...

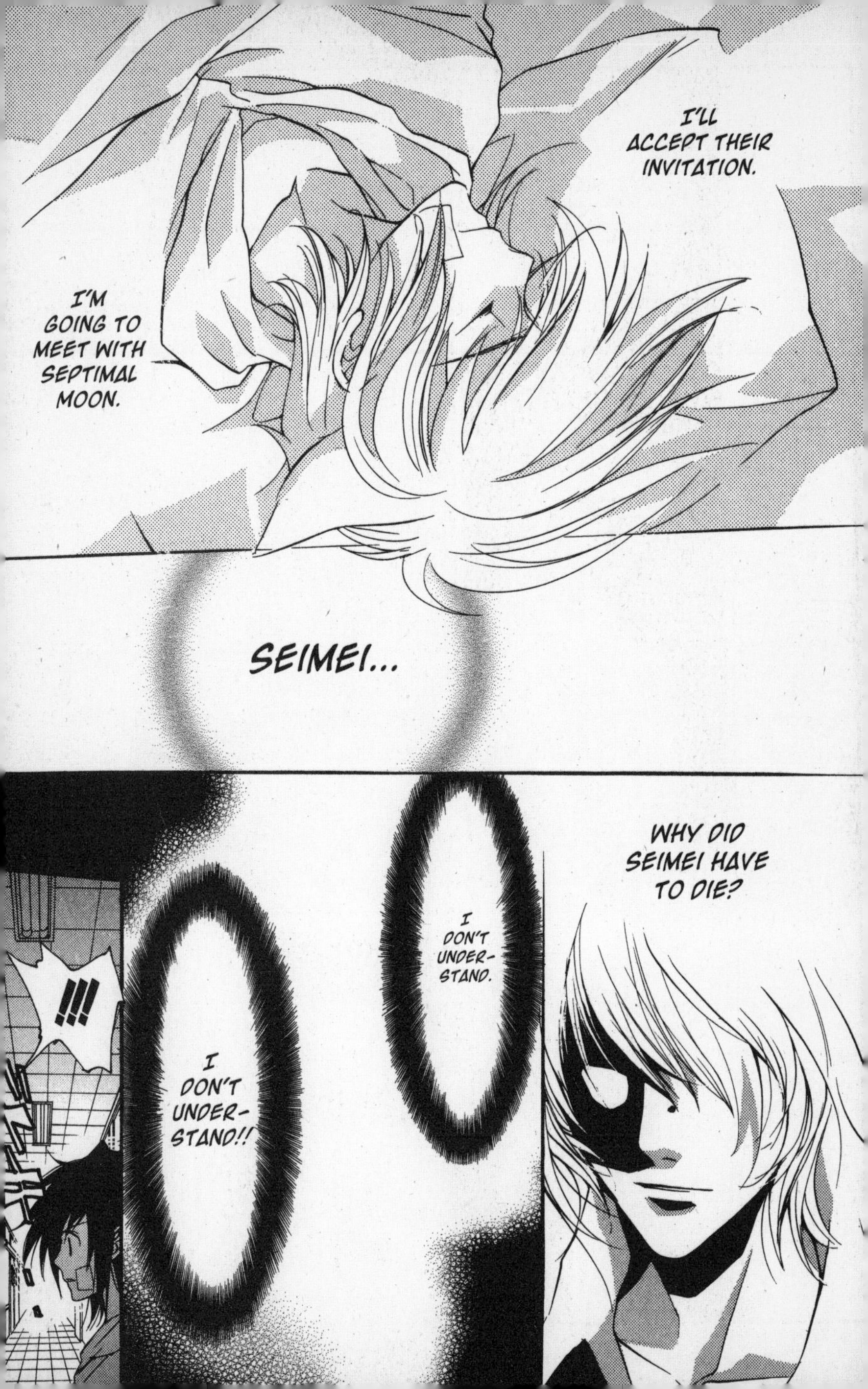
I'LL ACCEPT THEIR INVITATION.
I'M GOING TO MEET WITH SEPTIMAL MOON.
SEIMEI...
WHY DID SEIMEI HAVE TO DIE?
I DON'T UNDER-STAND.
I DON'T UNDER-STAND!!
!!!

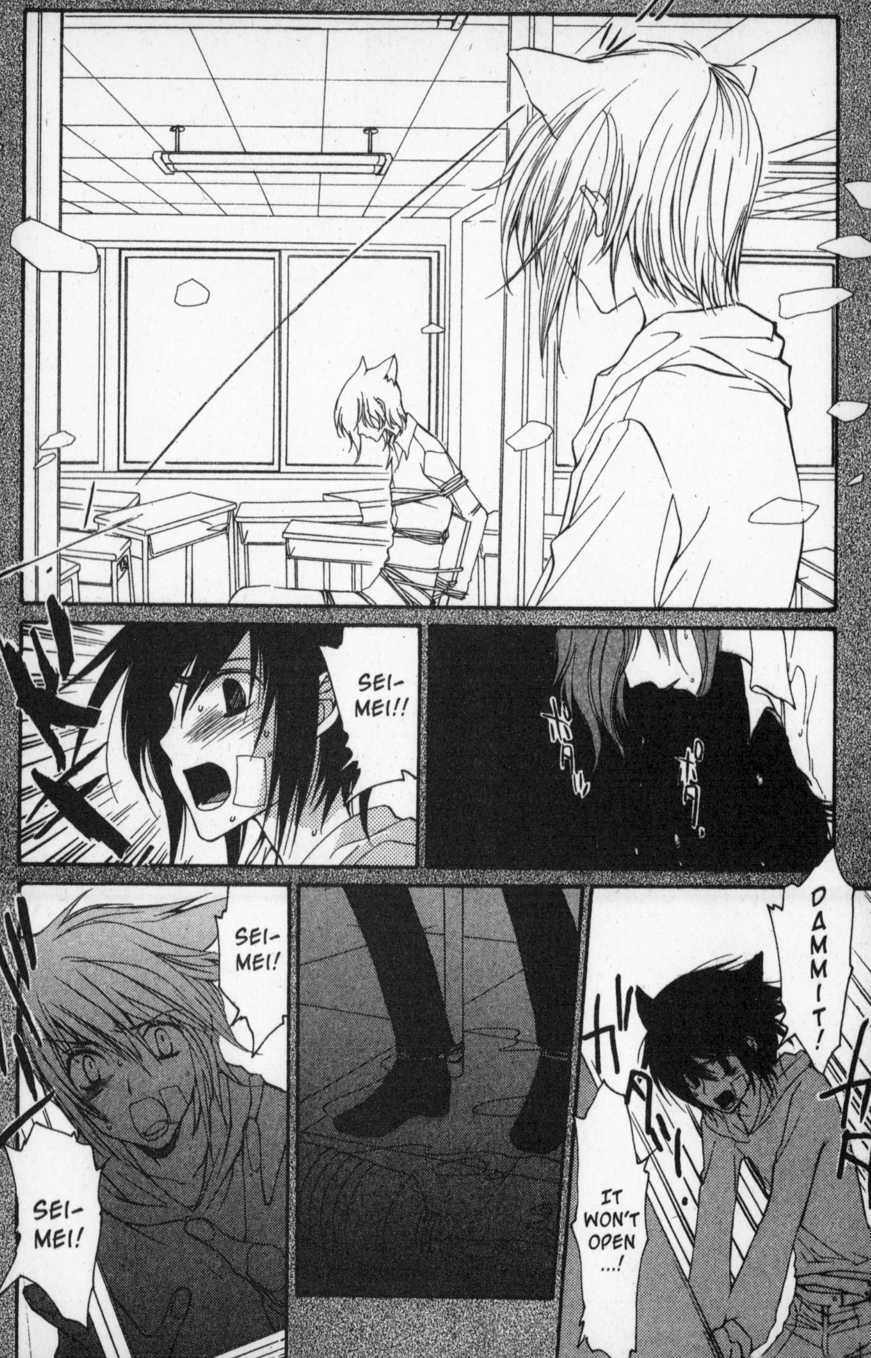
SEI-MEI!!
DAMMIT!
IT WON'T OPEN ...!
SEI-MEI!
SEI-MEI!

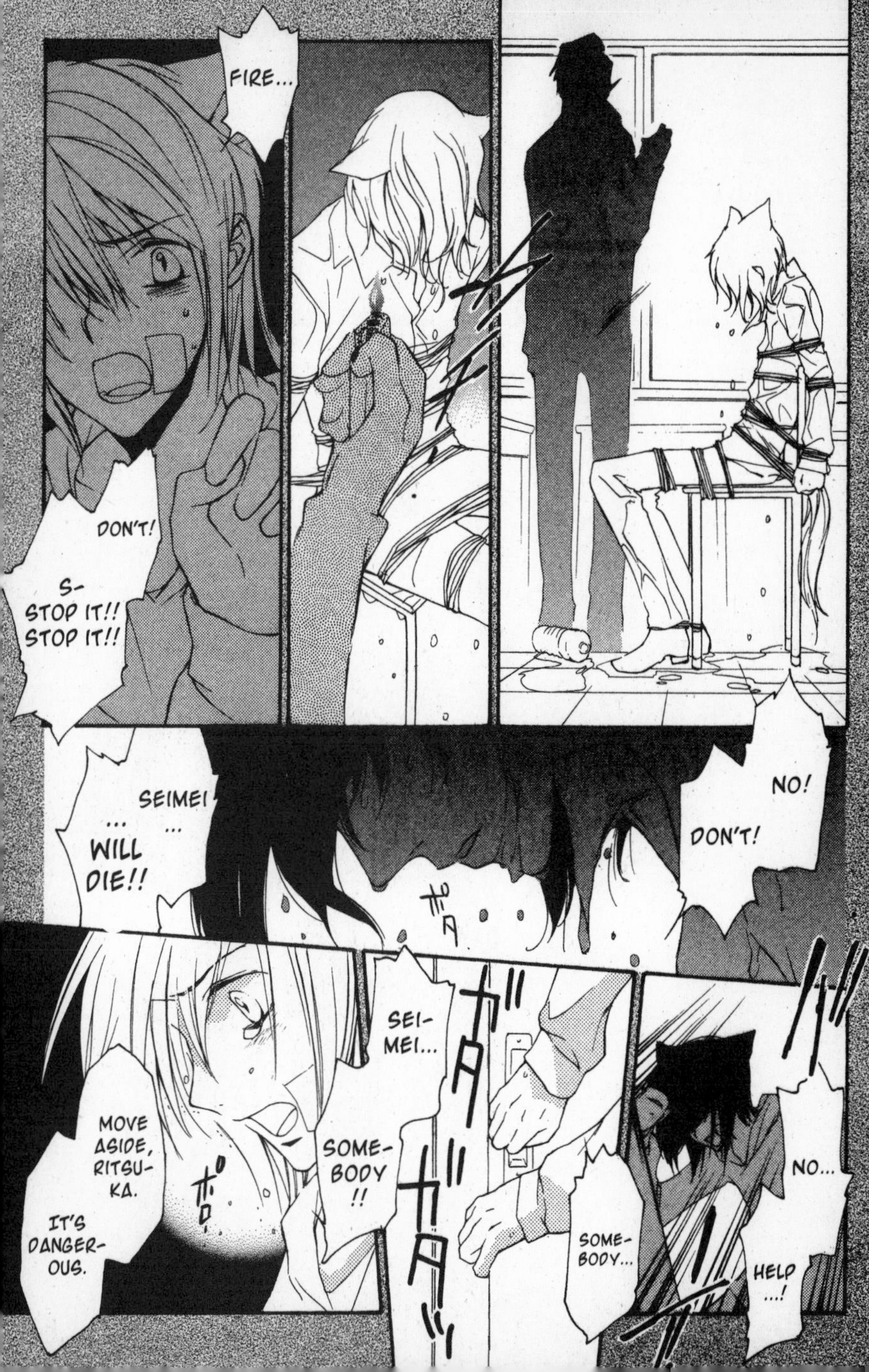
FIRE...
DON'T!
S- STOP IT!! STOP IT!!
NO!
DON'T!
SEIMEI ... ... WILL DIE!!
ポタ
NO...
SOMEBODY...
HELP ...!
SEI-MEI...
SOMEBODY!!
ガタ
ガタ
MOVE ASIDE, RITSUKA.
IT'S DANGEROUS.
ポロ

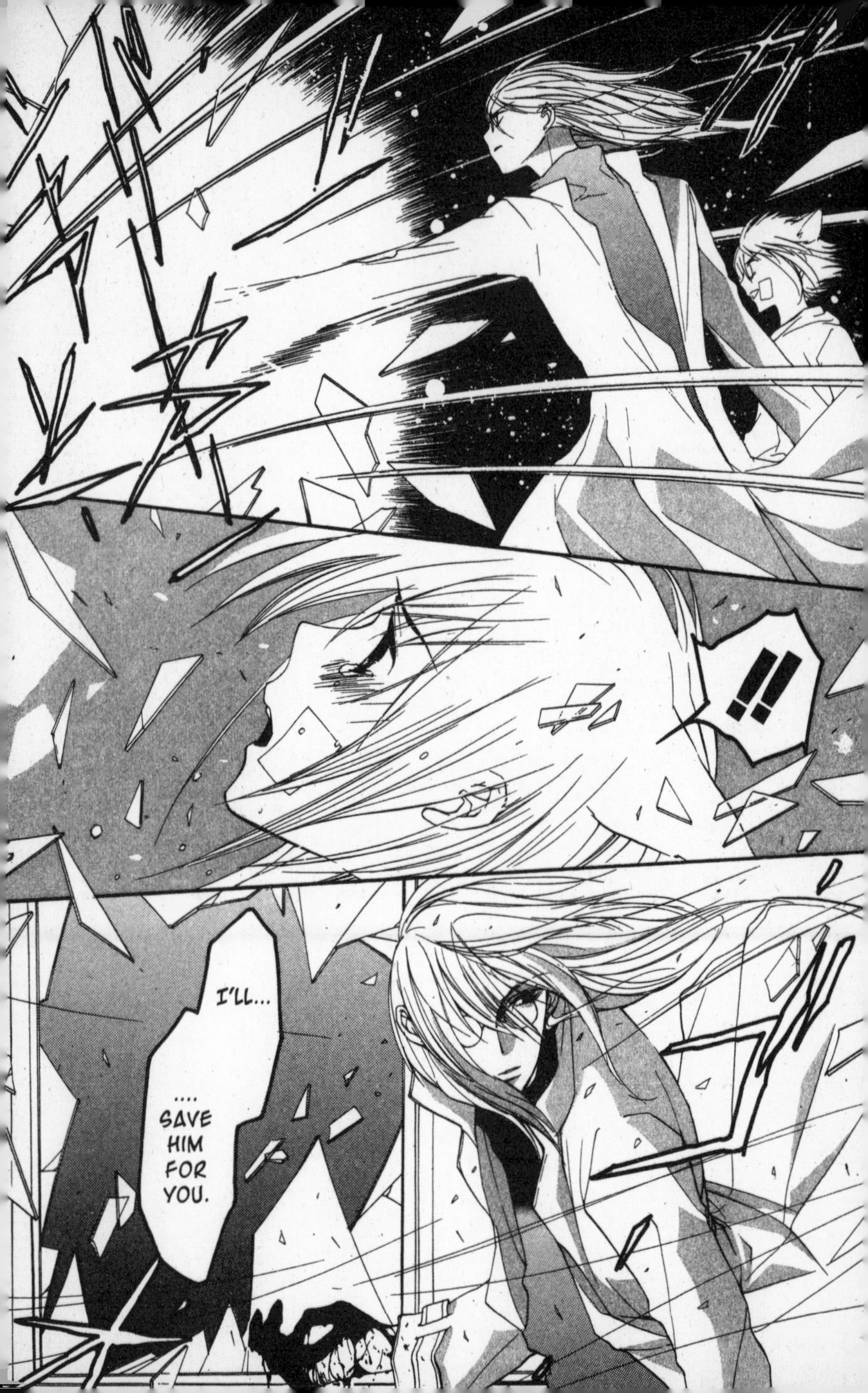
!!
I'LL...
....SAVE HIM FOR YOU.

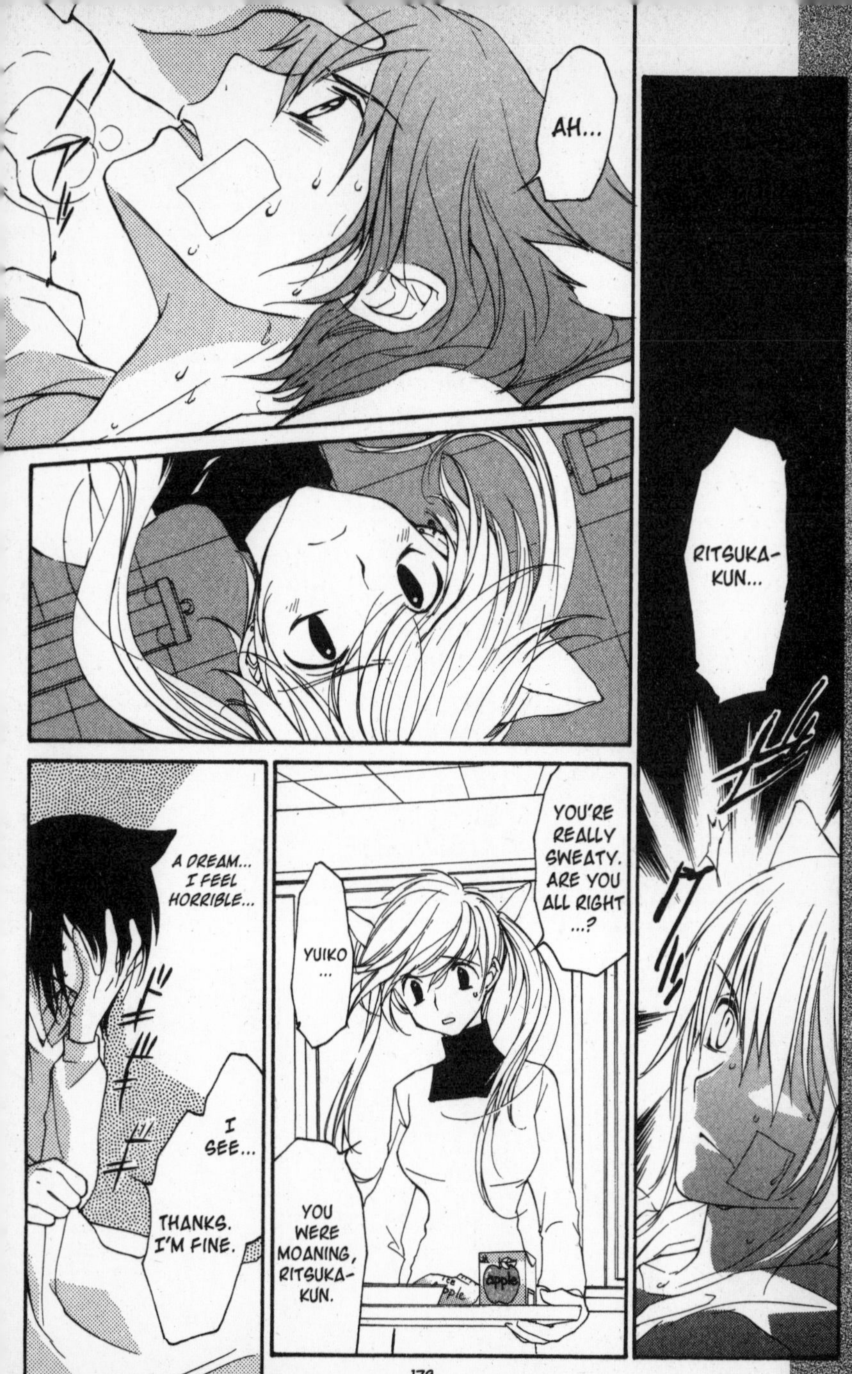

RITSUKA-KUN...
AH...
YOU'RE REALLY SWEATY. ARE YOU ALL RIGHT ...?
YUIKO ...
YOU WERE MOANING, RITSUKA-KUN.
A DREAM... I FEEL HORRIBLE...
I SEE...
THANKS. I'M FINE.

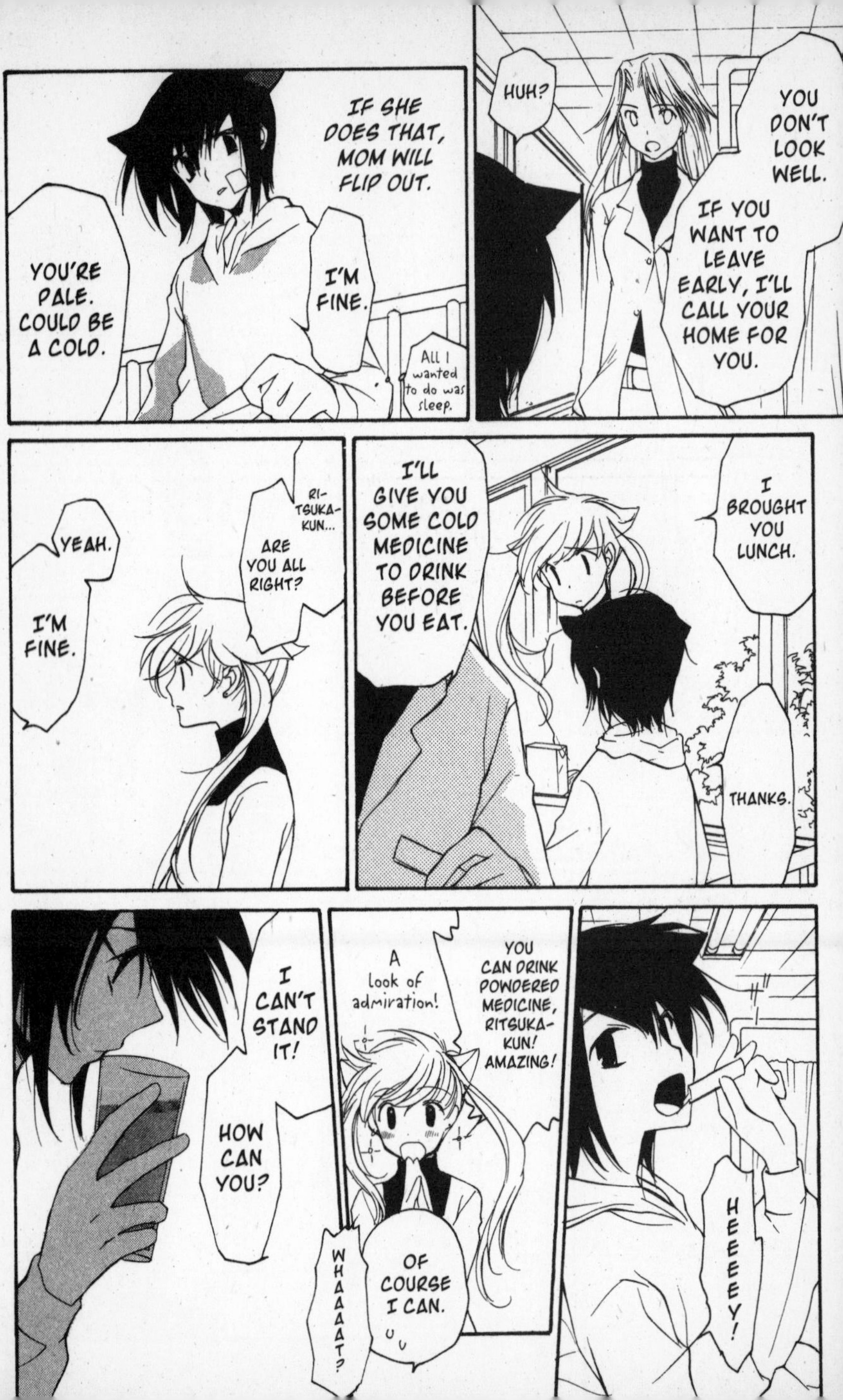
HUH?
YOU DON'T LOOK WELL.
IF YOU WANT TO LEAVE EARLY, I'LL CALL YOUR HOME FOR YOU.
IF SHE DOES THAT, MOM WILL FLIP OUT.
I'M FINE.
All I wanted to do was sleep.
YOU'RE PALE. COULD BE A COLD.
I BROUGHT YOU LUNCH.
THANKS.
I'LL GIVE YOU SOME COLD MEDICINE TO DRINK BEFORE YOU EAT.
RI-TSUKA-KUN...
ARE YOU ALL RIGHT?
YEAH.
I'M FINE.
HEEEEY!
YOU CAN DRINK POWDERED MEDICINE, RITSUKA-KUN! AMAZING!
A look of admiration!
OF COURSE I CAN.
WHAAAAAT?
I CAN'T STAND IT!
HOW CAN YOU?

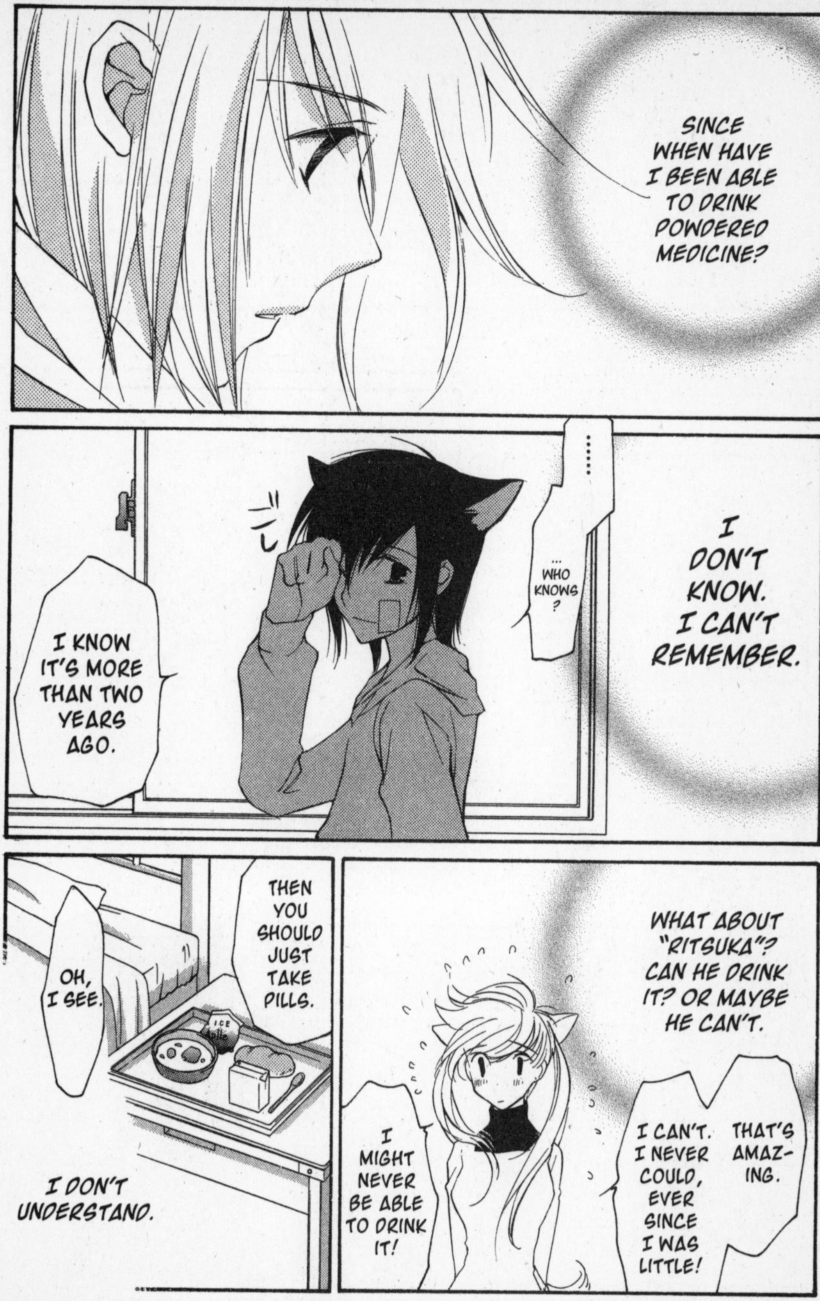
SINCE WHEN HAVE I BEEN ABLE TO DRINK POWDERED MEDICINE?
......
...WHO KNOWS?
I DON'T KNOW. I CAN'T REMEMBER.
I KNOW IT'S MORE THAN TWO YEARS AGO.
WHAT ABOUT "RITSUKA"? CAN HE DRINK IT? OR MAYBE HE CAN'T.
THAT'S AMAZ-ING.
I CAN'T. I NEVER COULD, EVER SINCE I WAS LITTLE!
I MIGHT NEVER BE ABLE TO DRINK IT!
THEN YOU SHOULD JUST TAKE PILLS.
OH, I SEE.
I DON'T UNDERSTAND.

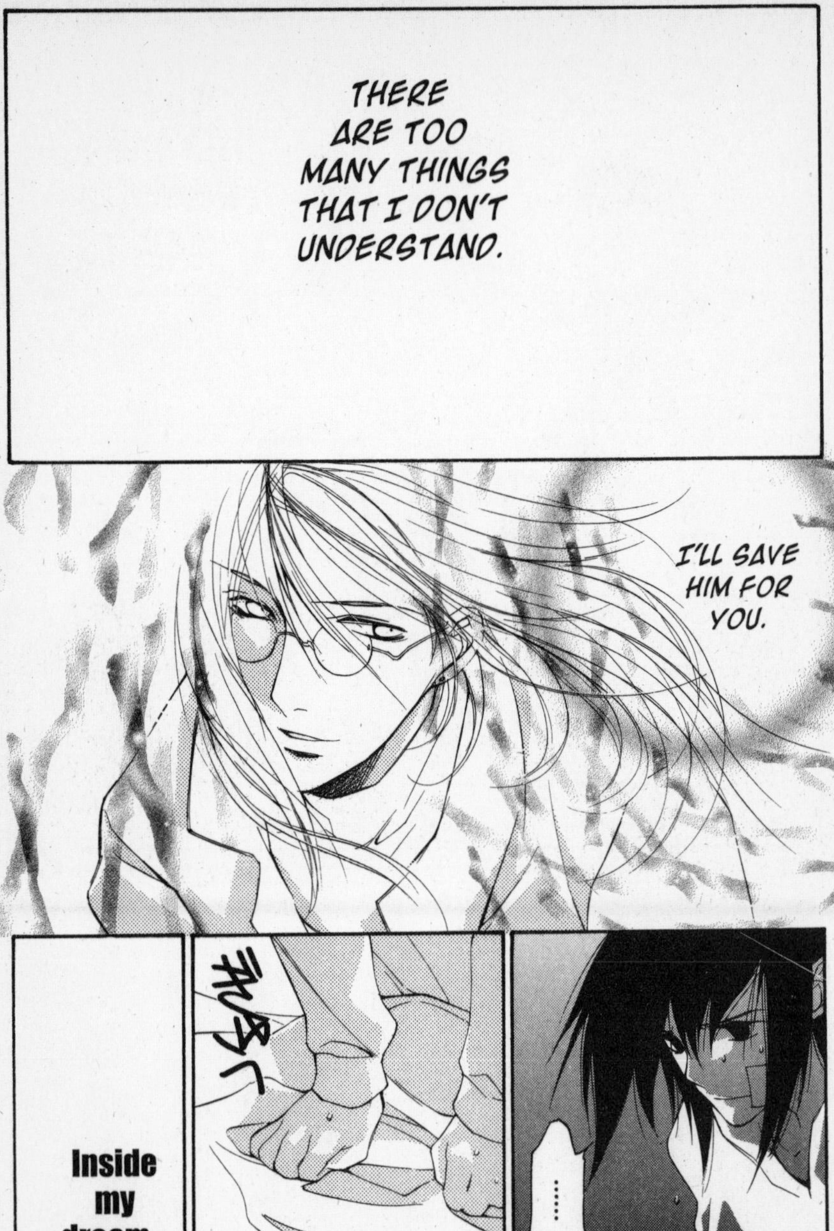
THERE ARE TOO MANY THINGS THAT I DON'T UNDERSTAND.
I'LL SAVE HIM FOR YOU.
......
Inside my dream...

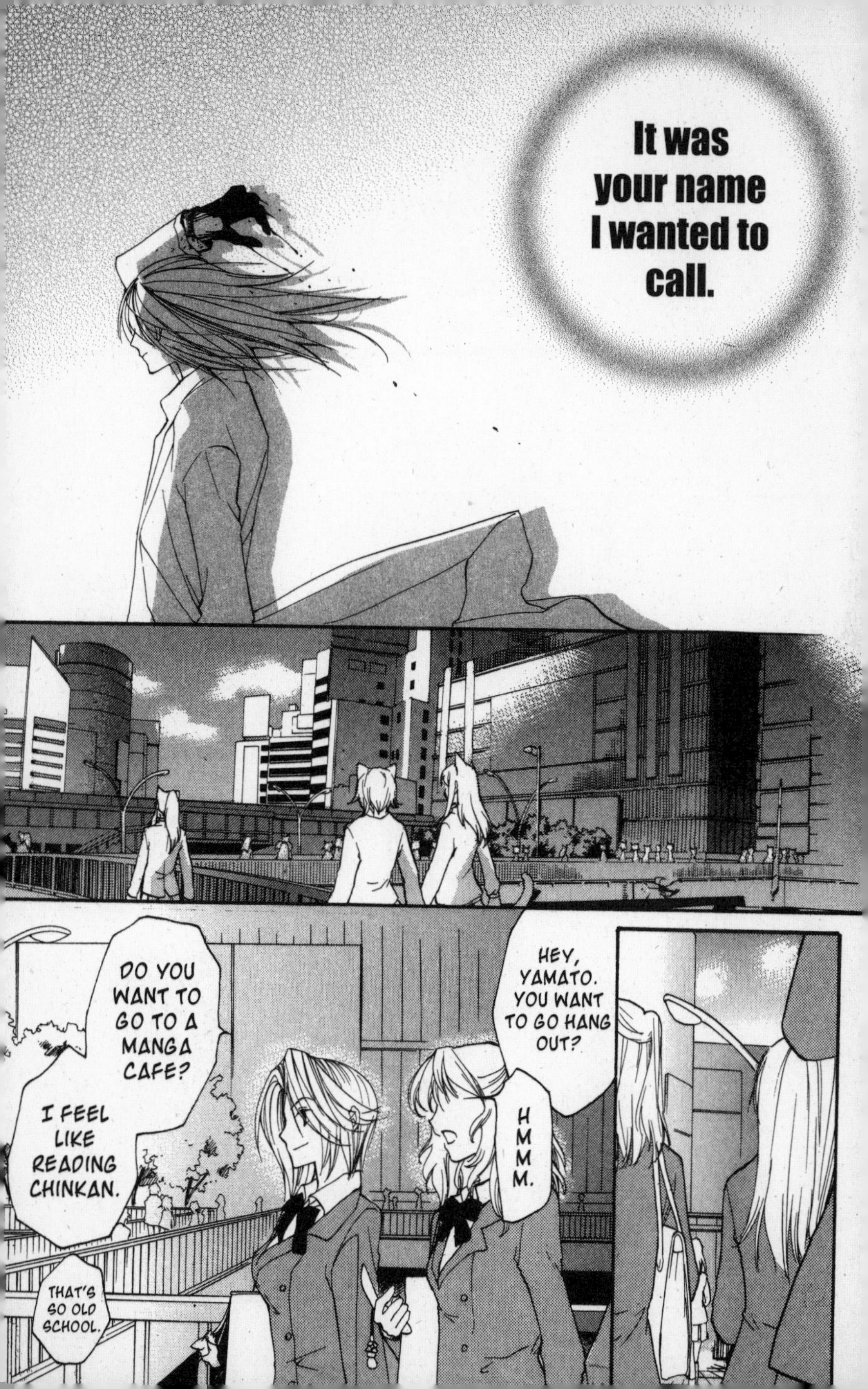
It was your name I wanted to call.
HEY, YAMATO. YOU WANT TO GO HANG OUT?
HMMM.
DO YOU WANT TO GO TO A MANGA CAFE?
I FEEL LIKE READING CHINKAN.
THAT'S SO OLD SCHOOL.

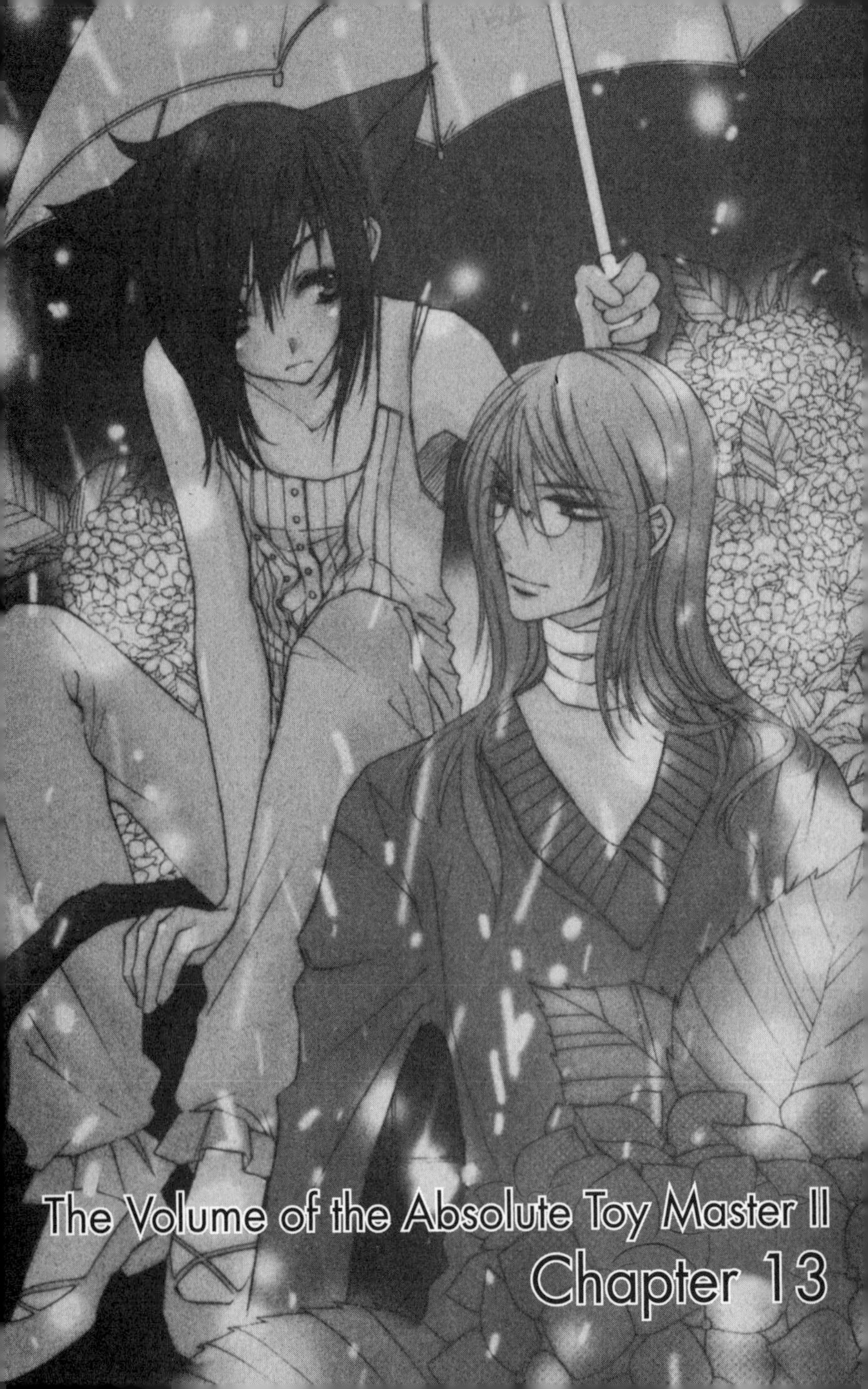
The Volume of the Absolute Toy Master II
Chapter 13

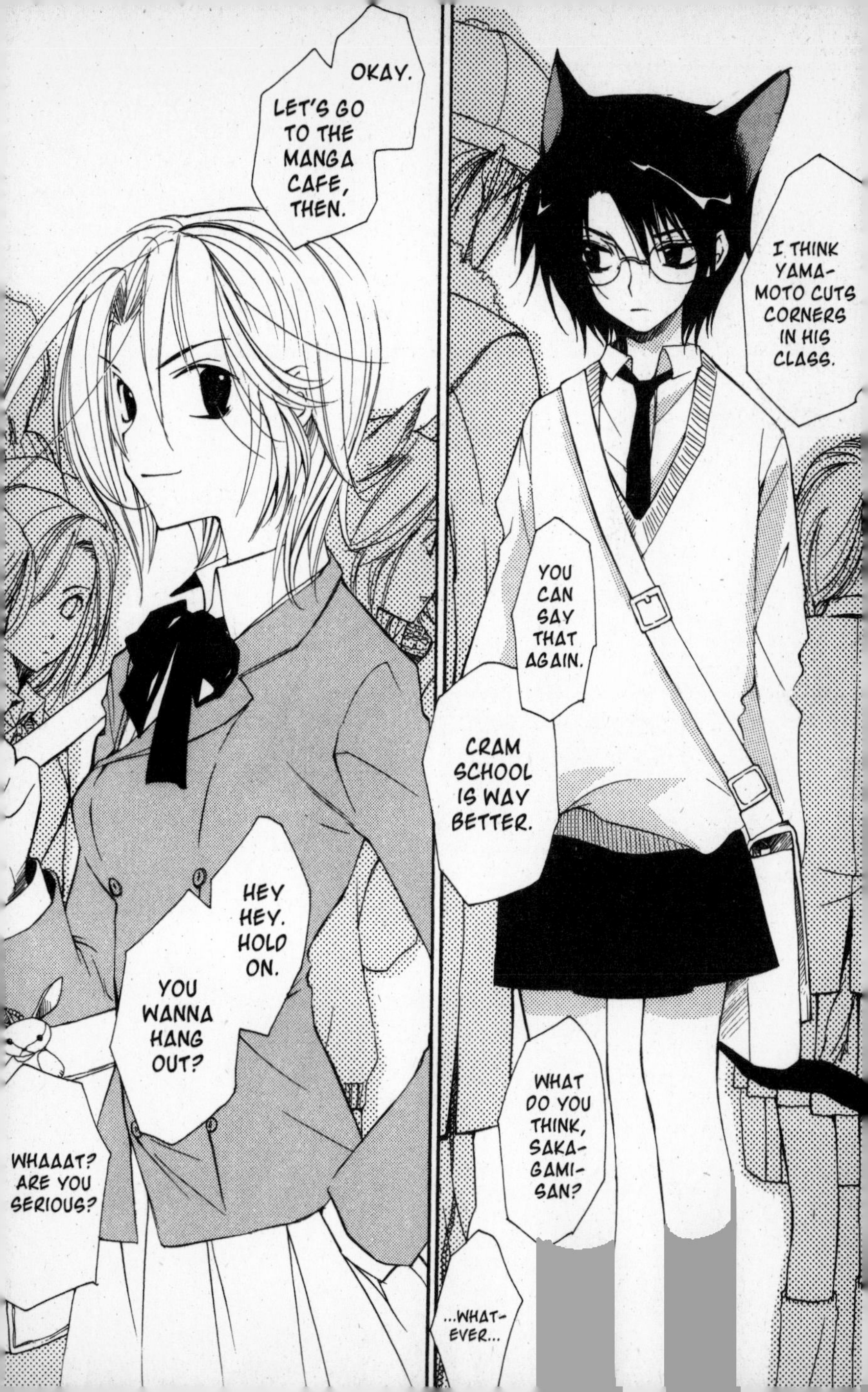
I THINK YAMA-MOTO CUTS CORNERS IN HIS CLASS.
YOU CAN SAY THAT AGAIN.
CRAM SCHOOL IS WAY BETTER.
WHAT DO YOU THINK, SAKA-GAMI-SAN?
...WHAT-EVER...
OKAY.
LET'S GO TO THE MANGA CAFE, THEN.
HEY HEY. HOLD ON.
YOU WANNA HANG OUT?
WHAAAT? ARE YOU SERIOUS?

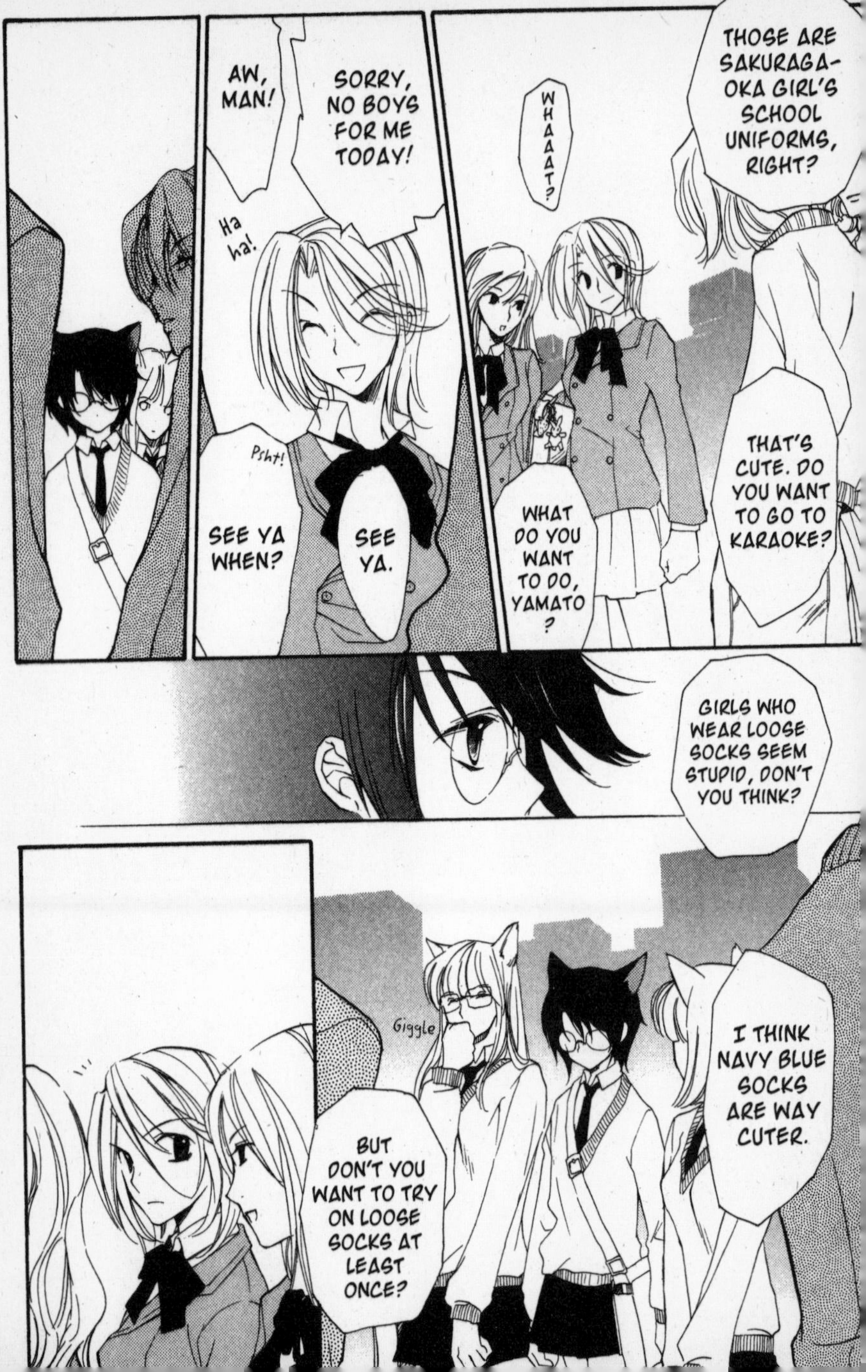
THOSE ARE SAKURAGA-OKA GIRL'S SCHOOL UNIFORMS, RIGHT?
WHAAAAT?
THAT'S CUTE. DO YOU WANT TO GO TO KARAOKE?
WHAT DO YOU WANT TO DO, YAMATO?
SORRY, NO BOYS FOR ME TODAY!
AW, MAN!
Ha ha!
Psht!
SEE YA.
SEE YA WHEN?
GIRLS WHO WEAR LOOSE SOCKS SEEM STUPID, DON'T YOU THINK?
I THINK NAVY BLUE SOCKS ARE WAY CUTER.
Giggle
BUT DON'T YOU WANT TO TRY ON LOOSE SOCKS AT LEAST ONCE?

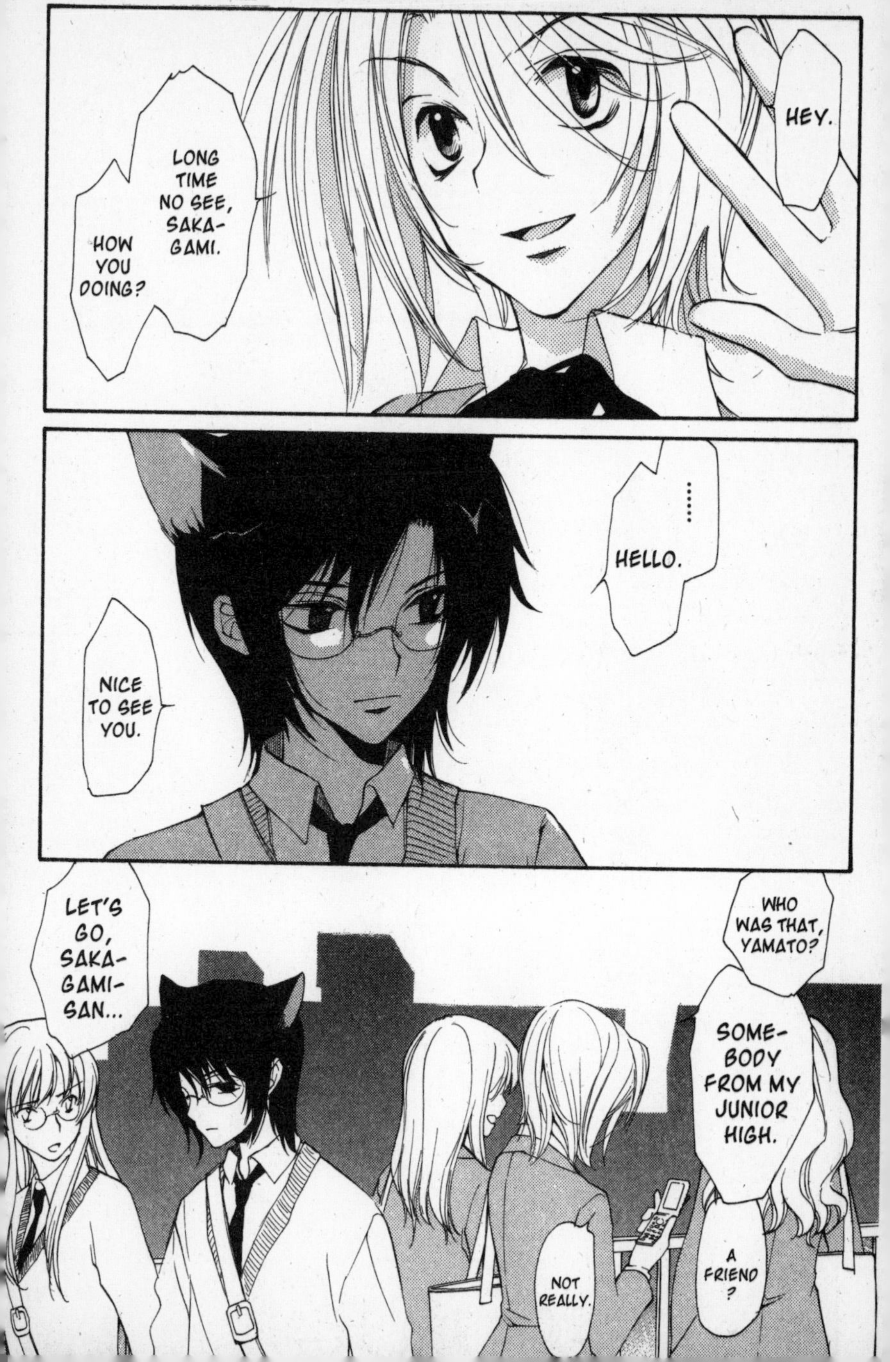
HEY.
LONG TIME NO SEE, SAKA-GAMI.
HOW YOU DOING?
......
HELLO.
NICE TO SEE YOU.
WHO WAS THAT, YAMATO?
SOME-BODY FROM MY JUNIOR HIGH.
A FRIEND?
NOT REALLY.
LET'S GO, SAKA-GAMI-SAN...

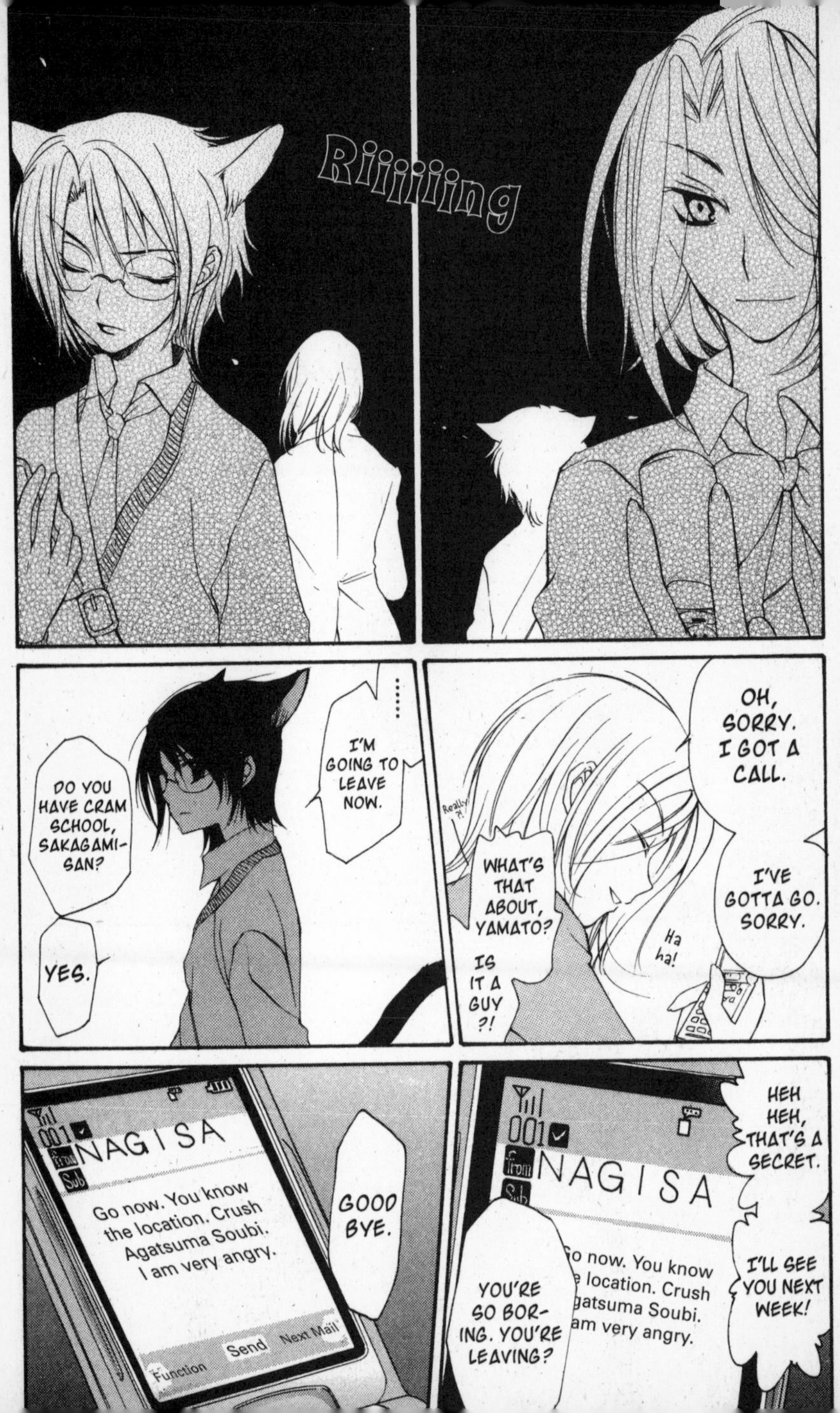
Riiiiiing
OH, SORRY. I GOT A CALL.
I'VE GOTTA GO. SORRY.
Ha ha!
Really?!
WHAT'S THAT ABOUT, YAMATO?
IS IT A GUY?!
......
I'M GOING TO LEAVE NOW.
DO YOU HAVE CRAM SCHOOL, SAKAGAMI-SAN?
YES.
HEH HEH, THAT'S A SECRET.
I'LL SEE YOU NEXT WEEK!
001 from NAGISA Sub
Go now. You know
e location. Crush
gatsuma Soubi.
am very angry.
YOU'RE SO BOR-ING. YOU'RE LEAVING?
001 from NAGISA Sub
Go now. You know the location. Crush Agatsuma Soubi. I am very angry.
Function Send Next Mail
GOOD BYE.

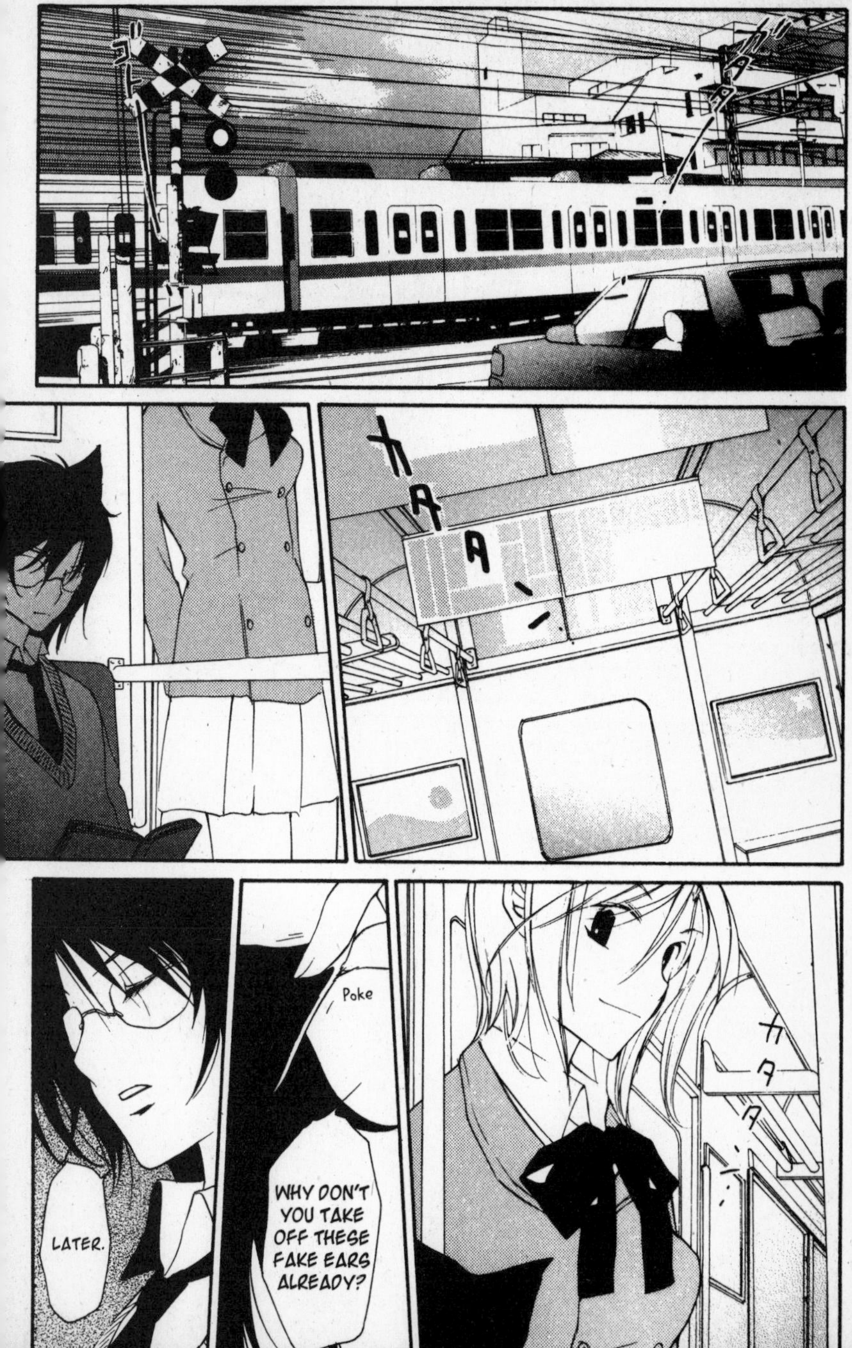
Poke
WHY DON'T YOU TAKE OFF THESE FAKE EARS ALREADY?
LATER.

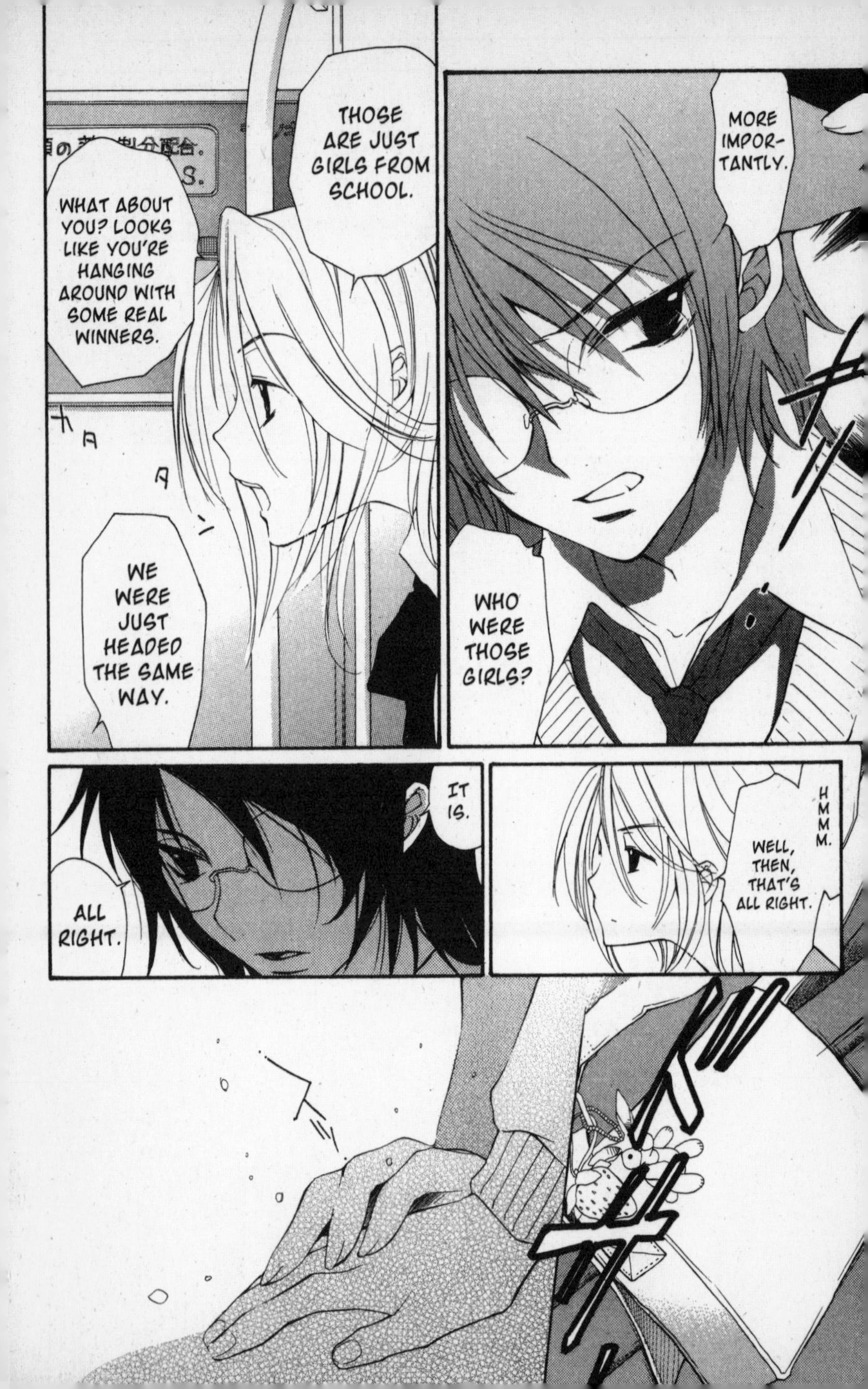
MORE IMPORTANTLY.
WHO WERE THOSE GIRLS?
THOSE ARE JUST GIRLS FROM SCHOOL.
WHAT ABOUT YOU? LOOKS LIKE YOU'RE HANGING AROUND WITH SOME REAL WINNERS.
WE WERE JUST HEADED THE SAME WAY.
HMMM.
WELL, THEN, THAT'S ALL RIGHT.
IT IS.
ALL RIGHT.

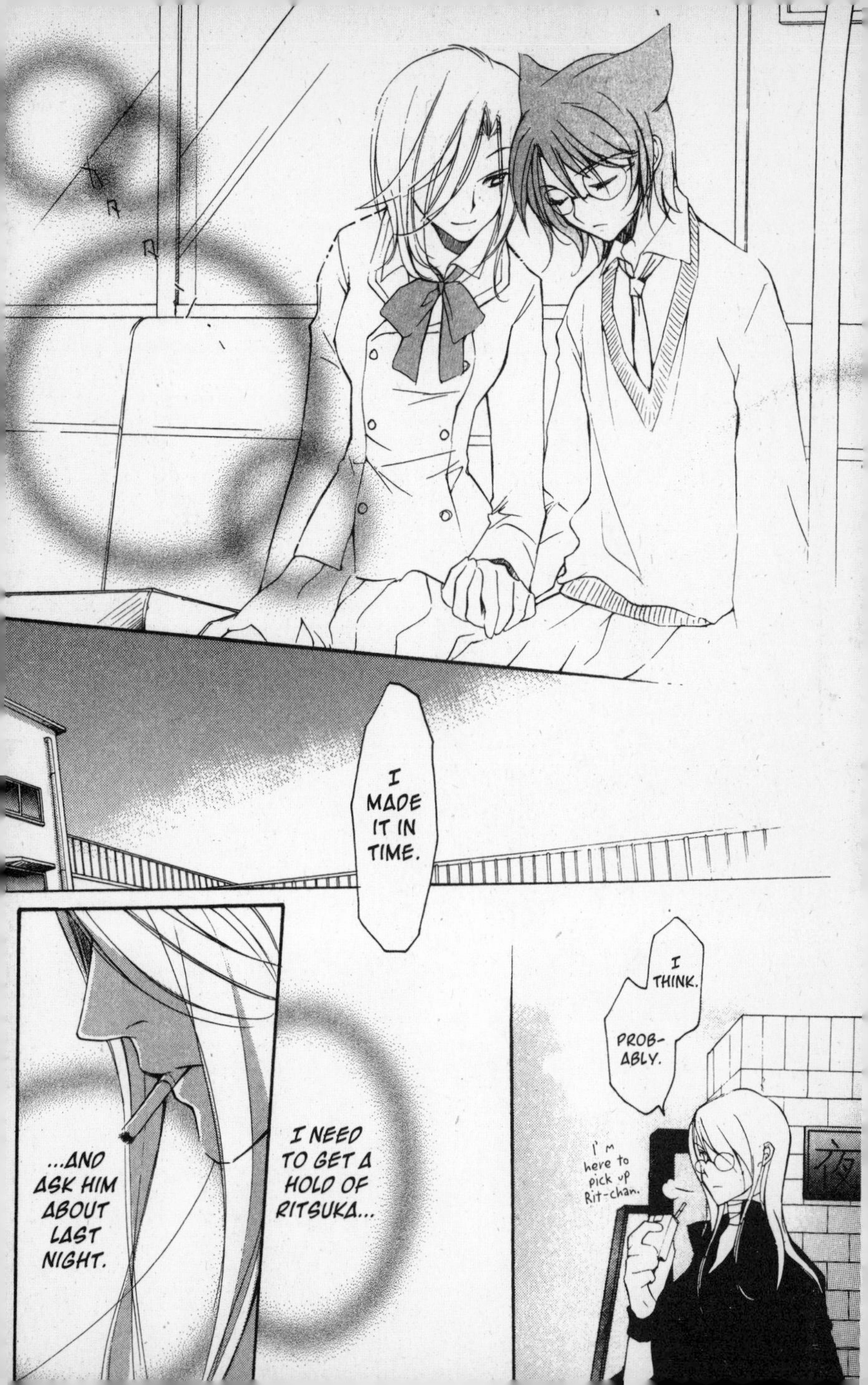
I MADE IT IN TIME.
I THINK.
PROBABLY.
I'm here to pick up Rit-chan.
I NEED TO GET A HOLD OF RITSUKA...
...AND ASK HIM ABOUT LAST NIGHT.

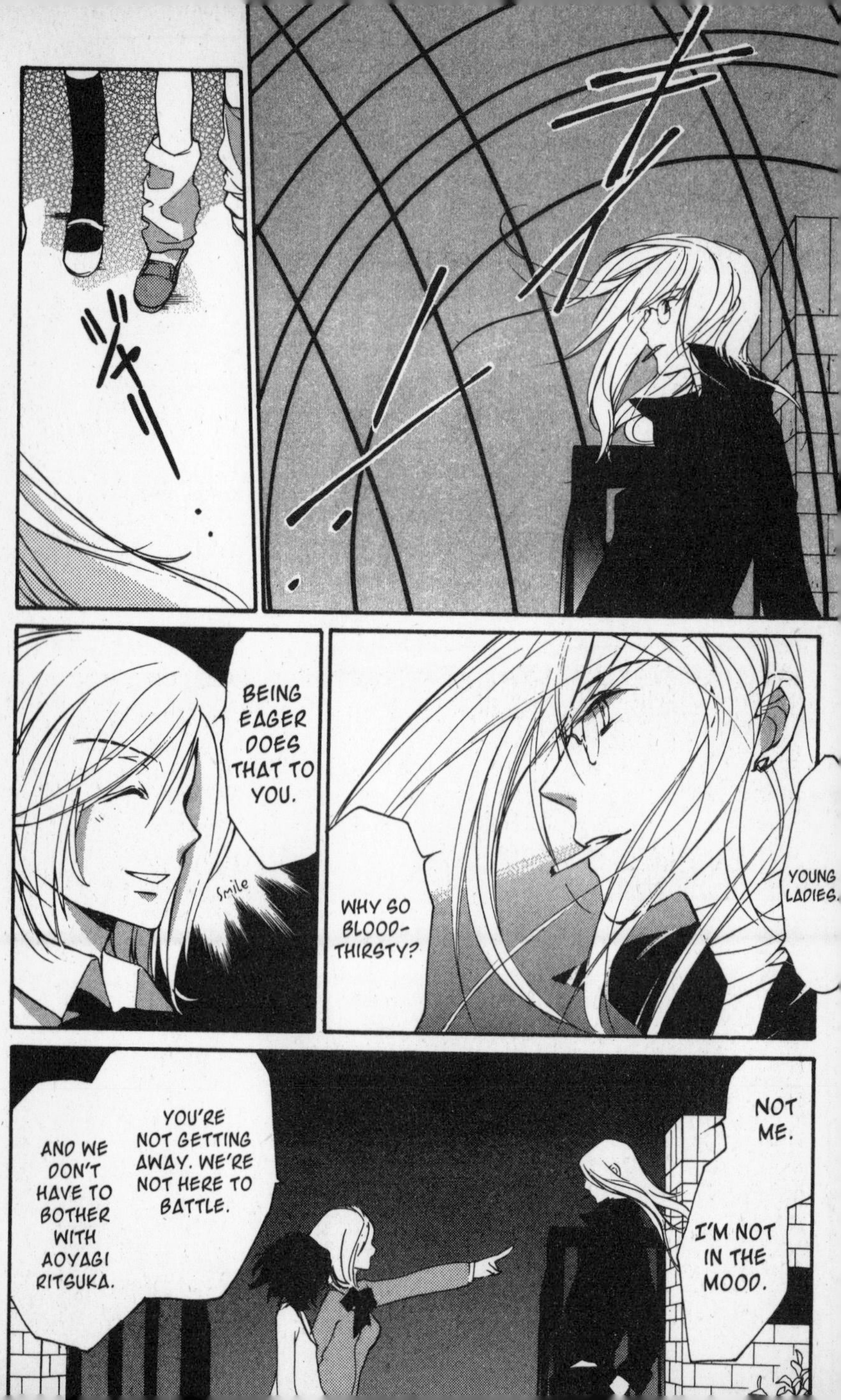
YOUNG LADIES.
WHY SO BLOOD-THIRSTY?
BEING EAGER DOES THAT TO YOU.
Smile
NOT ME.
I'M NOT IN THE MOOD.
YOU'RE NOT GETTING AWAY. WE'RE NOT HERE TO BATTLE.
AND WE DON'T HAVE TO BOTHER WITH AOYAGI RITSUKA.

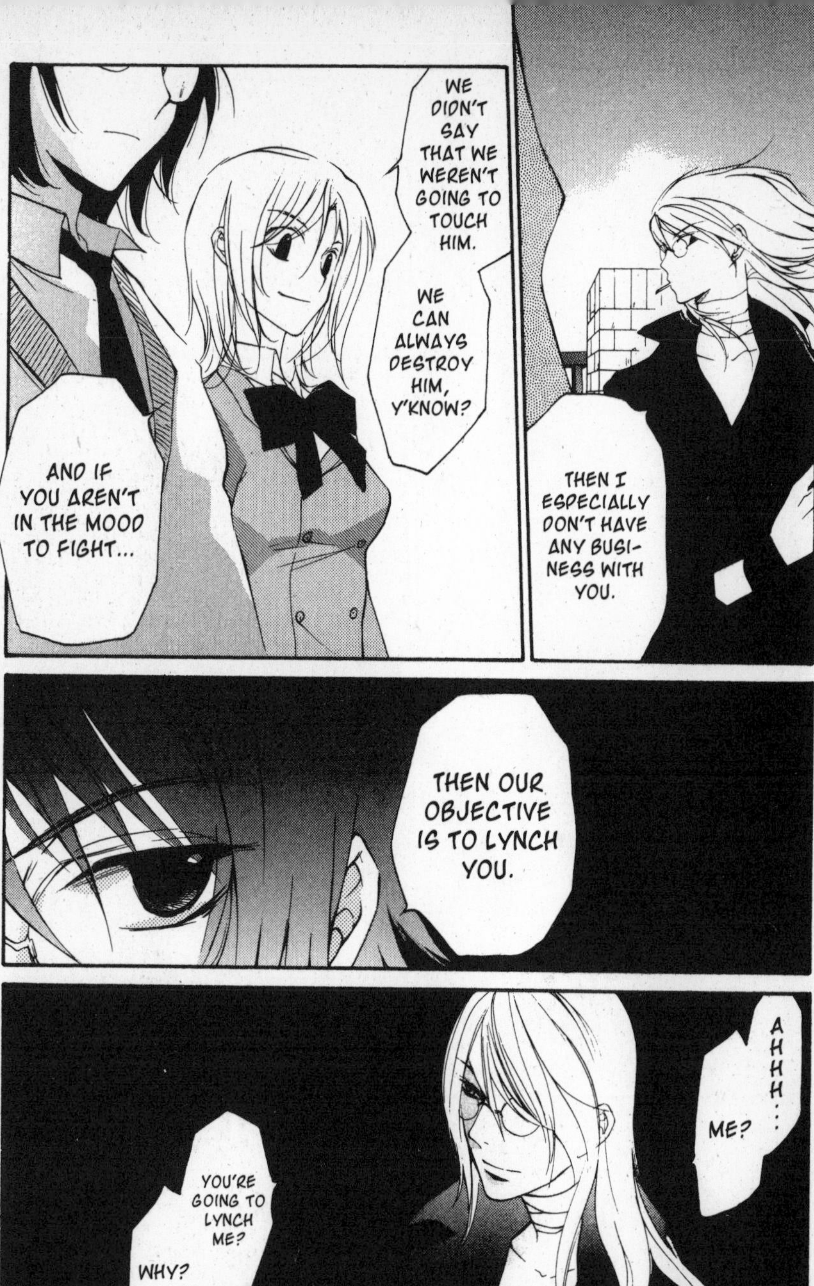
THEN I ESPECIALLY DON'T HAVE ANY BUSI-NESS WITH YOU.
WE DIDN'T SAY THAT WE WEREN'T GOING TO TOUCH HIM.
WE CAN ALWAYS DESTROY HIM, Y'KNOW?
AND IF YOU AREN'T IN THE MOOD TO FIGHT...
THEN OUR OBJECTIVE IS TO LYNCH YOU.
AHHH..
ME?
YOU'RE GOING TO LYNCH ME?
WHY?

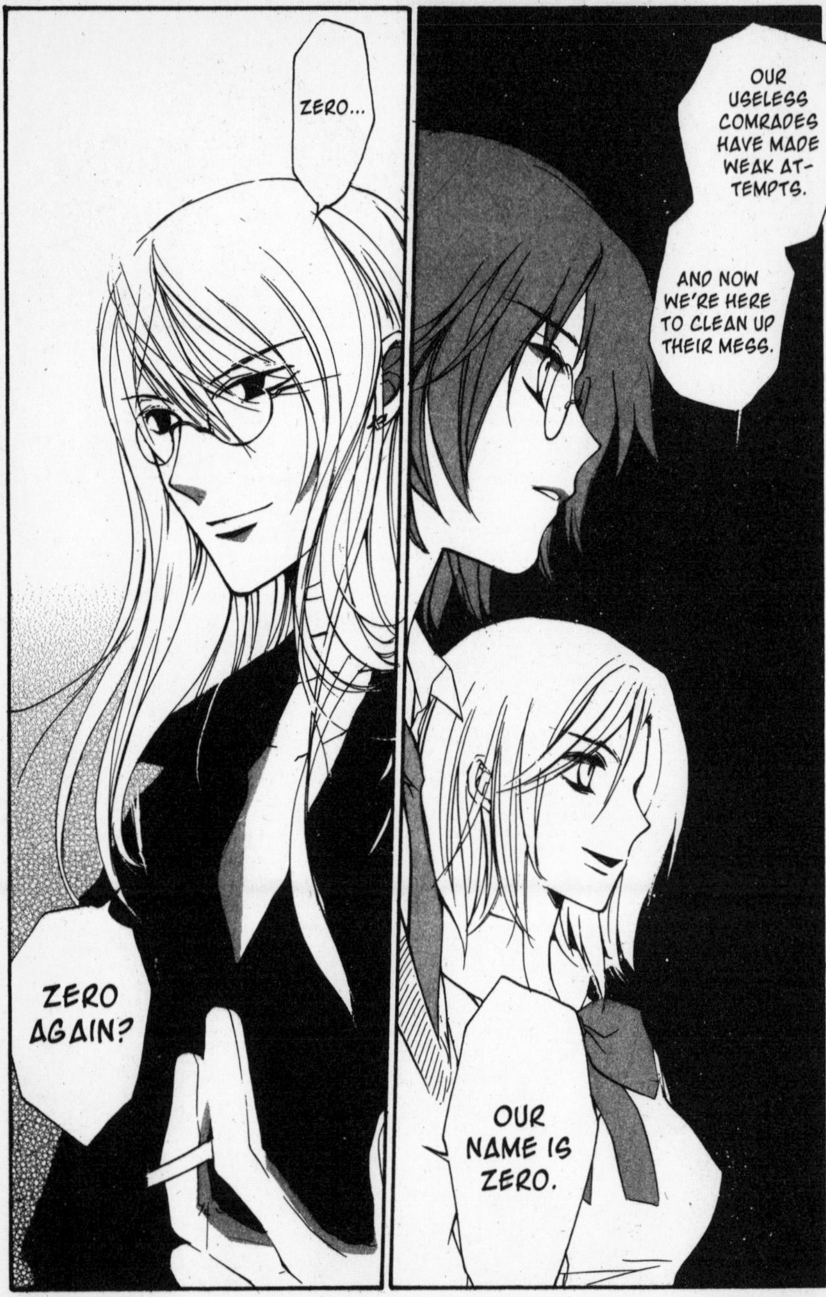
OUR USELESS COMRADES HAVE MADE WEAK AT-TEMPTS.
AND NOW WE'RE HERE TO CLEAN UP THEIR MESS.
OUR NAME IS ZERO.
ZERO...
ZERO AGAIN?

In The Next Volume of

LOVELESS

LOVELESS
4

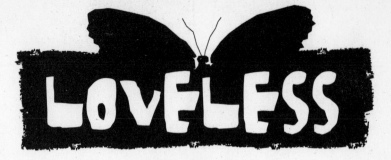

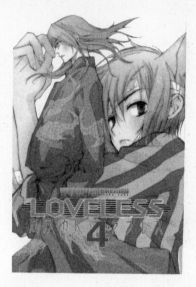

Up against the new Zeros, Soubi finally meets his match. Wounded physically and spiritually, he again turns away from Ritsuka, going instead to the exiled Zeros, Natsuo and Yoji, for comfort and aid. However, the new round of battles forces the three very different pairs to consider what it truly means to be a Fighter and a Sacrifice, and Ritsuka discovers that while he and Soubi do share something, what lies between them is quite different from that of a typical team. But what will this mean for their relationship, and those around them?

Loveless Vol. 4 Available February 2007

PAIN AND EDUCATION IN LOVELESS

Yun Kouga starts volume three of Loveless with a bold juxtaposition of two scenes: as Soubi, alone, fights a pair of Zeroes, he thinks back to his youthful lessons at the hands of a mysterious instructor, Ritsu, for his faults, is the best kind of teacher—one who teaches his students how to continue to learn. Soubi has broken away from Ritsu, for reasons unknown, but he cannot let go of the philosophies instilled in him, and these teachings, reluctantly recalled, save his life: "Pain triggers fear. But you must not fear pain. You must feel it. One who knows pain, Soubi-kun...knows strength." Ritsuka's pain is more shameful, less Romantic, though no less instructive. His mother beats him, and so he has the learned mental and physical tactics of appeasement and avoidance. He is made sensitive—monitoring his mother's tiniest shift in mood, so he can temper his own behavior accordingly.

The Zeroes' teacher, Nagisa, is petulant and naive. She designs her fighters to exist without feeling, so they can fight indefinitely. Zero seems the ultimate opponent because they are insensitive to pain—indeed, they know no pain. But experience makes the fighter as repetition makes the master—to feel once is to know forever. It's the carnal knowledge of pain that the Zeroes lack, and calm, attentive Ritsu knows better: "Insensitivity is dangerous. Pain is a signal to caution. Pain and fear are shields...if you learn how to use them."

But the ability to use pain requires a self-knowledge that the Zeroes cannot attain. "Feeling slows you down," says Yoji. While intellectually aware that they aren't immortal—the Zeros must be careful, for even they can die—they cannot feel danger, cannot feel that they are in trouble until it's far too late. It's the intellectual knowledge without the experience of emotion or physical sensation that eventually cripples them.

By contrast, Soubi's pain in battle inspires identification, then rough poetry: "They are cold. Like being stabbed all over with icicles." This turns to inspiration, and he fights the insensitive Zeroes by freezing the air around them, dragging their body temperatures down to dangerous lows. Their insensitivity means they aren't alerted to the threat—they just marvel at the pretty snow. Soubi has taught himself to use pain as an artist does, as a muse, as a creative tool. Every great work of art, Soubi the art student must have reasoned, has at least some small element of pain buried in its creation (this is a theme that will come up again in the series, when we see more of Soubi the painter, rather than Soubi the fighter). "Pain," concludes Soubi, completing his own education, "is proof that you're alive."

Yet the key is balance—there is a danger in being overly sensitive. Soubi saves Ritsuka's teacher from physical harm, but Shinonome's emotional pain, her fear of connecting with people her age and her loneliness show through when she bursts into tears in the middle of class. When pain is repressed, it forces itself to the surface violently, and at the worst times. But suffering felt, pain withstood and forged into inspiration—that is the spell of the magician, the discipline of the warrior, the art of the fighter and sacrifice.

~Christine Boylan

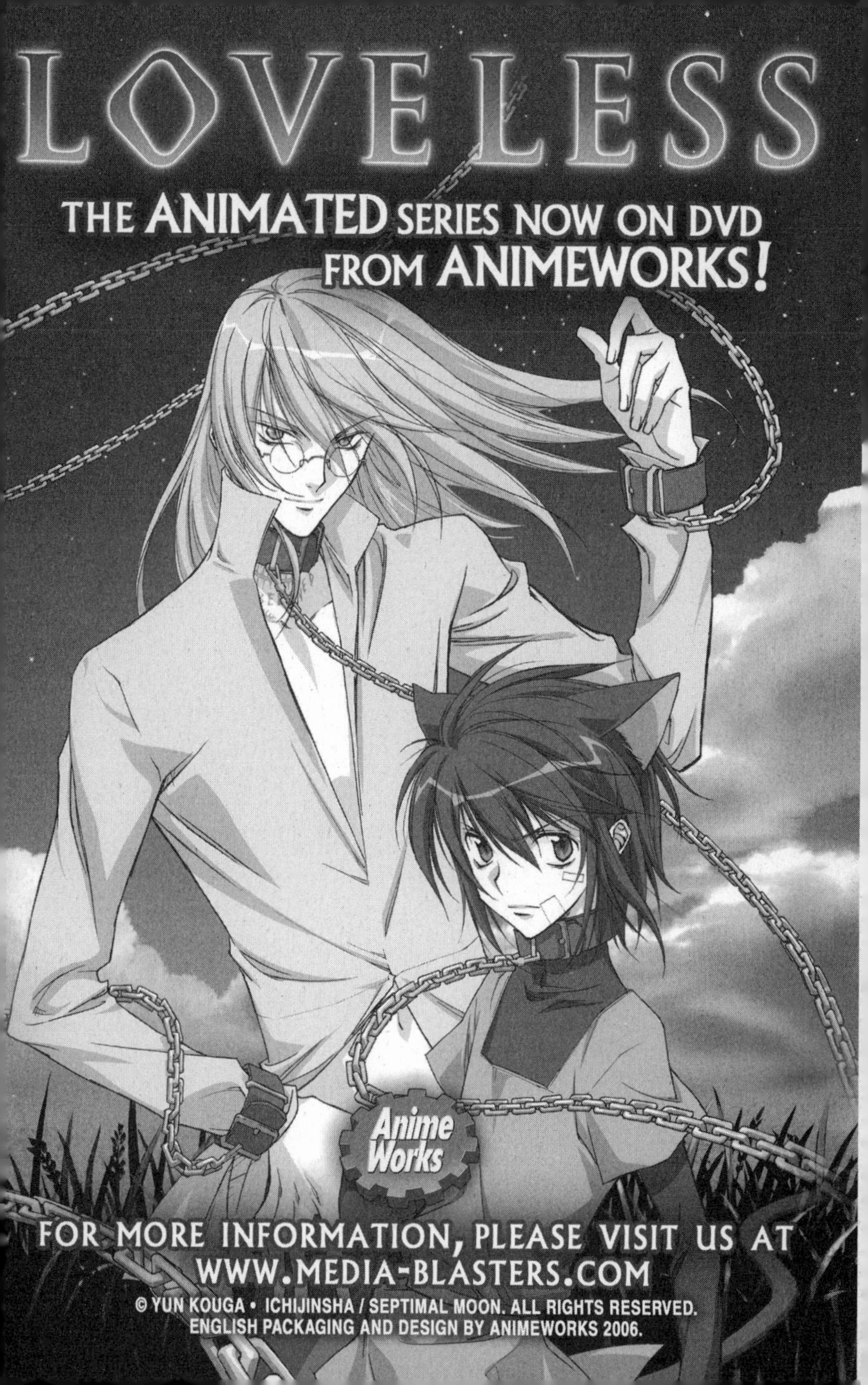
LOVELESS
THE ANIMATED SERIES NOW ON DVD
FROM ANIMEWORKS!
Anime Works
FOR MORE INFORMATION, PLEASE VISIT US AT
WWW.MEDIA-BLASTERS.COM
© YUN KOUGA • ICHIJINSHA / SEPTIMAL MOON. ALL RIGHTS RESERVED.
ENGLISH PACKAGING AND DESIGN BY ANIMEWORKS 2006.

How long would it take to get over...

losing the love of your life?

When Jackie's ex-lover Noah dies, she decides the quickest way to get over her is to hold a personal ritual with Noah's ashes. Jackie consumes the ashes in the form of smoothies for 12 days, hoping the pain will subside. But will that be enough?

From the internationally published illustrator June Kim.

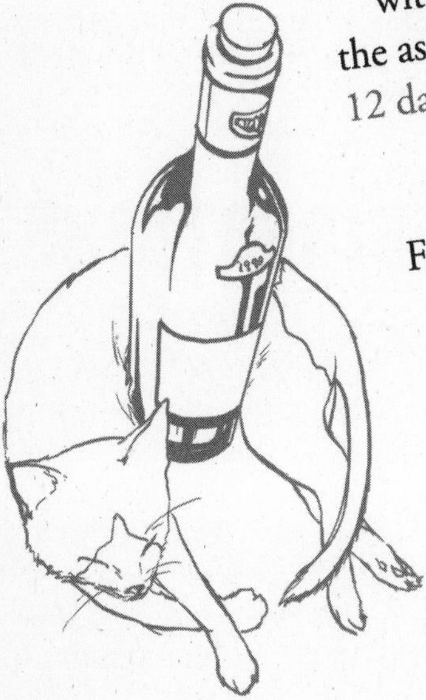

STOP!

This is the back of the book.
You wouldn't want to spoil a great ending!

This book is printed "manga-style," in the authentic Japanese right-to-left format. Since none of the artwork has been flipped or altered, readers get to experience the story just as the creator intended. You've been asking for it, so TOKYOPOP® delivered: authentic, hot-off-the-press, and far more fun!

DIRECTIONS

If this is your first time reading manga-style, here's a quick guide to help you understand how it works.

It's easy... just start in the top right panel and follow the numbers. Have fun, and look for more 100% authentic manga from TOKYOPOP®!